Violence at the Urban Margins

Recent Titles in

Global and Comparative Ethnography
Edited by Javier Auyero

Violence at the Urban Margins
Edited by Javier Auyero, Philippe Bourgois, and Nancy Scheper-Hughes

Violence at the Urban Margins

Edited by Javier Auyero
Philippe Bourgois
Nancy Scheper-Hughes

OXFORD
UNIVERSITY PRESS

OXFORD
UNIVERSITY PRESS

Oxford University Press is a department of the University of
Oxford. It furthers the University's objective of excellence in research,
scholarship, and education by publishing worldwide.

Oxford   New York
Auckland   Cape Town   Dar es Salaam   Hong Kong   Karachi
Kuala Lumpur   Madrid   Melbourne   Mexico City   Nairobi
New Delhi   Shanghai   Taipei   Toronto

With offices in
Argentina   Austria   Brazil   Chile   Czech Republic   France   Greece
Guatemala   Hungary   Italy   Japan   Poland   Portugal   Singapore
South Korea   Switzerland   Thailand   Turkey   Ukraine   Vietnam

Oxford is a registered trademark of Oxford University Press
in the UK and certain other countries.

Published in the United States of America by
Oxford University Press
198 Madison Avenue, New York, NY 10016

Library of Congress Cataloging-in-Publication Data
Violence at the urban margins / edited by Javier Auyero, Philippe Bourgois, and Nancy
Scheper-Hughes.
pages cm
Includes bibliographical references and index.
ISBN 978-0-19-022144-7 (hardcover : alk. paper) — ISBN 978-0-19-022145-4 (pbk. : alk. paper)
1. Urban violence—North America.   2. Urban violence—South America.   3. Urban poor—
North America.   4. Urban poor—South America.   I. Auyero, Javier.   II. Bourgois, Philippe I.,
1956–   III. Scheper-Hughes, Nancy.
HN50.V56 2015
303.609173'2—dc23
2014031024

9 8 7 6 5 4 3 2 1
Printed in the United States of America
on acid-free paper

CONTENTS

ACKNOWLEDGMENTS

This volume is the result of a two-day workshop that took place in April 2013 at the Lozano Long Institute of Latin American Studies (LLILAS) at the University of Texas at Austin. Heartfelt thanks to LLILAS, the Sociology Department, the Joe R. and Teresa Lozano Long Professorship in Latin American Sociology, the Rapoport Centennial Professorship of Liberal Arts, and the Office of Graduate Studies for their financial support, as well as Paloma Diaz (LLILAS senior program coordinator) for the wonderful organization of the event. Charlie Hale (LLILAS director) and Christine Williams (chair of the Sociology Deparment) were extremely supportive before, during, and after the workshop, and we are deeply grateful to them. We also wish to thank the graduate students who acted as discussants for the papers presented at the workshop: Jessica Dunning-Lozano, Erika Grajeda, Pamela Neumann, Elizabeth Velasquez, Katherine Jensen, Jorge Derpic, and Jacinto Cuvi.

The Editors

LIST OF CONTRIBUTORS

Javier Auyero is the Joe R. and Teresa Lozano Long Professor of Latin American Sociology at the University of Texas at Austin. He is the author of *Patients of the State*, and, together with anthropologist Debora Swistun, of *Flammable: Environmental Suffering in an Argentine Shantytown*.

Adam Baird is assistant professor and coordinator of the Urban Governance and Peace program at the United Nations-mandated University for Peace in Costa Rica. He is co-editor of *Paz, Paso a Paso: Una mirada a los conflictos Colombianos desde los estudios de paz*.

Philippe Bourgois is the Richard Perry University Professor of Anthropology and Family & Community Medicine at the University of Pennsylvania. He is the author of several books including, *In Search of Respect: Selling Crack in El Barrio, Righteous Dopefiend* (co-authored with Jeff Schonberg), and *Violence in War and Peace* (co-edited with Nancy Scheper-Hughes).

Randol Contreras is an assistant professor of sociology at the University of Toronto. He is the author of *Stickup Kids: Race, Drugs, Violence, and the American Dream*, which ethnographically analyzes the lives of Dominican drug robbers in the South Bronx.

Benjamin Fogarty-Valenzuela is a Guatemalan national, graduate of Columbia University (New York), and PhD student in the Princeton University Department of Anthropology.

Alice Goffman is an assistant professor of sociology at the University of Wisconsin, Madison. She is the author of *On the Run: Fugitive Life in an American City*.

Mo Hume is a senior lecturer in politics at the University of Glasgow, Scotland. She is author of *The Politics of Violence: Gender, Conflict and Community in El Salvador*.

Kristine Kilanski is a PhD student in the Department of Sociology and a graduate student fellow in the Ethnography Lab at the University of Texas at Austin. Her research focuses on poverty and gender, racial, and class inequality in the labor force.

Manuel Llorens is a clinical and community psychologist. He teaches at the Universidad Católica Andrés Bello of Caracas, Venezuela. He is the co-author of *Niños con Experiencia de Vida en la Calle* and of *Violencia Armada y Acuerdos de Convivencia en una Comunidad Caraqueña.*

Kevin Lewis O'Neill is an associate professor at the University of Toronto. He is the author of *City of God: Christian Citizenship in Guatemala* and the forthcoming *Killing Them Softly: Piety and Prevention in Postwar Guatemala.*

Dennis Rodgers is a professor of urban social and political research in the School of Social and Political Sciences at the University of Glasgow, UK. His recent publications include the edited volumes *Latin American Urban Development into the 21st Century: Towards a Renewed Perspective on the City* and *Global Gangs: Street Violence Across the World.*

Nancy Scheper-Hughes is a professor of anthropology at the University of Berkeley. She is the author of, among other works, *Saints, Scholars and Schizophrenics,* and *Death without Weeping: The Violence of Everyday Life in Brazil.*

John Souto is a psychologist. He is the coordinator of the School of Psychology at the Universidad Católica Andrés Bello (UCAB). In recent years, Mr. Souto has participated in care spaces for female victims of violence and children and youth with histories of abuse and neglect. He is the co-author of *Acuerdos de Convivencia en una Comunidad Caraqueña.*

Ana Villarreal is a PhD candidate in sociology at the University of California, Berkeley. Her dissertation examines the impact of increased drug violence and fear of crime on everyday life in urban Mexico.

Polly Wilding is a lecturer in gender and international development at the University of Leeds, United Kingdom. She is author of *Negotiating Boundaries: Gender, Violence and Transformation in Brazil.*

Verónica Zubillaga is a professor at the Universidad Simón Bolívar in Caracas. Her publications include *El nuevo malestar en la cultura,* together with Hugo José Suárez and Guy Bajoit, and *Violencia Armada y Acuerdos de Convivencia en una Comunidad Caraqueña,* together with Manuel Llorens, Gilda Núñez, and John Souto.

Violence at the Urban Margins

Introduction

KRISTINE KILANSKI *AND* JAVIER AUYERO

This volume is the outcome of a workshop held at the Lozano Long Institute of Latin American Studies at the University of Texas at Austin in the spring of 2013. The workshop, also entitled "Violence at the Urban Margins," brought together scholars conducting cutting-edge ethnographic research on the role of violence in the lives of the urban poor in South, Central, and North America. For two days conference participants discussed violence and its impacts in their respective field sites—as diverse as Philadelphia, Medellín, and Managua—and compared and contrasted their own findings with those of co-participants working across national or continental borders. Although each of the participants brought a unique perspective to the study of violence, they shared a commitment to shedding light on the suffering that violence produces and perpetuates, as well as the individual and collective responses it generates, among those living at the urban margins of the Americas. Participants' joint concern for the people at the bottom of the socioeconomic order, whose lives they have each labored so carefully to document, helped facilitate a productive dialogue even where disagreements emerged about field techniques or data interpretation. This volume combines, in printed form, the papers that were workshopped in Austin. Our hope is that when read side by side they will spark the same level and depth of dialogue across fields (disciplinary and sites of study) as when the authors themselves sat around a conference table in the center of UT-Austin's Benson Library, passionately discussing their research in front of (and sometimes with) graduate student and faculty observers.

Like those who attended the two-day workshop, the readers of this book are invited to see *theory in action*—the creative use of a diverse set of theoretical and analytical tools to illuminate particular aspects of the sources, experiences, uses, and effects of violence. There is no single, overarching theoretical framework shared by the contributors, just as there is no single, unified definition of violence employed in this volume. Reflecting the existing variation in social scientific studies of violence, some contributors draw on a more normative—and narrower—definition of violence, focusing mainly on the deployment of physical force and the intentional infliction of damage, while others rely on a more expansive understanding of violence, expanding their investigation to include symbolic and structural forms. Rather than asking authors to conform the research they presented at the workshop to achieve coherence across this volume, we encouraged them to maintain their distinctive approaches to the analysis of violence in the lives of the poor. This not only allows us to showcase the diversity of ways in which scholars have attempted to understand violence but also provides readers with the opportunity to weigh the benefits and drawbacks of each theoretical and conceptual approach through engagement with *actual* empirical work. We encourage readers, like the workshop attendees, to put the pieces into conversation with one another—and arrive at a greater whole than any individual author or set of authors can through their own field research and analysis.

While they come from unique perspectives, each of the authors in this book is attempting to understand how recent trends in violence have shaped the day-to-day lived experiences of the poor across the Americas. We explain these trends below, as well as some of the similarities and differences in the form violence has taken across continental borders, to provide context to the authors' ethnographic work. Then we provide a roadmap to the papers included in this volume, drawing out some of the initial insights and lessons that can be learned from drawing these diverse perspectives together.

While this book focuses specifically on the dynamics and experiences of violence at the urban margins, we undertake the project with caution and reserve. The tendency of ethnography to focus on the types of violence that shape daily life in poor black and brown communities—when read collectively—can help to (re)produce negative stereotypes of racial/ethnic minorities circulating in the wider culture. Scholars yield great power in the decisions they make about what constitutes "violence." The privileging of certain forms of violence, such as street-level gang violence, helps to construct certain racialized and gendered bodies, particularly young black and brown male bodies, as more capable of and implicated in violence than others (Muhammad 2010). Let us be clear right at the outset: the multiple forms of violence under scrutiny in this volume are a consequence of long-term exposure to intense and chronic victimization across multiple levels (Richie 2012; Smith 2005) and cannot be explained without considering factors external to the urban margins. A plethora of economic and political factors—from insulting levels of inequality, to the informalization of social relations and ensuing precarity, to a punitive and/or delinquent state—produce the urban margins *and* foster the violence that pervades them. In other words, the violence that tears at the fabric of the lives of the men and women living at the urban margins has its origins both in economic and political structures as well as in the actions and inactions of states and established political actors.

Another very basic point should not need re-telling, if not for the fact that public discussions in the Americas oftentimes ignore it. In the United States, as well as in Latin America, debates around issues of citizens' public safety (from debates that erupt after highly publicized events, such as the shootings of Jordan Davis and Trayvon Martin, to those that recurrently dominate the airwaves in Latin America) are dominated by members of the middle and upper-middle classes. However, a cursory count of the victims of urban violence in the Americas reveals that the people suffering the most from violence live (and die) at the bottom of the socio-symbolic order. Yet the inhabitants of the urban margins are hardly ever heard in discussions about public safety. They live in danger, but the discourse about violence and risk belongs to, is manufactured by, and is manipulated by others—others who are prone to view violence at the urban margins as evidence of a cultural (or racial) defect rather than question violence's relationship to economic and political marginalization. As a result, the experience of interpersonal violence among the urban poor becomes something unspeakable, and the everyday fear and trauma lived in relegated territories is constantly muted and denied. At a very basic level, this book seeks to counteract this pernicious tendency by putting under the ethnographic microscope (and making public) the way in which violence is "lived" and "acted upon" in the urban peripheries.

MARGINALITY AND VIOLENCE IN THE AMERICAS

As mentioned above, this project was inspired by the belief that scholars living and working across the Americas had much that they could learn from one another—and that through fostering conversation between scholars in the north and south, a better understanding of the causes, consequences, and lived experiences of urban marginality and violence might be collectively reached.

For what has now been more than four decades, urban sociologists in Latin America have been grappling with questions that have only emerged recently within mainstream urban sociology in the United States. For example, discussions about "marginality" and/or "informality"—while relatively new to debates among scholars studying urban poverty in the United States (Bourgois 1995; Duneier 2000; Venkatesh 2006)—have long been at the center of research on urban poverty in Latin America (Fernandez-Kelly and Shefner 2006). Similarly, a long and spirited debate about the economic and political relationships that "excluded" populations living in the urban peripheries establish with the rest of society (and whether or not the "marginal" can be considered "disposable" and/or fulfilling an economic "function") have long preoccupied Latin American social scientists. Those working north of the border can certainly profit from this established body of scholarship. Whether or not the debates have come to a satisfactory conclusion is beside the point.

In more than one way, this general theme encompasses a version of what Matthew Desmond (2012) recently called "the survival question"—that is, how do poor people survive in the absence of formal jobs and state assistance? Answers to this question north and south of the border have, on occasion, reached similar conclusions: for example, scholars in both the north and the south have documented the role of informal networks in helping the poor survive (Edin and Lein 1997; González de la Rocha 2004; Lomnitz 1978; Stack 1974). Other times, researchers have produced quite different assessments of how the poor "make ends meet." For example, Latin Americanists have written extensively about the key role played by "political networks" in the poor's survival (Auyero 2000; Gay 1994), while US-based work tends to focus on more formalized institutional state structures for supporting the poor, such as "welfare" (Collins and Mayer 2010; Edin and Lein 1997).

The recent and emerging concern with "urban marginality" and its spatial manifestations in the form of "hyperghettoes" (Wacquant 2007) also offers a formidable opportunity for meaningful and productive dialogue between both scholarly traditions. Almost three decades ago, in what would later become one of Latin America's most original and controversial contributions to the social sciences, a group of sociologists tackled the relationship between the structural character of unemployment in the region and the escalation of urban marginality. Working within a structural-historical neo-Marxist perspective, they recovered the notion of "marginality" from the realm of modernization theories (represented by sociologist Gino Germani and the DESAL school), which focused on the lack of integration of certain social groups into society due to their (deviant) values, perceptions, and behavioral patterns (DESAL 1969, 1970; Germani 1966, 1980; Perlman 1976; Portes 1972). Marginal groups, according to this approach, lacked the psychological and psychosocial attributes that were deemed necessary to participate in modern society. Emerging in the transition to modern, industrial society, marginality was thought to be the product of the coexistence of beliefs, values, attitudes, and behaviors of a previous, more "traditional" stage. Rural migrants to the city were seen as carriers of a "baggage of traditional norms and values which prevent(ed) their successful adaptation to the urban style of life" (Portes 1972, 272). Note the striking similarities between this behaviorist and value-centered approach to "marginality" and the emphasis on the alleged existence of a US "underclass," a term generally applied to the black and brown people who inhabit areas of urban blight. We should add in passing that the thorough criticism this approach to marginality was subjected to (Perlman 1976; Portes 1972) could still be a useful antidote to inoculate us against the pitfalls and political dangers of the ambiguous notion of the "underclass" (Gans 1995).

In contrast to this "culturalist" approach, the structural perspective on marginality focused on the process of import substitution industrialization and its intrinsic inability to absorb the growing mass of the labor force. As Mollenkopf and Castells (1991, 409) put it, this intellectual tradition "aimed to understand why and how increased industrialization and GNP growth, concentrated in the largest metropolitan areas, went hand in hand with accrued urban poverty and an ever-growing proportion of people excluded from the formal labor market and formal housing and urban services." At that time, Nun and colleagues (1968) understood that the functioning of what they called "the dependent labor market" was generating an excessive amount of unemployment. This "surplus population" transcended the logic of the Marxian concept of an "industrial reserve army" and led the authors to coin the term "marginal mass." The "marginal mass" was neither superfluous nor useless; it was "marginal" because it was rejected by the same system that had created it. Thus, the marginal mass was a "permanent structural feature" never to be absorbed by the "hegemonic capitalist sector" of the economy, not even during its expansionary cyclical phases. In more than a way then, the structural school on marginality anticipated the multiple effects of the structural character of "mass unemployment" (depressing of incomes, deterioration of working conditions, precarization of employment). Decades later, countries in the north and south began to experience, in addition to this "industrial" marginality, a novel kind of marginality related to the functioning of the globalized post-Fordist economy, from different forms of tertiarization to the passage of neoliberal policies (Wacquant 2007). The "old" debate about the causes and extent of marginality can help us to figure out whether or not there is a "new" marginality operating at the urban peripheries and, if so, to diagnose its dynamics and manifestations.

Absent in many discussions of emerging and/or durable forms of marginality, however, is a systematic assessment of the role that violence plays in shaping life in such contexts.

Over the last two decades, most countries in the Americas have witnessed a sharp increase in violence, as well as a mutation in the forms violence has taken (Koonings 2001; Koonings and Kruijt 2007; Rodgers et al. 2012). For example, violence in Latin America is "increasingly available to a variety of social actors," no longer an exclusive "resource of elites or security forces," and includes "everyday criminal and street violence, riots, social cleansing, private account selling, police arbitrariness, paramilitary activities, post-Cold War guerrillas, etc." (Koonings 2001, 403). As Imbusch, Misse, and Carrión (2011, 95) assert in their comprehensive review of violence research in the region, political violence "has now receded significantly in most countries of the continent," while other forms of violence (e.g., interpersonal violence, drug-related violence, domestic abuse, and sexual assault) have multiplied to such an extent that largely unchecked brutality appears to be besieging many of the newly established democracies in the region (Arias and Goldstein 2010; Caldeira 2001; Jones and Rodgers 2009; Pearce 2010). This does not mean that state violence has disappeared, as any cursory look at instances of police brutality in the region would immediately attest. These forms of violence are quite varied and, in contrast with past modes of violence, are now located mostly in urban areas. This new urban violence is stratified in that it affects the most disadvantaged populations in disproportionate ways (Brinks 2008; CELS 2009; Gay 2005), with poor adolescents and young adults most highly represented among its victims and perpetrators (Imbusch, Misse, and Carrión 2011). Most of this violence, furthermore, concentrates within the poor neighborhoods, slums, and shantytowns of the region (Moser and McIlwine 2004), to the point of becoming "the defining feature of life in such settlements at the beginning of the 21st century" (Rodgers et al. 2012, 15; see also McIlwaine 1999; Winton 2004).[1]

Those living at the urban margins in the United States today face many of the same challenges documented by urban sociologists in the 1980s and 1990s, such as limited job prospects, failing neighborhood social institutions, high levels of segregation, a predatory "poverty industry," and chronic interpersonal violence in the street and—for some—at home (Anderson 1999; Massey 1990; Rivlin 2010; Wilson 1996). Notably, the urban poor are also contending with disturbing trends in state surveillance, policing, containment, and punishment practices (Goffman 2009; Rios 2011; Soss, Fording, and Schram 2011; Wacquant 2009), spurred by the huge disbursement of federal funding to local government and policing agencies to fight the war on drugs (Jarecki 2012)—a "war" that has targeted poor communities of color through the institution of practices such as "gang injunctions," "round ups," and "stop-and-frisk" (Alexander 2010; Goffman 2009) and the increasing militarization of domestic police forces (Kraska and Kappeler 1997). Police violence in the United States is both too patterned and frequent to be reducible to "a cop gone bad," and the use of verbal, physical, and sexual threats and assaults by police officers against people of color, gender non-conformists and sexual minorities, and immigrants living at the urban margins is widespread, if not ubiquitous (Brunson and Miller 2006; Goffman 2009; Mogul, Ritchie, and Whitlock 2011; Richie 2012; Rios 2011). Racial and class bias in the U.S. police and judicial systems helps explain why African Americans, who use drugs in "a number consistent with their proportion of the population, [*sic*] account for '35 percent of those arrested for drug possession, 55 percent of drug possession convictions, and 74 percent of those sentenced to prison for drug possession'" (The Sentencing Project in Allard 2002, 26). As a result, and despite a decade-long decline in racial disparities among prison and jail populations (Mauer 2013), one in every nine black men between the ages of 20 and 34 is behind bars today, as is one in every hundred black women in her 30s (PEW 2008). The state-led war on drugs has devastated poor urban families and communities of color, ensuring and exacerbating their continued economic and political marginalization (Braman 2007; Goffman 2009; Roberts 2004).

In Latin America, state presence and state violence at the urban margins take a variety of forms: sometimes a militarized iron fist (Müller 2012), sometimes "localized 'states of exception'" in the form of "terrorizing raids that symbolically demonstrate the arbitrary power of the state" (Rodgers 2006, 325), and other times a police-criminal "collusion" of the kind described by Desmond Arias in Rio de Janeiro's favelas (Arias 2006a, 2006b; see also Auyero and Berti 2013). But the urban margins are not only besieged by state violence (in the form of police arbitrariness and brutality, for example) but also by a violence that, although causally linked with the operation of the state (Auyero, Burbano de Lara, and Berti 2014), takes a more "lateral" form.

The increase in interpersonal violence in urban settings has been associated with a number of potential causes—from increased economic precariousness, ethnic heterogeneity, and residential mobility (Kornhauser 1978; Shaw and McKay 1942), to the existence and operation of both informal and formal community networks (Sampson and Groves 1989;

Sampson 2012), to electoral competition and factionalization (Villarreal 2002). Social scientific studies of aggregate characteristics correlated with crime and violence have produced some important refinements and extensions of social control theory (Sampson and Groves 1989; Sampson, Raudenbush, and Earls 1997; Villarreal 2002) and highlighted the "risk" and "protective" factors that give rise to or deter violence (Krug et al. 2002; Turpin and Kurtz 1997). For example, studies cite governance failures or high levels of youth unemployment among the risk factors, and the presence of proactive community associations and productive employment opportunities among the protective factors (Muggah 2012). The dynamics of the informal drug economy are also a key source of interpersonal violence in both Latin America and the United States (see, e.g., Rodgers in this volume; Jones and Rodgers 2009; Ousey and Lee 2002; Reinarman and Levine 1997).

During the 1980s and 1990s, urban sociologists in the United States attempted to disentangle the causes feeding the depacification of daily life in ghettoes and inner cities, and to understand how residents experienced and dealt with chronic violence and insecurity (Bourgois 1995; Sanchez-Jankowski 1991). As essays by a number of authors in this volume attest, scholars conducting research in Latin America are now wrestling with similar issues and could benefit from a serious engagement with scholarly debates from the United States. While the drug trade was and is behind much of the violence ravaging what Loïc Wacquant aptly calls "territories of urban relegation" in both the north and the south, the state reaction to and/or clandestine involvement with drug trafficking marks a significant difference between regions and is in need of systematic study.

The pervasive violence experienced by those living at the urban margins can take a "chronic form" within marginalized communities (Brennan, Molnar, and Earls 2007; Schwab-Stone et al. 1995). Clark and her colleagues (2008) refer to chronic exposure to violence as a "mental health hazard," referencing its harmful developmental, emotional, and behavioral impacts on individuals (Farrell et al. 2007; Friday 1995; Holton 1995; Osofsky 1999; Popkin et al. 2010). The "trauma" of chronic exposure to violence and marginalization can impact individuals' schemes of perception, evaluation, and action (Black 2009; Bourgois and Schonberg 2009; Contreras 2013; Richie 1996, 2012). Importantly, responses to hostile surroundings vary drastically within a single neighborhood (Anderson 1999) and even by a single individual (Jones 2009; Auyero and Kilanski, this volume), pointing to the need for further contextualization for understanding how individuals make sense of (and deal with) danger and violence.

ROADMAP AND LESSONS LEARNED

The intensive field research that went into the production of each of these chapters varies according to the degree of embeddedness of the investigator in the community under scrutiny and the closeness he or she had to the phenomenon under investigation. Some, like Alice Goffman and George Karandinos and his co-authors, were on the scene when drug-related violence erupted or when the police came knocking at the door: these researchers shared the physical and psychological assault experienced by their informants on a more frequent basis. Others relied on interviews to reconstruct violent events and its immediate impact on those closest to them. Some contributors based their articles in (by now standard) ethnographic fieldwork strategies; others drew upon multiple ethnographic revisits to understand their field site. "Distortion of the events and context," writes anthropologist Anton Blok (2001, 105), "seriously hampers understandings and obstructs grasping any sense or meaning (of violence)." Aware of Blok's warning, and despite the variations in their approaches to the "field" or presentation of data, all contributors attempt to analytically reorganize their field material in order to simultaneously make sense (i.e., understand and explain) of the violence at their sites and reflect on the epistemic obstacles they faced while attempting to do so. As stated earlier, the chapters showcase a range of approaches to the subject of urban violence in the Americas. Despite differences in methodology or theoretical perspectives, there are some common themes that run through the chapters included in the four sections of this book. Let us highlight a few of those themes and some general takeaway points they may produce for readers.

In a now classic article, British historian E. P. Thompson attacks what he calls the "spasmodic view of popular history"—a perspective that views ordinary folks as occasional and compulsive intruders in history—by asking a simple but still essential question: "Being hungry, what do people do? How is their behavior modified by custom, culture, and reason?" (1993, 187). Eighteenth-century crowds were not simply responding to economic stimuli—a bad harvest or a sudden economic downturn, for example—but believed, Thompson shows, that they were "defending traditional rights or customs." Rapidly increasing prices, generalized hunger, or dealers' misconducts did spark collective (and sometimes violent) action, "but these grievances operated within a popular consensus as to what were legitimate and what were illegitimate practices in marketing, milling, baking, etc. This in its turn was grounded upon a consistent traditional view of social norms and obligations, of the proper economic functions of several parties within the community, which, taken together, can be said to constitute the moral economy of the poor" (Thompson 1993, 188). This moral economy is, in other words, a shared notion of what are appropriate and inappropriate economic practices. Dennis Rodgers and George Karandinos (with his co-authors) work with this notion to great effect by combining it with other theoretical traditions (Foucault's and Agamben's ideas about biopolitics, in the first; Marx's primitive accumulation, Bourdieu's habitus, Mauss's gift, in the second) in order to *simultaneously* make better sense of what they found in the streets of Managua and Philadelphia and understand these findings in their larger political and economic contexts. Without drawing explicitly on the notion of moral economy, a concern with morality also underlines the chapter by Kevin O'Neill and Benjamin Fogarty-Valenzuela—in which we see how, in postwar Guatemala, crack cocaine, and the violence it fuels, become the object of Pentecostal, "cruel and optimist," intervention. The rehab center is the specific physical (carceral) form this intervention takes, and the preaching of a "positive attitude" its moralizing trapping.

Taken together, the findings presented in these first three chapters act as a set of interrogating arrows pointing toward new kinds of inquiry centered around the shared understandings of violence: inquiry into the ways in which perpetrators actually "think and feel" about violence, the manifold ways credit and blame are assigned within violent worlds, the symbolic functions violent acts fulfill in local economies and politics, and the intricate relationships that all these have with larger structural contexts and transformations. How does violence work as a resource? How and why can it also become a "moral, social, and practical imperative"? How and why can violence—and its lethal outcome, death—change valence and significance? How and why can the supposed source of violence (addiction) become moralized and domesticated?

As George Karandinos and his colleagues reveal in their chapter, entitled "The Moral Economy of Violence in the U.S. Inner City," the notion of moral economy has an important gender dimension. The mandates of violence's shared assumptions, these authors show, dovetail with patriarchal obligations. The link between gender and violence is taken up in later chapters by Mo Hume and Polly Wilding (who offer a conceptual elaboration on the way analytical categories of gender and masculinity operate in their field research) and by Adam Baird (whose ethnographic data draws attention to the relationship between gender and gang violence). Both Karandinos et al. and Baird draw upon Bourdieu's notion of habitus to link the perpetration of violence to the reaffirmation of shared notions of manhood. Baird, along with Hume and Wilding, demonstrates that the pursuit of masculinity is one of the main motivations behind the perpetration of violence. While not a new argument, both chapters add to a deeper empirical and theoretical understanding of the relationship between gender and violence.

Reflecting on their extensive research in marginalized communities in Brazil and El Salvador, Hume and Wilding focus our attention on gangs as deeply gendered phenomena. Their feminist analysis is important not only because it places masculinities in relation to other axes of inequality in the explication of urban violence but also because it allows the readers to see that established distinctions between different types of violence (e.g., private and public) are arbitrary and misleading: they silence and hide specific experiences of fear and harm, and thus result in a highly partial understanding of violence at the urban margins. Violences are multiple and should be analyzed together and in relationship to one another, without prioritizing one (say, street crime) over another (say, physical and verbal disputes occurring within the household).

Hume and Wilding's comments about the stigmatizing descriptions of women who get involved with gang members should be read in tandem with Baird's piece on gangs in Medellín. Baird places gangs in the highly exclusionary socioeconomic context of Colombia's second largest city, and sees them as both a form of collective belonging and one of the few channels to forge masculine identities that poor youngsters have available. In the manufacturing of manhood that, according to his analysis, takes place inside gangs, interaction with girls and women is critical. Utilizing Bourdieu's concept of capital, he asserts that "sexual access to young women becomes another *capital* or 'glittering prize' of gang membership that has the unfortunate effect of reinforcing gang identities, hence perpetuating their existence." The search for masculine respect among men, and the pursuit of what Baird calls "the trickle-down of *capital* from the patriarchal dividend" among women are, according to his analysis, crucial dimensions in the perpetration and reproduction of violence in marginalized communities. Together, the two chapters compel us to transcend rigid distinctions among different types of physical and symbolic aggression.

Hume and Wilding raise the issue of the acute effects threat and fear have on daily life of poor communities, and alert readers about the gendered burden that violence places on women. The four chapters in the third section of this volume, "Being in Danger, What Do People Do?," take up the task of analyzing the specific things people at the margins, particularly women, do to confront and cope with danger.

Violence, as many social scientific accounts demonstrate (Anderson 1999; Bourgois 1995; Das 1990; Garbarino 1995), shatters and unravels routine existence. Chapters by Javier Auyero and Kristine Kilanski, Ana

Villarreal, Verónica Zubillaga (and co-authors), and Alice Goffman direct
attention to an understudied aspect of violence: the ways in which communities and individuals manage to respond to its deleterious effects.
Jointly, the chapters in this section seek to answer a version of E. P.
Thompson's (1993) straightforward question: being in physical danger,
beleaguered by a violent local environment, or besieged by state's policing and surveillance dragnet, what do people at the urban margins do?
While all of the authors avoid reproducing a sanitized or romanticized
rendering of the actions and beliefs of those living at the urban margins
(Gowan 2010; Contreras 2013; Wacquant 2002), they arrive at different conclusions. Some authors focus on how responses to violence can
operate to recreate forms of sociability. Reading Villarreal (and some of
the responses described in our chapter), for example, one is reminded of
the existence, even in highly volatile and dangerous contexts, of "small
acts [that] allow life to be knitted pair by pair" (Das 2012, 139). True,
even a cursory look at many areas of contemporary Mexico would reveal
that drug violence unravels everyday routines. But an attentive observer
should not miss the plethora of "raveling" practices that exist alongside
destructive violence. The chapters in this section seek to locate and analyze these particular expressions of sociality and mutual care amid a violence that corrodes community life. Fear, Villarreal reminds us, "tears the
social fabric and destroys public space," but also "brings people together
and creates new forms of social life." Interestingly enough, the chapters on
Mexico, Argentina, and Venezuela point to various (more or less stable,
more or less organized, more or less violent) forms of collective action
as one of the possible responses among the marginalized. In the poor
African American neighborhood where Goffman lived for six years, the
state's threat creates an atmosphere dominated by mutual "suspicion, distrust, and the paranoiac practices of secrecy, evasion, and unpredictability" where joint reactions seem quite unlikely. Our chapter and Zubillaga's
also scrutinize the social actions that, crafted in direct response to daily
violence, paradoxically reproduce interpersonal physical harm.

The volume concludes with two epistemological reflections about
entering and (never) leaving the field, and about the many difficult issues
that ethnographers studying violence encounter as they approach their
empirical universes and construct their objects of study. Drawing upon
his experiences in Los Angeles, California, Contreras engages in an
insightful meditation on the predicament of the ethnographer of violence, zooming in on the liminal moment where ambiguity and loneli-
ness define the position of the field researcher. In the last chapter, Nancy
Scheper-Hughes candidly reflects on her own career as an anthropologist

and *companheira* while providing a poignant examination of the changing politics of violence and death in Brazil.

Although diverse in styles, theoretical underpinnings, and substantive findings, the papers in this volume collectively demonstrate that any sociological sketch of urban marginality and its impacts on socially organized suffering should pay sustained and systematic empirical attention to the dangerous surroundings where the urban poor dwell. Together with income, employment, education and other conventional variables, social scientific analyses of the causes and manifestations of urban deprivation should take account of poor people's relentless exposure to violence, both interpersonal and state generated. In other words, if we want a better, more comprehensive understanding of "the texture of hardship" (Newman and Massengill 2006), the diverse forms of violence dissected in this volume are inescapable objects of analysis.

NOTE

1. For more on Rio de Janeiro, see Gay 2005; Arias 2006a; Penglase 2010; Perlman 2010; Wilding 2010; for El Salvador, see Hume 2009; for Managua, see Rodgers 2006; for Medellín, see Ponce de León-Calero 2014; for Guatemala, see O'Neill and Thomas 2011.

WORKS CITED

Alexander, Michelle. 2010. *The New Jim Crow: Mass Incarceration in the Age of Colorblindness.* New York: The New Press.

Allard, Patricia. 2002. *Life Sentences: Denying Welfare Benefits to Women Convicted of Drug Offenses.* Washington, DC: The Sentencing Project. Retrieved from http://www.sentencingproject.org/doc/publications/women_lifesentences.pdf.

Anderson, Elijah. 1999. *Code of the Street: Decency, Violence and the Moral Life of the Inner City.* New York: W. W. Norton & Company.

Arias, Desmond, and Daniel Goldstein, eds. 2010. *Violent Democracies in Latin America.* Durham, NC: Duke University Press.

Arias, Desmond. 2006a. *Drugs and Democracy in Rio de Janeiro.* Durham, NC: University of North Carolina Press.

Arias, Desmond. 2006b. "The Dynamics of Criminal Governance: Networks and Social Order in Rio de Janeiro." *Journal of Latin American Studies* 38(2): 293–325.

Auyero, Javier, and Maria Fernanda Berti. 2013. *La violencia en los márgenes.* Buenos Aires: Katz Ediciones.

Auyero, Javier, Agustín Burbano de Lara, and María Fernanda Berti. 2014. "Violence and the State at the Urban Margins." *Journal of Contemporary Ethnography* 43(1): 94–116.

Auyero, Javier. 2000. *Poor People's Politics.* Durham, NC: Duke University Press.

Black, Timothy. 2009. *When a Heart Turns Rock Solid: The Lives of Three Puerto Rican Brothers On and Off the Streets.* New York: Vintage.

Blok, Anton. 2001. *Honor and Violence.* New York: Polity.

Bourgois, Philippe, and Jeffrey Schonberg. 2009. *Righteous Dopefiend*. Berkeley: University of California Press.

Bourgois, Philippe. 1995 (2003). *In Search of Respect: Selling Crack in el Barrio*. Cambridge: Cambridge University Press.

Braman, Donald. 2007. *Doing Time on the Outside: Incarceration and Family Life in Urban America*. Ann Arbor: University of Michigan Press.

Brennan, Robert T., Beth Molnar, and Felton Earls. 2007. "Refining the Measurement of Exposure to Violence (ETV) in Urban Youth." *Journal of Community Psychology* 35(3): 603–618.

Brinks, Daniel. 2008. *The Judicial Response to Police Violence in Latin America: Inequality and the Rule of Law*. New York: Cambridge University Press.

Brunson, Rod K., and Jody Miller. 2006. "Gender, Race, and Urban Policing: The Experience of African American Youths." *Gender & Society* 20(4): 531–552.

Caldeira, Teresa. 2001. *City of Walls: Crime, Segregation, and Citizenship in São Paulo*. Berkeley: University of California Press.

Centro de Estudios Legales y Sociales (CELS). 2009. *Derechos humanos en Argentina: Informe 2009*. Buenos Aires: Siglo XXI.

Clark, Cheryl, Louise Ryan, Ichiro Kawachi, Marina J. Canner, Lisa Berkman, and Rosalind J. Wright. 2008. "Witnessing Community Violence in Residential Neighborhoods: A Mental Health Hazard for Urban Women." *Journal of Urban Health* 85(1): 22–38.

Collins, Jane, and Victoria Mayer. 2010. *Both Hands Tied: Welfare Reform and the Race to the Bottom in the Low-wage Labor Market*. Chicago: University of Chicago Press.

Contreras, Randol. 2013. *The Stickup Kids: Race, Drugs, Violence, and the American Dream*. Berkeley: University of California Press.

Das, Veena. 2012. "Ordinary Ethics: The Perils and Pleasures of Everyday Life." In *A Companion to Moral Anthropology*, edited by Didier Fassin, 133–149. New York: Wiley-Blackwell.

Das, Veena, ed. 1990. *Mirrors of Violence: Communities, Riots, and Survivors in South Asia*. Oxford: Oxford University Press.

DESAL. 1970. *Marginalidad, promoción popular e integración Latinoamericana*. Buenos Aires: Troquel.

DESAL. 1969. *Marginalidad en América Latina: Un ensayo de diagnóstico*. Barcelona: Editorial Herder.

Desmond, Matthew. 2012. "Disposable Ties and the Urban Poor." *American Journal of Sociology* 117(5): 1295–1335.

Duneier, Mitchell. 2000. *Sidewalk*. New York: Farrar, Straus, and Giroux.

Edin, Kathryn, and Laura Lein. 1997. *Making Ends Meet. How Single Mothers Survive Welfare and Low-wage Work*. New York: Russell Sage Foundation.

Farrell, Albert, Elizabeth H. Erwin, Kevin W. Allison, Aleta Meyer, Terri Sullivan, Suzanne Camou, Wendy Kliewer, and Layla Esposito. 2007. "Problematic Situations in the Lives of Urban African American Middle School Students: A Qualitative Study." *Journal of Research on Adolescence* 17(2): 413–454.

Fernandez-Kelly, Patricia, and Jon Shefner. 2006. *Out of the Shadows: Political Action and the Informal Economy in Latin America*. University Park: Pennsylvania State University Press.

Friday, Jennifer. 1995. "The Psychological Impact of Violence in Underserved Communities." *Journal of Health Care for the Poor and Underserved* 6(4): 403–409.

Gans, Herbert. 1995. *The War against the Poor: The Underclass and Antipoverty Policy*. New York: Basic Books.

Garbarino, James. 1993. "Children's Response to Community Violence: What Do We Know?" *Infant Mental Health Journal* 14(2): 103–115.

Gay, Robert. 2005. *Lucia: Testimonies of a Brazilian Drug Dealer's Woman*. Philadelphia: Temple University Press.

Gay, Robert. 1994. *Popular Organization and Democracy in Rio de Janeiro: A Tale of Two Favelas*. Philadelphia: Temple University Press.

Germani, Gino. 1980. *Marginality*. New Brunswick: Transaction Books.

Germani, Gino. 1966. *Política y sociedad en una época de transición: De la sociedad tradicional a la sociedad de masas*. Buenos Aires: Paidos.

Goffman, Alice. 2009. "On the Run: Wanted Men in a Philadelphia Ghetto." *American Sociological Review* 72: 339–357.

González de la Rocha, Mercedes. 2004. "From the Marginality of the 1960s to the 'New Poverty' of Today: A LARR Research Forum." *Latin American Research Review* 39(1): 184–203.

Gowan, Teresa. 2010. *Hobos, Hustlers, and Backsliders: Homeless in San Francisco*. Minneapolis: University of Minnesota Press.

Holton, John K. 1995. "Witnessing Violence: Making the Invisible Visible." *Journal of Health Care for the Poor and Underserved* 6(2): 152–159.

The House I Live In. 2012. Written and directed by E. Jarecki. Westminster: British Broadcasting Corporation.

Hume, Mo. 2009. *The Politics of Violence: Gender, Conflict, and Community in El Salvador*. Malden, MA: Wiley-Blackwell.

Imbusch, Peter, Michel Misse, and Fernando Carrión. 2011. "Violence Research in Latin America and the Caribbean: A Literature Review." *International Journal of Conflict and Violence* 5(1): 87–154.

Jones, Gareth, and Dennis Rodgers, eds. 2009. *Youth Violence in Latin America: Gangs and Juvenile Justice in Perspective*. New York: Palgrave.

Jones, Nikki. 2009. *Between Good and Ghetto: African American Girls and Inner-city Violence*. Rutgers, NJ: Rutgers University Press.

Koonings, Kees. 2001. "Armed Actors, Violence and Democracy in Latin America in the 1990s." *Bulletin of Latin American Research* 20(4): 401–408.

Koonings, Kees, and Dirk Kruijt, eds. 2007. *Fractured Cities: Social exclusion, Urban Violence & Contested Spaces in Latin America*. London: Zed Books.

Kornhauser, R.R. 1978. *Social Sources of Delinquency: An Appraisal of Analytic Models*. Chicago: University of Chicago Press.

Kraska, Peter B., and Victor E. Kappeler. 1997. "Militarizing American Police: The Rise and Normalization of Paramilitary Units." *Social Problems* 44(1): 1–18.

Krug, Etienne G., L.L. Dahlberg, James A. Mercy, Anthony B. Zwi, and Rafael Lozano, eds. 2002. *World Report on Violence and Health*. Geneva: World Health Organization (WHO).

Lomnitz, Larissa. 1978. *Cómo sobreviven los marginados*. Mexico: Siglo XXI.

Massey, Douglas S. 1990. "American Apartheid: Segregation and the Making of the Underclass." *The American Journal of Sociology* 96(2): 329–357.

Mauer, Marc. 2013. *The Changing Racial Dynamics of Women's Incarceration*. Washington, DC: The Sentencing Project.

McIlwaine, Cathy. 1999. "Geography and Development: Violence and Crime as Development Issues." *Progress in Human Geography* 23(3): 453–463.

Mogul, Joey L., Andrea J. Ritchie, and Kay Whitlock. 2011. *Queer (In)justice: The Criminalization of LGBT People in the United States*. Boston: Beacon Press.

Mollenkopf, John, and Manuel Castells, eds. 1991. *Dual City. Restructuring New York*. New York: Russell Sage Foundation.

Moser, Caroline, and Cathy McIlwaine. 2004. *Encounters with Violence in Latin America*. New York: Taylor and Francis.

Muhammad, Khalil G. 2010. *The Condemnation of Blackness: Race, Crime, and the Making of Modern Urban America*. Boston: Harvard University Press.

Muggah, Robert. 2012. *Researching the Urban Dilemma: Urbanization, Poverty and Violence*. Canada: IDRC.

Müller, Markus-Michael. 2012. "The Rise of the Penal State in Latin America." *Contemporary Justice Review* 15(1): 57–76.

Newman, Katherine S., and Rebekah P. Massengill. 2006. "The Texture of Hardship: Qualitative Sociology of Poverty, 1995–2005." *Annual Review of Sociology* 32: 423–446.

Nun, José, Juan Carlos Marín, and Miguel Murmis. 1968. *Marginalidad en América Latina*. Buenos Aires: Centro de Investigaciones Sociales, Instituto Torcuato di Tella.

O'Neill, Kevin L., and Kedron Thomas, eds. 2011. *Securing the City: Neoliberalism, Space, and Insecurity in Postwar Guatemala*. Durham, NC: Duke University Press.

Osofsky, Joy D. 1999. "The Impact of Violence on Children." *The Future of Children* 9(3): 33–49.

Ousey, Graham C., and Matthew R. Lee. 2002. "Examining the Conditional Nature of the Illicit Drug Market—Homicide Relationship: A Partial Test of the Theory of Contingent Causation." *Criminology* 40: 73–102.

Pearce, Jenny. 2010. "Perverse State Formation and Securitized Democracy in Latin America." *Democratization* 17(2): 286–386.

Penglase, Ben. 2010. "The Owner of the Hill: Masculinity and Drug-trafficking in Rio de Janeiro, Brazil." *The Journal of Latin American and Caribbean Anthropology* 15(2): 317–337.

Perlman, Janice. 2010. *Favela: Four Decades of Living on the Edge in Rio de Janeiro*. New York: Oxford University Press.

Perlman, Janice. 1976. *The Myth of Marginality*. Berkeley: The University of California Press.

PEW Center on the States. 2008. *One in 100: Behind Bars in America 2008*. Washington, DC: The PEW Center of the States. Retrieved from http://www.pewtrusts.org/uploadedFiles/wwwpewtrustsorg/Reports/sentencing_and_corrections/one_in_100.pdf.

Ponce de León-Calero, Alejandro. 2014. *Que la muerte se haga esperar: Cotidianeidad y confrontación armada en una barriada de Medellín*. Retrieved from https://www.academia.edu/2450788/ Que_la_muerte_se_haga_ esperar_ Cotidianidad_y_ confrontacion_armada_ en_una_barriada_ de_Medellin_2009_-_2012_.

Popkin, Susan, Tama Leventhal, and Gretchen Weismann. 2010. "Girls in the 'Hood: How Safety Affects the Life Chances of Low-Income girls." *Urban Affairs Review* 45(6): 715–744.

Portes, Alejandro. 1972. "Rationality in the Slum: An Essay in Interpretive Sociology." *Comparative Studies in Society and History* 14(3): 268–86.

Reinarman, Craig, and Harry G. Levine, eds. 1997. *Crack in America: Demon Drugs and Social Justice*. Berkeley: University of California Press.

Richie, Beth. 2012. *Arrested Justice: Black women, Violence, and America's Prison Nation*. New York: New York University Press.

Richie, Beth. 1996. *Compelled to Crime: The Gender Entrapment of Black Battered Women*. New York: Routledge.

Rios, Victor. 2011. *Punished: Policing the Lives of Black and Latino Boys*. New York: New York University Press.

Rivlin, Gary. 2010. *Broke, USA*. New York: HarperCollins Publishers.

Roberts, Dorothy E. 2004. "The Social and Moral Cost of Incarceration in African American Communities." *Stanford Law Review* 56(5): 1271–1305.

Rodgers, Dennis. 2006. "Living in the Shadow of Death: Gangs, Violence and Social Order in Urban Nicaragua, 1996–2002." *Journal of Latin American Studies* 38: 267–92.

Rodgers, Dennis, Jo Beall, and Ravi Kanbur, eds. 2012. *Latin American Urban Development into the Twenty-First Century: Towards a Renewed Perspective on the City.* New York: Palgrave.

Sampson, Robert J. 2012. *Great American City: Chicago and the Enduring Neighborhood Effect.* Chicago: Chicago University Press.

Sampson, Robert J., Stephen W. Raudenbush, and Felton Earls. 1997. "Neighborhoods and Violent Crime: A Multilevel Study of Collective Efficacy." *Science* 227(5328): 918–924.

Sampson, Robert, and W. Byron Groves. 1989. "Community Structure and Crime: Testing Social Disorganization Theory." *American Journal of Sociology* 94: 774–802.

Sánchez-Jankowski, Martin. 1991. *Islands in the Street: Gangs and American Urban Society.* Berkeley: University of California Press.

Schwab-Stone, Mary, Tim S. Ayers, Wesley Kasprow, Charlene Voyce, Charles Barone, Timothy Shriver, and Roger Weissberg. 1995. "No Safe Haven: A Study of Violence Exposure in an Urban Community." *Journal of the American Academy of Child and Adolescent Psychiatry* 34: 1343–1352.

Shaw, Clifford, and Henry D. McKay. 1942. *Juvenile Delinquency and Urban Areas.* Chicago: University of Chicago Press.

Smith, Andrea. 2005. *Conquest: Sexual Violence and American Indian Genocide.* New York: South End Press.

Soss, Joe, Richard C. Fording, and Sanford F. Schram. 2011. *Disciplining the Poor: Neoliberal Paternalism and the Persistent Power of Race.* Chicago: University of Chicago.

Stack, Carol. 1974. *All our Kin: Strategies for Survival in a Black Community.* New York: Harper.

Thompson, Edward P. 1993. *Customs in Common: Studies in Traditional Popular Culture.* New York: The New Press.

Turpin, Jennifer, and Lester Kurtz. 1997. *The Web of Violence.* Chicago: The University of Illinois Press.

Venkatesh, Sudhir. 2006. *Off the Books: The Underground Economy of the Urban Poor.* Cambridge, MA: Harvard University Press.

Villarreal, Andres. 2002. "Political Competition and Violence in Mexico: Hierarchical Social Control in Local Patronage Structures." *American Sociological Review* 67: 477–498.

Wacquant, Loïc. 2009. *Punishing the Poor: The Neoliberal Government of Social Insecurity.* North Carolina: Duke University Press.

Wacquant, Loïc. 2007. *Urban Outcasts: A Comparative Sociology of Advanced Marginality.* New York: Polity.

Wacquant, Loïc. 2002. "Scrutinizing the Street: Poverty, Morality, and the Pitfalls of Urban Ethnography." *American Journal of Sociology* 107(6): 1468–1532.

Wilding, Polly. 2010. "'New Violence': Silencing Women's Experiences in the Favelas of Brazil." *Journal of Latin American Studies* 42: 719–747.

Wilson, William Julius. 1996. *When Work Disappears: The World of the New Urban Poor.* New York: Vintage Books.

Winton, Ailsa. 2004. "Urban Violence: A Guide to the Literature." *Environment & Urbanization* 16(2): 1–23.

PART 1

Shared Understandings

CHAPTER 1

The Moral Economy of Murder

Violence, Death, and Social Order in Nicaragua

DENNIS RODGERS

INTRODUCTION

In his famous lectures to the College de France in 1975–1976, Michel Foucault (2003, 241) argued that politics in the modern era have become focused on life rather than death. While the power of medieval sovereigns was fundamentally based on their ability to kill with impunity, the contemporary epoch is the age of what he termed "biopower," that is to say, a politics organized around the control and regulation of life. Foucault pithily summarized this as the ability "to make live," which Stuart Murray (2006, 194) has contended effectively makes politics "a discourse on life that is *about* life as much as it appears, strategically, to *belong to* life itself, a natural extension of life's sacred—and thus unquestionable—value." As Andrew Norris (2000, 43) has pointed out, however, the inevitability of death means that it unavoidably assumes "a privileged place in the logic of the 'meaning' of human life," and by extension will always impact on the terrain of the political, if one accepts—following Georges Balandier's (1970) "maximalist" formulation—that the latter concerns the nature of collective social order at its most basic. Seen from this perspective—and against the grain of much recent theorizing on the biopolitical character of contemporary politics (e.g., Li 2009; Rose 2006)—I want to suggest that there is potentially much to be learned from adopting a focus on death rather than life in order to get to grips with the social "order of things" (see Foucault, 1970).

More specifically, through a consideration of the evolving norms, understandings, and significances associated with killing and dying in barrio Luis Fanor Hernández,[1] a poor neighborhood in Managua, the capital city of Nicaragua, where I have been carrying out longitudinal ethnographic research since 1996, I want to highlight how a "thanatopolitical" approach—that is to say, one based on a politics of death[2]—can reveal particular socioeconomic dynamics that are perhaps less obvious when our analysis is focused on life. I take as my starting point a conversation about a murder that I had with a barrio Luis Fanor Hernández gang member called Bismarck in the mid-1990s, which revealed what initially seemed to be a highly apathetic understanding of death. Drawing on the events that followed the demise of another gang member called Lencho, I then explore how dying constituted a critical element in the discursive social construction of individual gang membership, but also for the maintenance of a broader sense of collective community belonging and order. The transformation of Nicaraguan gang dynamics and the rise of new armed actors in the 2000s fundamentally changed local understandings associated with death, however, and led to the emergence of a particular moral economy of murder, which I discuss in relation to the killing of another gang member called Charola. Ultimately, what this particular metamorphosis points to is the fundamentally dystopian evolution of the broader political economy of post-revolutionary Nicaragua.

BISMARCKIAN PERSPECTIVES

I first met Bismarck in December 1996, moments after he thought he had committed his first murder. I had been carrying out a photo tour of barrio Luis Fanor Hernández, when I came across two teenage youths, Jader and Bismarck, boisterously taking turns riding what was clearly a new bicycle. Jader, with whom I was previously acquainted, hailed me over to proudly show off their acquisition, and asked me to take a photo of the two of them. As I snapped them, I asked where they had obtained the bicycle, and they explained that they had just stolen it from a "rich kid" in the nearby *colonia* Las Condes. "It was a piece of cake, we cornered him down a dead end," Jader elaborated, "although the *hijueputa* refused to hand it over at first, so we had to rough him up a bit."

"Yeah, and then he started screaming like a *cochón*, so we had to really do him in properly," Bismarck added excitedly.
"What do you mean, you had to do him in properly?," I queried.

"Hah! I dropped a concrete block on his head, that's what! It cracked right open, brains and all, and he stopped shouting forever," Bismarck exclaimed.

"Shit, *maje*, you killed him? For a bicycle? You're completely mad!"

"Yeah, Bismarck's crazy, real *dañino*," Jader injected, "but he'd never killed anybody before, you see, and you know how it is with first times, you get all excited and carried away, and *puf*, that's what happened, he got carried away and killed the guy for no good reason."

"Fuck you, *maje*, we got the bike, no?," Bismarck retorted. "Who gives a shit about the rest?"

As it happened, I did, because Bismarck was a member of the local neighborhood gang that I was studying. Despite the fact that I had become closely associated with the barrio Luis Fanor Hernández gang (see Rodgers 2007b), and the gang members' rather blasé attitude to murder was by no means unfamiliar, I had principally interacted with older members, whom I believed had become inured to death largely through their repeated exposure to the phenomenon. Bismarck, however, was a younger gang member who was just embarking on a murderous career, yet he seemed to display a similarly lackadaisical attitude toward death. I was therefore interested to learn more about the way he conceived of himself and his actions in order to understand the dynamics of what now seemed to me to possibly be a full-blown state of "cognitive dissociation" rather than simple habituation (see Festinger 1957). I asked Bismarck whether he was willing to let me interview him about both the murder and his life history more generally. He readily acquiesced, and we met regularly over the course of the next few months, as well as often seeing and greeting each other in the streets of barrio Luis Fanor Hernández.

Bismarck proved to be a hugely engaging informant. He was a happy-go-lucky sixteen year old, who always had a huge grin on his face and ready answers to my inquiries. He also displayed a lot of curiosity about my research, frequently responding to my questions with probing queries of his own or offering insightful commentary on my evolving analyses of gang life. It rapidly became obvious that my idea that gang members were "cognitively dissociating" from death—rather than simply habituated to the phenomenon—was a definite instance of academic over-theorization on my part. When I explained the concept of cognitive dissociation to Bismarck during our first interview, he listened patiently but then simply responded:

Death is death, Dennis. It's not something that you can avoid or ignore, it just happens. My father died when I was four, one of my sisters died when I was ten, and

several of my friends have also died over the past few years. You can't distance yourself from death, because you don't choose whether people live or die. Death just
happens.

I pointed out that this was not really true of the kid whose bicycle
he had stolen, but he summarily dismissed this and claimed that life in
poor Nicaraguan neighborhoods was governed by "the law of the jun-
gle" (*la ley de la selva*), by which you either killed or were killed. Death
was "a natural phenomenon, and you just ha[d] to accept it," according
to Bismarck.

Such an outlook toward death can certainly be linked to repeated
exposure to the phenomenon, in a manner reminiscent of the situation
famously described by Nancy Scheper-Hughes (1992) in the Alto do
Cruzeiro shantytown in Northeast Brazil, where she noted a ubiquitous apathy toward dying as a result of the high levels of child mortality,
extreme poverty, pervasive hunger, and political and criminal violence. At
the same time, however, Bismarck's fatalism in the face of death was by no
means constant. The contrast between his attitude toward the death of his
neighbor Don Antonio, and that of a fellow gang member called Lencho,
was striking in this respect.

Don Antonio was Bismarck's neighbor, linked to his family through
relations of *compadrazgo* (fictive kinship), yet his death in January 1997
seemed to barely register on Bismarck. He mentioned it matter-of-factly
a couple of times during our interviews, but otherwise it did not change
his usual routines. On the other hand, Bismarck experienced Lencho's
demise as a major bereavement, as did the other barrio Luis Fanor
Hernández gang members. Lencho was killed during gang warfare
against the neighboring *asentamiento* José Amador gang in February
1997. The evening after his death, the gang members gathered to mourn
him, sitting together on a street corner drinking and smoking late into
the night. Although there was some talk about Lencho's exploits and
achievements, the mood was generally rather somber, and there was little of the bittersweet humor often associated with wakes in Nicaragua.
The gang unanimously decided to change its graffiti from "SBV"—an
abbreviation of *Los Sobrevivientes*, a name the gang took from the neighborhood's pre-revolutionary name of *La Sobrevivencia*—to "Lencho,"
to honor his memory. Although this only lasted for a few months, even
today, almost twenty years after Lencho's death, one can still find old
graffiti of his name in barrio Luis Fanor Hernández.

To a certain extent, this emotional response to Lencho's death
was due to the fact that there existed strong ties of friendship and
camaraderie within the gang group that for many gang members

superseded kinship ties (both real and fictive). At the same time, however, when I subsequently asked Bismarck why he had reacted to Don Antonio and Lencho's deaths so differently, he did not distinguish between them on the basis of personal relations but rather claimed that his discriminating attitude was linked to the fact that as a gang member, Lencho had "lived in the shadow of death."[3] Unlike most neighborhood inhabitants, gang members regularly found themselves in dangerous situations and "lived" knowing that death was not an abstract concept but a very real possibility, which could strike at any time, and in any place. Certainly, during my first stay in barrio Luis Fanor Hernández between September 1996 and July 1997, four neighborhood gang members died violently,[4] and deaths occurred regularly over the subsequent years that I have been going back to the neighborhood. Seen from this perspective, as Silvia Kuasñosky and Dalia Szulik (1996, 57 [my translation]) remark in relation to their study of youth gangs in Argentina, death obviously "constitutes a dimension of the lives of gang members which must be considered a priori in order to understand the significance of the ways in which these youths relate to each other and to wider society."

At the same time, "living in the shadow of death" was more than just a corporeal state of being for gang members, who often actively used the expression to designate not only their predicament but also their attitudes, social practices, and even philosophy of life. For them, "living in the shadow of death" entailed displaying definite behavior patterns, such as flying in the face of danger, whatever the odds and whatever the consequences. It meant taking risks and showing bravado, neither asking oneself questions nor calculating one's chances, but simply going ahead and acting, almost daring death to do its best. It meant being violent and exposing oneself to violence, but with style, in a cheerfully exuberant manner reminiscent of Walter Benjamin's (1986, 301) famous "destructive character," who is "young and cheerful," and "always blithely at work." This could especially be observed during gang warfare, as gang members recklessly threw themselves into fighting, with an obvious enthusiasm and performative flamboyance which added to the highly ritualized nature of the fighting. A barrio Luis Fanor Hernández gang member called Julio, for example, was notorious for systematically exposing himself to gunfire during battles in order to "better defy" his adversaries, "daring them to do their best to injure [him] seriously," as he put it.

The idea of "living in the shadow of death" was also observable in more prosaic circumstances, including a botched attempt by Bismarck and Jader to rob a car in the neighboring *colonia* Las Condes in May

1997. The pair of them had heard that a party was being organized there and thought they might be able to mug a guest or break into a parked car. They quickly spotted a vehicle with a partially open window which they managed to jack down. As they searched for something of value, an obviously privileged young woman on her way to the party stopped and challenged them.[5] They told her to mind her own business, to which she responded, "What do you prefer, moving off or being shot?" Bismarck immediately answered "being shot," and posed defiantly with Jader by the car as the young woman alerted local security guards, who came running within seconds. The pair waited until the guards began shooting before running off. They were chased around Las Condes but managed to get away without suffering injury. Neither was at all disappointed by their failure to steal anything, however, and Bismarck in fact concluded his dramatic account of their escapade to an enthusiastic audience of fellow gang members with a self-satisfied and expressive "*¡Hijo de la setenta mil puta, maje, ni un cinco reales, pero ni verga, clase de alboroto!*" (Son of bitch, mate, not even half a *córdoba* for all that, but fuck it, what a brilliant uproar!), which generated great mirth and no little admiration.

Seen from this perspective, the act of "living in the shadow of death" was a primary constitutive social practice for gang members, playing a fundamental role in the construction of their individual self. Gang members asserted themselves through constant and high-spirited risk-taking that effectively corresponded to an "ethos". Indeed, they would often talk of their particular *onda*—a Nicaraguan slang term that can be loosely translated as "way of being"—which they would explicitly associate with "living in the shadow of death," arguing that this was what distinguished them most fundamentally from non-gang-member youth, frequently and aggressively repeating the expression in a quasi-talismanic manner during everyday discussions about their lives and activities.[6] As Bismarck and Jader's recounting of their botched theft illustrates well, *onda* also underpinned gang socialization, with tales of particularly dramatic, comedic, or tragic instances of risk-taking, bravado, or courage repeatedly recounted to younger gang members by older ones. Younger members often attempted to imitate them, although not necessarily with the same degree of success. Lencho had in fact died as a result of incautiously exposing himself to gunfire during a battle, explicitly imitating his fellow gang member Julio. Although he paid a high price for "living in the shadow of death," his death was considered distinctive from more prosaic, run-of-the-mill mortalities because of the actions that caused it.

SANCTIFIED SACRIFICE

The perception that Lencho's death was distinctive from other deaths went beyond the gang members. Almost half the neighborhood attended Lencho's wake or funeral, more than double the number that came to the wake or funeral of Don Antonio, despite the fact that he had been the patriarch of one of the original founding families of barrio Luis Fanor Hernández. But perhaps the most striking feature of Lencho's wake and funeral was the way that local inhabitants actively talked about how he had "sacrificed" himself for the neighborhood. This is not as implausible as it may initially seem to be. As I have written about more extensively elsewhere (see Rodgers 2006), although Nicaraguan gang wars in the 1990s seemed anarchic and disordered at first glance, they can be interpreted as having provided local neighborhoods with a functional sense of security. The first battle of a gang war was typically with fists and stones, but each new battle involved an escalation of weaponry, first to sticks; then to knives and broken bottles; and eventually to mortars, guns, and AK-47s. Although the rate of escalation varied, its sequence never did—i.e., gangs did not begin their wars immediately with firearms. On the one hand, the fixed nature of gang warfare constituted a mechanism for restraining violence, insofar as escalation is a process in which each stage calls for a greater but definite intensity of action and is therefore always under actors' control. On the other hand, it also provided local inhabitants with an "early warning system." Gang wars played out as "scripted performances," thereby offering local communities a means of circumscribing what Hannah Arendt (1969, 5) famously termed the "all-pervading unpredictability" of violence.

Even if gang wars often had negative consequences for local populations—bystanders were sometimes injured or killed in the crossfire—these were arguably indirect. The threat stemmed from other gangs, with whom the local gang engaged in a prescribed manner, thereby limiting the scope of violence in its own neighborhood and creating a predictable "safe haven" for local inhabitants. In a wider context of chronic violence, insecurity, and social breakdown, the inhabitants of barrio Luis Fanor Hernández very much recognized this as something positive, even if it was not always effective. As an informant called Don Sergio put it:

> The gang looks after the neighborhood and screws others; it protects us and allows us to feel a little bit safer, to live our lives a little bit more easily . . . Gangs are not a good thing, and it's their fault that we have to live with all this insecurity, but that's the problem about gangs in general, not of our gang here in the neighborhood. They protect us, help us—without them, things would be much worse for us.

Such a discourse was common among barrio Luis Fanor Hernández inhabitants of both sexes and all ages, but the esteem in which gang members were held was also obvious from the way neighborhood residents almost always cheerfully greeted and bantered with them on street corners, were happy to give them glasses of cold water during hot spells, or offered them shelter in their homes during flash downpours in the rainy season (none of which they necessarily did for non-gang-member friends and relatives).[7] The quasi-symbiotic relationship between the gang and neighborhood inhabitants was however especially evident from the fact the latter never called the police during gang wars, nor did they ever denounce gang members, often going so far as to actively hide them and provide false information to any authority figure asking questions about local gang members.[8]

Beyond the security that the gang provided the neighborhood, there also existed a clear sense of identification with the local gang and its highly performative violence. This was evident in the "aesthetic pleasure" (Bloch 1996, 216) that local inhabitants derived from swapping stories about the gang, particularly eye-witness accounts of dramatic acts by gang members, and spreading rumors and re-telling various incidents over and over again. As such, the gang and its violent ethos of "living in the shadow of death" can actually be said to have constituted something of an institutional medium for the symbolic constitution of a sense of collective communal identity in barrio Luis Fanor Hernández, one that was otherwise lacking due to the widespread poverty and the postwar political polarization, disillusion, and chronic insecurity that characterized Nicaragua at the time (see Rodgers 2007a, 2008a, and 2014). Certainly, it was common to hear the expression "*la pandilla es el barrio*" (the gang is the neighborhood) used by both gang members and non-gang residents in barrio Luis Fanor Hernández, and there was little beyond the gang that seemed to connect the neighborhood community.

Thus the notion that Lencho had "sacrificed" himself for the neighborhood makes sense, whether from a folk or an anthropological perspective (see Hubert and Mauss 1964, Girard 1977). At the same time, the notion of sacrifice also has particular resonances in Nicaragua considering its importance for *Sandinista* revolutionary politics, as Roger Lancaster (1988, 132–138) has described:

> Revolutions write and act out their own mythologies, which provide the new
> moral exemplars . . . and it is on the basis of their example of self-sacrifice that the
> Sandinistas ultimately rest[ed] their claim of being the "vanguard organization" of

the Nicaraguan people . . . Nicaraguan [revolutionary] history recounts itself as a succession of martyrdoms, and depicts itself as a series of martyrs. These martyrs become the icons of class consciousness.

It is interesting to note in this respect that the barrio Luis Fanor Hernández gang members actively and aggressively claimed the mantle of *Sandinismo* in a neighborhood that had otherwise politically gone "cold," as Doña Ursula Rivas, one of the neighborhood's historic *Sandinista* organizers, put it. Gang members claimed to be "the last inheritors of *Sandinismo*" and maintained that they engaged in violence due to their "love"—literally, "*querer*"—for their local neighborhood. "*Así somos, nosotros los bróderes pandilleros* [that's how we are, us gang member brothers], we show our love for the neighborhood by fighting other gangs," a gang member named Miguel claimed, while Julio told me that "you show the neighborhood that you love it by putting yourself in danger for people . . . You look after the neighborhood in that way, you help them."

To a certain extent, a conceptual parallel can be made here with the "love" that Ernesto "Che" Guevara (1969, 398) saw as the mark of "the true revolutionary."[9] At the same time, it was striking that the conversations about Lencho's "sacrifice" at his wake and funeral were not framed in political terms but had a more religious tinge to them. For example, Lencho's body was repeatedly described by well-wishers at his wake as "beautiful," "glowing," and even "saint-like." Almost everybody who went up to his coffin to pay their respects did so in a hushed and reverential manner that contrasted strongly with the behavior at other wakes I attended in barrio Luis Fanor Hernández, where emotions were generally very demonstratively expressed. In this respect, in his discussion of what he calls "the mythology of the guerrilla," Lancaster (1988, 132) notes how it is something that became intimately associated with religion in revolutionary Nicaragua, insofar as "by undergoing his ordeal of struggle, the guerrilla [was] purified . . . he [was] *sanctified.*" This notion of *sanctification through sacrifice* provided "powerful religious resonances" to the revolutionary regime, to the extent that Lancaster (1988, 133 and 139) argues that "Sandinista authority derive[d] from the same fount as priestly or saintly authority," and that "the rules of political authority so closely resemble[d] the rules of religious authority that the two very nearly merge[d]." Underlying this association is the fact that revolutionary praxis, like religion, can often be boiled down to certain repetitive tropes—e.g., good vs. evil, virtue vs. sin, bourgeois vs. proletariat, capital vs. labor, etc. Sacrifice, from this perspective, was "more than a mere event; it [was] more even than self-abnegation; it [was] a story, a narrative, an allegory of much wider significance" (Lancaster 1988, 138), one whereby the *Sandinista* revolutionary guerrilla was perceived as redeeming the social life of Nicaragua as a whole, in the same way that Jesus Christ is considered by Christians to have died for humanity's sins.

The religiosity that imbued conversations about Lencho at his wake and funeral suggests that he was similarly considered to have been sanctified through his sacrifice, which raises the obvious possibility of a conceptual parallel between gang and revolutionary guerrilla membership. A key difference between gang members in the 1990s and revolutionary guerrillas in the 1970s and 1980s, however, is that the former did not have a clear ideological agenda. At best, they constituted something of a Deleuzian "war machine," that is to say, "social phenomena that direct their actions against domination, but without necessarily having well-defined battle lines or standard forms of confrontation" (Jensen and Rodgers 2008, 231). The domination that the gang opposed was not that of a particular group or person but rather the more diffuse and generalized sense of insecurity, both real and ontological, that was a hallmark of Nicaragua in the 1990s, particularly in poor urban slums and neighborhoods (Rodgers 2007a and 2008a). This resistance can nevertheless be compared with the more explicitly political opposition of the sanctified *Sandinista* guerrilla insofar as it was fundamentally structural in nature, making the comparison between gangs and guerrillas at the very least symbolically appropriate.

Nicaraguan gang members' implicit resistance to their broader social circumstances can perhaps more plausibly be compared to the rage against oppression embodied in Eric Hobsbawm's (1959) famous figure of "social bandit." "Probably the single most influential idea in the modern study of bandits and outlaws" (Wagner 2007, 353), the notion of the social bandit refers to a particular type of criminal who, due to a (real or assumed) tendency to prey on the rich and to (sometimes) redistribute (some of) the proceeds of this delinquency to the poor, is seen as a hero and protector by the latter, who regularly aid, abet, and even hide the bandit from the authorities. Social bandits are therefore viewed as criminal by an oppressive state or a dominant class but are considered legitimate in the eyes of the local population, something that points to the existence of a differentiated morality of violence, clearly similar to the situation in barrio Luis Fanor Hernández in the 1990s, where gang violence was seen as morally legitimate and gang member deaths were considered symbolically more important than other deaths.

VALE VERGA LA MUERTE

Hobsbawm argued that social bandits were ultimately doomed to failure: they were not proper revolutionaries but rather markers of oppression and difference. Most died, were co-opted by the authorities, or became oppressors themselves. This certainly proved to be the case for the barrio Luis Fanor Hernández gang, which changed dramatically with the turn of the millennium. This transformation was principally due to the spread of crack cocaine from 1999 onward, which led to the gang shifting from being an organization that displayed a sense of social solidarity with the local community to a more exclusive and predatory group. This was partly because gang members became crack consumers, many to the point of full-blown addiction, which made them aggressive and unpredictable. They began to regularly attack, rob, and threaten neighborhood inhabitants in order to obtain the means to secure their next fix. Gang members also become directly involved in drug dealing, however, both as individual street dealers and collectively as the drug trade's security infrastructure. The gang as a group enforced contracts and guarded drug shipments whenever they entered or left the neighborhood, and engaged in a campaign of sustained terror against local inhabitants, arbitrarily threatening, beating, and intimidating to prevent denunciations and to ensure that drug dealing could occur unimpeded.

Not only did the gang generate significant insecurity for local inhabitants, but it also (violently) underpinned a process of localized capital accumulation that enabled a small group of drug dealers to flourish in an otherwise impoverished environment with few economic opportunities. This particular function—which bears comparison with the "primitive accumulation" of North Philadelphia drug dealing described by Karandinos et al. (this volume)—suggests that, ultimately, there existed overriding exogenous factors shaping the gang's evolutionary trajectory, and more specifically, the reduction of socioeconomic possibilities that has characterized post-revolutionary Nicaragua. Certainly, the basic thrust of Nicaraguan development since the end of the *Sandinista* revolution can be summarized in terms of ever-increasing levels of exclusion and impoverishment among the majority of the population combined with a continuous concentration of wealth in the hands of a small oligarchy, a situation that the second coming of the *Sandinistas* from 2006 onward has not challenged but in fact consolidated and accelerated (see Rodgers 2008b and 2011). To this extent, because gangs are always epiphenomena of broader structural processes (see Thrasher 1927), the barrio Luis Fanor Hernández gang's transformation from an institutional vehicle for community solidarity to a more predatory, parochial, and self-interested organization simply mirrors the broader dystopian—and rather Darwinian—developmental dynamics of contemporary Nicaraguan society.

This was also reflected in the transformation of the moral codes surrounding gang member deaths in barrio Luis Fanor Hernández, as events surrounding the break down of the symbiotic relationship between the gang and local drug dealers highlight very well. Drug dealing in barrio Luis Fanor Hernández developed initially in an informal manner around a single individual known as *el Indio Viejo* (the Old Indian). He had been a member of the first neighborhood gang and had drawn on a network of both former and current gang members in order to set up and run his drug-dealing business. Over time, however, he professionalized his organization and became more selective in picking his local partners. By 2005, he was leading a rather shadowy group that involved individuals from outside the neighborhood, although barrio Luis Fanor Hernández remained the main base of operations. This group was locally referred to as the *cartelito*, or "little cartel," and was highly feared, partly because it took on a more unknown quantity, involving individuals whom local inhabitants could not place or classify.

The *cartelito* developed its own security infrastructure, which rapidly clashed with the barrio Luis Fanor Hernández gang, at least partly in order to eliminate any potential challengers in the neighborhood for the local monopoly over violence. This led to a series of confrontations between the gang and the *cartelito* in mid-2006, which had rather predictable results, insofar as the latter was better armed and its members were not crack addicts and therefore much less prone to making stupid decisions. Members of the *cartelito* would wander around the neighborhood openly bearing arms, intimidating and sometimes shooting at any gang members they saw hanging around in the streets, to scare them and to warn them "not to get uppity," as local inhabitants put it. After a few months of this, the gang decided to retaliate and attacked *el Indio Viejo*'s house one evening, which led to a shoot-out between the gang and members of the *cartelito*, during which a gang member called Charola was badly wounded. The other gang members fled, leaving him behind, and a member of the *cartelito* named Mayuyu went up to Charola and shot him in the head, execution-style, "as a warning to the others," as he put it.

Charola's death was experienced very differently to Lencho's within barrio Luis Fanor Hernández. This was particularly obvious in the very different ways their wakes and funerals took place. Unlike Lencho's, Charola's death was met with widespread indifference. Although I was not present, by all accounts his wake and funeral were very poorly attended: there were no more than a dozen people at his wake, and only five—his immediate family—at his funeral. What I was able to directly observe, however, was that all discussion about Charola was extremely critical. While Lencho had been sanctified and was talked about in hushed, respectful terms for weeks on end after his death—at least, until the next gang member death created another "*santo pandillero*" (gang member saint), as a rather amused Bismarck put it during a 2012 interview when I discussed some of my preliminary ideas concerning gang members and death with him—Charola was not talked about at all. Whenever I brought him up in conversation, he was invariably described as a "parasite" or a "gargoyle" (which is a Nicaraguan slang term for a crack addict—due to the wasting effect that the long-term consumption of the drug can have), and his death was clearly considered to be of no significance, and even senseless.

Everybody I interviewed about the events that had led to Charola's death said that the gang's raid on *el Indio Viejo*'s house had been "stupid" or "illogical," and that it had served no purpose whatsoever. The general feeling was summarized very well by Julio, who during an interview in 2007 about Charola exclaimed, "*¡Vale verga su muerte!*" (Who gives a fuck about his death!) This sentiment was not just linked to Charola as an individual, but applied more broadly. The death of a gang member was no longer seen as anything socially significant within barrio Luis Fanor Hernández, partly due to the changed relationship between the gang and the neighborhood. Indeed, it was striking that local inhabitants no longer talked about gang members as having death "above them" but described them instead as "having death below them"—"*son muerte abajo*"—which in the context implied that death was something that was inevitably going to happen to them, sooner rather than later.[10] This was partly due to gang members' drug consumption, but it was also due to the new reality of the *cartelito*'s domination of the neighborhood and concomitant brutal attitude toward gang members, which local inhabitants rarely condemned. In other words, Charola's death was clearly not seen as a sacrifice in any shape or form, and was not sanctified.

Having said this, the *cartelito*'s violence also went beyond gang members—between 2006 and 2009, individuals associated with it would regularly commit acts of random brutality against barrio Luis Fanor Hernández inhabitants, including arbitrarily killing two non-gang members in 2008 and 2009. Although *Doña* Yolanda contended during a 2009 interview that such actions were "to train people," it was clear that they also contributed to reducing the significance of death generally. Certainly, it was striking that the three wakes and funerals I attended during my visits in 2007 and 2009 were all much less impressive events than any that I had been to in the 1990s. Even though the *cartelito*'s menace changed after it re-focused on drug trafficking in late 2009, and it became less present in the neighborhood, seeking invisibility rather than territorial control, death clearly continued to be experienced in a symbolically impoverished manner. This was particularly striking in relation to the death in July 2012 of Doña Bertha, the very popular widow of Don Sergio, the historic barrio Luis Fanor Hernández community leader. If there was anybody in the neighborhood whose death should have had the potential to lead to significant social mobilization, it was hers, but less than fifty people attended her wake and funeral. The processes that affected the morality of gang member death were, in other words, affecting the wider community as well. Seen from this perspective, the transformation of the moral basis for understanding the social significance of gang member dying and killing was very much a reflection of a broader underlying process.

CONCLUDING THOUGHTS

At its most basic, what I have discussed concerns changing norms, their evolving codification, and how social practices are embedded within them. Another way of putting this is in terms of "moral economy." The notion of the "moral economy" is usually associated with the works of E. P. Thompson (1971) and James Scott (1976), who respectively used it to explain the counterintuitive actions of food rioters in eighteenth-century Britain and peasants in twentieth-century Vietnam. More specifically, they were concerned with the fact that although human well-being and status are generally enhanced by productive economic activity, economic action is often policed by community norms, expectations, and values that do not necessarily respond to an economic logic. Both British food rioters and Vietnamese peasants for example displayed marked anti-market tendencies, acting to prevent unequal capital accumulation and to ensure the availability of a certain threshold of basic goods. Thompson and Scott argued that this kind of action reflected the embedded nature of the eighteenth-century British and twentieth-century Vietnamese economies. Such "pre-modern" economies, they argued, were moral because they were an integral part of social relations, while more "modern" (contemporary) economies were less moral because economic activity was disembedded from social relations. As Thompson (1971, 131–132) put it:

> It is difficult to re-imagine the moral assumptions of another social configuration.
> It is not easy for us to conceive that there may have been a time, within a smaller
> and more integrated community, when it appeared to be "unnatural" that any man
> should profit from the necessities of others, and when it was assumed that, in time of

dearth, prices of "necessities" should remain at a customary level, even though there might be less all round.

The concept of the moral economy is thus generally used specifically in relation to what might be termed "anti-economic" economic activity. Yet as Thompson (1971, 79) pointed out, "[w]hile this moral economy cannot be described as 'political' in any advanced sense, nevertheless it cannot be described as unpolitical either, since it supposed definite, and passionately held, notions of the common weal." Indeed, in many ways the moral economy can be seen as first and foremost political, even before it is economic. Pace Karandinos et al. (this volume), it can arguably be seen as a proto-theory of justice—thereby highlighting how justice is always positional—that at its most basic implicitly postulates a theory of political motivation and agency. As such, it offers a basis for both interpreting and explaining the evolving nature of collective social order. This is perhaps best understood from a thanatopolitical perspective. To properly get to grips with this, however, it is perhaps instructive to turn back to Foucault's ideas about biopolitics and, more specifically, to their articulation by the Italian philosopher Giorgio Agamben (1998, 103), who famously argued that the most basic form of power in the modern era rests upon the biopolitical categorization of persons into "valid" and "invalid" populations through the creation and re-creation of a fundamental distinction between what he terms "political life" (*bios*)—that which is imbued with sense—and "bare life" (*zoe*)—that which is nothing more than mere existence. This constitutes the "originary" point for the constitution of social order, according to Agamben, insofar as exclusion from "political life" establishes the limits of this order.

Many authors have pointed out both implicitly and explicitly that much of the population of the contemporary developing world, including in particular in its slums, is increasingly treated as being "bare life," that is to say, invalid populations that have no purpose and must be kept at bay from a shrinking "political life" that is more often than not elite oriented and driven (e.g., Biehl 2005; Davis 2006; de Boeck 2009; McIntyre and Nast 2011; Tosa 2009). When seen from this perspective—and also harking back to the parallels of his circumstances with social banditry—it can be argued that the reason Lencho was so feted and lauded was that he fought—and sacrificed himself—against the spread of "bare life," that is to say, against the exclusion of poor slum inhabitants from the body politic, and for the possibility of their being able to say "I am." But just as social banditry was, according to Hobsbawm, at best proto-revolutionary, so too the kind of political action that Lencho and the gang represented did not sustain itself and was transformed under the combined pressures of exclusion, poverty, and lack of opportunities that have characterized post-revolutionary Nicaragua. The gang's involvement in drug trafficking meant that it became more inwardly focused, more parochial, which transformed the moral landscape within the community, to the extent that Charola's death in 2006 was experienced as contingent and senseless.

One way of thinking about this change is in terms of a transformation of the underlying basis of the barrio Luis Fanor Hernández moral economy. If this was initially implicitly predicated on resistance to "bare life" in the 1990s, it subsequently became based on the predominance of what might be termed "bare death." This term was coined by Jean Comaroff (2007, 203) in her writings about the politics of HIV/AIDS infection in South Africa, to describe the way that victims of the disease are obliterated from memory, both locally and nationally (see also Decoteau 2008). As Stuart Murray (2006, 208) remarks, "this kind of death exceeds biophysical death. It is not the mere cessation of life and not even merely an attack on the conditions of possibility for life itself," but instead "a form of death . . . [that radicalizes] . . . our existential uncertainty" by negating the social significance of death. Kevin O'Neill (2012) has described this very well in a recent article exploring the interrelation between infrastructure and violence in Guatemala City's central cemetery, where overcrowding and new public administration measures have led to demands for the family of the dead to pay regularly for the cemetery plots of their loved ones, with failure to pay leading to disinterment and relocation into mass graves. In doing so, the dead are stripped of their social significance, cast aside as worthless within a neoliberal body politic.

In other words, just as Giorgio Agamben's notion of bare life distinguishes between two types of living—biological versus political—we can distinguish between two types of deaths. Lencho's death was obviously heavy with political significance, due to a particular moral economy regarding social action and agency, whereby gang members were seen as sacrificing themselves for the neighborhood. Charola's murder, on the other hand, was viewed as senseless and contingent, and was therefore a purely biological death, a "bare death." A critical distinction between "bare life" and "bare death", however, is that even if the former has been widely described as underpinning a new global politics of exclusion, it remains a fundamentally relational state of being—one that is implicitly defined in relation to "political life." In other words, "bare life" corresponds to an absence or a deficit, but always with regards to "political life." Indeed, Agamben (1998, 8) qualifies "bare life" as "inclusive exclusion." "Bare death," on the other hand, is not a relational form of categorization but an absolute one, corresponding to a state of pure nonexistence. As such, it can be said to represent something of a rupture, as it effectively constitutes a negation of the social that must necessarily underpin the political. When seen from this perspective, the obvious question raised by the thanatopolitical analysis presented here is whether such a rupture can be reversed, or whether in terms of the general political economy of Nicaragua's developmental trajectory it signals a point of no return down a dystopian road that is all the more tragic in view of the country's inspirational utopian past (see Rodgers 2008a).

ACKNOWLEDGEMENTS

I am grateful to Javier Auyero, Craig Jeffrey, Pamela Neumann, Tony O'Sullivan, and participants at the "Violence at the Urban Margins" workshop held at the University of Texas at Austin's Lozano Long Institute for Latin American Studies on April 4–5, 2013, for useful comments on earlier draft versions of this chapter.

NOTES

1. This name is a pseudonym, as are all the names of the individuals mentioned in this paper.
2. Foucault (2000, 416) used the expression *thanatopolitics* to describe "the reverse of biopolitics," but he associated it with specific instances of "wholesale slaughter" rather than the more generic application I am suggesting here.
3. My translation of the original Spanish—"*somos muerte arriba*"—is not literal, as I feel that the range of connotations the expression entails are not adequately conveyed by a more verbatim rendition of "we are [with] death above [us]."
4. While this may not sound like a very high number, it was equivalent to a 4 percent death rate for gang members. By contrast, the death rate for Union troops for the whole duration of the American Civil War (1861–1865)—often considered the bloodiest conflict in US history—amounted to 1.2 percent (calculated on the basis of Leland and Oboroceanu, 2010, 2, table 1).
5. I have no explanation why she challenged Bismarck and Jader, as this was rather unusual behavior for an unaccompanied woman, particularly considering her socioeconomic status.
6. Obviously, the ethos of "living in the shadow of death" can also be associated with the prevalent *machismo* characterizing Nicaraguan society, insofar as this very much revolved around activities such as "taking risk [or] displaying bravado in the face of danger" (Lancaster 1992, 195). To a certain extent, it is not dissimilar to the "riding" described by George Karandinos et al. (this volume).
7. This is not to say that neighborhood inhabitants never had anything negative to say about local gang members or did not quarrel with them, of course. Parents frequently

publicly expressed their worry about their offspring, for example, often berating them for the stress they caused them, and on several occasions during my first bout of field-work in 1996–1997, arguments broke out between neighborhood inhabitants and local gang members concerning the responsibility of the latter over damage caused to houses during gang warfare.

8. To a certain extent, this particular behavior was also due to the deep distrust of the police that existed in barrio Luis Fanor Hernández, partly related to the fact that they rarely came when called unless the caller explicitly indicated that they were willing to "pay for the gasoline" (i.e., pay a bribe). It should be noted that police patrols in the neighborhood were generally extremely infrequent during the mid-1990s.

9. This analogy is perhaps all the more relevant considering the strong associations between *Sandinismo* and the "Cult of Che" (see Lancaster 1988, 132 and 185).

10. Parallels can obviously be made here with the "mala conducta" ascribed to drug addicts in Guatemala, as described by Kevin Lewis O'Neill and Benjamin Fogarty-Valenzuela (this volume).

WORKS CITED

Agamben, Giorgio. 1998. *Homo Sacer: Sovereign Power and Bare Life*. Stanford: Stanford University Press.

Arendt, Hannah. 1969. *On Violence*. New York: Harcourt Brace.

Balandier, Georges. 1970. *Political Anthropology*. New York: Pantheon.

Benjamin, Walter. 1986. "The Destructive Character." In *Reflections: Essays, Aphorisms, Autobiographical Writings*, edited by Peter Demetz. New York: Schocken Books.

Biehl, Joao. 2005. *Vita: Life in a Zone of Social Abandonment*. Berkeley: University of California Press.

Bloch, Maurice. 1996. "La 'consommation' des jeunes hommes chez les Zafimaniry de Madagascar." In *De la Violence*, edited by Françoise Héritier. Paris: Odile Jacob.

Comaroff, Jean. 2007. "Beyond Bare Life: AIDS, (Bio)Politics, and the Neoliberal Order." *Public Culture* 19(1): 197–219.

Davis, Mike. 2006. *Planet of Slums*. London: Verso.

De Boeck, Filip. 2009. "Death Matters: Intimacy, Violence and the Production of Social Knowledge by Urban Youth in the Democratic Republic of Congo." In *Can there be Life without the Other?*, edited by Antonio Pinto Ribeiro. Manchester: Carcanet Press.

Decoteau, Claire Laurier. 2008. "The Bio-Politics of HIV/AIDS in Post-Apartheid South Africa." PhD dissertation, Department of Sociology, University of Michigan.

Festinger, Leon. 1957. *A Theory of Cognitive Dissonance*. Stanford, CA: Stanford University Press.

Foucault, Michel. 1970. *The Order of Things: An Archaeology of the Human Sciences*. London: Tavistock.

Foucault, Michel. 2000. *Power: Essential Works of Michel Foucault, 1954–1984*, Volume 3, edited James D. Faubion. New York: New Press.

Foucault, Michel. 2003. *Society Must Be Defended: Lectures at the Collège de France, 1975–76*. London: Penguin.

Girard, René. 1977. *Violence and the Sacred*. Baltimore: Johns Hopkins University Press.

Guevara, Ernesto. 1969. *Venceremos: The Speeches and Writings of Che Guevara*. New York: Simon and Schuster.

Hobsbawm, Eric J. 1959. *Primitive Rebels: Studies in Archaic Forms of Social Movement in the Nineteenth and Twentieth Centuries*. Manchester: Manchester University Press.

Hubert, Henri, and Marcel Mauss. 1964. *Sacrifice: Its Nature and Function*. Chicago: University of Chicago Press.

Jensen, Steffen, and Dennis Rodgers. 2008. "Revolutionaries, Barbarians, or War Machines? Gangs in Nicaragua and South Africa." In *Socialist Register 2009: Violence Today— Actually Existing Barbarism*, edited by Colin Leys and Leo Panitch. London: Merlin.

Kuasñosky, Silvia, and Dalia Szulik. 1996. "Desde los márgenes de la juventud." In *La Juventud es Más que una Palabra: Ensayos sobre Cultura y Juventud*, edited by M. Margulis. Buenos Aires: Editorial Biblos.

Lancaster, Roger N. 1988. *Thanks to God and the Revolution: Popular Religion and Class Consciousness in the New Nicaragua*. New York: Columbia University Press.

Lancaster, Roger N. 1992. *Life is Hard: Machismo, Danger, and the Intimacy of Power in Nicaragua*. Berkeley: University of California Press.

Leland, Anne, and Mari-Jana Oboroceanu. 2010. *American War and Military Operations Casualties: Lists and Statistics*, CRS Report RL32492. Washington, DC: Congressional Research Service.

Li, Tania Murray. 2009. "To Make Live or Let Die? Rural Dispossession and the Protection of Surplus Populations." *Antipode* 14(6): 1208–1235.

McIntyre, Michael, and Heidi J. Nast. 2011. "Bio(necro)polis: Marx, Surplus Populations, and the Spatial Dialectics of Reproduction and 'Race.'" *Antipode* 43(5): 1465–1488.

Murray, Stuart J. 2006. "Thanatopolitics: On the Use of Death for Mobilizing Political Life." *Polygraph* 18: 191–215.

Norris, Andrew. 2000. "Giorgio Agamben and the Politics of the Living Dead." *Diacritics* 30(4): 38–58.

O'Neill, Kevin Lewis. 2012. "There is No More Room: Cemeteries, Personhood, and Bare Death." *Ethnography* 13(4): 510–530.

Rodgers, Dennis. 2006. "Living in the Shadow of Death: Gangs, Violence and Social Order in Urban Nicaragua, 1996–2002." *Journal of Latin American Studies* 38(2): 267–292.

Rodgers, Dennis. 2007a. "'Each to their Own': Ethnographic Notes on the Economic Organisation of Poor Households in Urban Nicaragua." *Journal of Development Studies* 43(3): 391–419.

Rodgers, Dennis. 2007b. "Joining the Gang and Becoming a Broder: The Violence of Ethnography in Contemporary Nicaragua." *Bulletin of Latin American Research* 26(4): 444–461.

Rodgers, Dennis. 2008a. "Searching for the Time of Beautiful Madness: Of Ruins and Revolution in Post-Sandinista Nicaragua." In *Enduring Socialism: Explorations of Revolution and Transformation, Restoration and Continuation*, edited by Harry West and Paru Raman. Oxford: Berghahn.

Rodgers, Dennis. 2008b. "A Symptom Called Managua." *New Left Review* 49 (January–February): 103–120.

Rodgers, Dennis. 2011. "An Illness Called Managua: Urbanisation and 'Mal-development' in Nicaragua." In *Urban Theory beyond the West: A World of Cities*, edited by Tim Edensor and Mark Jayne. London: Routledge.

Rodgers, Dennis. 2014. "*Bróderes, Vagos*, and *Compadres* in the *Barrio*: Kinship, Politics, and Local Territorialization in Urban Nicaragua." In *Cities from Scratch: Poverty and Informality in Urban Latin America*, edited by Brodwyn Fischer, Brian McCann, and Javier Auyero. Durham, NC: Duke University Press.

Rose, Nikolas. 2006. *The Politics of Life Itself: Biomedicine, Power, and Subjectivity in the Twenty-First Century*. Princeton, NJ: Princeton University Press.

Scott, James C. 1976. *The Moral Economy of the Peasant: Rebellion and Subsistence in Southeast Asia.* New Haven, CT: Yale University Press.

Thrasher, Frederick. 1927. *The Gang: A Study of 1,313 Gangs in Chicago.* Chicago: University of Chicago Press.

Tosa, Hiroyuki. 2009. "Anarchical Governance: Neoliberal Governmentality in Resonance with the State of Exception." *International Political Sociology* 3(4): 414–430.

Wagner, Kim A. 2007. "Thuggee and Social Banditry Reconsidered." *The Historical Journal* 50(2): 353–376.

CHAPTER 2

The Moral Economy of Violence in the US Inner City

Deadly Sociability in the Retail Narcotics Economy

GEORGE KARANDINOS, LAURIE KAIN HART,
FERNANDO MONTERO CASTRILLO,
PHILIPPE BOURGOIS

George's fieldnote

A burst of loud yelling makes me glance out my bedroom window just in time to see a frail, middle-aged heroin addict slam into the side of my parked car. He is reeling from a punch to his jaw from Roland, one of my 22 year old neighbors. Alfredo, a gangling fifteen year old who lives two doors down from me, jumps on the fallen man, kicking him in the chest.

A few minutes later, I am sitting on the stoop with Roland, his mother Sol, and Juan, a heroin injector who regularly buys on the block, to hear the full story. Roland claps Juan on the back and explains: "Juan was the first to hit him."

Juan shrugs, "I only went to talk to him at first but to my eyes it looked like he was lifting his arm to hit you. So I punched him."

Sol adds, to make sure I understand, "See, George, this morning, a man thought I was staring at him and he cursed me. And when he came by again I pointed him out to Juan. Then when the trouble started, everybody came out to help me"

Roland interrupts: "Yeah, now if Juan has problems I'll ride for him, and for Alfredo too. I'll do that because they defended my mom."

Roland is currently on probation for seven counts of possession of narcotics, conspiracy to sell a controlled substance, attempted murder and gun possession. If he is arrested again on assault, he could face up to 10 years in prison for violating probation. When I ask him about this risk he shakes his head dismissively, "When I get in a fight or I'm really angry, I don't think of anything . . ." Roland explains that his mother's boyfriend, Carlos, "doesn't have that anger inside him where he can fight. Even if he said 'Okay let's fight,' and came down to fight someone, he would get his ass kicked because he doesn't have the anger to fight hard, and the other person will have that anger. I have that anger."

Sol nods in agreement, "I can't depend on Carlos."

Roland adds solemnly, "I am Sol's only son. Carlos doesn't fight. He won't get into my mom's problems. So I think God put me here for that reason. If I go to jail or if I die for my mom like this then I don't care, I'll die happy. I'll be smiling in my casket."

THE RIDER IN THE MORAL ECONOMY

Unlike Roland, Carlos is not a "rider," and his gentleness conjugates with a longer list of other failures as a man incapable of fulfilling patriarchal responsibilities. Sol does not hesitate to tell others, when she is depressed, that Carlos does not contribute financially to the household, cannot repair things in their crumbling apartment, does not help her resist the temptation to binge on crack, and is sexually impotent.

The importance of being a rider propels young men and women like Roland, Juan, Alfredo, and Sol into violent conflict on inner-city streets. They find themselves trapped in reciprocal exchanges of assistive violence and public displays of fearlessness and aggression. In an environment marked by scarcity at the margins of the legal labor market, buffeted by unstable influxes of cash from illegal drug sales, violence becomes an especially abundant and valuable resource in a larger, morally regulated gift economy that facilitates sociability and day-to-day survival through exchanges of goods, services, affective bonds, small sums of money, and—perhaps most importantly—access to just-in-time subcontract employment in the drug economy. An act of assistive violence creates a debt that becomes the basis for an ongoing relationship generating social obligations and hierarchies of prestige. Failure to reciprocate makes an individual vulnerable to defamation, social isolation, and ultimately violent victimization. It also excludes that individual from the narcotics industry, the largest local source of employment and income. Participating in violence, consequently, becomes a moral, social, and practical economic imperative for many of the young men and women who are invested in maintaining public credibility in street-based interactions.

Historically, anthropology's contribution to understanding violence has been to explore its structural-organizational effects and local moral valences. To avoid the romanticizing, essentializing, or racializing trap of projecting valorizing humanistic visions of popular justice and order onto "traditional heroic peoples," spectacularized black gangsters, or the "unworthy poor," (see critiques by Meeker 1980; Thomas 2011; Wacquant 2002), we need to unpack the local ethics for interpersonal and criminal violence in their relationship to external fields of power and economic forces.

Social historian E. P. Thompson developed the concept of "moral economy" in his analysis of small-town food riots in eighteenth-century England (Thompson 1971). He documented the ways an emerging capitalist market economy violated "customary norms . . . and practices" resulting in violent outbreaks of class conflict (Thompson 1991, 271). Political scientist James C. Scott brought the concept to the attention of anthropology with his analyses of rural resistance to super-exploitation by landlords and market speculators in Southeast Asia (see review by Edelman 2012; Scott 1976).[1] These works highlight the ways terms of exchange—the price of bread, sharecropping arrangements, rents, access to common land, crop prices—are locally embedded in moral expectations about appropriate behavior that make power-holders socially accountable to the poor in times of scarcity. In normal times, moral economies form part of patronage systems, with checks and balances against aberrant abuse that, paradoxically, ultimately legitimize an exploitative and hierarchical status quo to the benefit of the powerful. When the terms of these moral economies break down under pressure from commodification, crises such as a crop failures can precipitate revolutionary movements (Wolf 1969).

Anthropologists, following Durkheim (1938 [1895]), use the term *moral* to describe collective socially obligatory practices, and explicitly disassociate it from its transcultural positive ethical valence. Nevertheless, the word's vague commonsensical implications have led to an analytical slippage in the use of "moral economy," and its association with a supracultural implication of justice. S. J. Tambiah (1996, 319–323), in his analysis of ethnonationalist conflicts in South Asia, specifically rejects the use of a concept of a "moral economy of collective violence" because it mischaracterizes ethnic pogroms as subaltern resistance. Several critics have also warned against the term's "banalization" (Edelman 2012; Fassin 2009). In a careful analysis of the ways Thompson's original formulation has traveled through the social sciences, Marc Edelman criticizes the loss of Thompson's concern with the mediation of highly unequal class relations as well as his focus on the role of the marketplace as "a nexus for class conflict and struggle."

Thompson's own use of the term *moral*, however, is not by any means neutral. His analysis valorizes the violence of subaltern mobilizations against the rise of eighteenth-century agrarian capitalism (for example, see Thompson's 1991 response to the polemics that "moral economy" elicited among anti-Marxist British historians). Our anthropological usage of the term, by contrast, makes no argument that intracommunity/intraclass street violence represents political or prepolitical mobilization (still less, that it should elicit positive valorization). Nevertheless, Thompson's concept is useful for an anthropological exploration of, on the one hand, the contradictory pressures of extra-state customary justice and, on the other hand, the reverberations of disjunctive shifts in modes of production. In adapting Thompson's interclass model to our own case, we draw on an a Maussian (Mauss [1924] 1990) interpretation of gift exchange in non-market societies.[2] Mauss's early twentieth-century functionalist insight on the structuring effects of reciprocity, however, does not help us see the negative articulation of local social formations within broader class hierarchies and global processes in twenty-first-century segregated urban enclaves (though, arguably, his analyses of potlatch hint at a more complex critique of reciprocity, hierarchy, and global circulation).

We suggest that to understand the disruptive effects of market and state forces, especially those shaping the drug economy, we need to combine Thompson's emphasis on disenfranchisement in relation to commoditized market relations with Mauss's analysis of the moral regulation of everyday intraclass reciprocities by bringing Marx's theory of primitive accumulation (1972 [1867], Part VIII) to bear on the exploitative productivity of violence in the everyday state of emergency that rules the US inner city. Marx's emphasis on the centrality of violence to new processes of capital formation helps us conceptualize the ways value can be destructively extracted from the human body by state violence as well as by interpersonal and instrumental criminal violence when other productive resources are unavailable. Riding relationships produce valuable social capital at the expense of violated bodies. The inelastic demand of the pained bodies of addicted customers elevate cash profits in the drug economy; drug bosses capitalize on the hyperexploitation of piece-rate street-level sellers who are subject to chronic incarceration and physical maiming by rivals and thieves. Finally, the state's prosecution of a zero-tolerance war on drugs elevates prices in the drug market, destabilizing supply and creating cycles of scarcity and plenty. Violence consequently becomes a practical necessity in a volatile illegal drug economy that obviously cannot rely on law enforcement to regulate the orderly exchange of its commodity in a safe, stable marketplace.

Our hybrid moral economy concept facilitates an ethnographic documentation of the ways in which the apparently individualized acts of violence that erupt intermittently in the neighborhood are embedded in the historical context of deindustrialization and the contemporary facts of inner-city hypersegregation, infrastructural desertification, and coercive policing.

It renders more comprehensible the emergence of contradictory destructive-and-solidary survival practices that are part of the fallout from both scarcity and the hierarchically accumulated volatile profits of the drug economy. Ethnographies of spectacular violence in West African war zones at the turn of the 21st century have also emphasized violence's "productivity" in relationship to extractive local and global economies and parasitical states with shrinking resource bases (Hoffman 2011; Vigh 2006. See also Abdullah and Muana 1998; Bayart 1993).

RESOURCE SCARCITY IN THE DEINDUSTRIALIZED INNER CITY

We have been conducting fieldwork as a team since the fall of 2007 on a block in the predominantly Puerto Rican section of North Philadelphia. According to the 2010 Census, our tract and those surrounding it are over 70 percent "Hispanic," primarily Puerto Rican, with significant Dominican and African American populations and a small Mexican, Central American, and South American presence. Forty-seven percent of the residents in our census tract have annual incomes below the poverty line, almost twice the citywide rate of 24 percent and three and a half times the national rate of 13.5 percent. According to the Census Bureau's American Community Survey 2005–2009, three of the census tracts surrounding us have poverty

rates over 54 percent, and five of the eight poorest census tracts in the city are in the Puerto Rican section of North Philadelphia.

Philadelphia has not yet recovered from deindustrialization. It is the poorest of the ten largest cities in the United States and, beset by the classic US pattern of white and middle-class outmigration to the suburbs, it has lost residents every year from 1951 to 2009 (Philadelphia Research Initiative 2011; Davis 1990; Wilson 1987). Demographers identify Philadelphia as one of five hypersegregated metropolises in the United States (Wilkes and Iceland 2004). Puerto Ricans migrated to Philadelphia in large numbers immediately after World War II seeking factory jobs in the city and agricultural work in the suburban counties (Whalen 2001). Over the next three decades, however, over 75 percent of those manufacturing jobs disappeared. Additionally, Philadelphia has some of the highest rates of vacant and abandoned property in the country, and North Philadelphia's infrastructure is especially devastated (Fairbanks 2009, 5).

The block on which two members of our ethnographic team (George Karandinos and Fernando Montero Castrillo) lived between 2009 and 2012 is literally in the shade of an enormous abandoned curtain and upholstery fabric factory that occupies a full square block. As late as 1962, there were fourteen factories producing rugs, textiles, and tools within five square blocks of our fieldwork site (Department of Public Works 1962). At its height in the immediate post-World War II years, our street had sixty-six row houses. Six are now abandoned, uninhabitable ruins. A further thirteen have been demolished. Seven are vacant and strewn with garbage, and five have been converted into parking spaces. From the window of Fernando's apartment, we could see another full-square-block vacant lot, where a yarn mill formerly stood. From his roof, we could count eleven more abandoned factories.

As in many US inner cities beset by public- and private-sector disinvestment, the drug economy has filled the economic vacuum and become the most readily accessible "equal opportunity employer" for poor male high school dropouts (Anderson 1999; Bourgois 2003). In the context of the US war on drugs, this effectively condemns a large portion of local residents to lives of chronic incarceration (Goffman 2009; Wacquant 2009). In 2006, Philadelphia had the highest per-capita rate of county jail incarceration in the nation (Petteruti and Walsh 2008).

The poorest section of Puerto Rican North Philadelphia is also the city's most active open-air drug market for heroin and powder cocaine. It attracts primarily white injectors from other impoverished Philadelphia neighborhoods and some wealthier clients from the surrounding tristate regional suburban sprawl (Pennsylvania-New Jersey-Delaware). Within two hundred meters of our apartment,

buyers can purchase heroin, cocaine (both crack and powder forms), PCP (referred to locally as "wet" or "embalming fluid"), marijuana, and diverted prescription pills (primarily benzodiazepines such as Xanax and opiates such as Percocet) at virtually any time of day and night. The growth of the drug economy is most intelligible when understood as one of the few remaining sources of significant income generation accessible to neighborhood residents. It valorizes the cultural skills, knowledge of the streets, and ability to mobilize violence of the most impoverished members of the inner city. In contrast, the low levels of education and the limited social capital of most residents restrict their access to the lowest rung of the dwindling service, commerce, and factory jobs remaining in their community.

The prevalence of drugs is well documented in police statistics: in 2006, officers made 1,100 narcotics-related arrests in the neighborhood we are studying. This represented over 10 percent of total narcotics arrests in the city that year and 62 percent more than any other of sixty-eight localities identified by the University of Pennsylvania's Neighborhood Information System's CrimeBase. In 2006, the drug arrest rate in the fifteen census tracts with the highest number of Hispanic residents in Philadelphia was 30.4 per 1,000 inhabitants, almost four times the citywide rate of 8.5 per 1,000 inhabitants. The primitive accumulation processes that have turned the neighborhood into a sprawling open-air supermarket elevate local rates of petty and major violent street crime.

Addicts steal opportunistically and mug local residents for cash to ward off painful withdrawal symptoms, and dealers fight for territory, enforce (or violate) contracts, and intimidate police informers. This section of North Philadelphia, consequently, is one of the most violent in the city. In the late 1990s and early 2000s, it had Philadelphia's highest rate of shootings and murders, and in 2011 the city of Philadelphia as a whole logged the most per-capita murders of the ten largest US cities.

Violence becomes both a risk, and a resource to be managed intimately through social relations, because the state mechanisms of regulation taken for granted in wealthier neighborhoods are ineffective at best and hostile at worst. Classic anthropological studies of segmentary societies have noted that fragile economic capital in the absence of effective centralized state authority elevates the practical and cultural value of violence (Meeker 1979). A reputation for mobilizing violence and rage skillfully becomes a form of cultural capital (Bourgois 1989) that translates into useful social capital through networks of reciprocity based on kinship, friendship, romance, and utilitarian economics. Ironically, the moral economy of violence cannot exist without the personal disposition to generosity that is inculcated in those residents who seek security in the Maussian economy of face-to-face exchanges of basic resources. On most days, the neighborhood is a friendly place. Many of our neighbors respond

to the routine boredom that unemployment and poverty impose
by investing their energy in warm sociability. On sunny days, neighbors
sit on stoops, chatting, listening to music, and playing spades and dominoes. Most blocks regularly organize block parties, and children play in
the street. Spectacular incidents of violence irregularly erupt, however,
in the midst of this dense sociality. In a two-month period during our
first spring here, there were fifteen shootings, three of them fatal, within
four blocks of our apartment. There were also three stabbings and eleven
aggravated assaults. The following spring was just as violent and just as
spectacular, including a prolonged afternoon fusillade a few blocks away
from us that left one man with fifteen bullet wounds.

TRANSGRESSIONS IN THE MORAL ECONOMY
OF DRUG SELLING

While an ethics of reciprocity propels individuals into violent acts, these
same social relations of mutual obligation and dependence also impose
restraints on overly transgressive violence. During the first two years of
our fieldwork, our block was an active open-air heroin sales spot. Benito
was the *bichote* (a Puerto Rican colonial Hispanicization of the English
phrase "big shot"), which means that he controlled the rights to drug selling on our block. He lived in another neighborhood but was recognized
as *el dueño* (the owner), and he had an ex-wife, a child, and many friends

residing on the block. He charged Rico, a local drug entrepreneur, several thousand dollars a week for the privilege of selling heroin on the corner, which a rival *bichote* jokingly referred to as "waterfront property." Rico's workers opened the "*punto* [sales point]" at dawn and, on good days, sold over a thousand ten-dollar packets of heroin and cocaine to streams of primarily white addicts who arrived on foot, often dressed in rags and limping from abscesses. Occasionally, cars would swoop in from the suburbs to buy wholesale quantities.

Competition for preferential access to scarce resources in a limited territory is a classic generator of violence (Peters 1975, xxiii), but the drug economy also requires a limit on non-instrumental violence that is bad for business. For example, the beating of the heroin addict in George's opening vignette conflicted with the immediate instrumental logic of the drug market. It risked attracting police attention and produced an undercurrent of tension over who rightfully controlled public space: Rico, the manager of drug sales on the block, or Roland, the local resident. Rico ultimately reasserted his authority over the public space by beating up the lowest status participant in the fight: Juan, the heroin addict who had thrown the first punch. He also sent out a warning to fifteen-year-old Alfredo, but did not punish the teenager physically. He did not dare confront Roland and Sol, but neither did Roland step in to defend Juan or Alfredo, despite his recent public promise to ride for them. Their incipient rider relationship was too fragile, not buttressed by kinship or the kind of status and economic incentives that Rico commanded within his own larger network of retainers as a drug boss.

A few months later, a more dangerous transgression in the moral economy occurred when Benito's guarantee to Rico that no one else be allowed to compete with his sales on the block broke down with a midday shoot-out that left Benito on the run and his girlfriend with a wounded foot. Benito was lucky. The customized extension of his assailant's semiautomatic pistol caught in the sag of his "short-pants" as he was drawing it out, giving Benito time to duck for cover. His opening salvo went wild, and Benito put four bullets into his assailant's back and chest before speeding off in his SUV. Over a dozen bullets sprayed into the brick facades of six row houses on the block.

The shoot-out proved to be a tipping point. Its magnitude and carelessness violated the delicate conventions that, for the past sixteen months, had granted Benito an undisputed fear-based respect and begrudging, semi-amiable tolerance by neighbors on the block who benefited directly or indirectly from his occasional financial generosity. Over the next few weeks, criticisms began circulating about Benito's greed. He was accused of having provoked the

attack by trying to take over someone else's corner five blocks away. "He already owns this block and two others. What kind of a person thinks he needs four blocks?" We also heard complaints that "Benito and Rico ain't done nothin' for us this summer." When the block captain organized a city-sponsored clean-up of the block's back alleys, he noted angrily that Rico failed to pay any of his hustling crew to help us pick up garbage. Several residents commented that on the July 4 block party, neither Rico nor Benito bought meat for the barbecue or fireworks. A mother grumbled to George, "He didn't even buy the kids one of those plastic swimming pools, to cool down on hot days." These criticisms of the *bichote's* lack of generosity approximate a more Thompsonian hierarchical moral economy process,[3] which demands proper resource sharing from patrons who hoard economic resources; Benito and Rico diplomatically shut down sales on our block in the shooting's aftermath.

Over the next winter and spring, in the market vacuum created by Benito's retreat, several attempts were made by two different *bichotes* to "reopen the punto [open air sales spot]," but both failed following multiple police raids allegedly prompted by calls to the police by "the mothers." The "snitching" was rumored to be coordinated by Luisa, the mother of a twenty year old who had been accidentally killed five years earlier by a stray bullet from a gunfight between low-level drug sellers. She obliquely took responsibility for calling the police, noting her concern for

her eleven-year-old daughter and four-year-old nephew: "We [the mothers on the block] are trying to raise kids here, we don't want to be a *punto*
anymore [*ya no queremos ser punto*]." Zubillaga et al. (this volume) provide further insight into the unique cultural position of mothers who at
times are able to carve out a fragile united legitimacy to mediate and even
dare to protest the violence destroying their communities. The stakes are
unimaginably high for these mothers who are often implicated in the violence they condemn. Their sons are often both perpetrators and victims
of the shootings, and their mourning for lost sons propels surviving sons
to participate in cycles of revenge. Furthermore, their own vulnerability
in the precarious environment of extreme urban relegation obliges their
sons to mobilize violence to protect them in the nexus of local struggles
for respect and resources.

Several years before we moved into the neighborhood, a row home
across the street from our apartment had been firebombed after the owner
reported drug-dealing activities to the police. During this five-month-long
drug market hiatus, however, even Benito's former sellers celebrated the
newfound calm brought on by Luisa's alleged snitching: "Now the mothers can let the kids out to play without having to worry." They all emphasized the gendered and age-graded legitimacy of a mother's right to protect
her children from violence. They all also unproblematically ignored their
own recent pasts as drug sellers and participants in violence. Goffman

(this volume) subtly notes a similar flexibility among participants in the quasi-ubiquitous underground economies of inner-city Philadelphia to redact problematic inconsistencies in their adherence to kin-and-gender-scripted moral codes in the struggle for survival.

Eight months later, to our surprise, Benito returned and smoothly reestablished drug sales. The previous criticisms of him were forgotten, and it was business as usual. We asked Benito how he managed to "reopen the block" when two other operations had collapsed in his absence under police pressure brought on by snitching. He answered, without hesitation:

> Respect . . . and then the love of the neighbors. You get that by looking out for them. If anybody else tries to open the block, the neighbors will call a cop quick. But they respect me and they know they can talk to me, and I talk to them, so it's not a problem with me. If they need help with rent or bills they know they can come talk to me. So when I come around and I speak to them they be like, "That's fine." And when shit's doin' alright, you look out for the neighbors, like if they doin' a little barbecue and want to close the block, we just buy a whole bunch of stuff for the kids and do it right.

Benito had also cultivated a unique relationship to Luisa five years earlier following the collateral death of her son. Benito had paid for her son's funeral, and commissioned both a reggaeton song and a thirty-foot mural in Luisa's son's honor. According to Benito, Luisa had been sending

neighbors around with a box to raise money for her son's funeral, unbeknownst to him, and

> . . . someone came over to me with that box and I said "No, no, no. We don't do that on
> this block, you ain't going to be asking for money with boxes for your son's funeral."
> That's a loss that lasts forever. How does it look I am out here making all this money
> and Luisa is sending out a box to collect money for her son's funeral? So I told her,
> "Get whatever you want, and I'm gonna pay for the whole thing. Get whatever casket
> and do the service the way you want it."

The "thanatopolitical" insight from Rodger's provocative call (this volume) to attend to the politics of death can be productively extended to highlight the social solidarity-building effects of the death of Luisa's son. Benito, the *bichote*, resuscitated his self-serving commitment to a local moral economy just-in-time, and managed to cement the legitimacy of his monopoly of drug-dealing rights on the block by publicly funding Luisa's mourning for the senseless death of her son in a crossfire of drug-market violence.

EARLY HABITUS FORMATION: FAMILY, GENDER, AND SCHOOL

On an embodied level, the moral economy of violence requires the propensity to flare into rage at a moment's notice over apparently trivial insults. Bourdieu's concept of habitus (defined as an individual's socioeconomically and culturally patterned deepest likes, dislikes, propensities, and "schemas of perception") is useful for understanding how behaviors, conceptualized as embodied "practices," operate on both a conscious and preconscious level in a relationship to encompassing fields of power (Bourdieu 2000,128–163).

Roland, for example, was proud of having a habitus-level well of rage that prompts him to fight effectively ("I have that anger . . . to fight hard"). His habitus resonates with the insecurity of inner-city streets to make him an effective rider, but it simultaneously puts him at a disadvantage in his relationship to the state and the larger economic and social field ("When I'm really angry, I don't think of anything, not even getting locked up"). Riders, consequently, are especially vulnerable to being imprisoned in the current era of hyperincarceration. At the time of the beating described earlier, Roland was living as a financial parasite of his mother with his pregnant fifteen-year-old girlfriend. In contrast to his failure to fulfill his responsibility as a father and as an only son, he excels at violence and consequently embraced the opportunity to reaffirm his love for his mother by attacking her insulter. Rather than regretting the risk of long-term incarceration on a probation violation, he felt mystically empowered afterward, invoking God and an epiphanal purpose in life.

Roland's mother and the elderly addict who was beaten are also dispositionally sensitive to imagined or real insults. The beatdown itself was triggered by a hyperalert habitus: Juan delivered the proactive first punch as a protective reflex to preempt another punch that, in fact, might never have been thrown. Finally, Alfredo, the fifteen year old, had no qualms about repeatedly kicking a fallen, emaciated, elderly addict. He did not need to know why the man deserved punishment.

Instrumental interests were also entangled with the dispositional response of each of the participants in that particular beatdown. Juan was raising his fragile status as a lowly heroin addict by siding with Sol, a street dealer, and her son Roland. Juan had only known Sol for a couple of months, but he regularly brought her syringes to sell to the injectors purchasing heroin next door to her, and she often gave him food. She enjoyed conversing with him and sometimes lent him money when he was short a dollar or two for a packet of heroin. His participation in the fight extended this incipient relationship with Sol into a rider relationship with her son, publically acknowledged as a debt by Roland: "Now I will ride for you." More mundanely, Alfredo, the fifteen year old, took advantage of the beatdown to demonstrate his budding masculinity, proving himself for the first time in his life to be a worthy rider among adults.

Adolescence and early childhood are crucial moments in habitus formation. Benito's transgressive shoot-out offered us a glimpse into the powerful habitus-level effects of spectacular violence when experienced in early childhood. We interviewed a father and mother whose row house caught the brunt of the crossfire during Benito's last gunfight on the block. Three bullets had pierced their front door, blasting through their television speakers, shattering a glass angel figurine on their coffee table, and ricocheting off their DVD player before lodging in the plaster wall. Our conversation was interrupted by the couple's precociously articulate three-year-old daughter, Cindy. Her words illustrate how the traumas of spectacular, terrifying violent incidents become powerful conscious teaching moments for parents.

Mother: I had actually just walked in from work, and closed my door, and there were a bunch of gunshots.
Cindy: Yeah, a bunch of it. Bad people just shoot at the door. And then mommy started dragging me and pushed me down. And that's when I got scared. And I was crying. And mommy started crying too. And

Papi fell down, and he just went under the table, and I just did too. And then someone knocked [shot] our glass [angel figurine] down. See! [Pointing at the coffee table] Look!

Father: As soon as I went down, the bullet hit the speaker, boom! Then I felt glass hit me in the back.

Mother: [To Cindy and pointing at the hole in the front door made by the bullet] What is that in the door?

Cindy: A bully?

Mother: No, a bullet hole.

Cindy: [Nodding] That's a bullet hole.

Struggling with learning the difference between a bully and a bullet hole, Cindy tries to manage her fear by opening up an imaginary space for engagement with the "bad people," offering a glimpse into the psychodynamic interface between the conscious and preconscious dimensions of early habitus formation that normalizes a self-protective moral engagement with more powerful potential aggressors:

Mother: . . . she won't sleep in her room. No, she stays in my room now because she says she's too scared.

Cindy: [pointing to the three bullet holes in the door with a worried voice] Little people could come in here? They might hit me?

Mother: No, they're not going to touch you.
Cindy: They're not?
Mother: No.
Cindy: You mean, they like my flower pants? [cheering up] They like 'em?
Mother: Who?
Cindy: The bad people. They like 'em?
Mother: I don't know baby.
Cindy: They better be nice!

Cindy's father, furthermore, attempts to manage his daughter's insecurity through a scenario of exaggerated retributive violence in the face of the state's failure to guarantee personal security:

Father: She wakes up with nightmares screaming about "Daddy! Daddy, no, no, no!" That bullet in the wall could've been her. If that happened, and my daughter would have got shot, I would've went to war.
I tell them [drug sellers] "get off my steps" but they don't listen. It's turning me to the point that one day I'm going to chop somebody's head and heave it down the block. The cops don't do nothing. They just pass right by them [drug sellers] like nothing happens. If it's not their people [other police who are shot] they don't do nothing.
The next person I see on my steps . . . I got that bat right there, it's going right in their head.

The imperatives of the moral economy of violence resonate with gender and age-graded patriarchal responsibilities to defend family ("[If] . . . my daughter would have got shot, I would've went to war"). Our fieldnotes coded "violence" abound with between-the-lines references to these bravado-tinged, high-stakes responsibilities. In the opening fieldnote, for example, Roland was able to resolve the failure of Carlos to defend his mother by becoming a violent son in his emasculated stepfather's stead. Roland's epiphanal solidarity through sacrificial risk-taking for his mother (including exposing himself to the likelihood of long-term incarceration) contrasts with the mutual distrust that otherwise pervades his family's everyday interactions over money, caretaking, and household responsibilities. The precariousness of their economic situation, exacerbated by their addictions, provokes frequent humiliating public squabbles over unpaid loans, pilfered money, and missing possessions. Nevertheless, Roland is ready at a moment's notice to fight for his mother's street respect, despite the consequences.

The insecurity in which families are embroiled in North Philadelphia problematizes the mid-twentieth-century anthropological application of kinship's "axiom of amity" whereby family relations represent a binding force of social structure (Fortes 1970). It also complicates Bloch's (1973) insight that the security offered by the sphere of kinship enables relationships based on longer-term cycles of exchange that tolerate short-term imbalance. According to Bloch, fragile "non-kin" alliances with neighbors and friends require buttressing by frequent, egalitarian exchanges of gifts or labor with immediate benefits. In twenty-first-century North Philadelphia, in the fallout of an illegal drug economy that imposes conditions of primitive accumulation on its customers and its labor force, the reliability of kin relationships, especially when strained by chronic drug consumption, cannot be taken for granted. In a nearby poor, segregated African American neighborhood in the same city, Goffman (this volume) documents an additional level of institutional strain on kinship solidarities as police harass mothers and romantic partners to capture young black men. Zubillaga et al.'s (this volume) analysis of the overlapping, contradictory peacemaking and revenge-demanding role of the solidarity of mother-son relationships in a poor Caracas barrio reveals further violence-producing permutations of kinship solidarity under siege. The relegation of growing surplus populations into outlaw urban neighborhoods overwhelmed with fear and survival insecurity throughout the Americas intensifies the salience of violent solidarity as the most accessible currency of intimate kinship relations.

In the insecure inner-city environment, brothers are also often conspicuously called upon to protect their sisters from insult or physical aggression. For example, when we asked Robert, a young African American man living on our block, whether he had fought much when he was a teenager, he responded, laughing, "I'm an only brother with 14 sisters!," as if the implications were commonsensical: "Of course!"

> They knew they only had one brother. And I'm not just a little brother. I got so many calls. My phone would stay ringing. You know what I mean?

In fact, we only vaguely understood what Robert meant, but when we later documented his kinship network, the everyday emergency of families fragmented by unstable unemployment, incarceration and polarized gender relations emerged more clearly:

Robert: I never grew up with none of my other sisters. Ain't none of us ever lived together like that. My dad wasn't in my life. Like, he came out of jail and then I met his other kids. From him I have fourteen . . . no, thirteen sisters. I have one from my mom. Altogether I've got fourteen sisters. I'm only a little brother to three of them and two of them I haven't met yet, because of my dad's trifling ass. But all the rest of them, they was younger than me, so I stayed getting phone calls.

George: To fight for your sisters?

Robert: Hell yeah. I been fighting for them ever since I was little as fuck, dawg. A man is expected to provide, to protect, dawg. Not be tooken lightly. Half the time if a bitch has got a problem, they call a big brother, or a dad, or an uncle. Niggas is always on time, always on the clock, always being called for something. And you ain't even gonna be the type of man that should be able to stand up with your chest out and deserve the title "big brother" or "dad" or "uncle" if you're not gonna show up for the occasion ready to ride.

Ethnographers working on inner-city gendered violence have repeatedly documented the phenomenon of older kin socializing the younger generation to become fighters as a survival skill (Bourgois and Schonberg 2009; Jones 2010; Ness 2010). Robert was following his mother's directives when he developed the ability to "black out" in rage:

> My mom was like, "Anybody ever touch your little sister, you gotta almost kill that motherfucker, baby." This one time I seen my sister fighting this dude in the school yard and I blacked out. I almost killed the motherfucker. They called the police and my mom had to come to school. But my mom ain't even really care that I almost killed that little boy because I was defending my sister and in her book that was right. I was the best dude in the world: best big brother in the world for that.

Robert's ability to fulfill his role as a brother was founded on earlier lessons his mother had given him in anticipation of his middle school's ritual hazing day-of-welcome for sixth graders. He remembers that first day of middle school vividly because it was the first time he "blacked out" and knocked out an upperclassman. Robert's institutionalized experience of school violence and his internalization of the value his mother placed on aggressive self-protection positioned him well as he matured to become an adolescent rider despite his small physical stature. He and his peers fought hard to establish rigid boundaries of loyalty around violence, thereby raising the surrounding micro-neighborhood's daily level of unpredictable insecurity:

> Back in the day we used to beat up random niggas every week just for fun. Point the motherfucking direction. I'm ridin'. [Giggling] We called it "catchin' bodies."

The terms of exchange were enforced by violent group shaming when abrogated.

> If someone even looked in your direction the wrong way and you ain't get him, and we seen that, we on your ass. If you ain't riding, then you can't walk with us, dawg, don't even act like you with us.

Shifting performatively from a narration of isolated embattlement to one of peer-group solidarity to one of kin-based reciprocity, Robert showed us how he ultimately sought refuge in the violent potential of solidary consanguinity. His extended set of consanguineous relations attempted to maintain unity through frequent exchanges of assistive violence, but the sodality ultimately, nonetheless, imploded:

> Later, my squad was family. Ain't none of us going to cross each other. We blood! All us has this RNR tat [pointing to the letters tattooed on his forearm]. Real Niggas Ride. About like twenty-five of us had it though. I've got a big family. It wasn't nobody outside the bloodline.
>
> After that, I didn't fight alone most of the time because you could get rolled on. But now most of them dead, locked up, or had to leave Philly.

RIDERS IN THE DRUG ECONOMY

Robert's overdetermined, "bloodline"-enforced rider habitus was not produced by the drug economy, but it is rewarded by it. To rise in the hierarchy of high-risk street-level drug selling one needs to have a rider reputation. Not surprisingly, street-level drug selling became Robert's employment refuge when he was fired from his job at a meat-packing plant following an occupational injury. The profits, extracted from drug markets by *bichotes*, are augmented by the dispositions to rage and generous violent solidarity that are inculcated in early childhood. The narcotics industry coopts and capitalizes the skill that charismatic young men and women develop for fist fighting, braving gunfire, and evaluating aggressive threats.

More subtly, collective dependence on income from drug sales and appreciation for the cultural capital of violence creates a dynamic of symbolic violence (Bourdieu 2000,164–205) that naturalizes and mystifies the exploitative power of the drug bosses, persuading low-level employees that they must enforce the monopoly ownership of their *bichote's* corner and absorb the risks of violence as a matter of self-respect. Jay, the owner of a competing heroin and cocaine sales spot on an adjacent block, laughed when we asked him how much he would have to pay someone to have a customer beaten up for ripping off his workers. "I don't have to pay for that; my people are riders." Roland's first felony case, for example, was for possession of a handgun that he had brought to the drug corner where he worked as a street seller in order to chase off someone encroaching from a competing drug boss's corner. It did not occur to Roland to ask the *bichote* to enforce his own territorial control. Instead Roland interpreted the rival seller's unauthorized proximity as a personal insult. Had Roland requested assistance from his boss to chase off the competitor, he would likely have been ridiculed with the misogynist insult, "pussy." Asserting one's masculinity by defending the economic interests of one's boss with deadly force is a classic manifestation of the symbolic violence bolstering profitable drug economy hierarchies.

There was a dramatic illustration of masculine shaming for failure to mobilize violence in defense of a drug corner's profits during our second year of residence on the block. Paul, a well-liked twenty-three year old night-shift manager on Jay's corner, was pistol-whipped and robbed of both "the cash and the stash." This was the second successful stickup of this corner in the two-week period since John, a new street seller, had been hired on the afternoon shift's sales crew. Because both holdups occurred strategically at the transition from the graveyard to the morning shift, it was assumed to be an inside job, and John, the newcomer on the afternoon shift, became the primary suspect. Paul brought a revolver to work the next day and drew it on John when he reported for his shift, and demanded an explanation. The morning shift manager, off duty at the time but visiting his girlfriend on the block, proactively punched John in the face when he pled his innocence. Evidently party to the conspiracy and fully prepared for foul play, two of John's cousins suddenly appeared with handguns drawn. The off-duty shift manager dove into his car to grab his weapon. After a brief standoff, followed by a wild exchange of gunfire, John and his two cousins fled. Hakeem, a boisterous fifteen year old, noticed that Paul was not shooting his revolver and grabbed it from him to lead the chase, firing at the fugitives until he ran out of bullets. Hakeem

was eager to prove himself as a rider, because he had only recently joined Jay's sales crew after cutting off his court-imposed home-arrest ankle bracelet for a previous drug case from another neighborhood. Paul lost so much credibility from his failure to shoot that Jay, the drug boss, demoted him from night-shift manager to street seller.

Perhaps the most insidious dimension of the symbolic violence legitimizing internecine brutality is the fact that these shoot-outs, which reassert the monopoly control of drug bosses and sometimes hurt neighbors, are experienced as fun, exciting events rife with potential (cf. Meeker 1979). Paul's peers maligned him for his lack of nerve for several weeks after the shoot-out. To them, the gunfight was an exciting reaffirmation of their masculinity and sense of solidarity.

THE PUNITIVE INTERFACE WITH STATE INSTITUTIONS

The state interfaces incongruently with the inner city's moral economy of violence, which simultaneously overlaps with, contradicts, reacts against, and thrives on the parallel but institutionally buttressed moral logics of "street-level [law enforcement] bureaucrats" (Lipsky 2010 [1980]). Riders and street-level drug sellers are periodically swept up by the carceral dragnet, and attempts to rely on police aid are exceptional and often counterproductive. When Arlena, a popular older woman on the block, was being severely beaten by Willie, her unpopular partner, a neighbor called 911. The call, however, led to the incarceration of Arlena and three kinsmen who rode to avenge her in the face of police inaction and mixed messages:

Fernando's fieldnote

There are two police cars from the local police district outside Arlena's house. I hear a woman yelling [in Spanish] "It's about time they locked Willie up! Desgraciado [that good-for-nothing]!"

Moments later, an officer is explaining to Arlena that he cannot arrest Willie "just like that, without a restraining order!"

Pookie and Efrain (Arlena's two oldest sons) and Papo (her favorite brother-in-law), demand an explanation from the officer, who, in sympathy with their outrage, and perhaps moved by Arlena's sobbing and her swelling right eye, tells them with a wink, "Wait till we leave and do what you need to do."

As soon as the police leave, Efrain, led by Papo with a baseball bat and Pookie gripping a golf-club, run into the house to punish Willie. Sol, an ex-girlfriend of Papo's, warns them not to get involved, reminding Papo of his three outstanding bench warrants for unresolved drug cases. Someone else notes that Pookie and Efrain are both on probation for drug sales.

Ten minutes later a highway patrol car screeches to a stop. Someone must have called 911 again. Highway patrol officers are nicknamed "*los embotados* [the ones with boots]" because of their reputation for kicking people with their heavy boots. They drag everyone out of the house in front of the gathering crowd. To everyone's astonishment, the officers ask Willie to identify his assailants and they arrest Papo, Pookie, Efrain, and even Arlena, despite her now dark black swollen right eye. Willie is not arrested and everyone suspects he is receiving special treatment from the police for being a "*chota* [snitch]."

The police are unpredictable but powerful arbiters of conflict. Despite the apparent rigidity of the code of law, individual officers have tremendous discretionary authority in face-to-face interactions. They too are informed by a moral code that at times overlaps with local logics ("Wait 'till we leave and do what you need to do"). But often the quasi-sovereign punitive power of the police and the courts asserts itself in direct opposition to these logics. Papo, Pookie, Efrain, and Arlena were each held in the county jail on detainers for periods ranging from three to eleven months.

The three men had thought they had police permission as responsible kinsmen to protect a vulnerable female family member from an abusive lover. All of them eventually received a combination of time served, house arrest, and two additional years of probation that left them vulnerable to lengthy reincarceration if found guilty of another felony or a routine "technical probation violation" (such as failing to report a change of address or delivering drug-tainted urine on a random drug test).

Trust in the police is further eroded by routine police malfeasance, especially that of narcotics officers. Many residents of our micro-neighborhood, including all the members of our ethnographic team, have been verbally harassed by the police. A significant number of local residents, including one member of our ethnographic team (Philippe), have been physically abused and/or falsely arrested. Local and national press have documented major scandals of police brutality and corruption in Philadelphia during every decade since the 1970s (Klein 1987; National Public Radio 2010; *Time* magazine editors 1978). According to a 1998 Human Rights Watch report: "[Philadelphia has] the worst reputation of big city police departments in the United States . . . Officers raided drug houses, stole money from dealers, beat anyone who got in the way and, as one judge . . . stated, 'squashed the Bill of Rights into the mud' "(Collins 1998, 314–335).

Despite the common-sense assumption that the police cannot be fully trusted, neighborhood residents (like the mothers on our block following Benito's midday shoot-out) desire police protection and occasionally seek it. Nevertheless, even our neighbors who are not involved in the drug economy, such as the family caught in the crossfire of the midday shoot-out, feel the necessity to enforce justice on their own. In this context of multiple levels of violence and antagonistic citizen-state relations—ranging from institutionalized police malfeasance and unpredictably punitive courts, to territorial conflicts in the drug economy, instrumental criminal assaults, and idiosyncratic interpersonal disputes—a common sense emerges valorizing violent self-help. The emergent logic for a self-sufficient moral economy of violence, however, further exposes self-respecting "riders" to arrest and incarceration.

CONCLUSION: PRIMITIVE ACCUMULATION ON THE BODY AND THE POLITICAL INVOLUTION OF VIOLENCE

Applying Marx's theory of primitive accumulation to the drug economy helps us combine Thompson's original formulation of the moral economy with Mauss's analysis of reciprocal obligations of gift giving to analyze the political and economic effects of the involution of US inner-city violence. The mothers on our block imposed a moratorium on drug-dealing violence by tentatively engaging with the police. Like the rioters Thompson analyzed in eighteenth-century England, the mothers mobilized charismatically, but only temporarily, around transgressions of "social norms and obligations of the proper economic functions of several parties within the community" (Thompson 1971, 71). Following Mauss's insights, we can understand why so many of our neighbors, especially the young men and women involved in the drug economy—but also schoolchildren, brothers and cousins like Robert, and middle-aged kinsmen like Pookie, Papo, and Efrain—mobilize so readily to protect themselves and others in social networks of "riders" despite the extraordinary risk of bodily harm and incarceration to which this solidarity exposes them .

Although based on a disposition to sociality and generosity, the moral economy of violence requires a facility for rage and an anxiety over insult that exacerbates community insecurity. Consequently, despite a dramatic overall national trend of decreasing violent crime rates since the mid-1990s (Blumstein and Wallman 2006), shootings, stabbings, and assaults continue to occur at unacceptably high rates in US inner cities. Unlike the incipient class solidarity identified by Thompson in the eighteenth-century's moral economy of grain riots, "riding" in the twenty-first-century inner city generates a destructive solidarity predicated on intraclass interpersonal violence. The spectacular nature of each violent incident amplifies the prevailing sense of physical insecurity and further elevates the symbolic and practical importance of commanding violent resources. In short, violence is converted into a valuable but fragile resource: unstable cultural and social capital that meshes ethically with gender and kin-based roles and is cast not as choice but as obligation to both individuals and the local community. It is interesting to contrast this example of violent response to insecurity in Puerto Rican Philadelphia to the multiple typologies of "poor people's responses to urban violence" identified by Auyero and Kilanski (this volume) in the particularly distressed urban margin of metropolitan Buenos Aires they studied. The responses they documented included much more formal, politically informed, collective organizing—including protests against police corruption and public-sector abandonment, as well as the shaming of local drug dealers. These solidary responses went far beyond the limits of immediate kinship, friendship, and market relations that anchored the moral economy of violence we documented in the case of the US inner-city.

The moral economy of violence pervading our Philadelphia neighborhood benefits the drug bosses and also legitimizes a coercive response by the state that ironically augments the profitability of the drug economy.

Marx defined *ursprüngliche Akkumulation* (literally "original accumulation") as the creation of capital through physical or military coercion resulting in the total exhaustion, rather than the maintenance or reproduction, of the original resource base. We extend this primitive accumulation lens to understand how value can be extracted destructively from the human body in both the drug economy and in the moral economy of assistive violence depleting the nonrenewable resources of organic life and health. Drug bosses profit from the painful addiction of their clients (see figure 2.15) and from the eagerness of riders to build valuable reputations by shooting and maiming the bodies of the bichotes' rivals.

The utility of violent capital, however, extends well beyond the drug workforce. In the context of some zones of intensive imbrication in the drug economy and social isolation, it seeps into the common sense of what becomes desirable in family, friends, and lovers, generating social capital and reaffirming fraught kinship bonds through solidary violence. Obviously, some residents, especially those who are less dependent on the drug trade (or have been galvanized by experience) self-reflectively object to the normalization of intracommunity and interpersonal violence. Furthermore, there is abundant fear and anger concerning the physical insecurity imposed by the drug trade. The moral economy of violence is not a universal consensus or a habitus of poverty but the social product of a particular form of capital.

Thompson's original moral economy formulation and Scott's application of it to Southeast Asia recognized that moral economy practices often

reinforce hierarchical relationships despite providing the potential for an emergent class consciousness. In the inner city, in the context of extreme spatial class segregation and disenfranchisement from the legal labor force, however, the moral economy of violence profoundly depoliticizes the poor, turning violence inward—neighbor on neighbor. The violence that is irregularly but spectacularly reported on local television news stations pathologizes the poor as dangerous "others," legitimizing zero-tolerance carceral repression in the name of public safety and moral retribution and fueling more rounds of institutional and structural violence (disinvestment by the private sector and decreases in public funds for welfare, health, education, and housing). Perhaps most important, the de facto apartheid boundaries of the US inner city are normalized by the fact that most people in the United States fear they will be ripped limb from limb if they set foot in the ghetto.

CORRESPONDING AUTHOR: pbourgois@gmail.com.

PHOTOGRAPHY CREDITS: Photographs 1, 2, 5, 7, 9, and 11-15 copyright by Fernando Montero. Photographs 3, 4, 6, 8, and 10 copyright by George Karandinos.

ACKNOWLEDGMENTS: A preliminary version of this chapter appeared in *Current Anthropology* 55(1): 1–22, 2014. Research funding was provided by National Institutes of Health (NIH) grants DA 010164, as well as the John Simon Guggenheim Foundation, the American Council on Learned Societies, the School for Advanced Research in Santa Fe, the Paul and Daisy Soros Fellowship for New Americans, the National Endowment for the Humanities and the Haverford Faculty Research Fund. Comparative and background data supported by NIH grants DA027204, DA027689, DA27599, and AA020331. Editorial assistance by Jeff Ondocsin.

NOTES

1. Scott (1985) later deemphasized "heroic" peasant rebellions in favor of attention to Brechtian forms of indirect everyday resistance—"foot dragging, feigned ignorance, sabotage . . . theft"—thus reducing the focus on violent mobilization of incipient class consciousness as the primary response to exploitation. Taussig (1986) creatively brought the concept to bear on internecine conflict, envy, and witchcraft among Colombian peasants beset by rising social inequality and a legacy of colonial and capitalist extractive violence. In the 2000s, a more classically Thomsponian moral economy framework has been usefully applied to transnational peasant mobilizations against free-market globalization policies imposed by the World Trade Organization (Edelman 2005). For another application of the concept of moral economy to illegitimate violence in drug markets, see Rodgers's article in this volume.
2. Mauss's gift exchange framework has been applied to the drug economy among heroin injectors in the post-industrial US inner city to explore sharing practices that build

community and guarantee access to resources and drugs, but also propagate infectious diseases (Bourgois 1998).
3. Pace Thompson's (1991, 339) explicit admonishment against extending his concept to the "uses and customs [of] Pirates," we find it useful to highlight mechanisms for mobilizing restraint and demanding mutuality in the illegal economy.

WORKS CITED

Abdullah, Ibrahim, and Patrick Muana. 1998. "The Revolutionary United Front of Sierra Leone: A Revolt of the Lumpenproletariat." In *African Guerrillas*, edited by Christopher Clapham. Bloomington: Indiana University Press, 172–193.

Anderson, Elijah. 1999. *Code of the Street: Decency, Violence, and the Moral Life of the Inner City*. New York: W. W. Norton.

Bayart, Jean-François. 1993. *The State in Africa: The Politics of the Belly*. New York: Longman.

Bloch, Maurice. 1973. "The Long Term and the Short Term: The Economic and Political Significance of the Morality of Kinship." In *The Character of Kinship*, edited by Jack Goody. Cambridge: Cambridge University Press, 75–87.

Blumstein, Alfred, and Joel Wallman. 2006. *The Crime Drop in America*. New York: Cambridge University Press.

Bourdieu, Pierre. 2000. *Pascalian Meditations*, translated by R. Nice. Stanford, CA: Stanford University Press.

Bourgois, Philippe. 1989. "In Search of Horatio Alger: Culture and Ideology in the Crack Economy." *Contemporary Drug Problems* 16(4): 619–649.

Bourgois, Philippe. 1998. "The Moral Economies of Homeless Heroin Addicts." *Substance Use & Misuse* 33(11): 2323–2351.

Bourgois, Philippe. 2003. *In Search of Respect: Selling Crack in El Barrio*. New York: Cambridge University Press.

Bourgois, Philippe, and Jeff Schonberg. 2009. *Righteous Dopefiend*. Berkeley: University of California Press.

Collins, Allyson. 1998. *Shielded from Justice: Police Brutality and Cccountability in the United States*. New York: Human Rights Watch.

Davis, Mike. 1990. *City of Quartz: Excavating the Future in Los Angeles*. London, New York: Verso.

Department of Public Works. 1962. *Philadelphia Land Use Map, 1962: Land-Use Zoning Project No. 18313*. Federal Works Progress Administration for Pennsylvania: Map Collection, Free Library of Philadelphia. http://www.philageohistory.org/rdic-images/view-image.cfm/LUM1962.Index, accessed January 5, 2015.

Durkheim, Émile. 1938 [1895]. *The Rules of Sociological Method*, translated by Sarah A. Solovay and John Henry Mueller, edited by George Catlin. Chicago: University of Chicago Press.

Edelman, Marc. 2005. "Bringing Moral Economy Back." *American Anthropologist* 107(3): 331–345.

Edelman, Marc. 2012. "E. P. Thompson and Moral Economies." In *A Companion to Moral Anthropology*, edited by Didier Fassin. Oxford: Wiley-Blackwell, 49–66.

Fairbanks, Robert P. 2009. *How it Works: Recovering Citizens in Post-welfare Philadelphia*. Chicago: University of Chicago Press.

Fassin, Didier. 2009. "Les Economies Morales Revisitées." *Annales. Histoire, sciences sociales* 64(6): 1237–1266.

Fortes, Meyer. 1970. *Kinship and the Social Order: The Legacy of Lewis Henry Morgan*. London: Routledge.

Goffman, Alice. 2009. "On the Run: Wanted Men in a Philadelphia Ghetto." *American Sociological Review* 74(3): 339–357.

Hoffman, Danny. 2011. *The War Machines: Young Men and Violence in Sierra Leone and Liberia.* Durham, NC: Duke University Press.

Jones, Nikki. 2010. *Between Good and Ghetto: African American Girls and Inner-city Violence.* New Brunswick, NJ: Rutgers University Press.

Klein, Howard B. 1987. "Fighting Corruption in the Philadelphia Police Department: The Death Knell of the Conspiracy of Silence." *Temple Law Quarterly* 60: 103–116.

Lipsky, Michael. 2010 [1980]. *Streel-level Bureaucracy: Dilemmas of the Individual in Public Services.* New York: Russell Sage Foundation.

Marx, Karl. 1972 [1867]. *Capital,* translated by Samuel Moore and Edward Aveling. New York: International Publishers.

Mauss, Marcel. 1990 [1924]. *The Gift: The Form and Reason for Exchange in Archaic Societies,* translated by W. Halls. London: Routledge.

Meeker, Michael E. 1979. *Literature and Violence in North Arabia.* Cambridge, New York: Cambridge University Press.

Meeker, Michael E. 1980. "The Twilight of a South Asian Heroic Age: A Rereading of Barth's Study of Swat." *Man* 15(4): 682–701.

National Public Radio. 2010. "Covering 'Tainted Justice' And Winning A Pulitzer." Fresh Air hosted by Terry Gross. May 3. http://www.npr.org/templates/transcript/tran-script.php?storyId=126386819.

Ness, Cindy. 2010. *Why Girls Fight: Female Youth Violence in the Inner City.* New York: New York University Press.

Peters, Emrys L. 1975. "Forward." In *Cohesive Force: Feud in the Mediterranean and the Middle East,* edited by Jack Black-Michaud. New York: St. Martin's Press, xxiv–xxvii.

Petteruti, Amanda, and Nastassia Walsh. 2008. "Jailing Communities: The Impact of Jail Expansion and Effective Public Safety Strategies." Justice Policy Institute Report.

Philadelphia Research Initiative. 2011. *Philadelphia 2011 State of the City Report.* Philadelphia: PEW Charitable Trusts.

Scott, James C. 1976. *The Moral Economy of the Peasant: Rebellion And Subsistence in Southeast Asia.* New Haven, CT: Yale University Press.

Scott, James C. 1985. *Weapons of the Weak.* New Haven, CT: Yale University Press.

Tambiah, Stanley Jeyaraja. 1996. *Leveling Crowds: Ethnonationalist Conflicts and Collective Violence in South Asia.* Berkeley: University of California Press.

Taussig, Michael T. 1986. *Shamanism, Colonialism, and the Wild Man.* Chicago: University of Chicago Press.

Thomas, Deborah. 2011. *Exceptional Violence: Embodied Citizenship in Transnational Jamaica.* Durham, NC: Duke University Press.

Thompson, Edward P. 1971. "The Moral Economy of the English Crowd in the Eighteenth Century." *Past & Present* (50): 76–136.

Thompson, Edward P. 1991. "The Moral Economy Reviewed." In *Customs in Common.* New York: New Press, 259–351.

Time Magazine Editors. 1978. "The Cop Tamers." *Time* 111:19. http://www.time.com/time/magazine/article/0,9171,919555,00.html, accessed September 19, 2011.

Vigh, Henrik. 2006. *Navigating Terrains of War: Youth and Soldiering in Guinea-Bissau.* New York: Berghahn Books.

Wacquant, Loïc. 2002. "Scrutinizing the Street: Poverty, Morality, and the Pitfalls of Urban Ethnography." *American Journal of Sociology* 107(6): 1468–1532.

Wacquant, Loïc. 2009. *Punishing the Poor: The Neoliberal Government of Social Insecurity.* Durham, NC: Duke University Press.

Whalen, Carmen Teresa. 2001. *From Puerto Rico to Philadelphia: Puerto Rican Workers and Postwar Economies*. Philadelphia: Temple University Press.

Wilkes, Rima, and John Iceland. 2004. "Hypersegregation in the Twenty-first Century." *Demography* 41(1): 23–36.

Wilson, William J. 1987. *The Truly Disadvantaged: The Inner City, the Underclass, and Public Policy*. Chicago: University of Chicago Press.

Wolf, Eric. 1969. *Peasant Wars of the Twentieth Century*. New York: Harper & Row.

CHAPTER 3

On the Importance of Having a Positive Attitude

KEVIN LEWIS O'NEILL *AND*
BENJAMIN FOGARTY-VALENZUELA

"Sometimes I feel kinda locked up." It was an unnerving comment. The house was empty. The front door was ajar. He could have walked out, into the streets of Guatemala City, and no one would have stopped him. No one. But it was not that easy, nor that obvious. This man had been held captive, against his will, since 1989. The stated reason, as scribbled on his file, was the use of drugs and *mala conducta* (misconduct). For some twenty-three years, he had been held at a Pentecostal rehabilitation center.

These are for-profit, unregulated Christian centers that hold men for months, sometimes for years. They have proliferated in postwar Guatemala, punctuating the capital city with hundreds of anonymous houses, each dedicated to the sin of drug addiction. They are a public secret, so to speak. The police rely on them. Families need them. And churches benefit from them, sometimes financially but always spiritually. In fact, those held captive are oftentimes their only critics. Beyond the reach of natural light, with the smell of urine and mold often framing their captivity, these men want out, and they want out now.[1]

Frener, the man in the empty house, was one such captive.

His cell was an almost windowless house, with bars and razor wire punctuating every ray of natural light. He stood motionless. Frozen by freedom, he asked a simple question. "Where do I go?" In the absence of an answer, he offered an impromptu tour of Central America's oldest and most notorious Pentecostal rehabilitation center. Abandoned after a police raid and shut down for harboring members of organized crime, the

Figure 3.1
Reto a la Juventud (2012).
Photograph by Benjamin Fogarty-Valenzuela.

Figure 3.2
Frener (2012).
Photograph by Benjamin Fogarty-Valenzuela.

house lay stage to a slow-moving conversation, one that shuttled between this man's life and a sermon preached inside this very house. A few months earlier, during the course of fieldwork that led to this essay, an itinerant preacher had delivered a sermon on the importance of having a positive attitude. Delivered to twenty-five men and five women, each seemingly forsaken by society, the pastor insisted that each person should cultivate a positive attitude—to strengthen his will, to conquer her sins, to overcome drugs.

This photo essay thinks through juxtaposition, between the reality of captivity and the rhetoric of positivity, to consider the politics of what Lauren Berlant (2011) would call "cruel optimism." It is this juxtaposition that helps capture the dire circumstances of those held inside these houses. It also reflects larger insights about the moral economy underlying Central America's war on drugs (see Rodgers this volume; Karandinos et al. this volume). As we collected the life histories of those held inside this house, as well as dozens of similar houses, we reflected on the political theology that undergirds these centers. For drug-market violence, amid an ever-shifting war on drugs, finds rhetorical sustenance as well as material resources from Pentecostal Christianity. This is because Pentecostalism mixes with prohibitionist drug policies to foment a growing genre of drug-market violence in postwar Guatemala. Frener is not the only one who feels locked up. With hundreds of Pentecostal rehabilitation centers dotting Guatemala City and more Guatemalans held captive inside these centers than locked up in maximum-security prisons, thousands find themselves beyond the reach of not just natural light but also due process, proper medical treatment, and the most basic of human rights.

To walk with Frener, remembering this particular sermon, is to chronicle (critically, descriptively) an otherwise untold story. More than a decade into the second millennium, attention justifiably rushes to Mexico, where tens of thousands of men, women, and children have died in the name of drugs (Beittel 2013; Felbab-Brown and Nieto 2013; Molzahn, Rodriguez Ferreira, and Shirk 2013). The numbers are astounding. At the same time, the Andes remains a point of concern for anyone interested in the production of cocaine and its corollary toll on human life. Colombia is at war (Holmes, Gutiérrez de Piñeres, and Curtin 2008; Thoumi 2003). Yet, between these two increasingly militarized zones stands Central America, which has witnessed its own spike in drug use and drug violence due to increased levels of drug trafficking (Beckley Foundation 2013a, 2013b; UNODC 2012b, 21).

At the same time, Pentecostal Christianity surges in postwar Guatemala. Once overwhelmingly Roman Catholic, Guatemala is now as much as 60 percent Pentecostal and charismatic Christian. This mix of cocaine and Christianity sets the conditions for captivity. And they are conditions that ultimately silence structural forces while laying blame on individual action. Addiction is not a sickness, these centers say. Addiction is a sin (Committee Against Torture 2013). There is no cure, pastors plead. There is Jesus. Beyond a rapid influx in cocaine, the factors at play include the aftermath of Guatemala's thirty-six-year genocidal civil war, the implementation of economic reforms usually labeled "structural adjustment," and the rapid expansion of transnational criminal organizations (O'Neill and Thomas 2011). Contrary to prohibitionist drug policies and at odds with Pentecostal theologies, each of which emphasizes the individual, this photo essay shuttles between a series of images and recordings to argue, in classic anthropological fashion, that Frener is not the cause. He is the effect.

Pastor: So let's talk about having a positive attitude. If you think you can do something, you can do something. When people change their attitude, they change their life. Jesus Christ came to change our lives, and he wants to help us change our lives. Jesus came to set the captives free, to give freedom to the prisoners and to the oppressed. And the biggest discovery of his generation is that human beings can change their lives by changing their mindset. In other words, all people can change, but what do you need to have? You need to have a positive attitude. We all have problems in life in one or another way, and God has the solution for us. Jesus is the way. He is the truth. He is life, and no one comes to the Father except through the Son. Jesus has something special for you today. I want you to tell the person next you something. Tell him:
"Jesus has something special for you." (Group members repeat to neighbors.)
"He wants to change your life." (Group members repeat to neighbors.)
"God has miracles for you. God will do extraordinary things in your life." (Group repeats.)
"God will change your attitude." (Group repeats.)

Drugs are not new to Guatemala. Neither is cocaine. But the scale of it all has changed. It is a story that starts beyond the streets of Guatemala City and its Pentecostal rehabilitation centers, and rather in the nostrils of North Americans. A gourmet soft drug in the 1960s, cocaine found its clientele courtesy of President Richard Nixon (Mares 2006; Musto 1999). His 1969 Operation Intercept, with its aerial sprays of Mexican hemp fields and its crackdown on Mexican marijuana smugglers, prompted the American middle class to seek out alternative thrills (Gootenberg 2009). As demand soared, cocaine corridors connected Medellín to Miami and Cali to Northern Mexico—all by way of the Caribbean. The United States responded with hugely militarized anti-drug policies (Andreas and Nadelmann 2006; Vellinga 2004; Youngers and Rosin 2005), yet its Navy and Coast Guard patrols ultimately accomplished very little. By the early 1990s, the Andean region produced an estimated one thousand metric tons of cocaine every year. Twenty years and one trillion US tax dollars later, the region still does, making the war on drugs, by all accounts, a complete and unwavering failure (Loveman 2006).

Yet this failure has not been without effect. Increasingly expensive, progressively effective maritime blockades have prompted traffickers to shift their transport operations from sea to land, making Central America their principal transit route (UNODC 2012b, 21). Today planes, boats, and submarines ferry cocaine along the Pacific coast to northern Guatemala. There, in the jungles of Petén, beyond the reach of US interdiction efforts, traffickers prep their product for its eventual trip north. The only challenge of late has been keeping up with traffic. In 2004, an estimated 10 percent of the cocaine produced for the United States passed through Guatemala (Jordan 2004). This number jumped to 23 percent in 2006 and then 44 percent in 2008. In 2011, in the shadows of Plan Mexico, a US-led $1.6 billion security initiative, 84 percent of the cocaine produced for the United States moved through Guatemala (Archibold and Cave 2011). This means that more than $100 billion of narcotics now touches Guatemalan soil every year. This is three times Guatemala's legitimate gross domestic product (Viviano 2012).

The mass movement of all this cocaine requires considerable logistics. Equipment, labor, infrastructure—traffickers need all of these but pay for none of them in cash. Instead, they pay with cocaine, which actually holds very little value in Guatemala. There are simply not enough Guatemalans who can afford the drug. To monetize this material—that is, to turn cocaine into cash—laboratories mix the drug with baking soda to make crack cocaine. Now sold throughout Guatemala City, crack cocaine is far more affordable and far more addictive than powder cocaine; it is the very substance that hit Los Angeles, New York, and Miami in the mid-1980s (Bourgois 2003). Smoked through a pipe one rock at a time, it is as intense as it is cheap as it is fleeting. Crack leaves the user hungry for more. In the United States, this observable desperation met growing urban violence and decidedly racist anti-drug policies in ways that tripled the country's prison population (Alexander 2010). Yet in Guatemala City, with a homicide rate nearly ten times the US average, crack cocaine has not only been criminalized (UNODC 2012a). It has become the subject of Pentecostal intervention.

Pastor: We can change. But it all depends on us. You have to have the desire. If I have the desire to change, then you will. You need to say to yourself, I'm going to do it. And success lies in your habits and customs. People who have bad habits fail. People who have good habits succeed. Let me put it this way. Your attitude determines your actions. A winner is not born super-gifted or with high intelligence. A winner's advantage is his attitude, not his fitness. Attitude is the standard for success. Your attitude is crucial because it determines the way you act . . . Here in Guatemala it is obviously very difficult. It's difficult to get a job. People complain about the price of everything. But I want to say something. God has something special for you. But it all depends on your attitude. You have to have a positive attitude. If you say that you can do something, then you can do something. Because everything you do comes through Christ. He strengthens you. He strengthens your attitude.

Christianity is not new to Guatemala. Neither is Protestantism. But, much like cocaine, the scale of it all has changed. Guatemala's slow transition from a genocidal civil war (1960–1996) to a formal democracy (1981 to the present) coincided with the rapid evangelization of its once overwhelmingly Roman Catholic population (1976 to the present). As mentioned, more than half of Guatemala is Pentecostal or charismatic Christian (Pew Forum 2006). These denominations are conservative takes on Christianity that emphasize the power of personal conversion, the need for evangelization, belief in the Bible's authority, and the understanding that Jesus Christ's crucifixion was a sacrifice made on behalf of humanity's fallen nature (Bebbington 1989).

This transformation of Guatemala's Christian contours began with an act of God. At 3:03 a.m. on February 4, 1976, an earthquake measuring 7.5 on the Richter scale rocked Guatemala. The quake's epicenter lay to the west of Guatemala City, near Chimaltenango, but the entire nation felt the effects: 23,000 dead, 77,000 wounded, and 370,000 houses leveled. As residents braced themselves for aftershocks, the Protestantization of Guatemala took hold. The earthquake set into motion a number of processes that all contributed to a sustained expansion of Guatemala's Protestant population. The first, and possibly most important, was that Protestant aid agencies from the United States came to Guatemala soon after the earthquake. They provided much appreciated relief in the short term and, in the long term, "saturated [Guatemala] with Scripture" (Garrard-Burnett 1998, 121). As immediate relief gave way to efforts at sustainable development, many of these Protestant relief agencies established regional offices in Guatemala City, continuing their work to rebuild both the nation and its soul. The strategy worked. Protestant church membership jumped by 14 percent only a few months after the earthquake, while the annual growth of Protestant conversion in Guatemala rose to 26 percent by 1982. This number was nearly four times what it had been a decade prior (Garrard-Burnett 1998, 121–122).

The earthquake also initiated a wave of migration from the rural interior to Guatemala City, as survivors moved to the capital looking for work (Camus 2002; Gellert and Pinto Soria 1990). Pentecostal churches provided these newcomers with basic resources, such as food and shelter, while also offering them spaces where they could cultivate a sense of belonging in uncertain times and unfamiliar places. Amid it all, the Roman Catholic Church was nowhere to be seen. In rural areas, the institutional presence of the Catholic Church literally disappeared between 1880 and 1950. In the 1940s in Huehuetenango, there were only two priests for a population of 176,000 (Sierra, Siebers, and Samandú 1990, 9). In 1966, only 530 priests served a nation of four million Catholics, and 434 of those clergymen and women were foreign born. Many of these priests chose to minister in the countryside instead of Guatemala City, for reasons that most likely ranged from the practical to the romantic. The ratio of Catholic priests to congregants in Guatemala City's poorer *zonas* was even lower—one to 30,000 by 1978 (Garrard-Burnett 1998, 123). The Catholic Church, at this level, was simply outmanned and out-hustled by Pentecostal churches willing and ready to provide material and social support to poor residents. A less calculable reason is that the Catholic Church, captained by a conservative bishop, proved itself to be too oafish, in a bureaucratic sense, to compete with the dexterity of grassroots churches. The rest, as they say, is history.

Pastor: When are you going to improve your attitude? Today! Today is the day when the weak will become strong. Today is the day that the fool will become smart. God gave us special gifts. God gave us talents. And God has special things for each of us. But everything depends on us. We need to have the desire to do these things. Look, your attitude is very important. I am constantly amazed by how many people have a poor attitude but still want others to be optimistic. If you have a poor attitude and tell your family, "Well, that's just how it goes," then what? You have to be excited. You have to be motivated. You have to set a good example for your wife, for your children, and for your neighbor. And I know you need to do this. God changed my life thirty-four years ago. For thirty-four years I have not taken alcohol. I have not smoked for twenty-six years. I do not smoke. And so do like me. Change your way of thinking, the way you act, but you can only change your life through Jesus Christ.

Figure 3.3
After the police raid (2012).
Photograph by Benjamin Fogarty-Valenzuela.

Frener was all alone in the house when we visited, except for three women on the roof. They did not know where to go either. "I just feel locked up sometimes," Frener repeated. "I can't really get through the door. I'm locked up . . . I can't leave." He wandered through the main hall, where his fellow inmates (*internos*) once lived. Inmates—this is what the house, the entire industry, calls those held inside Pentecostal rehabilitation centers. They have been "sentenced" in ways that blur, at least at the level of subjectivity, any distinction between a prison and a patient.

"The penalty [for leaving] is kind of bad, you know," Frener explained. "They keep you locked up in the morgue or cage (*jaula*) [if you try to escape], or we need to be against the walls." The morgue is a small room. It is a cage. Itself fortified, it holds new inmates, the ones reeling from the pangs of withdrawals. It is also used to restrain those inmates who prove resistant. But Frener proved a docile subject. He initially had to be put "against the walls," which means standing naked on a concrete staircase for twelve, twenty-four, and sometimes thirty-six hours. With some twenty-three years of captivity under his belt, he had since then surrendered to this house. With the voice of a child, he confessed, "They mostly be mean with us." But the guards weren't there, we noted. "But they don't think that releasing us is going to affect us well," he replied. And so he stayed.

Frener came to this Pentecostal rehabilitation center on March 3, 1989. He had been in the United States without proper documentation for years. In the 1980s, he worked in Maryland, learning English and building a life for himself. He worked small jobs. As the story goes—though the details are hardly established—he slipped into a kind of depression, started using drugs, and then spiraled out of control. One day, in a terrible state, he walked to a gas station, doused himself with gasoline, and then swallowed a lit match. His body erupted into flames, from his mouth outward. He survived, but only after a long stretch in a public hospital to treat the third-degree burns that cripple his body. His hands, which he uses to draw, even to this day bend inward, their tips having been melted off in the fire.

When telling the story, he explains with pride about how they medevacked him to a hospital in Annapolis, Maryland. "I flew in a helicopter," he notes, less to stress its novelty than to mention that someone, somewhere, took such an interest in him that they hired a helicopter. They did not just let him die in the streets. They did not abandon him. He mattered to someone, somewhere.

Once he was stable, the United States deported Frener. After he convalesced in a Guatemalan hospital, Frener's family planted him in Reto a la Juventud, the first rehabilitation center of its kind in Central America. It is the house that started this movement. Graduates of this center, so

Figure 3.4
Drawings (2012).
Photograph by Benjamin Fogarty-Valenzuela.

to speak, soon started their own centers, whose own eventual graduates also started their own. Over the last thirty-five years, some two hundred centers have emerged, many with connection to Reto a la Juventud. The network mushroomed, especially as demand began to soar after a shift in US interdiction efforts in 2004. Rarely does such a decentered network have such a clear origin story. It is a story that begins and ends with captivity, with the felt reality of being locked up and tied down. Much of this has to do with the built form. Neither unlawful nor illegitimate, although inhumane and illiberal, these Pentecostal rehabilitation centers provide a practical solution to a concrete problem. Drug use is up. State resources are down. And Pentecostalism is *the* discourse of change in Guatemala. Jesus saves. Nobody else.

Pastor: Thomas Edison was the one who invented the light bulb. And how often did he fail? He failed nine hundred times. But he also succeeded. He just kept trying over and over again. You have to persist over and over again. Because you don't have to stay here. You can get up. You must get up! God has special things for you, and God wants to bless you. He wants you to prosper. He wants the best for whatever you touch. Whatever you do in life—be blessed. And I'll tell you something. Listen to me. Your family is my family. It doesn't matter if you tell me that your dad is involved in drugs or that that your mom is doing drugs. Those things do not matter. God wants something special for you. I'm telling you that you have the ability to change your life. You can leave this house. You can leave this house. You can do it, but it all depends on your desire to do so. Is your desire weak? Or is your desire strong? You have to want to change your life.

Reto a la Juventud may have been founded with the best of intentions, but the situation quickly spiraled out of control. By the end of its run, only a few weeks before the police raided the place, men from the house would go "hunting"; they would form a hunting party (*grupo de cacería*). This is what the industry calls the four or five men tapped to collect users from the streets. More often than not these men are themselves in rehab, also under lock and key, but they are bigger, stronger, and sometimes smarter than the average user. Hunting (*cacería*) is a privilege, and the rewards are immediate: status, adventure, and a bit of sunlight. The work pays for itself. But Frener would never hunt. This was not his role. He was too slow, physically and mentally, to keep up with the pack. His role was different. He would wait for the men to return. And after the new inmates had been strip searched in front of everyone, had been told to bend over and then squat down, Frener would then join the circle. Prompted by the attendant (*encargado*), Frener would approach each new inmate, stand close to his face, and say: "Welcome to hell." Everyone would laugh, except for the new inmates. The joke lay in that the whispering Frener, because of his burned body, resembled the primary character from the *Nightmare on Elm Street* film series: Freddy Krueger. Frener Krueger, they called him.

The founder of Reto a la Juventud would not have stood for this treatment, it is said. He was a convicted criminal, yes, but he was also a changed man. He was a Christian. In his early years, he went by the name *Malasuerte* (bad luck) and served multiple prison sentences. On July 5, 1970, he was sentenced to twenty-four months of prison for theft. On June 11, 1971, while still in prison, he was sentenced to another forty-eight months for disorderly conduct, and on August 8, 1977, he was sentenced to prison for three and a half years for drug trafficking. But, as the title of his autobiography notes, "Malasuerte died in Pavon" (Corleto 1992). By this, he means that he found Christ in Guatemala's largest maximum-security prison, Pavon. It is also the place where Malasuerte learned the most about incarceration. These were lessons that he would articulate through the classic Christian idiom of warfare. "One wonders if it is worth it," Malasuerte writes. "I mean to engage in a direct war against evil, when in most cases one becomes a victim of the very system that one fights" (1992, 18). In search of higher ground, amid his conversion to Christianity, Malasuerte took aim at drugs and delinquency.

Reflecting further on humanity's inherent weakness, its predilection toward sin, Malasuerte narrates his life as folding along a binary. He sinned *before* his conversion, while in prison, but thrived as a Christian *after* his conversion, with his rehabilitation center. His correction, he insists, was by the grace of God. The prison itself did nothing to better him. It only made him more of a criminal. What he longed for was a context in which people could change, where the individual could come to terms with sin. And so, amid an ever-changing capital city, one riddled by unemployment and gross inequalities, Malasuerte's attention landed on a daily schedule for a new kind of context. The schedule was institutional, for sure, if not penal, but it was directed at drug rehabilitation. "Is it surprising," Michel Foucault writes, "that prisons resemble factories, schools, barracks, hospitals, which all resemble prisons?" (1995, 228). This is the schedule that sparked Malasuerte's imagination:

5:00 a.m.	Bath
5:30 a.m. to 6:00 a.m.	Hygiene, housework, and breakfast preparations
6:00 a.m.	First church service

During the next two hours, the inmates (*internos*) will dedicate themselves to prayer, praise, testimonies, sermons, and choir practice. Sermons will also be delivered by Brother Pastor Carlos Celda. Meditation of the word. The end of worship and choir.

8:00 a.m.	Breakfast
9:00 a.m.	Cleaning

The following hour will also be dedicated to playing ping pong, chess, and reading, until the start of the second church service.

10:00 a.m. to 12:00 p.m.	Church service
12:00pm to 2:00pm	Lunch
2:00 p.m.	Cleaning
3:00 p.m.	Afternoon church service

One can also practice "fencing" (*esgrima*) in between the church services. This is a game to see who can recall Bible verses the fastest.

4:30 p.m.	Visits

Family visits will last until 7:30 p.m. At any moment during the day one will take time to maintain and repair the vehicles used to transport preachers, assistants, visitors as well as pick people up from the streets.

7:30 p.m.	Dinner
8:00 p.m.	Spiritual action

Pastor: Look at Warren Buffet. He will give thirty billion dollars to an organization. Thirty billion dollars is a pretty penny. And he has always given to the poor. He has helped. And how did he do it? Not by finishing his studies. No! What he had was a dream. And that's what we have to have. We have to have dreams. We have to have big dreams. We have to have a dream and then say, "I will change. I'm going to do it." But if you do not want it, then it's not going to happen. Again, it depends on the attitude you have. You must have a positive attitude. And keeping a good attitude is easier than getting one. You have to stay positive, but how will you do it? You have to read inspirational books that motivate you. You have to read the Word of God every day. You have to go to church. You have to meet people at church. You have to find a way to be motivated. You have to find people that will minister to your soul. God has the power and authority to get ahead, and God has special things for us, and God is the one we need to get ahead.

Rather than recreating prison life, Malasuerte planted the seed for a new kind of captivity. There are as many as two hundred Pentecostal rehabilitation centers in the metropolitan area. Frener is subject to but one. A quick mapping of some of these structures calls to mind Michel Foucault's notion of the carceral archipelago (1995, 297). Yet Foucault's metaphor is static. This is no archipelago. These centers are not islands. They close. They relocate. They reopen. As already mentioned, users also graduate and start their own outfits. Others escape but then return (and return and return). Recidivism is common. This assemblage, put simply, is in constant motion.

This movement is productive, because Guatemala City is not a particularly large metropolis. With approximately three million residents, the city cannot support what a growing literature describes as "fortified enclaves." These are internally complete spaces of privilege where the wealthy live in peaceful solidarity. Mexico City, Bogotá, and São Paulo—each of these mega-cities typifies what Teresa Caldeira (2004) understands as a "city of walls." Guatemala City does not fit this model (O'Neill and Thomas 2011). There are simply not enough wealthy Guatemalans to wall themselves off from the world. The quick fix, however, has been to invert private security's infrastructure—its steel bars, razor wire, and reinforced concrete—to keep users in rather than out, to wall them off from the rest of the world. "At least this place is safe," I mentioned to one inmate offhand. Facing a security wall, one topped with shards of broken glass, he corrected me. "That doesn't keep people out," he said. "It keeps us in."

Figure 3.5
Door wide open (2012).
Photograph by Benjamin Fogarty-Valenzuela.

This in, as opposed to this out, is also existential. Frener is evidence enough. While Foucault's notion of the carceral archipelago is not fitting, at least not here, his reflections on the internalization of discipline are directly pertinent. These centers believe that drug users, through the saving grace of Jesus Christ, are capable of watching themselves—of internalizing the panopticon—when no one else is watching. "A real subjection is born mechanically from a fictitious relation," Foucault writes. "He who is subjected to a field of visibility, and who knows it, assumes responsibility for the constraints of power" (1995, 202–203). Frener stood at the front door. His family was nowhere to be found. The state had no space for him. He was fit for neither a prison nor an asylum. "He makes them play spontaneously upon himself," Foucault continues, "he inscribed in himself the power relation in which he simultaneously plays both roles; he becomes the principle of his own subjection." Frener, the principle of his own subjection, had learned to watch himself "so that the police, the guards and the doctors do not have to" (Cruikshank 1996, 330). So he stood. Almost parodying the last two lines of Samuel Beckett's *Waiting for Godot*, we say, "Well, shall we go?" (1982, 59, 109). And Frener says, "Yes, let's go." He does not move.

Figure 3.6
Free to go (2012).
Photograph by Benjamin Fogarty-Valenzuela.

Pastor: Some people fall into a rut of negativity, because they feel like they are not progressing. If this is the case, begin to set daily goals that you can achieve. And make those goals tangible. Make them stuff that you can measure. I stopped taking liquor, and I do not sleep with women. I like women, but I respect and love my wife, and I have to be true to her and true to my children. So it is very important. But then what do you want to do? Set a goal every day. Each day, have a goal. Keeping a positive organized life will help you develop positive thinking. In other words, if you change the way you think, then you will change the way you act. It's easy. Do not think that the change will be difficult. Think that change will be easy, and as you think so, it will be so. Visualize yourself in a church, raising their hands to heaven, being free from all these chains. And imagine that you have a vehicle, a car. Don't work about the brand. Don't worry if it is Toyota, Mazda, or Mitsubishi. Just visualize a car, with a cute wife. Imagine some children. Visualize nice things for your life.

Frener is not alone. The estimated six thousand Guatemalans held captive inside Pentecostal rehabilitation centers join those held in similar sites in Brazil and Peru. In Asia alone, there are an estimated three hundred thousand people held captive in compulsory drug detention and rehabilitation centers (Human Rights Watch 2011; Open Society Foundations 2011; Radio Free Asia 2013; UNAIDS 2012). While the vast majority of those in Asia are state run and do not subscribe to any Christian assumptions, these centers in Guatemala force their inmates to inhabit a kind of cruel optimism. Lauren Berlant's definition is key. Cruel optimism is the "kind of relation in which one depends on objects that block the very thriving that motivates our attachment in the first place" (Berlant 2012). For it seems perverted to preach about having a positive attitude, about bootstrapping an almost unattainable kind of subjectivity, in such dire circumstances, especially when a far more macro-scale, far more critical analysis is certainly in order. Drug use is on the rise in postwar Guatemala not because of a weak will or a lack of faith, but rather because of the United States' concomitant need for and war against drugs.

The cruelty comes when the inmate is forced to submit, under the pressure of torture, to a belief that their use of drugs is moral rather than material. The cruelty comes when these inmates have been left alone, by the state and by their families, to genuflect themselves in the hope that something will change. And the cruelty comes when political theology, the onetime engine of liberal politics in Latin America, gets diverted in ways that support not just subjugation but outright captivity. This optimism is cruel because it promises salvation by way of modern slavery.

Pastor: We're going to kneel on our knees. We are going to ask the Lord to help us. If you want to raise your hands to heaven, you can do so. If you want to repeat the words that I say, you can do so. (Pauses for group members to repeat in unison.) Lord Jesus, today, this afternoon, I put my life in your hands. I ask you, Lord, to forgive me. I have sinned against you, and I have done evil in your eyes. Today I put my life in your hands, and I ask you with all my heart, with all my strength, to help me. I give you my addictions, and I ask you to help me. (Pastor starts to cry.) Have compassion and mercy on me. Forgive me. I have misbehaved with my mother. I have misbehaved with my father. I have misbehaved with my children. Forgive me, in the name of Jesus. Thank you, Lord, I know you're going to do a miracle in my life. I know there is rejoicing in heaven for every sinner who repents. In the name of Jesus, I receive my salvation. Thank you, Lord, Amen!

NOTES

1. Parts of this argument have been developed further elsewhere. See Kevin Lewis O'Neill, "On Liberation: Crack, Christianity, and Captivity in Postwar Guatemala City," *Social Text* 32, no. 3 (Fall 2014):10–28.

WORKS CITED

Alexander, Michelle. 2010. *The New Jim Crow: Mass Incarceration in the Age of Colorblindness.* New York: The New Press.

Andreas, Peter, and Ethan Nadelmann. 2006. *Policing the Globe: Criminalization and Crime Control in International Relations.* New York: Oxford University Press.

Archibold, Randal C., and Damien Cave. 2011. "Drug Wars Push Deeper into Central America." *The New York Times,* March 23, A1.

Bebbington, David William. 1989. *Evangelicalism in Modern Britain: A History from the 1730s to the 1980s.* New York: Unwin Hyman.

Beckett, Samuel. 1982. *Waiting for Godot: Tragicomedy in 2 Acts.* New York: Grove Press.

Beckley Foundation. 2013a. "Paths for Reform: Proposed Options for Alternative Drug Policies in Guatemala." Project Director Amanda Feilding. January 11. http://www.beckleyfoundation.org/Paths-for-Reform.pdf.

Beckley Foundation. 2013b. "Illicit Drugs Markets and Dimensions of Violence in Guatemala." Project Director Amanda Feilding. May 30. http://www.beckleyfoundation.org/Illicit-Drug-Markets.pdf.

Beittel, June S. 2013. "Mexico's Drug Trafficking Organizations: Source and Scope of the Violence." Congressional Research Service Report for Congress, April 15. http://www.fas.org/sgp/crs/row/R41576.pdf.

Berlant, Lauren. 2011. *Cruel Optimism.* Durham: Duke University Press.

Berlant, Lauren. 2012. "On Her Book Cruel Optimism." *Rorotoko.* Cover interview, June 5. http://rorotoko.com/interview/20120605_berlant_lauren_on_cruel_optimism/.

Bourgois, Philippe. 2003. *In Search of Respect: Selling Crack in El Barrio.* Cambridge: Cambridge University Press.

Caldeira, Teresa P. R. 2004. *City of Walls: Crime, Segregation, and Citizenship in São Paulo.* Berkeley: University of California Press.

Camus, Manuela. 2002. *Ser Indígena en Ciudad de Guatemala.* Guatemala: Facultad Latinoamericana de Ciencias Sociales.

Committee Against Torture. 2013. "Concluding Observations on the Combined Fifth and Sixth Periodic Reports of Guatemala, Adopted by the Committee at Its Fiftieth Session (6–31 May 2013)." June 21. §20.

Corleto, Manuel. 1992. *Malasuerte murió en Pavón: vida, pasión, muerte de un drogadicto y delincuente.* Artemis Edinter.

Cruikshank, Barbara. 1996. "Revolution Within: Self-Government and Self-Esteem." In *Foucault and Political Reason: Liberalism, Neo-Liberalism, and Rationalities of Government,* edited by Andrew Barry, Thomas Osborne, and Nikolas Rose. Chicago: University of Chicago Press.

Felbab-Brown, Vanda, and Peña Nieto. 2013. "Piñata: The Promise and Pitfalls of Mexico's New Security Policy against Organized Crime." Washington, DC: The Brookings Institution. February.

Foucault, Michel. 1995. *Discipline and Punish: The Birth of the Prison.* Translated by Alan Sheridan. New York: Second Vintage ed.

Garrard-Burnett, Virginia. 1998. *Protestantism in Guatemala: Living in the New Jerusalem.* Austin: University of Texas Press.

Gellert, Gisela, and J. C. Pinto Soria. 1990. *Ciudad de Guatemala: Dos Estudios Sobre Su Evolución Urbana (1524–1950).* Guatemala City: Universidad de San Carlos de Guatemala.

Gootenberg, Paul. 2009. *Andean Cocaine: The Making of a Global Drug.* Chapel Hill: University of North Carolina Press.

Holmes, Jennifer S., Sheila Amin Gutiérrez de Piñeres, and Kevin M. Curtin. 2008. *Guns, Drugs and Development in Colombia.* Austin: University of Texas Press.

Human Rights Watch. 2011. "Vietnam: Torture, Forced Labor in Drug Detention." September 7. http://www.hrw.org/news/2011/09/07/vietnam-torture-forced-labor-drug-detention.

Jordan, Mary. 2004. "Pit Stop on the Cocaine Highway: Guatemala Becomes Favored Link for US-Bound Drugs." *The Washington Post,* October 6, A20.

Karandinos, George, Laurie Hart, Fernando Montero Castrillo, and Philippe Bourgois. 2014. "The Moral Economy of Violence in the US Inner City." In *Violence at the Urban Margins,* edited by Javier Auyero, Philippe Bourgois, and Nancy Scheper-Hughes. New York: Oxford University Press.

Loveman, Brian, ed. 2006. *Addicted to Failure: U.S. Security Policy in Latin America and the Andean Region.* New York: Rowman & Littlefield.

Mares, David R. 2006. *Drug Wars and Coffeehouses: The Political Economy of the International Drug Trade.* Washington, DC: CQ Press.

Molzahn, Cory, Octavio Rodriguez Ferreira, and David A. Shirk. 2013. "Drug Violence in Mexico: Data and Analysis Through 2012." Trans-Border Institute (TBI). February.

Musto, David F. 1999. *The American Disease: Origins of Narcotics Control.* New Haven: Yale University Press.

O'Neill, Kevin Lewis, and Kedron Thomas, eds. 2011. *Securing the City: Neoliberalism, Space, and Insecurity in Postwar Guatemala.* Durham: Duke University Press.

Open Society Foundations. 2011. "Treated with Cruelty: Abuses in the Name of Drug Rehabilitation." http://www.opensocietyfoundations.org/sites/default/files/treatedwithcruelty.pdf.

Pew Forum. 2006. *Spirit and Power: A 10-Nation Survey of Pentecostals by the Pew Forum on Religion and Public Life*. Washington, DC: Pew Research Center.

Radio Free Asia. 2013. "Rights Group Calls for Closure of Cambodian Drug Detention Centers." December 9. http://www.rfa.org/english/news/cambodia/drugs-12092013183433.html.

Rodgers, Dennis. 2014. "The Moral Economy of Murder: Toward a Thanatopolitical Understanding of Social Order in Nicaragua." In *Violence at the Urban Margins*, edited by Javier Auyero, Philippe Bourgois, and Nancy Scheper-Hughes. New York: Oxford University Press.

Sierra, Oscar, Hans Siebers, and Luis Samandú. 1990. *Guatemala: Retos de la Iglesia Catolicá en una Sociedad en Crisis*. San José: DEI.

Thoumi, Francisco E. 2003. *Illegal Drugs, Economy and Society in the Andes*. Baltimore: The Johns Hopkins University Press.

UNAIDS. 2012. "Joint Statement: Compulsory Drug Detention and Rehabilitation Centres." March. http://www.unaids.org/en/media/unaids/contentassets/documents/document/2012/JC2310_Joint%20Statement6March12FINAL_en.pdf.

UNODC. 2012a. "Intentional Homicide, Count and Rate per 100,000 Population (1995–2001)." http://www.unodc.org/documents/data-and-analysis/statistics/crime/Homicide_statistics2012.xls.

UNODC. 2012b. "Transnational Organized Crime in Central America and the Caribbean: A Threat Assessment." http://www.unodc.org/documents/data-and-analysis/Studies/TOC_Central_America_and_the_Caribbean_english.pdf.

Vellinga, Menno, ed. 2004. *The Political Economy of the Drug Industry: Latin America and the International System*. Gainesville: University Press of Florida.

Viviano, Frank. 2012. "A Vacation Goes South." *California* (Summer), http://alumni.berkeley.edu/news/california-magazine/summer-2012-north-south/vacation-goes-south.

Youngers, Coletta A., and Eileen Rosin, eds. 2005. *Drugs and Democracy in Latin America: The Impact of U.S. Policy*. Boulder, CO: Lynne Rienner Publishers.

PART 2

Gender and Masculinities

CHAPTER 4

"Es que para ellos el deporte es matar"

Rethinking the Scripts of Violent Men
in El Salvador and Brazil

MO HUME *AND* POLLY WILDING

INTRODUCTION

"Their sport is killing" is how a Salvadorean gang member describes his fellow "homeboys." His description is of an extreme form of violent masculinity that has widespread purchase, both within gang structures and across wider public debates of gang members as the violent "other." While it is acknowledged that gangs are predominately made up of young men, many of whom engage in violent behavior, they are rarely analyzed as a gendered phenomenon. As Yllo observes, "male aggression is so closely bound to popular perceptions of violence that it has become a 'nonissue' . . . is that fact so thoroughly taken for granted that it is not regarded as requiring explanation?" (1993, 51). This lack of gendered analysis is indeed true of public forms of violence more generally. Through an examination of what we call the "everyday scripts of violence," we analyze some of the tensions in researching different forms of violence in El Salvador and Brazil from a gendered and class perspective. We situate this in a wider discussion of debates on men and masculinities, paying particular attention to the "pull" of the stereotypes related to extreme forms of masculinities—against which researchers are not immune.

The larger goal of the chapter is to make political connections between different types of violence at the urban margins, and thus we emphasize the importance of locating gender relations within the broader political economy of violence in Latin America. Drawing on data from our separate research processes, we explore how chronic levels of violence in different contexts reproduce similar silences, as well as discourses of blame and judgment, and how these are highly gendered. These are used both to explain violence and to distance the narrator from it. We employ these narrative tools—silence, blame, and judgment—to structure the following discussion. Based on feminist methodologies, underlying this is the imperative to prioritize normal and everyday experiences, as an antidote to the male frame of violence and insecurity.

In contrast to the ungendered world portrayed in mainstream discussions of urban violence, we argue that if violence is to be tackled holistically, we must acknowledge its multiple interconnected manifestations and the factors that facilitate it. This involves looking at violence both materially and discursively. This chapter is a product of many conversations over some years which have explored the shared experiences and tensions of carrying out feminist research on violence in different contexts across Latin America. Both authors have conducted research in urban marginal communities over several years—Hume in El Salvador and Wilding in Rio de Janeiro. Rather than claiming to be a comparative ethnography, this chapter comprises the interrogation of questions arising from both contexts that inform our frustration about the arbitrary distinction between different types of violence, and the implications this has for both the research process and our knowledge of violence. By bringing together these two cases in this way, we do not suggest that experiences of urban violence are universal, but that we have identified certain tensions common to these settings and prevalent more generally in research on violence.

Our starting point here is to reject the normative separation between "gender-based" violence and other forms, and the resultant sidelining of violence against women from public scrutiny. Our ethnographic research in Brazil and El Salvador has shown that popular understandings of violence are often underpinned by gendered assumptions that affect understandings of violence (Hume 2009a; Wilding 2012). On a very simple level, this makes it challenging at times to explain the type of research we do, since we are often pushed to disconnect "gender violence" or so-called "private violence" from "violence," as if they can be separated so neatly. In practice this indicates that private violence is deemed of lesser importance than the more public manifestations of violence and crime and are seen as something analytically distinct. This forced compartmentalization not only misses that violence against women takes multiple forms and that all forms of violence have gendered impacts, but it also reveals a certain reduction of gender analysis to women and, by default, to what happens in the private sphere. In part, this is explained by normative assumptions that violence against women is largely a private or family matter. In the case of more public expressions of violence, the notion is that these types of violence are ungendered, whereas violence against women can only be discussed as a gender or women's issue. This belies the fact that violence in marginalized communities is highly visible, ever present, and interconnected.

The chapter is divided into three substantive sections. The first situates the political economy of violence at the urban margins as complex and multifaceted in order to provide a backdrop for the subsequent discussion. Here we problematize some of the existing debates on men and masculinities in order to argue for an analysis of men's violence as gendered and to caution against pushing for politically appealing, but potentially simplistic, causal explanations for men's violence. The second section interrogates the theme of silence. In particular, we are concerned with what stories and data inform the everyday scripts of violence and how these silences are gendered. Finally, we look at how violence is judged by those who live with it on a daily basis in order to illuminate the ways in which everyday scripts are underpinned by normative gendered assumptions that allow certain types of violence to go unquestioned. At the heart of this chapter is the tension between the gendered public scripts of violence and the reality of violence playing out in its multiple forms on an everyday basis.

GENDERING THE POLITICAL ECONOMY OF VIOLENCE

Latin America stands out as one of the most violent regions in the world. The issue attracts the attention of policy makers, scholars, and journalists. Violence related to crime, drugs, militias, and the police frequently hits the headlines, and—more often than not—the stories are presented in highly sensationalist terms and rely on a predetermined cast of actors. These stereotypical actors are usually young, poor (black) males who live on the urban margins. This representation of the violent actor is not only partial, but it also reveals deep societal biases around class, gender, and— in many Latin American contexts—ethnicity and race. In Rio de Janeiro and the cities of El Salvador, male gang members, marginalized by their class and social origins, are seen as the primary protagonists of violence. Grotesque images of spectacular acts committed in the name of feuds, territoriality, and punishment feature heavily in the everyday scripts of violence that dominate all strata of society. The very title of this chapter speaks self-consciously to such scripts. This representation of violent masculinity lacks rigorous and nuanced examination and fails to interrogate masculinities as *relational, complex,* and *multidimensional.*

(Mis)representing violence in this way leads to a curious impasse in our thinking, which is often underpinned by embedded and pre-scripted notions of gender and class. The fact that men are the key perpetrators and victims of lethal violence is taken for granted, while the obvious gendered dynamics are for the most part ignored. Where gender is addressed, the perpetrators' masculinity is often cited as the "reason" for their violence—otherwise men only appear "as men" when they engage in overtly gendered forms of violence against women, such as domestic violence and rape. In short, that the key protagonists of violence in the region are male is taken as a given, rather than being worthy of analysis.

Feminist research has argued the importance of recognizing the "thin line" between "*identifying* male power" and "*accepting* it implicitly" as a cause of violence (El-Bushra 2000, 82). We maintain here that the *acceptance* of male power as a cause both reproduces and naturalizes a simplified model of masculinity built on violence. Rather than looking at the intersectionality of different forces on men's lives and how these inform the use of violence (or not), causality is reduced to a somewhat abstract notion of masculinity or machismo. Yet it is at the intersection of race, class, and gender that violence is most productively understood. As Baird emphasizes (this volume), not all men benefit equally from patriarchy, so the relationship between masculinities and violence must be understood as both complex and changing. The risk in relying on simplified scripts of violence is that it serves to reproduce easy explanations that bolster exclusionary power structures around race, economics, and politics in which different forms of violence are embedded.

Both of us have asked our research participants about the positive and negative elements of their neighborhoods, and, although the localized dynamics may be distinct, the theme of violence dominated these narratives of community in both research contexts. As Evelia (age forty-nine) says in the following quote, you cannot "remain indifferent":

> [Violence is] not only here in our community, but in all communities in general. It's just that in the favela we are more exposed to it because we live here and we hear about a lot that goes on—you can't shut your eyes to everything that is going on. Even if you can't help someone change their attitude, you still don't remain indifferent. So this ends up affecting you, being worried about your kids, when they go to school, when they come back, shootings, stray bullets.

Evelia pinpoints a crucial concern: violence crosscuts class and ethnic groups—"[it is] in all communities"—but those who live in the precarious political economy of the urban margins have less capacity to insulate themselves from its pernicious effects. Focusing our attention on the margins does not mean that the poor are more prone to violence than other groups, and we have an ethical responsibility to situate violence in its broader political economy. However, its impact is felt differentially. The lack of material resources has very real implications for how citizens respond to violence and try to protect themselves. The middle and upper classes may respond to perceived insecurity by physically insulating themselves against the perceived "threat." This crudely translates into urban spaces being segregated along class lines through the growth of luxurious malls and gated communities and the growing presence of private security guards (Caldeira 2000). Those who do not have the means to negotiate the urban space through consumption, such as the participants in both our research contexts, have more permanent and more intimate contact with violence. In both research contexts, the presence of violence in the urban margins has profound effects on the way people live their lives. How people negotiate the urban space is shaped by threat and fear (Pain 2001). Gangs' use of violence to impose fear, for example, is achieved through a variety of mechanisms, including direct violence as well as ostensibly benevolent methods. Notably, however, both the directly aggressive and the more coercive aspects of their behavior are reliant on dominant models of masculinity: either the disciplinarian/protector or patriarchal provider (Wilding 2014; Hume 2007a).

Basic decisions, such as how to get home through your own community, whether to go to the local shop, and whether to speak to neighbors are therefore colored by the threat of violence. Delmy, a twenty-nine-year-old school teacher in Greater San Salvador suggests:

> Maybe what we see most is social violence, gangs. If you go to the shop at 7 p.m., you are afraid because just the fact that it is dark means that it is deserted.

Other women spoke about how the growing problem of extortion in marginal areas of El Salvador has particularly negative repercussions for local residents: "You have to pay to work" (Paty, 58 years old). Many in Paty's neighborhood have "paid" for non-payment with their lives (Hume 2009). Violence therefore destroys livelihood strategies in very direct ways. Threat and force are used by and against different groups for a range of ends. This has multiple ramifications for people, who are positioned differently in their communities according to their social networks and standing, as well as their social identity factors like age, race, and gender.

Not leaving the house, especially at night, is a common way of "protecting" oneself against the threat of violence, particularly for women and older residents. This sets certain expectations or implicit *rules* for how to behave in violent areas. However, this modification of routines is not possible for residents who work shifts or have to travel late to get home from work. More precisely, it is not possible for many people who engage with the neoliberal economy. Eighteen-year-old Alfonso works delivering bread for a local baker, so his economic needs mean that he must leave the house in the middle of the night. He says:

> [Violence] affects me because there is no normal security that allows you to feel ok and let you sleep well because you don't know what time *they* might come to kill you. Maybe you don't know if they arrive they might not take it out on you but with someone in your family or who means something to you, or someone you care about.

"They" in Alfonso's narrative refers to the local gang. Similarly in Brazil, "they" is interchangeable with "the boys" (*os meninos*) to describe violent actors, which is only understood in context, alerting us to the importance of listening to local scripts. As Wheeler (2009) found, while doing participatory videos with favela residents, participants spoke about violence without once naming the gangs or militia as the sources of this insecurity. This is one example of how the threatening presence of gangs in people's lives is discernible, but the reality of violence is much more complex, and what is unsaid can be as revealing as what is said (Hume 2009b). For example, Carmen (age fourteen) lists a number of interconnected forms of violence that affect her community in Greater San Salvador. She cites the gang as the major source of these different forms of violence.

> In the community, there are gangs, rapes. There are gang problems when others come here, drug pushing, gangs who beat up men. The gang mistreats people who visit, drugs, vices, lack of respect and gossip. Think about it, here, inside the community there are gangs and they have problems with outsiders, sometimes their blood gets up and they hit people. Rape, they rape kids and they grab them and take them away . . . Lack of respect.

Carmen's narrative reveals that in these contexts violence has multiple sources and many expressions. While it may be tempting to reduce all causality (and therefore, blame) to gang violence—a pattern very evident in narratives from both Brazil and El Salvador—both actors and expressions of violence are more dynamic. When asked about the negative aspects of her Rio community, Rosária (age sixteen) speaks not only of gangs, but also her fear of the police:

The traffickers are abusive to the girls. Police officers hit and verbally abuse people who don't have anything to do [with trafficking]. I am scared of the police because they come into the community, drugged up, saying bad things. Once I answered back to an officer and he gave me a slap in the face.

Rosária's fear reminds us that discrimination against these communities comes from the state as well as local gangs. In fact, community members are readily critical of the police violence. Although gang members are known for the acts they carry out in the name of the gang, there is a tension between the desire to distance gang violence, as a product of the "other," and the knowledge that gang members are socially embedded in the community: somebody's brother, son, and friend. In contrast to the horror stories of brutal acts of violence they commit, opinions expressed about gang behavior often suggest they observe a moral code: "They don't go from door to door, they only sell [drugs] to those that want it' (Sérgio, twenty-two, Brazil). Rosa echoed Sérgio's view, stating that she had "nothing against them" and that each could live as they desired, despite the fact her teenage son had been shot dead as a result of police-gang conflict. She did not openly criticize the part the gang played in the reproduction of violence and who the police had ostensibly come in to find. This is distinct from El Salvador, where the gang is highlighted as the key protagonist of violence in the community, as suggested in the above quote from Carmen. Limiting the scripts of violence to its most visible – or speakable – forms potentially silences the multiple actors involved in its localized production. What is clear from our research is the need to be alert to the interplay between criminal, interpersonal, and state-sanctioned violence.

Understanding the complex linkages between multiple violences poses a very real challenge for research and obliges us to situate violence within its gendered political and moral economy. Understanding linkages is not the same as determining causality, which requires a more complex mapping of violent processes and actors. Since the 1990s, there has been a burgeoning literature that seeks to understand the interplay between men and violence in an effort to tease out these political connections (Greig 2000). The impetus to bring men and a "masculinities perspective" into a sharper focus identifies men both as allies in achieving gender equality and as having their own gendered needs (e.g., Sweetman 1997 and 2013; Chant and Gutmann 2000; Cleaver 2002; Cornwall 1997 and 2000). Many of the arguments given for the inclusion of a male perspective appear to mirror, and complement, feminist goals by focusing on the reproduction of harmful gender regimes. However, while feminists' primary goal is to end women's oppression by tackling inequality within and between men and women, the comparatively recent masculinities literature tends to focus on men in isolation, constructed primarily as victims of oppressive gender norms, but failing to recognize the role that these play in perpetuating hierarchies *between* men and women. Further, large sections of this literature ignore the insights gleaned from decades of feminist research on violence against women.

In this vein, men are often presented either as vulnerable victims at risk of being targeted by drug gangs or as the dangerous protagonist in need of containment/diversion. One tendency has been to construct men as victims of limited job and education opportunities and social exclusion, and therefore left without a legitimate means of "achieving manhood" (Barker 2005). The premise is that young, poor men from low-income communities are left with limited possibilities for productive and fulfilled lives by virtue of their identity and where they live. Both popular and academic representations of men in the context of neoliberalism have made allusions to men or masculinities "in crisis," referring to the process by which traditional male roles are being undermined by the *emasculating* nature of the neoliberal economy. The increasing precarity of labor, for example, strips men of their "traditional" pathways to becoming men. In response to this process of dispossession, Bourgois (1996, 412) has argued that men can develop a "street culture of resistance" which "celebrates a misogynist predatory street culture that normalises gang rape, sexual conquest, and paternal abandonment. Marginalized men lash out against the women and children they can no longer support economically nor control patriarchally." In a similar vein, Baird (this volume) persuasively suggests that male gang members from low-income backgrounds in Medellín have few legal opportunities to pursue masculinity and thus violence becomes a key tool to achieve patriarchal dividends. The everyday scripts of violence are awash with convincing reasons why men lash out against women and other groups. Unemployment, alcohol, and drug use often feature heavily in such accounts:

> He drinks and then comes home and hits the children. . . . The financial situation is very influential. . . . If a father is unemployed it disrupts (*desestrutura*) everything, he will get drunk, go to the corner to take drugs, because he sees his wife and child going hungry, getting ill, without medicine, and his hands are tied. He will end up looking for a way out in drink and drugs. (Evelia, focus group, Rio de Janeiro)

This characterization of men as victims of a harsh socioeconomic system that leaves them no opportunities but to lash out at those less powerful than themselves is appealing and it usefully situates violence in the intersection of multiple forms of domination in men's lives. However, it is also problematic. Not all marginalized men respond through the use of violence, and not all men who use violence are marginalized. Feminists have been vocal in cautioning against overly simplistic causal analyses of men's use of violence, and we suggest here that a more rigorous and indeed historically situated analysis of gendered relations is necessary. Male domination (of women) crosscuts time, place, and social class. The fact is that not only marginalized men "celebrate" or indeed benefit from misogyny and patriarchy. Without acknowledging the centrality of unequal gender relations to the reproduction of violence, we risk suggesting that male domination is a response to a particular economic climate, shifting the blame away from oppressive gender relations but also silencing the multiple ways violence is used by men who are not considered "marginalized." Indeed, it is specifically to the issue of silencing that the discussion now turns.

SILENCE

The questions asked by feminist scholars of violence against women offer important lessons for the study of violence more generally, particularly for the examination of the narratives of those who live in intimate contact with its multiple forms on a daily basis, such as many of those who live on Latin America's urban margins. A key challenge of feminist research has been to shatter some of the silences and myths that surround violence against women, many of which implicitly or explicitly blame victims of certain forms of violence (Kelly 1988). We understand silence here not only as the "unsaid" but also as productive of these everyday scripts of violence. A notable achievement of the feminist movement has been to expose the immediacy and intimacy of different forms of male domination expressed through both overt and hidden violence in women's lives. This runs contrary to popular assumptions that continue to inform fear and danger, which typically root violence as something "committed by strangers in public places" (Stanko 1990, 78) and, as argued above, silences much of the violence used by powerful men and groups. Feminist literature exposes the misconception that violence is something that is "out there," rather than being constitutive of relationships of both intimacy and oppression. This insight has helped open up space to talk about other forms of violence and abuse that involve close relationships, such as intergenerational abuse. But it also has lessons for understanding other social relationships and groups that involve both trust and oppression, such as gangs. Approaching violence in this way calls attention to the arbitrary separation between what is perceived as two distinct phenomena—that is, "real" violence and that perpetrated in intimate relations—or indeed the notion that intimacy and oppression are mutually exclusive. This poses a direct challenge to popular conceptualizations of real violence as "mindless," "incomprehensible," "unpredictable" (Dobash and Dobash 1998, 141), and most commonly committed by a stranger.

In an attempt to address these connections between actors and acts, Liz Kelly (1988) suggests that sexual violence is best understood as a continuum of overlapping male behavior ranging from, for example, a shouted insult to rape. The utility of the continuum can be extended to an analysis of violence more generally since it forces us to challenge the notion that violence can be reduced to a discrete act removed from everyday and otherwise harmonious human relations. This has two key implications. First, it demands an examination of the relations that underpin violent processes and behaviors, which are normally imbued with inequalities. Second, it emphasizes the importance of the dynamism and interconnectedness of different forms of violence, which we have looked at elsewhere (Hume 2007a and 2009a; Wilding 2010 and 2012). Such lessons are crucial for the Latin American context, where violence is increasingly seen as a "normal option" for citizens to pursue their goals (Koonings and Kruijt 1999, 11).

The very way in which violence is measured exposes certain gendered silences. The principle mechanism for assessing levels of violence in a society is through homicide rates, which are taken as a proxy for overall levels of violence. Young men dominate in statistics of both perpetrators and victims of violence and crime, accounting for just under 90 percent of murder victims in both Brazil and El Salvador (89.8 percent for Brazil and 89 percent for El Salvador in 2012, according to UNODC, 2014). Young men are specifically vulnerable. Of 52,198 killed in Brazil in 2011, over half were between fifteen and twenty-four years old; 71 percent were black (*pretos* and *pardos*); and 93 percent were male (Waiselfisz 2013, 9); equating to 53.4 per 100,000 population (ibid., 11). Meanwhile in El Salvador, homicide rates reached 69.9 per 100,000 in 2011, dropping to 41.2 per 100,000 in 2012. In 2008, the homicide rate for Salvadoreans aged fifteen to twenty-four was 94 per 100,000 (UNODC, 2014). Despite this statistical salience, data disaggregated by gender is difficult to come by and rarely used in policy development. Even less reliable are the data for non-lethal violence, which suffer from both chronic under-reporting and under-recording. It is still worth pointing out that homicide data may be the most reliable available to researchers and can be compared across countries and cities, even though numbers only shed light on extreme forms of violence that result in death, without providing a more general picture of the low intensity violence and insecurity that marks everyday lives for many in Latin America's urban margins.

Nevertheless, it is through this prism of death rates, that young, poor (black) men, often from informal settlements, are depicted as both dominant victims and perpetrators. This truism is used to fuel class-based stereotypes of violent young men killing each other. With reference to a more general "talk of crime," Caldeira (2000, 32) has termed this both "a kind of knowledge and a misrecognition," suggesting it has much in common with other forms of classificatory thinking such as racism. Men are seen to be more vulnerable to outbursts of "natural" aggression; more likely to meet conflict and frustration with violence; and more easily lured by the temptations and glamour of crime, violent networks, and the desire to dominate. However, we should be clear that when we speak about men, we cannot do so in isolation from class. "Violent men" are normatively and implicitly working-class men. In Brazil, this also has racialized dimensions. The failure to interrogate the use of violence by men from higher social classes leaves working-class men to be the protagonists of these violent scripts even within critical scholarship, as suggested above. So while some men's violence is interrogated and challenged, the violence of others is about overlooked.

Therefore, although men may dominate over women in many settings, it is not simply the case that all men benefit equally from patriarchy. Indeed, differences within genders may be as significant as differences between men and women (El-Bushra 2000, 80). Connell's (1987) work has shown how some expressions of masculinity are privileged over others, with those who can perform to the dominant models benefiting the most. This is particularly evident within the hierarchical structure of gangs, which are often buttressed by specific notions of masculinity and reinforced through the threat of violence.

Interrogating what is silenced and omitted from these everyday scripts of violence becomes a challenging but crucial task for the researcher. Caldeira (2000, 33) argues that the pervasive "talk of crime" elaborates prejudices. She suggests that in order to make sense of the violent reality, one must adhere to the available stereotypes: "The categories are rigid: they are meant not to describe the world accurately but to organise and classify it symbolically. They are meant to counteract disruption at the level of experience, not to describe it" (ibid.), which allows people to construct a feeling of safety in spite of the actual risks they face (Wilding 2012). Our research suggests that one reason these simplified representations of men have such purchase is that they are based on partial realities, such as those presented in crude statistics or sensational headlines that appeal to commonsense assumptions of what a violent actor is. Hume (2009a, 24) has suggested they are "seductive in their simplicity" because they insulate those who see themselves as upstanding citizens from those they label as violent criminals. These same citizens are often the ones to support heavy-handed and even extrajudicial measures to deal with criminals (Hume 2007a). This automatically distinguishes types of violence as acceptable or unacceptable. In this sense, such scripts are a "constant form of moral discourse" (Liebling and Stanko 2001, 428). It is therefore important to understand the everyday (gendered) scripts of violence and the ways in which these draw on judgments made about the acts and actors involved (Wilding 2014). Judgments are reinforced by wider political and social norms, as discussed in the following section.

BLAME AND JUDGMENT

In spite of the fact that gender identities are generally only acknowledged when violence is considered to be overtly "gender based," which is most often reduced to violence against women, the way in which men and women construct femininities and masculinities is done in conversation with one another—both symbolically and materially. This making of categories, what it means to be or become a man, draws on particular notions of what it means to be a woman as a counterpoint. As research into gangs in Brasilia has identified, "masculinity is not only reproduced through interaction with violence, but through gender relations, with femininity a co-producer of models of virility" (Abramovay 2010, 242). In El Salvador, Vladimir, a member of the Mara Salvatrucha gang suggests that central to his participation in the gang is precisely a specific masculine identity premised on violent domination: "What makes me a man are my balls because I haven't borrowed them . . . I have them because God gave them to me and I show them that with tattoos or without tattoos, I sleep with who I want. No matter how big a guy is, I'm better than him." Emphasized here is both an aggressive sexuality and competition among men. Research has suggested gangs can provide a sense of belonging for young men, but such belonging has its costs. Intragang violence is common. One of the ways Vladimir (age twenty-three) has rectified problems with other members of his gang has been by carrying out executions on their behalf:

The guy spoke up for me and he brought me here at night. I told him I thought they were going to kill me. No, you silly bastard, there is no hassle. So we came up. . . . They asked me did I want to fix [the problem I had with them], so I said yes and they told me to go kill someone. I said, great, just give me the gun to do it right. I went and I pumped him with nine bullets and left him there in the [community], here in that street, up there.

MH: And was he from another gang?

No, from a [criminal] gang. Maybe you have heard of los Ricos gang? He was one of those guys. They called him "el Limpio." I shot him straight, in that fucking street. I left him lying with nine bullets in him. That was how I fixed getting back in. From then on, thanks be to God, they treated me like they had done beforehand. Now there is no conflict in the gang.

In this case, Vladimir recognizes that he had a choice: to kill or be killed. Others do not have this "choice." A common example that portrays the brutality of the gangs in both Brazil and El Salvador involves the spectacular act of displaying victims in public places: gangs and other violent groups often leave the heads or hearts of "traitors" in public spaces, such as sports pitches and street corners. Such rituals are presented as a warning to potential rule breakers or "traitors," but they also reinforce gang power through their display of ruthlessness. These tactics have a long history in Latin America, most notably during the period of authoritarian rule when the state used such displays to spread terror in the population.

Similar to the politically motivated state terror and despite the fear and disgust that these contemporary displays generate among the wider population, narratives of victim blaming continue to resonate in everyday scripts. Some residents have expressed their relief that "criminals" are killing themselves, while others are vocal in their support for both legal and illegal social cleansing policies (Hume 2007a and b; see also Snodgrass Godoy 2006 on Guatemala). Such scripts underpin a moral discourse of guilt and innocence, which distinguishes between "good" and "bad" citizens, "worthy" and "innocent" victims. According to Ana María, a resident of a marginal area in Greater San Salvador:

> I think that we're okay now because all those, all of them who were thieves here, they're all dead and others are in prison. That guy that lived up beside Don Chepe, the one they called "the chicken," he's left here. I mean, thank God, they are killing themselves and now there are some thieves, not like that though, those other thieves that went about robbing clothes, hens.

Such symbolic acts of violence are reliant on the construction of a brutal and brutalized masculinity, whereby gang members' own involvement in violence validates their victimization.

Following Caldeira (2000), we argue that such "classificatory" thinking, which compartmentalizes actors and simplifies their motives, underpins some of the key ways in which violence is judged. These hegemonic scripts are nourished by stereotypes that offer a particular ordering of social reality that eliminates the possibility of ambiguity and are reliant on the construction of a dangerous "other." As everyday scripts, stereotypes insulate citizens from the complexities and closeness of violence. As mentioned above, this narrative also has a protective function. It can insulate other residents, who believe that they can protect themselves: "As long as I abide by the rules, I am safe" (Wilding 2012). Likewise, "belonging" to a particular group or community can foster protection, however illusionary this may be in reality (Hume, 2007b). In this way, stereotypes are both reflective of and complicit with bigger exclusionary narratives that operate to sanitize and stamp an "official" value on violence.

As researchers, we are not immune from such scripts. The quote at the start of this paper, "their sport is killing," is evocative of a particular image of the young violent gangster that dominates much research on the issue. As researchers of violence, we are often drawn to the extreme in our efforts to understand violence. We self-consciously used this to attract attention and to problematize the issues under discussion. When we present this quote in context, a more complex picture of Vladimir's life emerges that unsettles the somewhat one-dimensional notion of the gangster concerned only with supposed glamour, consumption, and violence.

> I have been in the gang for almost seven years. I don't regret it. I know that at some stage it will be my turn [to die]. Their sport is killing, robbing, you could say, raping girls. That was my thing before, I can tell you, but that child [his daughter] changed my mind a fuck load. Even though I am what I am because for people who have money, what are we gang members? We're rubbish. I mean I am not interested; as long as I feel alright what people say doesn't interest me—it goes in this ear and out that one. It's hard to forget the past.

Here we see a young man who has spent a large part of his life in the violent structure of the gang. He faces discrimination on a daily basis, both because of his gang status and his poverty. He is also a man who has been profoundly affected by fatherhood. At the time of the interview, he was an active member of the Mara Salvatrucha and main caregiver for his young daughter. Both lived with his mother, who had been tortured by the security forces during the war because of her leftist sympathies. Her partner (Vladimir's father) had been killed. As a result, she had suffered a severe breakdown when Vladimir was a baby and he was brought up by relatives. For him, joining the gang was a way of escaping the local bullies who picked on him because he was considered "small" for his age, but now that he had taken on responsibility for his daughter's care (the girl's mother was living with another gang member), he found he no longer enjoyed the "vacil" or gang life.

Presenting Vladimir in this more complete way allows a more complex understanding of violence to emerge. We see how different forms of violence can create conditions where violence is reproduced and challenged. It also humanizes the violent actor and destabilizes any potential for a neat account of violent masculinities. Yet everyday scripts of violence cannot allow such ambiguity. Media portrayals of both actors and victims of violence rely on caricature, showing images of body bags emerging from the urban margins and presenting one-dimensional portrayals of brutal gang members. In such cases, the victims are constructed to have been at best foolhardy or at worst complicit in their own deaths. In contrast, middle-class victims of violence are portrayed in terms of the lives cut short and the pain and loss of family members. Their innocence is emphasized. Greer (2004) has termed this a hierarchy of victimization that ranges from "ideal" to "undeserving" victims.

Both our research contexts have shown that in cases of violence against women generally, men use women to explain and excuse their behavior, and absolve themselves of responsibility for the violence they have inflicted. Men impose their own definitions of violence in order to neutralize or minimize women's experience of abuse. For example, in El Salvador, men argue it is "her" fault that they are being held to account for their behavior (Hume 2009a). Similar narratives have been identified in other contexts such as Trinidad (Sukhu 2013) and the United Kingdom (Cavanagh et al. 2001, 695). Of interest here is less what men say or how they try to excuse and explain their violence, and more the ways in which wider society engages with and reinforces these scripts that allow women to be blamed.

Blame is frequently ascribed to women for tolerating the abuse. Women's dress, speech, greed, infidelity, and even walking down the street after dark have all been used to "explain" men's use of violence. Widely held assumptions include that women are complicit in the violence against them because they should have known better and are responsible for protecting themselves. According to Tulio (fourteen years old, focus group in San Salvador): "Women even wear miniskirts and you can see almost everything and he goes and fucks her and worse if he is drunk or on drugs, he grabs her more." Such scripts leave the male violence unquestioned. Women's presumed financial dependence on men is also cited as the key reason women endure abuse, but such explanations can border on accusations of greed. One fourteen-year-old boy in Rio commented,

"Men end up taking this [violent] attitude due to the fact that the women accept it. Because much of the time, women get abused and they don't leave the man, they stay with him, so that they don't get stuck without clothes, money and so on." The risk of abuse is particularly acute for women in relationships with gang members. Interviewees in Brazil suggested that girls go so far as to show off their bruises as a symbol of their relationships, which not only reinforces the connection between sex and violence but also reinforces popular perceptions that some women actually enjoy violence. Although this framing may appeal even more when it concerns young women in relationships with gang members, it should be noted that it is not exceptional and indeed forms part of a broader logic in which women are seen as complicit in the violence that is carried out against them.

However, it should be pointed out that Hume's research in El Salvador suggests that the much-cited financial rationale for staying in violent relationships is often overstated and itself a product of gendered scripts. Although their economic contribution is all too often rendered invisible, women often have sole economic responsibility for their families' well-being. Also pertinent are the cultural obstacles to leaving, such as fear of what people will say. "If she leaves that man, she will have to be with another and if he doesn't want her because of the children then she will have to get another" (Mary, El Salvador). This is a clear indication of the cultural value placed on "having a man" and the shame associated with being alone. It also reveals women's lack of autonomy in terms of her own sexuality and provides a caution against accepting at face value the "reasons" for women's apparent tolerance of violence.

Nevertheless, women are not only vulnerable to violence because of their roles as girlfriends and partners, and we should be careful about reducing all forms of violence against women to intimate relations. One of the most pressing problems in Central America for women is the growing problem of femicide. Interviews with police in El Salvador suggest that the murder of women is growing in both scale and brutality. Increasingly, women's bodies are used as sites for retaliation and punishment. In San Salvador, Hume's research participants talked about one particular case of a young woman who was taken from the street in front of her house, brutally tortured and mutilated, then dumped on a football pitch because her father worked in the police. Media stories speak of partners and mothers who have been targeted in gang rivalries. Women's bodies have long been an acceptable site of men's violence in both public and private. Placing this historical fact at the center of our analysis opens up the possibility to reveal the gendered connections of violence.

CONCLUSION

As we have shown, male gang members are seen to be the primary pro-tagonists of violence in Rio de Janeiro and the cities of El Salvador, with grotesque images of spectacular acts—committed in the name of feuds, territoriality, and punishment—imprinted on the public memory. These images feature heavily in the everyday scripts of violence that dominate all strata of society. Yet those who live in the communities affected can't "shut their eyes to everything that is going on," as Evelia stated in a focus group in Rio.

Both Brazil and El Salvador have high levels of violence, which have reached chronic proportions. Each country has at various times been labeled as having levels of violence comparable to war zones. However, the violence that this invokes is the violence of the street, "real violence" that occurs in public places, supposedly by "public" actors. This image curtails alternative voices, experiences, and interpretations that might give a fuller depiction of violence. Studying violence in these contexts from a feminist perspective requires that different forms of violence be studied together, challenging the implicit hierarchy that prioritizes the visible over the invisible, the "ungendered" over the "gendered," men's experiences over women's. But more importantly, it requires us to not treat them as separate phenomena that can somehow coexist in the same locale without sharing any common source or logic. Rather, the connections between different forms of violence and the gendered dynamics that underpin all forms of violence need to be considered as mutually constitutive. Everyday forms of violence need to be studied alongside the spectacular, criminal, and institutional in order to better understand the reproduction of violence in all its forms.

In seeing violence as gendered, we do not wish to cite gender to "explain" why violence occurs but rather to understand the contextual-ized gendered relations, dynamics, norms, and contradictions that under-pin violence and its relation to everyday human relations. We have argued that so-called mainstream understandings of violence, which see gender as at best secondary to the analysis, result in a partial understanding of violence, silencing subaltern voices and ignoring the everyday dynam-ics of conflict and aggression. In particular, silencing voices that are not constructed as being part of the problems deemed to constitute "hard" security overlooks and may legitimize certain forms of violence. Given that social relations are informed by gender stereotypes and norms, and violence occurs in the context of these social relations, gender norms therefore provide meanings and logic to the performance of violence, the actors involved, and their relationships and apparent motives. As such, acts of violence—and which forms are legitimized and which are challenged—can only be understood in combination with an analysis of localized gender scripts and practices.

WORKS CITED

Abramovay, Miriam. 2010. *Ganges, Gênero e Juventudes: Donas de Rocha e Sujeitos Cabulosos*. Brasília: Ministro da Secretaria de Direitos Humanos da Presidência da República (SDH), Central Única de Favelas (CUFA).

Barker, Gary. 2005. *Dying to be Men: Youth and Masculinity and Social Exclusion*. Oxford: Routledge Taylor & Francis Group.

Bourgois, Philippe. 1996. *In Search of Respect: Selling Crack in El Barrio*. New York: Cambridge University Press.

Caldeira, Teresa P. R. 2000. *City of Walls: Crime, Segregation, and Citizenship in São Paulo*. London: University of California Press.

Cavanagh, Kate, R. Emerson Dobash, Russell P. Dobash, and Ruth Lewis. 2001. "'Remedial Work': Men's Strategic Responses to Their Violence Against Intimate Female Partners." *Sociology* 35(3): 695–714.

Chant, Sylvia, and Matthew C. Gutmann. 2000. *Mainstreaming Men into Gender and Development: Debates, Reflections, Experiences*. Oxford: Oxfam.

Cleaver, Frances. 2002. *Masculinities Matter! Men, Gender and Development*. London: Zed Books.

Connell, R. W. 1987. *Masculinities*. Oxford: Polity Press.

Cornwall, Andrea. 2000. "Missing Men? Reflections on Men, Masculinities and Gender in GAD." *IDS Bulletin* 31(2): 18–27.

Cornwall, Andrea. 1997. "Men, Masculinities and 'Gender in Development.'" *Gender and Development* 5(2): 8–13.

Dobash, R. Emerson, and Russel P. Dobash. 1998. *Rethinking Violence Against Women*. Thousand Oaks: Sage.

El-Bushra, Judy. 2000. "Transforming Conflict: Some Thoughts on Gendered Understandings of Conflict Processes." In *States of Conflict: Gender, Violence and Resistance*, edited by Susie Jacobs, Ruth Jacobson, and Jennifer Marchbank. London: Zed Books, 66–86.

Greer, Chris. 2004. "Crime, Media and Community: Grief and Virtual Engagement in Late Modernity." In *Cultural Criminology Unleashed*, edited by Jeff Ferrell, Keith Hayward, Wayne Morrison, and Mike Presdee, 109–120. London: Cavendish, 109–120.

Greig, Allen. 2000. "The Spectacle of Men Fighting." *IDS Bulletin* 31(2): 28–32.

Hume, Mo. 2007a. "Mano Dura: El Salvador Responds to Gangs." *Development in Practice* 17(6): 739–751.

Hume, Mo. 2007b. "'(Young) Men With Big Guns': Reflexive Encounters with Violence and Youth in El Salvador." *Bulletin of Latin American Research* 26(4): 480–496.

Hume, Mo. 2009a. *The Politics of Violence: Gender, Conflict and Community in El Salvador*. London: Wiley-Blackwell.

Hume, Mo. 2009b. "Researching the Gendered Silences of Violence in El Salvador." *IDS Bulletin* 40(3): 78–85.

Kelly, Liz. 1988. *Surviving Sexual Violence*. Cambridge: Polity

Koonings, Kees, and Dirk Kruijt. 1999. *Societies of Fear: The Legacy of Civil War, Violence and Terror in Latin America*. London: Zed.

Liebling, Alison, and Betsy Stanko. 2001. "Allegiance and Ambivalence: Some Dilemmas in Researching Disorder and Violence." *British Journal of Criminology* 41(3): 421–430.

Pain, Rachel. 2001. "Gender, Race, Age and Fear in the City." *Urban Studies* 38(5/6): 899–913.

Snodgrass Godoy, Angelina. 2006. *Popular Injustice: Violence, Community and Law in Latin America*. Stanford: Stanford University Press.

Stanko, Elizabeth. 1990. *Everyday Violence: How Women and Men Experience Sexual and Physical Danger*. London: Pandora.

Sukhu, Raquel. 2013. "Masculinity and Men's Violence against Known Women in Trinidad: Whose Responsibility?" *Men and Masculinities* 16(1): 71–92.

Sweetman, Caroline. 1997. "Editorial: Special Issue on Men and Masculinity." *Gender and Development* 5(2): 2–7.

Sweetman, Caroline. 2013. "Introduction: Working with Men on Gender Equality." *Gender and Development* 21(1): 1–13.

UNODC. 2014. *Global Study on Homicide*. Available at https://www.unodc.org/gsh/Accessed 23 April 2014.

Waiselfisz, Julio. 2013. *Homicídios e Juventude no Brasil: Mapa da Violência 2013*. Secretaria-Geral da Presidência da República, Secretaria Nacional de Juventude.

Wheeler, Joanne. 2009. "'The Life That We Don't Want': Using Participatory Video in Researching Violence." *IDS Bulletin* 40(3): 10–18.

Wilding, Polly. 2010. "'New Violence': Silencing Women's Experiences in the Favelas of Brazil." *Journal of Latin American Studies*. 42: 719-747.

Wilding, Polly. 2012. *Negotiating Boundaries: Gender, Violence and Transformation in Brazil*. Basingstoke: Palgrave Macmillan

Wilding, Polly. 2014. "Gendered Meanings and Everyday Experiences of Violence in Urban Brazil." *Gender, Place and Culture: A Journal of Feminist Geography* 21(2): 228–243.

Yllo, Kersti. 1993. "Through a Feminist Lens: Gender, Power and Violence." In *Current Controversies on Family Violence*, edited by Richard Gelles and Donileen Loseke. Newbury Park: Sage.

CHAPTER 5

Duros and Gangland Girlfriends

Male Identity, Gang Socialization, and Rape in Medellín

ADAM BAIRD

INTRODUCTION: NEGOTIATING PATHWAYS TO MANHOOD THROUGH GANG MEMBERSHIP

Youth gangs are paradigmatic of urban violence[1] and are generally associated with socioeconomic exclusion[2] Poor young men overwhelmingly provide the human capital for continued gang membership and at the same time are the principal victims of homicidal violence.[3] There is also increasing acceptance of the connection between gang membership and the construction of masculine identities (Covey 2003; Barker 2005; Rodgers 2006; Dowdney 2007; Hagedorn 2008). Muncie (2009) has argued that much poor, male youth violence is perpetrated as a "maverick" form of masculinity by those who have grown up in economically deprived areas at the margins of mainstream society. Over fifty years ago, Cloward and Ohlin (1960) observed the "aberrant behaviour [that] may result" when individuals encounter obstacles to growing up. Similarly, other studies that link versions of masculinity to violence (see Barker 2005, 71, 82; Yablonsky 1997, 172; Hume in Pearce 2006, 70) point to structural exclusion, which fosters the development of youth gangs. Disadvantaged youths use violent and macho activities to restore esteem through the "glittering prizes" of the gangland lifestyle, regarded as "indissoluble" from masculine identity (Pitts 2008, 94-95). This chapter seeks to understand the relationship between masculinities and violence in a nuanced, multidimensional way; as Hume and Wilding point out, it is at the "intersection between race, class and gender, that violence is most productively understood" (this volume).

The gang as a manifestation of "protest masculinity" amid socioeconomic exclusion is not new (Adler 1928). Enduring exclusion generates a collective sense of emasculation among marginalized young men as they are blocked from achieving the traditional male identities they are expected to live up to, which can lead them to embrace rebellious processes of masculinization. Bloch and Niederhoffer claim that where male adolescents are "cut off from the possibility of manhood for a prolonged period," gangs function as vehicles for satisfying their urge for male adulthood (Yablonsky 1997, 171–172). Bourgois makes similar observations in his study of Puerto Rican drug gangs in New York. While men with business acumen and diverse progeny command "respect," these masculinizing processes are hindered by social exclusion: "The former modalities of male respect are no longer achievable within the conjugal household . . . One can discern the gender-specific form of the experience of social marginalization in the Puerto Rican diaspora" (Bourgois 2003, 293–295). Puerto Rican drug gangs emerged as epiphenomena of systematic exclusion tied to the political economy of a city that blocked access to the opportunities that defined dignified pathways to manhood (Bourgois 2003, 319).

Similarly, Vigh contends that young men in Guinea Bissau face "social death" as the conventional pathways to achieving male adulthood with esteem and dignity have been closed by economic decline. To avoid the shame and frustration of emasculation, many male youth seek alternative means to becoming "men"—through migration, drug trafficking, or becoming child soldiers because "war becomes a terrain of possibility" rather than a terrain of death (Vigh 2006, 31; Adams 2012, 22). In an excellent body of research into gangs and exclusion in Cape Town, South Africa, Jensen has likewise analyzed the *agterbuurte* gang member who becomes a "bad mother fucker" through heroic identification with the gang in order to invert a sense of masculine disempowerment (Jensen 2008, 92).

Emasculation contributes to the reproduction and reinforcement of youth gangs because they are tools for mitigating such feelings and thus become instrumental in negotiating pathways to manhood (Baird, 2012a). Where gangs persist across generations in a given neighborhood, they become a masculine system of influence (Baird 2012b), symptomatic of continual marginalization from the productive sociocultural and economic practices of urban life. Latin America has widespread poverty and weak systems of governance. It suffers chronically from inequality, most visible in its cities, where the rich and poor live in closer proximity. This situation contributes to many youths' gravitation toward gangs, so much so in many Central American countries that some scholars liken them to forms of dystopian social organization or collective movements (Beall and Fox 2009, 186; Rodgers 2006, 288; Rodgers and Baird, 2015).

Conceptually I examine social exclusion and masculinization as the basis for the (re)generation of youth gangs and violence. The endeavor is to understand the processes that lead to male youths being socialized, generation after generation, into gangs. Bourdieu's concepts of *habitus* and *capital* (1977) have been used to examine how masculine identity is reproduced in circumstances of deprivation, how masculine *habitus*—latent subjective urges or dispositions to become men—animates new generations of boys to accumulate masculine assets—or capital —through gang membership.

The interaction with girls and women is crucial to the process of male identity formation in the gang and receives particular attention in this chapter, not least because women's roles in gangs are so understudied but also because singular focuses on male-dominated homicide rates obfuscate the range of other violences suffered by women (see also Hume and Wilding, this volume). Here I examine how sexual access to young women becomes another capital or "glittering prize" of gang membership that has the unfortunate effect of reinforcing gang identities, hence perpetuating their existence.

RESEARCH IN CONTEXT

Medellín, Colombia's second largest city with some 2.5 million dwellers, has a long history of gang-related violence and drug trafficking linked to the dynamics of the broader armed conflict. Growing up in these neighborhoods is challenging: generalized poverty, socioeconomic exclusion, and the traumas of everyday violence severely limit opportunities for young people. The ubiquity of the drug trade and gang presence across generations has led to chronic levels of violence, in turn promoting social and family disorder. In fact, fatherless households are the norm. Sexual and domestic violence is pervasive, as are levels of alcoholism and drug addiction—local drug sales being the principal income generator for gangs. Amid such challenges, these neighborhoods are also sites of tremendous resilience, agency, and *rebusque*—the creative capacity for day-to-day survival. However, the focus here is upon gang socialization, violence, and gender.

This chapter is based on interviews with a range of gang members and their (ex)girlfriends, and non-gang residents, supported by a broad body of ethnographic work conducted intermittently between 2007 and 2012 (Baird 2009). It should be noted that all of the gang members cited here except Junior—who was ten years old and running drugs and guns around the neighborhood—smoked marijuana, took cocaine, and drank alcohol, most of them heavily. Peludo stands out, as he entered the gang as a *sicario* assassin at the age of twelve. The two non-gang individuals cited here—Sammy and Pepe—could be described as proactive or "prosocial" members of the community, because they worked at a youth-based community organization (see Baird 2012). The (ex)girlfriends cited are Negra, Femina, and Diabilis, all in their twenties. They had all headed out in their early teens to "party" with gang members but have now left that life behind. Negra and Femina had children by ex-gang-member boyfriends. They all took a lot of cocaine and ecstasy in their earlier years of partying with gang members. Femina euphemistically said that in her past she had exchanged sex for "material things," which she distinguished from being a sex worker, and Diabilis recounted a harrowing story of rape. All names used in this chapter are pseudonyms chosen by the interviewees themselves.

GANGLAND MASCULINITIES
Exclusion as Emasculation

We should be careful not to oversimplify or stereotype male identity, and we should rightly speak of *masculinities* and not *masculinity*. However, the most common and somewhat exaggerated version of hegemonic masculinity across Latin America is defined by the notion of *machismo*, the visible symbols of which are male displays of wealth, sexual conquest, and power over others. *Machismo* is culturally rooted in gender inequalities that cut across class divisions and encompasses the attributes of social status, material wealth, sexual prowess, and a predilection to violence (Gutmann and Viveros Vigoya 2005, 118). *Machismo* in Medellín is somewhat exaggerated. Sammy, one youth who was not in a gang, articulated: "Being a man is to be strong, a brute, bringing home money, a protector, skillful, a womanizer, a chauvinist, macho, having power, being respected" (Sammy, March 6, 2008). Yet navigating pathways to manhood and "doing" gender in this performative sense varies according to the possibilities of accessing diverse "masculinization opportunities." In Medellín these depend considerably on the "tools at hand" linked to the socioeconomic circumstances male youths grow up in, which vary dramatically in such an unequal city.

One evening I spent in the wealthy neighborhood of Parque Lleras contrasted starkly with the previous night spent in a poor part of town called La Salle. In Lleras, the popular image of the "successful" macho man is one who has a well-paid executive job, comes from a "good" family, drives a prestigious 4x4 car, wears expensive Ralph Lauren polo shirts or suits, drinks Chivas Regal whisky, and has several attractive female friends or a beautiful wife. These displayed trappings of wealth and status are the bases of his masculinity identity (in public at least). The popular perspective of the macho man in La Salle is one who owns a fast Pulsar motorcycle, wears expensive sneakers and jeans, and likewise has the capacity to captivate attractive girls. In both Lleras and La Salle, macho "success" and status were established through the accumulation of masculine capital, which is at once material and symbolic. Although the specific material capital they accumulated was not the same given the differentiated "masculinization opportunities" they had, the way masculine habitus— that disposition to seek locally accepted male identity, esteem, and "success"—played out in both locations—was actually the very same process. In La Salle "success" was displayed most visibly by gang members, whereas the macho men in Lleras were more likely businessmen from "good families." I could not help thinking that if the businessmen had been born in the poor neighborhoods around La Salle, they would have grown up to become gang members to achieve the same macho, alpha-male, or hegemonic status. This shows how diverse tools or masculinization opportunities lead to decidedly different actions in pursuit of the same goals of male status and power (Kersten 2001).

Exclusion generates emasculation. When the acquisition and accumulation of masculine capital is denied to men by structural obstacles rooted in a city's prevailing sociopolitical economy, men will invariably consider alternative means of attaining it. They do so in part because masculine habitus will dispose them to reproduce culturally valued male practices in their neighborhood. Emasculation makes the relative riches of gang membership a standard-bearer of male success. Masculine habitus is more likely to lead youths to join gangs in such circumstances rather than in more affluent contexts with less gang presence and other attractive and legal masculinization opportunities. Therefore, urban exclusion creates fertile grounds for gang membership. This was articulated best by gang members themselves. Sayayo talks about growing up fast, selling sweets on the street at the age of nine. At the age of fourteen he became a gang member:

Sayayo: I hit the streets to work when I was nine . . . by the time I turned fifteen I had my own *plaza* [drugs corner], I was earning well, had my own place.

Adam: How old were you when you felt like an independent man then?

S: At fifteen.

A: And whom did you admire as a kid?

S: There were a lot of guys round here who were always in shoot-outs. When I was a kid I admired Pablo Escobar [cartel boss], you know, a man like that who manages to get so much money and so much power, you see? They're the role models we've seen in this country. We live in a country where violence, cocaine an' all the money that follows. Round these neighborhoods the chances of you becoming a professional, a lawyer, and doctor are real slim . . . round here people paint the houses of the rich. The difference between the two is huge.

Kids round here admire gang members because they drive about in luxurious cars with pretty girls . . . you can't go to university, get a degree, buy a car, a house an' all that . . . you don't have any opportunities to get that stuff honestly . . . you gotta think how you can get it, if not you're gonna be poor your whole life, your whole life a poor man.

You know how many of my friends they've killed? They've killed more than forty of my friends. I've taken eight to hospital. About ten of my friends have survived all this time, but that's because they've left these parts for good . . . The only one left alive who's still here is my friend from the football club . . . all of the rest they killed, the motherfuckers. All of my friends from childhood, my brother, my cousin, they've killed all of them.

[pause]

A: D'you think that violence can become almost normal?

S: Of course, human beings become accustomed to it. It's about getting used to it, you know. But we did some good stuff, we killed a few rapists . . . The thing is, when you have to live in a bad place, and you're not a bad person, you've still got to defend yourself. When I picked up a gun for the first time I felt content because I had something to defend myself with, you understand? (Sayayo, November 30, 2011)

The poor neighborhoods of Medellín perpetually lack legitimate social mobility opportunities for most male youth. They are denied the education and steady remunerative work that would otherwise enable them to attain dignified masculinization. Sayayo is an example. He began working as a street vendor at nine years old and is acutely aware of the inequalities in his city and the dearth of dignified opportunities growing up. This is reflected in his narrative when he compares the impossibility of becoming a doctor or lawyer to the reality of low-paid manual labor painting wealthy people's houses. The sheer violence of gang life is also made terrifyingly clear by the number of his friends who have been killed.

Half of the gang members interviewed explicitly referred to limited opportunities borne out of poverty as a causal factor that led them to gang membership, precisely because gangs stand out as instruments to mitigate the effects of emasculation, presenting themselves as an alternative pathways to male identity and an outlet for youthful ambition. Pepe, in his early twenties, worked for a community-based organization and was highly critical of gang membership. He spoke lucidly about how gangs present themselves as alternative pathways:

> I reckon it's easier to join gangs because there's economic motivation. I think that when a lad has difficulties at home—and I'm not saying that I don't have them—you run out of ideas and you think, "What am I going to do?" Any opportunity that comes along seems like a good one in those contexts. The first way out that comes along is their first option—I think that they are models that reproduce themselves and they reproduce with great ease and efficiency—imagine during this kid's whole life at home there's not enough food or basic utilities; there are no loving relationships and high levels of domestic violence; and the whole time they see this bloke who lives locally who enjoys "accessories." He's got a motorbike, designer trainers, girls, expensive clothes, all that sort of stuff. But he's also got respect, recognition, power. So of course the young lads round here say, "Fuck me, this is the ticket!" (Pepe, April11, 2008)

This suggests that gangs are a consequence of a struggle for male dignity within an urban context of poverty and exclusion. Masculine habitus is a powerful motivator, and it can encourage socialization into the gang when other pathways are unattractive or undignified. While it helps us explain why the vast majority of gang members in Medellín are poor, young men, we should be careful not to romanticize the gang as a popular movement in a dystopian cityscape. This would be to deny youth in such neighborhoods their agency and obfuscate the fact that the majority of youths do not actually join gangs, even in the most violent neighborhoods (see Baird 2012b).

Accumulation of Masculine Capital

The conceptual framework laid out in this chapter implies that youths navigate pathways to manhood by accumulating culturally valued masculine capital. For many young men in Medellín, the gang is perceived in utilitarian terms, that is, as a reputational and economic project, a mechanism to obtain wealth and status. Where exclusion impedes many male youths from the legal and socially positive accumulation of such capital, the gang emerges as an attractive vehicle for obtaining and displaying it. Fast motorbikes, money in hand, sexual access to women, and ostentatious drinking and partying are predominant cultural signifiers of masculine capital among gang members. As one gang member, Ceferino, noted:

> The other thing is that you want to show off in a lot of ways, to be noticed by other men, to make women look at you. Well, you get to a point where, it's like, you gotta stab someone up, ya know, the bloke who makes a name for himself, gets the girls— Firing a gun gives you a fright first of all, but afterwards you don't feel a thing, you take it in your stride—It's not the women's fault though, gang members are promiscuous, men are promiscuous. (Ceferino, November 5, 2011)

These performances provide reassurance for these young men of their masculinity. Wielding a gun—or a knife—is a particularly symbolic reflection of masculine capital that provokes fear, which gang members interpret as respect. In fact, respect and fear are so synonymous for gang members that when they say "they respect me," what they actually mean is "they fear me." One gang member, Notes (16/07/2008), pointed out the link between guns and masculinity in a matter-of-fact way: "Yeah bro, you know what happens? The same thing that happens to all of us youngsters; picking up a gun for the first time means putting on the big trousers." This "respect" helps generate a sense of self-worth for these young men, and the "big trousers" help them develop a macho identity, countering feelings of inadequacy and low self-esteem.

Socialization, Admiration, and *Duros*

It was not uncommon for youths to indicate that they felt swept along by gang influences and violence in their neighborhood, shrugging their shoulders to say engaging with gangs was beyond their control. This was often described as a matter-of-fact process.

> The energy of the other person begins to stick to you. If you're with a bad person, you're always gonna be with that negative energy, it sticks to you, so—you know, no one's like, "Yeah I wanna go an' kill someone," it's just that this stuff creeps up on you bit by bit, bit by bit, bit by bit—until pfffffum! It's got you. And you're in it. You get me? (Tino, November 20, 2011)

Gang ubiquity has a profound impact among children and youths in these neighborhoods in Medellín. As most of the interviewees related, male youth often find themselves socialized into gangs because of the influence of friends on the street or siblings with whom they have grown up. Yet there was a clear masculine logic underlying many youths' decisions to join gangs. Peludo was a mid-ranking gang member in his twenties who had followed his older brother into the gang.[4] He controlled a lucrative drug vending point at night on the edge of his neighborhood high up on the hillside overlooking the lights of the city below. From up there, he chuckled, we're "just like the bourgeoisie."[5]

> [I joined a gang] to get a motorbike and girls. The girls, we're never short of women, never! They like our cars, our money from drug deals . . . You get used to that life, you know. Women like men with guns, the shooters, because it gives you power . . . [So younger lads] look up to you and say, "Wow! I want to be just like you."

The pursuit of masculine capital and the admiration of older gang members were indivisible from processes of gang socialization. Niñez explained why the older gang members—particularly the gang leaders or *duros*—were so admired:

> The [*duros*] stand out because they're well dressed, they've got cash in their pockets, drinking, they ride a nice motorbike . . . You know what, a kid round here who's fifteen or eighteen years old riding a good looking *Pulsar* [sports motorbike], with a chick on the back . . . and he takes out one of those pistols . . . so a load of children see that "wow! I wanna be like that guy on the corner with a *Pulsar*, a flashy pistol and a good looking chick." So that's the role model that kids look up to nowadays, right? It's very powerful. (November 20, 2011)

Here, space in the city is not just about geographic terrain but also social relations (Rodgers 2010). These relations are gendered, and as others have noted, male socialization often figures prominently as a form of violence transmission (Pearce 2006; Gayle and Mortis 2010; Barker 2005). This is none more evident than in gangland territories.

Gender relations with street gangs in Medellín are both inclusive and exclusive. The gang's "core" or "full" membership is a homosocial domain, a place of "homosocial enactment" (Kimmel 2004) that only permits, with very rare exceptions, hegemonic masculine identities. This excludes femininities and a range of nonhegemonic masculine identities, such as homosexual ones. Girls and women are almost never allowed to become core members of the gang nor take part in the homosocial enactment of violence. These core activities are those that generate a series of economic benefits of gang membership.

Girls and women in Medellín take on gang functions that do not involve direct violence, for example, collecting extortion money or transporting drugs around a community, into a prison, or into a football stadium. Assassinating someone who does not pay up or engaging in gang combat over turf is exclusively carried out by male gang members. Males are sanctioned to use violence, to do this "work"; females are not. This gives men a position of dominance in the gang structure and control of its economic rewards.

On the rare occasion women do become core members by engaging in systematic violence and taking on leadership roles within the gang, they are obliged to go through a process of masculinization to successfully negotiate gang patriarchy. One "retired" gang member in his forties who was one of Pablo Escobar's[6] "lieutenants" during the 1990s commented: "There was once a gang member who was a girl, but she became just like one of the men. In fact she was even worse than the gang bosses, because being a woman she had to prove herself" (Jose). The oxymoronic "hyper-masculinized woman" reflects the extreme measures women must take to negotiate the patriarchal system within the gang. This casts light on why women very rarely become leaders or power-holders. It was notable that during the research period, which spanned six years from 2007 to 2012, I did not meet one female "core" gang member.[7]

Likewise, homosexuals or nonhegemonic masculine identities are excluded or marginalized by the gang. *Loquitas*[8]—softies or sissies—are gang "hangers on" who seek the dividends of gang life without engaging in the risky crime and violence that pays for it. Other gang members, unsurprisingly, frown upon *loquitas*. Junior, a thirteen-year-old *carrito*[9] and aspiring gang member revealed that the older gang members he looked up to were "the most cunning, the slickest, the 'baddest.' The ones who kill the most earn respect and fear. You don't want no *loquitas*" (Junior, June 19, 2008).

The Medellín gang is a socialization space of male work and play where norms are deeply gendered, reflecting an exaggerated form of patriarchy.[10] This is not to say that girls do not interact with gangs; they do so intensively, and on a daily basis. These relationships deserve more of our scholarly attention, to which we will now turn.

GANGLAND GIRLFRIENDS

A pillar of hegemonic masculinity is sexual access to women. In the patriarchal communities of Medellín, men are expected to buy gifts and pay other expenses as part of the ritual of wooing women, concomitant with globalized forms of Western hegemonic masculinity. Most young men living in poor neighborhoods in Medellín, however, do not have the financial and material resources to perform this ritual. One mother was asked if her son had a girlfriend, to which she replied curtly, "Of course my son doesn't have a girlfriend, he's got no money" (Field Diary 2011). This appears to be a somewhat overstated response, but it is a reflection of the pervasive grip of patriarchy on gendered relationships in the communities where I conducted my research. It was the norm for the youths interviewed to refer to sexual access to women and girls as a reason for joining the gang and admiring the *duros*. In their perceptions at least, girls pay much more attention to gang members than those outside gangs. Ceferino's narrative earlier went so far as to claim women are at fault for compelling young men to become gang members where "you gotta stab someone up [to] get the girls" (Ceferino, November 5, 2011). This connection between gang membership and the sexual objectification of women underscores gang culture in Medellín.

Little is understood about why some girls and women apparently seek to become girlfriends of gang members. A better grasp of gang dynamics in this area could help address some of the abuses faced by a number of these women

Gang Displays in La Salle

Gang socialization is undoubtedly complex. I focus on how gang members' interaction with girls and women serves to reinforce gangland identities by facilitating sexualized masculine performance. In doing so, of course, it highlights women's position of vulnerability. What is the role of girls and women in the construction of gang masculinities? If male youths are motivated to join gangs in part to gain sexual access to women, what is the nature of the relationship between gangsters and their "girlfriends"?

The benefits of gangster life are performed publically—a display of masculine capital. The heavy partying, designer clothes, women, drinking, and drug taking are an entitlement, the fruit of their labors or "spoils of war." Gang member capital is an assertion of masculine identity and status, a locus of macho pride and self-esteem rooted in territory. The gang's socialization with girls and young women is couched within these boundaries, where their bodies are frequently sexualized, commodified, and subject to control and domination.

Gangland displays and relationships with girls and young women stand out on weekend evenings. One notorious place where gang members would party is known as La Salle. By day La Salle is a typical main street in a poor neighborhood way up the northeastern hillside of Medellín. It has mini-markets, bakers, butchers, and the like. On weekend nights it transforms into a drinking and partying strip—or *zona rosa*—lined with bars blaring out a cacophony of *vallenato, porra,* and *reggaeton* music. From around 10 p.m., the motorbikes of gang members begin to pull up and park in long rows outside bars where they sit looking out onto the street and drinking *girafas*—tall tubes of beer with a small serving tap at the bottom— *aguardiente,* and rum. One former girlfriend of a gang member said, "In those bars you only find junkies and gangsters. There are no law-abiding people there, not one" (Negra, October 11, 2011). It was unnerving to see girls as young as eleven and twelve years old,[11] although most were between sixteen and twenty, dressed in short skirts and made up, parading past the tables of men drinking outside the bars.

The scene is in some ways reminiscent of a fashion catwalk. Girls would gradually accompany the men at the tables and join them in drinking, which would progress to dancing and drug taking—normally ecstasy and cocaine—inside the bar later in the evening. This would continue well into the next day, or even afternoon. La Salle can be described as hedonistic and decadent. It is not uncommon for moneyed gang members to get girls to dance naked inside the bars, competing for half a bottle of *aguardiente*. Normative assumptions underlie these relations; men pay, and the girls have sex with them later.

What is striking about these exchanges is that young girls demonstrate agency, albeit within the constraints of the social structures of La Salle, in their first interactions with gang members. This happens despite the significant power imbalance, frequent humiliation and sexual objectification, prevalence of sexually transmitted infections, and numerous accounts of abuse and rape—all of which point to the insidious influence of gangland patriarchy. In a similar vein, Hume and Wilding (this volume) argue that the extreme nature of rape suffered by some women engaged with gangs "highlights the role of loyal and submissive femininities in reinforcing dominant masculinities." Ironically, female agency plays a role in the construction of the "successful" male identity where "the gangster gets the girl," perpetuating the very system of "masculine domination" (Bourdieu 2001) that subjugates them. Where does this agency stem from and why do girls seek out gang members in places like La Salle?

"*El Power*" of the Gang

The young women interviewed concurred that gang members had numerous girlfriends. "Girls round here say that gang members are sexy, exciting risk-takers and so attractive because they've got guns. Boys join gangs to get the girls . . . I think 80 percent of girls in these neighborhoods are after gang members. If you're not a gang member you're not gonna be very popular! [laughing]" (Negra, October 11, 2011). Femina explained why she was attracted to gang members:

> The father of my son is a gang member. And I've had a few gang member boyfriends. I like the adrenaline, the fear that you might get caught by the police, *el power*,[12] and everything... a gang member is interesting; they tell you stuff about their adventures and all that, but a kid who's not in a gang, well, the conversation is really monotonous." (October 13, 2011)

Many young girls feel attracted by the identity and dynamics of gangs (Aguila Umaña and Rikkers 2012, 3), but they are also attracted to the possibility of access to money, material benefits, status, and "el power" associated with having a gang-member boyfriend. Gang displays in La Salle, where "money is power," are captivating for both poor boys and girls (Femina, October 13, 2011). As Negra stated:

> You've gotta understand that a girl growing up round here will ask her parents for a pair of jeans or sneakers, and the parents will say, "Wait until Christmas or your birthday." Then they can go out with one of these gang members and they give them the jeans, the sneakers, straight away. The girls always say they go out with them because they are in love, but that's just bullshit, they go out with them for the stuff they can get out of them. (October 11, 2011)

Girls are attracted to the "successful" males in the community, in part because it is one of the few ways they can access the trickle-down of capital from the patriarchal dividend. In this sense, the motivations of girls and women to engage in relationships with gang members has a certain logic—where girls' options and opportunities to "get jeans and sneakers" are hampered by exclusion, entering into a relationship with a gang member becomes increasing appealing. This is powerful enough to offset the risks of abuse and guaranteed infidelity of gang members:

Adam: So how is it that a girl gets together with a gang member?
Negra: They just come up and talk to you, but also the girls go up and talk to the *duro*. The *duro* stands out the most because he's got money, the money, the clothes he wears, they drive 4x4s and motorbikes.
A: Do the girls go out with them because they don't even have the money to buy themselves a beer?
N: It's not like that. They go out with gang members because they want to, because the gangster fame rubs off on them, so if they're *duro's* girlfriend, if anyone talks down to her, the *duro* will turn up and give them a beating.

A: What, you mean power transfers from the *duro* to his girlfriend?

N: Yeah, to his *girlfriends* [indicating the author's naiveté at suggesting that the *duro* had just one girlfriend]. All Colombian men are unfaithful and gang members are *really* unfaithful . . . and even knowing that the *duro* has a wife and kids at home, we still chase after them. (October 11, 2011)

Girls' reasons to become involved with gang members reflect the motivations of male youths to join gangs: to achieve identity, status, and esteem. In other words, their ambition has been ontologically contorted by socioeconomic exclusion and generations of gang domination. For both boys and girls, this leads to gangs being perceived as a site of opportunity, mirroring Vigh's (2006, 31) analysis of war as "terrain of possibility" for the most disenfranchised.

It was argued that male youths are utilitarian in their approach to gangs; they use the gang as a vehicle to access masculine capital in contexts of exclusion. Without discounting the complexity and nuances of genuine reciprocal attraction and the possibility of loving and lasting relationships, many girls are similarly utilitarian in their engagement with gang members. The difference is they are seeking to secure the multiple transfers of capital, such as clothes, mobile phones, or motorbikes; payment for silicone breast implants, buttock implants, or teeth whitening (*un diseño de dientes*); as well as "respect" and status as a derivative of gang association: "Girls think that if they are sleeping with the *duro* [gang leader] then they're gonna be respected by everyone" (Diabilis, October 13, 2011). Such relationships are immediately attractive because they can alleviate, in the short term at least, the corrosive effects of exclusion on young women's esteem.

Mosas, Mujeres, and Rape

We should caution against reducing young women's relationships with gang members to stereotypes or simplistic forms of transactional sex. Two of the women spoken to here, Femina and Negra, fell in love and had children with gang-member boyfriends. They weren't abandoned by these men; instead, their boyfriends have since left the gang, and they both appeared to be in a happy relationship. Gang members also have female friends, such as neighbors, school friends, and sisters. However, the sexual objectification of girls largely stems from partying and wild nights out with a particular group of girls. Gang members are complex individuals. Often victims of traumatic childhoods, they are not committed to one single type of male identity, behavior, or "gangster" performance all of the time. They are renowned for revering their mothers because you "only have one mother, but your father can be any old son of a bitch" (Salazar 1990). It is not uncommon for gang members to have *la mujer*—the serious partner, wife, or mother of their children "at home"—whom they treat with respect, but also have fleeting sexual encounters with and sexually abuse young women and girls called *las mosas* (also *amiguitas* or *grillas*). This reflects divisions between wives and mistresses who become involved with gang members in other violent urban contexts in Latin America (see Hume and Wilding, this volume).

There is not always a clear division between the respected *mujer* and the *mosa* party girls. It is common for the *mosas* to aspire to become the *mujer* of a gang member, although as there are always multiple *mosas* and just one *mujer*, only a minority of girls ever make that transition. Diabilis's narrative explains that young girls are attracted to the *duros's* power and aspire to become the *mujer*, but that they are destined to remain the *amiguita*.

Diabilis: I like the gang members that treat us nice, I mean they call us baby, sweetheart, cutie, and if you need something they're there to listen to you. He [ex-boyfriend in gang] was really kind, he dressed well. Me, as a woman, I like a man who dresses well, who's clean, who's got clean shoes on. [laughs]

Adam: I'm glad I've got clean shoes on today. [laugh together]

D: He's gotta smell nice, ya know, he's gotta be well turned out.

A: And most girls think the same?

D: Yep. But I don't like to get mixed up with gang members that have got the most money, or the best motorbike, or the best car. I don't like to get mixed up with them, 'coz that's always gonna be more problems, 'coz he's always gonna have loads of women and we're gonna fight and they'll rip my hair out. No, those guys I don't want to go out with.

The higher rank he's got, the more girls he's gonna have. Why? Because those girls nowadays think that because he's got *power* [*porque tiene power*] and a motorbike he's gonna give me money, and he's gonna give me a good lifestyle, or he gonna give me something. But then, I mean the men, they aren't looking for that, that's what the girls want, and all the men want is, excuse me for being vulgar, all they want is sex, to have their way with us, and that's all. When they've gone out with you just three times then they say, "Ah ya know, I don't like this one so much, she's a bit of a pain in the arse," and they leave you. So you're dumped there, still in love with them, and that's it.

Girls think that if they are sleeping with the *duro* then they're gonna be respected by everyone . . . They've got a saying, "The *mujer* is the *mujer* [*la mujer es la mujer*], the other women are just bitches from the street." But they're not good boyfriends.

A: So why do they have so many girlfriends then?

D: Because we let ourselves get seduced by the attractive stuff, the motorbike, money, like they say. 'Coz the young girls today think that because they go round on their bikes they're gonna become the *mujeres*, but they're never gonna be the *mujeres*, they're only ever gonna be the *amiguita* . . . yeah they've got loads of *amiguitas*. (October 13, 2011)

While *amiguitas* or *mosas* often knowingly enter into this exchange, they are objectified by the gang, and their bodies become sites of domination, reproduction, and pleasure (Umaña and Rikkers 2012, 15). *Mosas* become an object for male sexual gratification and a fundamental part of gang socialization and displays. These complex relationships reinforce the gang as a symbolic site of male success, drawing the gaze of aspirational young boys, tapping into the dispositions of their male habitus, and contributing to the cycle of gang membership. The domination of women's bodies is palpable in the attitudes of male gang members who "pay" for a night out, which is synonymous with unfettered sexual access to *mosas* they are with. Sexual expectation is compounded overtime as a girl becomes stigmatized as a *mosa* who is easy to have sex with: "They start [having sex with gang members] when they are eleven or twelve and by sixteen they're complete sluts, and by eighteen their reputation is in the gutter" (Femina, October 11, 2011).

Relationships involving these types of exchanges and transactions are common in patriarchal and *machista* societies.[13] However, they become exaggerated or perverse in ganglands, given the extreme power imbalances at play. Objectification and domination make *mosas* vulnerable, and any initial feelings of empowerment they might have can swiftly evaporate.

When I went out with the duro I felt powerful, I was content. I felt like no one could touch me, they're gonna have to respect me, they're not gonna talk down to me. I thought [the duros] were gonna take care of me, but that was a lie. (Femina, October 11, 2011)

Sexual objectification shifts easily to obligation whenever a *mosa* does not consent to sex. When she was sixteen years old, Diabilis was raped by several members of the gang in one of their houses after she did not consent to group sex:

> The gang did a lot of damage to me. I met this guy in my neighborhood, a well-known guy [infamous for being a gang member]. Supposedly it was love, a beautiful love, an eternal love, but him and his friends raped me. She knows [indicating Maria, who later told me details about the rape. Diabilis has tears in her eyes]. So, from one moment to the next I left all that stuff behind. The only thing before that that I cared about was going out with friends, going down the plaza, getting on one motorbike or another, parties . . . my parents would come and drag me out of nightclubs. (October 13, 2011)

Maria later told me that Diabilis was beaten and her clothes taken away from her as punishment, probably for resisting, so she had to walk naked through the streets back to her house. Such incidents of rape, which are unfortunately common in gang-dominated neighborhoods in Medellín, reflect the exaggerated male sexual entitlement that emerges through gang socialization with girls and young women. This phenomenon has been noted by other authors who note that the "relationship between poverty and rape perpetration is mediated through ideas of masculinity and the quest for 'success' " (Jewkes et al. 2011, 2).

Lamentably, gang socialization is a symbolic beacon that has a gendered impact on young boys and girls. Many boys aspire to *el power* that comes with gang membership. There is logic to these aspirations, but this process also functions at a less than conscious level as boys are disposed by the latent desires of the masculine habitus to seek out adult male identity.

A number of girls also seek *el power* through a gang-member boyfriend. Again, like boys, they aspire to the material and symbolic capital the gang can offer and the corresponding female identity and status of being a gang-member girlfriend. The glittering prizes, and the sheer fun, drugs, drink, and adrenaline of a night out with the gang are strong lures. It is not surprising that many aspire to be a gang member's girlfriend, despite the risks. The tragedy is that girls expose themselves to potential abuse by going out with gang members, and in doing so reinforce the cycle of "successful" gang life, which leads to the regeneration of gang membership itself. La Salle is always busy on a Saturday night.

CONCLUSIONS

As other scholars have argued, we should not separate youth decisions to join gangs from the settings of poverty and exclusion in which they live (Barker 2005; Jensen 2008; Koonings and Kruijt 2009; Maclure and

Sotelo 2004; Rodgers 2003). In such contexts, the tools at hand to become men vary dramatically, and exclusion blocks dignified pathways to manhood. In territories where gangs are prevalent, gang members stand out through overt displays of masculine capital, and as such are often seen as the most appropriate vehicles to achieve male adulthood that satisfies the dispositions of the masculine habitus.

Places such as La Salle distill the experience of gangland displays and bring to our attention how gang riches are flaunted. This dynamic raised the issue of girls and women and their engagement with gangs. The gang's masculine capital is generated by threatening, dominating, and controlling their communities in Medellín. The bodies of the *mosas* are also subject to the same domination, becoming disposable and prone to abuse and rape. Ironically, the agency that the *mosas* show to engage in relationships with gang members only perpetuates the symbolism of the gang as an iconic site of male identification in the eyes of local boys and young men. While we cannot reduce all gang activity to such nightlife performances, nor all gang relationships with girls and women to transactional sex, the displays of wealth and wild partying stand out dramatically amid local struggles for existence in impoverished contexts.

These processes facilitate the continuum of gang membership. Worryingly, the presence of gangs across generations, intensity, and territory[14] influences local ontologies of what it *means* to be a successful man, while simultaneously offering the vehicle for achieving that success.[15] As such, gangs in Medellín have emerged as a significant masculine system of influence (Baird, 2012a), which compounds the reproduction of gangs and hence the possibilities of social violence.

Gang membership and socialization is a deeply gendered process and should be regarded as a dystopian expression of inequality and exclusion generated by the prevailing political, socioeconomic, and cultural circumstances of the city. I have found that young men do not aspire to become violent, drug dealers, or rapists; they aspire to a dignified male identity. Above all, they want status and social belonging.

NOTES

1. Research for this paper was conducted as part of the Drugs, Security and Democracy program at the Social Science Research Council, funded by the Open Society Foundation (both United States), and the International Development Research Centre (Canada).
2. These can be understood as "structural" factors. Galtung (2002) has described factors such as inequality, exclusion, racism, or sexism as forms of "structural violence." Moser et al. (1999) add that political legacies provided the foundations for present-day

violence in Latin America, and the rapid rise in urban violence is interrelated with factors such as rapid urbanization, poverty, exclusion, weak governance, the increasingly organized nature of crime, and increased drug proliferation.

3. The 2011 UNODC Global Study on Homicide revealed that "at one extreme, where homicide rates are high and firearms and organized crime in the form of drug trafficking play a substantial role, 1 in 50 men aged 20 will be murdered before they reach the age of 31. At the other, the probability of such an occurrence is up to 400 times lower."

4. In 2007 I interviewed Peludo's brother and cousin. In 2012 they had been arrested and were serving terms in Bellavista prison for drug-trafficking offences.

5. Peludo was interviewed on three occasions between 2007 and 2012, allowing me to build a relationship with him. One interview took place at night on his drug corner.

6. Former cartel boss and archetypal drug baron killed by Colombia police and DEA in 1993.

7. Medellín here differs from Central American countries with *Mara salvatrucha* and *Calle 18* gangs in which female gang membership, through gruesome initiation, is more common.

8. Discursively, it is telling to note that men are called *loquitas*, the feminine gendered ending, and not *loquitos*, the masculine ending.

9. Carrito translates as cart or trolley. These are young, normally prepubescent boys, who carry guns, ammunition, money, and drugs for gangs around the neighborhood. They are popular among gang leaders because they become new recruits, but particularly because the police are not legally permitted to search them.

10. It should be noted that female participation in gangs ranges depending on context, location, etc. For example, female *Maras* gang members appear to be more common than Medellín female gang members, although gang patriarchy remains pervasive (see Aguila Umaña and Rikkers 2012, 14). "Male domination and the reproduction of the patriarchal model reach exaggerated proportions in gang culture. Male domination is present in all gang activities . . . while men perceive infidelity and the possibility of having more women as a way to reinforce their domination and their masculinity, they strictly prohibit women the same liberty."

11. Negra calls this a "biological moment"; when girls reach puberty, they head to the *zona rosa* to party. (Negra, 11/10/11)

12. Femina was speaking in Spanish but used the words "el power."

13. "This is a characteristic trait of courtships in societies and groups ruled by patriarchy, in the same sense that in these societies the men with greater social 'prestige' . . . are the ones most attractive to women, and that the women seek these types of men because it gives them access to better security better resources and a better social position, etc." (Aguila Umaña and Rikkers 2012, 4).

14. The three-dimensional concept of gang presence is derived from Pearce's (2006) thinking on chronic violence. This tendency toward illicit and violent pathways to manhood is compounded when young males are growing up in circumstances where a "gangland" pattern of exclusion and chronic violence has been established across generations.

15. Rodgers (2010, 4) argues that disorder and ontological insecurity play indirect roles in the emergence of gangs as forms of "social sovereignty."

WORKS CITED

Adams, Tani M. 2012. "Chronic Violence and its Reproduction: Perverse Trends in Social Relations, Citizenship, and Democracy in Latin America." *Citizen Security and Organized Crime*. Washington, DC: Woodrow Wilson Center.

Adler, Alfred. 1928, Understanding Human Nature, Allen & Unwin, London.

Baird, Adam. 2009. "Methodological Dilemmas: Researching Violent Young Men in Medellín, Colombia." *IDS Bulletin. Violence, Social Action and Research* 40: 72–77.

Baird, Adam. 2011. *Field Diary*. Medellín.

Baird, Adam. 2012a, The violent gang and the construction of masculinity amongst socially excluded young men, *Safer Communities*, 11(4): 179–190

Baird, Adam. 2012b. "Negotiating Pathways to Manhood: Rejecting Gangs and Violence in Medellín's Periphery." *Journal of Conflictology* 3: 28–39.

Barker, Gary. 2005. *Dying to be Men: Youth, Masculinity and Social Exclusion*. London: Routledge.

Beall, Jo, and Sean Fox. 2009. *Cities and Development*. Abingdon: Routledge.

Bourdieu, Pierre. 1977. *Outline of a Theory of Practice*. Cambridge: Cambridge University Press.

Bourdieu, Pierre. 2001. *Masculine Domination*. Cambridge: Polity Press.

Bourgois, Philippe. 2003. *In Search of Respect: Selling Crack in El Barrio*. New York: Cambridge University Press.

Cloward, Richard. and Ohlin, Lloyd. (1960), Delinquency and Opportunity: A Theory of Delinquent Gangs, The Free Press, New York, NY.

Covey, Herbert C. 2003. *Street Gangs Throughout The World*. Springfield, IL: Charles C. Thomas Publisher Ltd.

Dowdney, Luke. 2007. *Neither War Nor Peace*. Rio de Janeiro: COAV.

Galtung, Johan. 2002. *Searching for Peace: The Road to Transcend*. London: Pluto.

Gayle, Herbert, and Nelma Mortis. 2010. "Male Social Participation and Violence in Urban Belize: An Examination of Their Experience with Goals, Guns, Gangs, Gender, God, and Governance." Belize City: Ministry of Education.

Gutmann, Matthew C., and Maria Viveros Vigoya. 2005. "Masculinities in Latin America." In *Handbook of Studies on Men and Masculinities*, edited by Michael Kimmel, Jeff Hearn, and R. W. Connell. London: Sage Publications.

Hagedorn, John. 2008. *A World of Gangs*. London: University of Minnesota Press.

Jensen, Steffen. 2008. *Gangs, Politics & Dignity in Cape Town*. Oxford: James Curry Ltd.

Jewkes, Rachel, Yandisa Sikweyiya, Robert Morrell, and Kristin Dunkle. 2011. "Gender Inequitable Masculinity and Sexual Entitlement in Rape Perpetration South Africa: Findings of a Cross-Sectional Study." *PLoS ONE* 6(12): e29590.

Kersten, Joachim. (2001), "Groups of violent young males in Germany." In *The Eurogang Paradox: Street Gangs and Youth Groups in the US and Europe*, edited by Malcom Klein, Hans-Jürgen Kerner, Cheryl Maxson and Elmar Weitekamp, Dordrecht: Kluwer Academic Publishers.

Kimmel, Michael. 2004. "Masculinity as Homophobia: Fear, Shame, and Silence in the Construction of Gender Identity." In *The Masculinities Reader*, edited by Stephen Whitehead and Frank Barrett. Cambridge: Polity Press.

Koonings, Kees, and Dirk Krujt. 2009. "The Rise of Megacities and the Urbanisation of Informality, Exclusion and Violence." In *Mega-Cities: The Politics of Urban Exclusion and Violence in the Global South*, edited by Kees Koonings and Dirk Krujt. London: Zed Books.

Maclure, Richard, and Melvin Sotelo. 2004. "Youth Gangs in Nicaragua: Gang Membership as Structured Individualization." *Journal of Youth Studies* 7: 417–432.

Moser, Caroline, and Bernice Van Bronkhorst. 1999. "Youth Violence in Latin America and the Caribbean: Costs, Causes and Interventions." In LCR Sustainable Development Working Paper No. 3. Urban Peace Program Series. Washington, DC: World Bank.

Muncie, John. (2009), Youth and Crime, 3rd ed., Sage, London.

Pearce, Jenny. 2006. "Bringing Violence 'Back Home': Gender Socialisation and the Transmission of Violence through Time and Space." In *Global Civil Society 2006/7*, edited by Marlies Glasius, Mary Kaldor, and Helmut Anheier. London: Sage Publications.

Pitts, John. 2008. *Reluctant Gangsters: The Changing Face of Youth Crime*. London: Willam Publishing.

Rodgers, Dennis. 2003. "Youth Gangs in Colombia and Nicaragua: New forms of Violence, New Theoretical Directions?" In *Breeding Inequality—Reaping Violence: Exploring Linkages and Causality in Colombia and Beyond*, edited by Anders Rudquivst. Uppsala, Sweden: Uppsala University Collegium for Development Studies.

Rodgers, Dennis. 2006. "Living in the Shadow of Death: Gangs, Violence and Social Order in Urban Nicaragua, 1996–2002." *Journal of Latin American Studies* 38: 267–292.

Rodgers, Dennis. 2010. "Urban violence is not (necessarily) a way of life: towards a political economy of conflict in cities." In *Beyond the Tipping Point: The Benefits and Challenges of Urbanisation*, edited by Jo Beall, Basudeb Guha-Khasnobis, B. and Ravi Kanbur Oxford: Oxford University Press

Rodgers, Dennis & Baird, Adam. Forthcoming, Understanding Gangs in Contemporary Latin America. In *The Wiley Handbook of Gangs*, edited by Scott Decker and David Pyrooz, Oxford: John Wiley & Sons, 2015.

Salazar, Alonso. 1990. *No Nacimos Pa'Semilla*. Bogotá: CINEP.

Vigh, Henrik. 2006. *Navigating Terrains of War: Youth and Soldiering in Guinea-Bissau*. New York: Berghahn Books.

Yablonsky, Lewis. 1997. Gangsters: Fifty Years of Madness, Drugs, and Death on the Streets of America. New York and London: New York University Press.

PART 3

Being in Danger, What Do People Do?

CHAPTER 6

Fear and Spectacular Drug Violence in Monterrey

ANA VILLARREAL

D on José spread a coat of paint over the words *Taquería Goyo* written on the front of his house, giving modest publicity to his daughter's taco stand in a working-class neighborhood of the Monterrey Metropolitan Area. "Are you closing?," asked a neighbor passing by. "Yes . . . bad people come asking for money and there's none to give; you close to avoid trouble." His daughter had received a phone call from armed men standing outside their house threatening to kidnap her if she did not provide an unaffordable sum of money. Don José and his family sought shelter with relatives for weeks before returning home. "They got the tamales guy yesterday as well," his neighbor told him. Don José recalled this conversation in an interview and proceeded to detail the recent history of crime in his neighborhood: the corner store closed due to repeated extortion, the fruit seller and the baker kidnapped and killed, the butcher's fifteen-year-old daughter kidnapped with no ransom request. "And it's the same thing in other neighborhoods, the *malosos* are asking for quotas . . . kidnapping innocent people." He closed the taco stand and his daughter moved in with a sister in another neighborhood where she now sells household supplies (Interview, March 9, 2013).[1]

A wave of gruesome, spectacular drug violence (2009–2012)[2] and related forms of crime imposed practical constraints on the simplest everyday activities for residents of Monterrey, Mexico. Like Don José and his daughter, many changed their address, work, even physical appearance in an attempt to avoid crime or harassment by public authorities. I spent two years (2012–2013) observing how upper- and lower-class residents adapted to these new forms of violence. Residents frequently spoke of a "before" when they didn't think twice about carrying out everyday activities versus an "after" when they had to think through things. In the words of a local newspaper reporter observing this phenomenon prior to my arrival in the field, a "momentary analysis" was required to fulfill everyday activities:

> Fear originated by violence and insecurity has slowly but steadily paralyzed *regio-montanos* [Monterrey residents]. Activities that used to be carried out without prior thought now require a momentary analysis: "Is the neighborhood I am heading to safe?" "Should I go out at night?" "What street should I take to arrive safely?" (Menchaca 2010)

New fears required developing new logistics. Hence, a great part of my fieldwork consisted in tracing these new logistics of fear or practices reorganizing everyday activities to cope with fear of heightened violence and crime. The term logistics, a military term in its origins, is particularly adequate to describe the practices documented here, given that these are military strategies down-scaled and extended into civilian life: armoring, camouflaging, caravanning, and regrouping.

Unlike most scholarship on violence and everyday life focusing on the living conditions of the urban poor (Auyero and Lara 2012; Goffman 2009; D. Goldstein 2004; D. M. Goldstein 2003; McIlwaine and Moser 2007; Wacquant 2004), this study began as an examination of the impact of violence and fear on the upper classes. It is precisely this entry point that allowed me to detect the four strategies I develop in this chapter, as these were far more visible with the resources of the wealthy. I then set out to examine whether these strategies held true across the class spectrum. I found that both upper- and lower-class residents sought to armor their neighborhoods and homes, camouflage themselves and their businesses out of fear of kidnapping and extortion, travel in caravans to avoid hijacking, and regroup to compensate for the loss of previous social spaces and practices. While the first two strategies reconfirm what most scholarly work on urban violence has documented in terms of fear tearing the social fabric and destroying public space, the last two strategies attest to a less examined dimension of fear. The central claim I make in this chapter is that fear may both tear the social fabric and bring people together, both destroy public space and create new forms of social life. I begin with a brief overview of the escalation of spectacular drug violence in the Monterrey Metropolitan Area. I then turn to how each of these strategies was implemented in working-class neighborhoods and conclude with a brief outline of pending questions around these less-examined dimensions of fear.

ON FEAR AND ITS LESS EXAMINED DIMENSIONS

Current debates on fear in the social sciences are heavily structured around the question: why are individuals so afraid? Whether we examine the extensive interdisciplinary literature on "fear of crime" (Dammert 2012; Farrall, Jackson, and Gray 2009; Lee 2001; Pain 2000) or more recent sociological work on "cultures of fear" (Furedi 2006; Glassner 2009), this scholarship tends to assume that individuals should not feel as afraid as they do. Fear is explained in relation to exaggerated media portrayals of violence or dominant political agendas redefining citizens as crime victims (Simon 2006). Although focused on explaining fear, this scholarship provides little evidence on what fear is; how it is experienced; or how increased fear can come to reconfigure everyday spaces, practices, and relations. A recent exception is the work of Alice Goffman on how poor young black men in Philadelphia respond to their fear of capture and confinement in a time of unprecedented policing and imprisonment (Goffman 2014). In this volume, she provides evidence of the numerous fears that police rely on in their "techniques of persuasion" as they seek to turn women into informants on the men they hold dear. Yet for the most part, the core question implicit in most of these studies—why are individuals so afraid?—is almost irrelevant when we turn to contexts where the monopoly over the means of exerting violence has been lost.

In Latin America, there is a nascent literature seeking to examine widespread fear more closely. Sociologists working on Argentina, Mexico, Venezuela, and Colombia are laying out the principles for a sociological examination of fear (Kessler 2009), tracing the processes whereby fear is socially constructed (Reguillo 2002). One of the conclusions derived from these studies and consistent with previous scholarship on fear of crime is that fear is an isolating emotion: it makes us stay at home, diminish nightlife activities, abandon parks, and suspect others (Cárdia 2002). Fear of crime and insecurity perception surveys are indeed designed to measure these negative facets of fear leading to a "loss of city" (Briceño-León 2007). At an urban scale, fear has provided a language and justification to increase social segregation in the form of rising walls and gated communities (Caldeira 2000; Capron 2006; Low 2006). More recent cross-class empirical examinations of the meanings attributed to everyday security practices demonstrate how these reproduce social inequalities (Rebotier 2011). Although all these aspects exist in my empirical examination of fear, I found that fear is a double-edged emotion: it both tears the social fabric and brings people together, both destroys public spaces and creates new forms of social life.

In *The Civilizing Process*, Norbert Elias (1989 [1939], 527) writes that, accustomed to monopolies of violence, we are barely aware of their importance for the structure of our behavior and of how quickly our "logics" would collapse if the balance of fear within us and around us were to change abruptly. This is exactly what happened in Monterrey during a period of gruesome and spectacular drug violence (2009–2012). Fear of being caught in the range of fire between different fractions of organized crime and the military emptied the streets. Nightlife centers were shut down. Informal curfews were enforced. Discourses of good versus evil or *los buenos* against *los malitos* began to burgeon in everyday conversations across the class spectrum as Monterrey residents sought to explain to themselves who was hanging bodies from their overpasses and leaving headless corpses on the streets. New moral boundaries between an "us" and a "them" were drawn in classic Durkheimian style (2008 [1912]) forming a new social whole, a "fearful citizenry" (Rotker 2002).

Some residents left the city (Durin 2012), while others accommodated their lives to these new forms of violence. In order to cope with feared trajectories, individuals turned to caravanning, showing how fear may be structural to the formation of spontaneous social ties. In order to cope with the loss of individual leisure practices, individuals and families grouped in *vías recreativas*, that is, streets blocked by local governments for pedestrian use on weekends. Fear fluctuated into trust in these sites reminiscent of classical arguments in the social sciences on social morphology and collective effervescence (Durkheim 1998 [1893]). Monterrey residents retreated and lived increasingly compartmentalized lives with their nuclear families due to fear. Yet on weekends they came together on these closed streets knowing that they would be safe in their greater number. In this sense, I found that fear, like a harsh winter climate, generated specific spaces of sociability where social ties were denser and capable of generating feelings of trust, solidarity, and community (Mauss 2006 [1905]). Granted, increased violence and fear produced deep tears in the social fabric, but it is precisely for this reason that individuals regrouped to create the new social spaces and practices described at the end of this chapter.

DOCUMENTING FEAR

My insomnia began in the late summer of 2010. Although studying abroad, I experienced violence escalating in Monterrey through the worried voices of my loved ones and the Facebook posts of old friends turned peace activists in my hometown. Friends of friends were shot, kidnapped, and disappeared. I was not thinking of studying fear back then, but I was already immersed in the field. During the summer of 2011, I went back to my family's home for a few weeks. I took notes on how family, friends, and acquaintances felt the constant need to update me on what I could or could not do and where I could or could not go. I experienced how much urban life had changed, as I became a tourist in my hometown.

I decided to conduct fieldwork on this topic in early 2012, knowing a first necessary step would be to relearn how to live in Monterrey. Located in northeastern Mexico, the Monterrey Metropolitan Area is comprised of nine municipalities (*municipios*) with a high degree of government autonomy. The total population is around 4.5 million inhabitants. I moved into an apartment located in the old quarter of the wealthy municipality of San Pedro where I was raised, now referred to as the "armored municipality." I took notes as I reconnected with old friends and previous fieldwork acquaintances I had not seen in years. The beginning of my fieldwork was thus a revisit (Burawoy 2003) of a site I used to know. Each of these contacts provided an update from their perspective on all that had changed: the places they were not going to anymore, the sites that had closed, and the cautions they had to adopt. These updates allowed me to regain a sense of place, recover my sleep, and draw the basis for a systematic examination of fear in the socio-spatial dimensions analyzed in my dissertation (Ana Villarreal n.d.).

San Pedro is the municipality where traditional local elites and high-ranking drug traffickers took refuge from increased drug violence in the Monterrey Metropolitan Area. In the words of a former mayor interviewed for a documentary, "if you see San Pedro is [politically marketed as] the safest municipality in Mexico, then that is an invitation not only for good people but also for bad people" (Altuna, Rossini, and Osorno 2012). Although local elites had already begun a process of suburbanization in the 1950s, moving their homes from downtown Monterrey to this valley located on the skirts of the Sierra Madre Mountains, increased violence intensified this process. Business centers, upper-class nightlife, and leisure were quickly relocated within this municipality, further impoverishing the rest of the metropolitan area. For many San Pedro residents, the borders of this municipality represent rigid limits for their everyday activities. This is the municipality where I focused much of my fieldwork through 2012 and 2013.

Given the focus of this edited volume, I selected observation and interview material from fieldwork carried out in traditionally marginalized areas such as La Independencia and Sierra Ventana neighborhoods in the municipality of Monterrey, as well as working-class neighborhoods from five municipalities of the Monterrey Metropolitan Area: Guadalupe, San

Nicolás de los Garza, Juárez, Escobedo, and Monterrey. The sample provides evidence of the widespread impact of these new forms of violence
in the metropolitan area. Thus, this chapter draws on in-depth interviews
conducted with several working-class residents on shifts in their everyday lives, as well as interviews with one photojournalist, two prominent
human rights activists, one artist, and one fashion scholar on their perceptions of violence in the city. I also draw on ethnographic observations
of peace protests conducted by local human rights groups and new leisure practices in the city. In order to reconstruct the escalation of drug
violence, as well as the beginning of armoring and caravanning practices
taking place prior to my fieldwork, I rely on the observations of journalists
writing for a widely read local newspaper, *El Norte*.

SPECTACULAR DRUG VIOLENCE IN MONTERREY (2009–2012)

Following the Hague International Opium Convention of 1912, Mexico
passed its first antidrug laws in 1920 and marked the start of a national war
on drugs (Campos 2012). Ensuing the efforts of influential doctors urging
the state to define drugs as an issue of public health and not public security, drugs were legalized in Mexico in 1940, then prohibited again a few
months later under pressure from the United States (Enciso 2014, n.d.).
There is extensive data on drug production and trafficking in Mexico during the twentieth century (Astorga 2005), yet incidents of drug violence
in this period were rare compared to the wave of grotesque homicides
and disappearances that increased significantly following former president Felipe Calderon's decision to lead a frontal attack against all drug
traffickers in 2006. Sociologists and political scientists argued increased
violence is correlated with democratization, for electoral competition
disrupts local patronage networks (Andrés Villarreal 2002) or breaks
down "state-sponsored protection rackets" (Snyder and Durán-Martínez
2009), thus eroding peaceful configurations between state and criminal
organizations (Osorio 2013). Moreover, a policy of indiscriminate frontal
attacks against all drug-trafficking organizations provided no incentives
to decrease violence (Lessing 2012). In terms of consequences, journalists were the first to document the horrors in detail (Baltazar et al. 2012;
Gibler 2011; Osorno 2012), providing sharp accounts of life and death in
"drug war zones" (Campbell 2009).
    The state of Nuevo León in northeastern Mexico was initially spared
from the upsurge of drug violence that spiked homicide rates in northern states such as Chihuahua, Sonora, Durango and Sinaloa in 2008 and

2009 (Heinle et al. 2014, 27). Homicide rates for Nuevo León, the state where Monterrey is located, remained steadily below the national average until 2010, then doubled the national average in 2011 (see figure 6.1). Beginning in 2009 and throughout 2010, newspapers began to report the appearance of abandoned corpses, numerous shootings, and the kidnapping and killing of public officials in Monterrey and neighboring towns. The military was deployed to enforce security on the streets. Public officials affirmed all deaths corresponded to criminals killing each other, yet the deaths of civilians became increasingly visible with high-profile cases such as the killing of two students at the exit of a highly reputed private university on March 10, 2010. Human rights activists argued soldiers left guns by their side as supposed evidence that they were killers or *sicarios*. Four years later, the case continued to garner media attention as family members, friends, and activists demanded that the military "clean their names" (Campos Garza 2014).

Pedro is a photojournalist from Ciudad Juárez, the city with the highest homicide rates in Mexico. He received an offer to cover violent events in Monterrey in early 2012, a job other photojournalists did not stand for more than a month. When offering him this appointment, the international press agency he works for told him, "If you're going to Monterrey, you know what the situation is like, we think that since you come from Ciudad Juárez you might last longer [than other photojournalists] but we also understand if you don't want to go" (Field notes, August 26, 2013). Pedro had covered violence in Ciudad Juárez for sixteen years. "I was used to working with violence, amidst shootings," he said, a bulletproof vest resting in the chair between us. "I arrived and they would tell me there

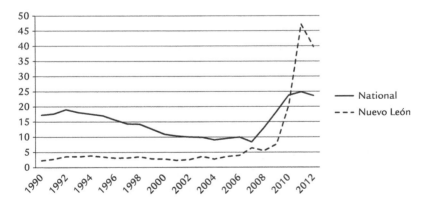

Figure 6.1
Homicide rates for Mexico and Nuevo León (1990–2012)
Data from *Estadísticas de mortalidad* (Instituto Nacional de Estadística y Geografía 2013) and *Indicadores demográficos básicos* (Consejo Nacional de Población 2013).

were three deaths at a bar and I'd be like, so what? What's the big deal?" Yet despite the lower homicide rates, Pedro explained that the characteristics of violent deaths in Monterrey were different, "bloodier" than the workings of organized crime in Ciudad Juárez.

In an exhaustive examination of twenty-two violent death methods used by organized crime in Mexico as reported in the media, Angélica Durán-Martínez (2013, 94) finds that most violent deaths in Ciudad Juárez are the result of a "simple use of fire gun," "hitmen," and "simple use of knives," while less common methods include "wrapped in blanket," "head in cooler" and "mutilation or incineration with note." The category "dismembered" does not appear, as this extremely cruel method of killing is more closely related with the workings of the Zetas (for more on their "Battle for Monterrey," see Dudley 2012; Osorno 2012). In relation to the multiple dismembered bodies that appeared in different points of the Monterrey Metropolitan Area, including forty-nine on a nearby highway in 2012, I asked Pedro if these human beings were executed and then dismembered. "I know they cut them alive," he answered. I asked how he knew this. "I know, don't ask me, I know." I asked no more (Field notes, September 9, 2013). A local artist took one such dismembered body as a centerpiece in his painting, "The Streets of Monterrey Smell Delicious, Like *Carne Asada*" (see figure 6.2). For a local art critic, the painting accurately depicts how Monterrey residents or "regios" learned to "flow" with escalating violence:

> López paints a caustic portrait of *regio* idiosyncrasy. He shows the pastimes and prides that are almost a faith dogma for *regios*: beer, football and *carne asada*. All flavored with the new and omnipresent ingredient of exacerbated violence. The main character, mustached, bellied and hairy, seems undisturbed by reality and, doing nothing about it, flows with the situation. It's sad, but the scene is so verisimilar it borders the obscene. Even sadder, as it seems we have misplaced our shock in regard to escalating violence, perhaps under the gambling tables. (Granados 2011)

Fascinated by this painting, a geographer invited the artist to a seminar on urban violence I regularly attended at a public university. For the artist the painting showed "how beer can work as an aspirin sometimes, and *carne asada* as well, those family gatherings, football, all part of ... ignoring ... what is going on" (Field notes, February 11, 2013). The painting referenced a main alternative to nightlife clubbing I found in my interviews:

> My friends no longer get together to go to a bar or a club, they get together in somebody's house and they have their *carne asada* . . . somewhere close to everyone . . . (forty-eight-year-old male, Monterrey, March 5, 2013)

Figure 6.2
The Streets of Monterrey Smell Delicious, Like *Carne Asada*
Painter José López depicts exacerbated violence in *Las calles de Monterrey huelen bien rico, a carne asada* (2011).
Photograph courtesy of Ricardo Lazcano.

> Before, you would go to the *Barrio Antiguo* to some bar . . . have a beer . . . now, we
> get together in somebody's home . . . four, five friends, *carne asada*, tacos or whatever
> until 11 . . . (fifty-seven-year-old male, San Nicolás, October 21, 2012)

The hills with little grey houses in the background of the painting reminded us of Sierra Ventana and La Independencia, two neighborhoods stretching along opposite sides of a hill defining the limits between Monterrey and wealthy San Pedro. Its first inhabitants were migrants from the southern state of San Luis Potosí who came to Monterrey looking for work. Both neighborhoods have been stigmatized as some of the most violent in the metropolitan area. The artist confirmed that this hill was indeed the inspiration for the painting and then clarified our question regarding a white UFO-like disk hovering over them: "A reference to this not knowing what will happen to them, a UFO can arrive and take them and nobody will know" (Field notes, February 11, 2013).

The UFO raises the question of the inexplicable kidnappings, disappearances, and enforced disappearances that began to take place in these neighborhoods and beyond. The local human rights group *Ciudadanos en Apoyo a los Derechos Humanos* (CADHAC) documented over 1,007 cases of disappearances in Nuevo León between 2009 and 2012 (Human Rights Watch 2013, 92). Both Amnesty International and Human Rights Watch collected evidence on multiple cases of state involvement in disappearances "committed by members of every security force involved in public security operations, sometimes acting in conjunction with organized crime" (Amnesty International 2013; Human Rights Watch 2013, 1). The local human rights group *Fuerzas Unidas por Nuestros Desaparecidos en Nuevo León* (FUNDENL), founded by family members of the disappeared, began to lovingly document these stories in embroidered handkerchiefs exhibited in public plazas in 2012 (a regrouping technique discussed in greater detail later in this chapter). One of these handkerchiefs (see figure 6.3) reads:

> Detained and disappeared by municipal police of Monterrey, Nuevo León, patrol
> cars 534, 538 and 540 on February 25, 2009. "I have your smile tattooed on my heart

Figure 6.3
"I Have Your Smile Tattooed On My Heart."
One of several hundred handkerchiefs exhibited in downtown Monterrey as part of the Embroidering Peace initiative of FUNDENL. Picture taken by author on September 30, 2012.

I love you my son." Your parents and brothers do not stop looking and waiting for you. Embroidered by: Mom.

Other embroidered stories of the disappeared as summarized by their family members provide evidence of the everyday circumstances in which these crimes took place. The following stories were displayed among two hundred others during a peace protest I observed in front of the governor's office on October 26, 2013:

> Disappeared August 12, 2010 when he went to work, together with his brother-in-law in Villa de Juárez, Nuevo Léon. Both are still missing.

> 23-year old. Apodaca, Nuevo León. "A woman cried out her name. She came out and gave her a kiss. Ten minutes later they took her." February 2010.

> 18-year old. La Estanzuela, Monterrey. After taking a taxi with three neighbors, none of them have returned ...

> March 2011. He went out with his brother and four friends to a store in San Nicolás de los Garza, none of them returned. The six are still missing.

Going off to work, stepping out of the house for a moment, taking a taxi, going to a store—these are the incomplete stories family members repeat to themselves and to others of lives inexplicably interrupted. Hence, when considering increased violence in the region, it is essential to look beyond crime statistics to consider these qualitative shifts: gruesome, spectacular violence on one side attributed to organized crime fighting a turf war, but also the terror surrounding these mysterious and more hushed crimes. In a couple years, fear of disappearances, kidnappings, extortion, and being caught in the range of fire gripped Monterrey residents, urging them to transform their everyday lives in response. Confronted with this challenging scenario, they began to armor their everyday spaces.

ARMORING

1. defensive covering for the body; *especially*: covering (as of metal) used in combat
2. a quality or circumstance that affords protection
3. a protective outer layer[3]

A few years before the wealthy municipality of San Pedro was politically marketed as the "armored municipality" of the metropolitan area (2009–present), political actors of primarily middle- and working-class municipalities were already discussing and implementing "armoring" policies. Indeed, escalating drug violence hit working-class municipalities like Guadalupe first, making neighbor municipalities like San Nicolás nervous about violence spillover. As a result, a former mayor of San Nicolás sought to build a wall between these two municipalities in February 2008, arousing public debate and rejection before increased violence brought its approval two years later (Rodríguez 2008a, 2008b; Rodríguez and Martínez 2011). This mayor spearheaded local initiatives to gate parks, soccer fields, and neighborhoods starting in 2007 under the "Armoring Neighborhoods" program, which paved the way for the following administration (2009–2012) to gate twenty-eight neighborhoods. A newspaper article in 2009 gathered comments from residents and authorities from several municipalities to assert that in the face of increased violence and crime,

> many city residents have made a decision: to lock themselves up . . . together with their neighbors, they have decided to gate their neighborhood and control its access. Means used to isolate themselves include fences, chains and even large flowerpots. (Montes de Oca 2009)

For Memo, a fifty-seven-year-old San Nicolás resident who paid for his education by making one thousand tamales per week, such policies may have contributed to emptying public spaces like the park across from his house:

> You used to be able to go out on the block, with kids . . . there were shootings nearby but people still got together . . . now they're empty even by day, on Sundays . . . they gated almost all parks in San Nicolás, they put steel fences around them . . . cameras in some of them . . . they call it armoring . . . the municipality asked the people to vote . . . they voted yes . . . but now with the armoring, they don't use it. (Interview, October 21, 2012)

For Memo, armoring his home in San Nicolás took the form of locking a front gate at all times that was previously left open during the day. This move involved convincing and training family members to enforce this family policy. "We all have keys [to the front lock] . . . my sister is the one who is still too trusting [*muy confianzuda*], she hasn't gotten used to the key and she leaves it open and we call her attention" (Interview, October 21, 2012). In the last three years, he recalls hearing at least thirty shootings, with deaths of between four and ten people in five of them. Nevertheless, his father did not want to lock the front gate. Memo recalled his exact words: "No, we can trust each other here [*aquí hay confianza*] . . . I hate being locked up like an animal." Then Memo's father was harassed by youth in his neighborhood and changed his mind about the lock; he stopped his daily walks, spending increasingly more time at home. "How our life is changed by all this," Memo added, "such a strong violence."

Guadalupe, home to many factory workers, followed San Nicolás with its "Safe Neighborhood" program, gating seventeen neighborhoods in this same period (2009–2012). However, some Guadalupe residents did not wait for authorities to approve closing off their neighborhoods; they set up fences instead (*El Norte* 2011). Residents of other municipalities applied similar armoring practices using "chicken wire, wooden or metal poles, security booths, guards, bars, barrels, block walls, barbed wire, cameras and even laboriously crafted iron fences" (Vázquez 2013). Where walls were already in place, some residents opted for increasing their height. For example, thirty-year-old Juan spoke of his municipality Juárez as "no man's land, the police is there to harass and not protect, a lot of corpses have been found in nearby hills, people are just looking for opportunities to rob" (Field notes, April 12, 2013). In response, he raised the walls of his home an extra 2.5 meters.

Gating, closing streets, and raising walls are all indicators of increased fear and tears in the social fabric. Although some neighbors approve and endorse these "armoring" policies, others do not, creating conflicts at the neighborhood level. Conflicts are extended into households as family members debate the adoption and enforcement of further security measures. There is some evidence that these policies may lead residents to withdraw from the spaces they are supposed to render secure. Nevertheless, armoring may draw more attention to individuals or businesses attempting to avoid crime. Hence, in the next section I turn to a sample of camouflaging techniques they may employ instead.

CAMOUFLAGING

1. the disguising especially of military equipment or installations with paint, nets, or foliage; the disguise so applied

Leslie has followed the closing of multiple small businesses, including a butcher and a car lot, on an avenue in San Nicolás where she works. She likes to eat at a small food stand that has managed to stay in business.

Although the place is clean on the inside, the broken paint on the outside suggests that the place is rundown:

> What he sells does not match the appearance of the stand, it's horrible on the outside, but then he has kept it as a strategy . . . "don't let it seem like business is going too well and add chains" . . . no, he keeps it as a stand inside a building that does not draw attention. (Interview, September 9, 2013)

Rather than armoring his small business by adding chains or other security measures, this owner turns to aesthetics and adopts a camouflaging technique. That is, contrary to broken windows theory (Wilson & Kelling 1982) asserting that untended property may attract criminal attention, broken paint in an extortion-plagued setting may actually deter crime. Susana, a long-time resident of a very poor neighborhood in Monterrey, offered an example of another camouflaging technique. One by one, the small businesses in her street closed due to extortion. Samuel, who sold beer to his neighbors, was no exception. Needing a new job, he got a small van to work as a mover. According to Susana:

> He is careful not to park his van outside his home. Instead, he parks a couple of blocks away from his house. His number is listed on the van and if he receives a call that he thinks is trustworthy, he takes the job. (Field notes, June 30, 2011)

Like Samuel and the owner of the food stand mentioned above, many small business owners adopted poor aesthetics, removed signs, or devised other methods of dissimulating their worksite. Similarly, Monterrey residents during the early period of my fieldwork were preoccupied with becoming "invisible." For example, Elena, a fifty-nine-year-old public school teacher living in Guadalupe said,

> They have kidnapped a bunch of people here . . . they were keeping them [kidnapping victims in a security house] four blocks away because it looked like they had a lot of money; they had a mega-pick-up truck [*un camionetón*] . . . I have tried to become invisible, and I think a lot of people have experienced that as well. (Interview, June 8, 2013)

Kidnapping became so widespread in Monterrey that residents across the class spectrum began to refer to themselves as *secuestrables* or kidnappable (Ana Villarreal 2013). To avoid this and other forms of crime, residents changed their clothes, hairstyles, and even facial hair. For example, Memo from San Nicolás shared his personal strategies on how to stay safe:

Don't carry anything in your hands, dress as austerely as possible . . . I've heard some guys [office employees] carry their ties in a plastic bag . . . I used to wear dressy pants [*pantalón de vestir*], shirt, shoes, now, around here, tennis shoes, jeans . . . don't carry anything of value. (Interview, October 21, 2012)

Individuals may alter their appearance out of fear of being mistaken for someone involved in organized crime. Luis, a male resident of Sierra Ventana in his late forties, shaved his mustache and cut his hair shorter after two pick-up trucks followed him home from the bus stop after work. Luis concluded he had been followed because he was mistaken for Raúl who lives a few blocks away:

They confuse me because some people say to me, "Aren't you Raúl?" "You're not the Raúl that I know." I know he lives further down but he has been confused with me and I have been confused with him . . . I used to wear a mustache and longer hair . . . ever since I realized I could be mistaken [for someone who he thinks might work for organized crime], I won't lie, I'm afraid. (Field notes, September 7, 2013)

In 2008, fashion scholar Amanda Watkins began to document a very particular style developed by the young men and women of La Independencia. "I thought wow! This is so cool! It's quite LA-ish . . . a Mexican hip-hoppy kind of thing" (Interview, August 27, 2013). She showed me pictures of the style (see figure 6.4) defined by these men and women as *Cholombiano*, a look "combining *cholo* and Colombian aesthetics" (Watkins 2014). Fashion observers highlighted the centrality of their haircut,

which draws equal parts inspiration from American hip-hop, Puerto Rican reggaeton, and ancient depictions of Aztec warriors . . . Snoopy-like sideburns that start at the top of their heads and are glued to their cheeks with sickeningly large handfuls of hair gel. (Loyola and Ruiz 2011)

Watkins remained in touch with the young men and women she began studying prior to the escalation of drug violence (2009–2012). More recently, she learned that several men had changed their hairstyle due to military and police harassment:

If they [police and military] got hold of them, they cut it [the hair] off . . . they developed a kind of bullying . . . this is something a lot of them told me, the reason why the fashion has almost disappeared, they're a little bit scared, everyone thinks they're the bad boys . . . it seems to me that they were the scapegoats. (Interview, August 27, 2013)

Figure 6.4
The *Cholombiano* signature haircut
Picture by fashion scholar Amanda Watkins.

I confirmed this observation at her book presentation a few months later. Several of the men photographed in her project were invited to share the stage and comment on the experience, yet none of them wore the haircut anymore (for more examples of the haircut, see Watkins 2014, 200–210). On stage, "Toughman," a leading figure in this community, said they had to change their style due to "marginality." When he stepped down to get a beer, I approached him to ask how exactly they had changed their style:

> I used to wear my bangs down here [he marked the spot with his hand halfway down his chest] . . . the military cut it off . . . "Hey, who are you working for?" [he recalled the military asking him] I work for nobody . . . the guy on the [book] cover [also had his hair cut off] . . . neighborhood police, military and they don't cut it with scissors, they use a Rambo knife in the *granadera* [police van or truck]. (Field notes, March 15, 2014)

Young men toned down a prideful fashion as a means of avoiding harassment by state authorities. Older men stopped wearing dressy pants to avoid crime. Women sought to become "invisible." Taco stand owners and movers developed techniques to dissimulate their worksites. Like armoring practices, camouflaging techniques provide evidence of tears in the social fabric as residents become increasingly suspicious and fearful of each other. Fear brought great isolation, yet it also fostered the formation of new social ties as examined in the next section.

CARAVANNING

1. a: a company of travelers on a journey through desert or hostile regions;
   b: a group of vehicles traveling together (as in a file)

Traveling in caravans is a security practice that predates the modern state. This is how military, police, and organized crime groups travel in conflict zones today, and this is also how Monterrey residents sought to confront feared trajectories on highways or within the metropolitan area. A 2011 newspaper article documents the caravanning practices of Monterrey migrants traveling home for Christmas from the United States:

> Fear of violence lead a great majority of *paisanos* who arrived for Christmas vacations to travel by day and in groups through the highways of Nuevo León and this is how they plan to return to the United States. Many of these caravans were spontaneously formed, given that individuals sought to continuously travel near others, even if they did not know them. (Villasáez and Rodríguez 2011)

Alternatively, individuals chose to ride a bus in order to travel in the company of others. Elena reported:

> I used to travel [to McAllen, Texas] on Fridays, I would go there and come back on Sunday in my car, all women, my sisters, my daughters, my little nephews. I don't do that anymore ... I feel safer in the bus. (Interview, June 8, 2013)

Elena travels with a bus company she believes has some arrangement with organized crime, as it has not suffered attacks as other bus companies have. Although there is no way of knowing how many individuals opted to travel by bus instead of by car, a newspaper article from 2011 suggests that the demand for this service was higher than usual. Bus drivers also relied on caravanning as a security measure:

> Transportation between McAllen and Monterrey was in high demand over Spring Break ... some buses travelled in caravans for security reasons. Bus drivers explained that the demand was so high buses were leaving every five minutes ... bus companies

preferred to increase their offer by day and eliminate night or early morning travel. (Domínguez 2011)

Similarly, a San Nicolás resident no longer drives to the neighboring state of Tamaulipas for his routine doctor visits out of fear of hijacking. He takes a bus (Field notes, June 28, 2013). Memo now walks his teenage daughter to the bus stop day and night. Although there are different strategies to cope with fear of crime in a given trajectory, the main denominator I found was some kind of grouping. These examples highlight how fear may be structural to the formation of spontaneous social ties as individuals seek to improve their safety by increasing their numbers.

The practice of caravanning reached a political dimension in 2011. Following the murder of his son, poet Javier Sicilia launched a widely mediatized Caravan for Peace from Mexico City to Ciudad Juárez. Over ten days, the caravan stopped at a dozen cities collecting testimonies of victims and their families. I documented its passing through Monterrey that summer:

White paper bodies hang from the ropes circling a plaza in downtown Monterrey . . . Slowly but surely federal police trucks start to line up on the street across from the plaza with soldiers holding long guns as the sun sets . . . "Lock your arms together in case someone tries to break the line!" "Who will try to break the line?," a friend standing next to me asks. "Let's hope nobody does," the organizer says nervously and continues his way. His nervousness is contagious, especially given the increasing number of military and police surrounding us. My friend reassures us, "Nah, there have been no cases of shootings at peace marches." As a precaution, many have brought their cameras or smart phones and film the arrival of more police cars and finally, the appearance of a bus followed by a few passenger trucks [the caravan]. The crowd starts cheering, "You're not alone! You're not alone!" A mob of reporters halt the first members of the caravan to get off the bus . . . The crowd cheers and dances as Javier Sicilia and other members of the caravan make their way up to the podium . . . A few introductory speeches give way to the main purpose of this gathering: a woman takes the microphone and begins to tell the story of her disappeared son . . . "You're not alone! You're not alone!" She gathers her breath to continue and states the numbers of the police patrol cars responsible for the disappearance of her son. Her voice breaks again and the crowd cheers again. She describes the frustration of being turned away by officers reluctant to investigate the case but assures us that as long as she is alive she will not stop looking for him. "They took him alive! I want him alive!" . . . A dozen parents share their grief, their pain, their anger but also their hopes for justice as soldiers in civil clothes continue to stroll around the crowd. "Where is everyone?," a father cries out. "Are they at work? Are they watching television? Are they lazy? We need to stop being afraid!" (Field notes, June 7, 2011)

The passing of the Caravan for Peace fostered the formation of local human rights groups dedicated to finding their disappeared family members such as FUNDENL. One of their core activities has been to embroider hundreds of handkerchiefs with the names of the dead in red and the disappeared in green. They exhibit these handkerchiefs at a public plaza in downtown Monterrey, the first of two regrouping activities I turn to in the next section.

REGROUPING

1. to reorganize (as after a setback) for renewed activity
2. to alter the tactical formation of a military force

"Public space is the first thing to go, public space is the first thing we need to take back," said Maria, a local human rights activist (Field notes, February 25, 2013). Seated beside her, Laura rearranged a pile of handkerchiefs she had brought with her, including several she embroidered for her son. She was at home when it happened. Armed men irrupted into her house and took her son in front of her eyes. Two years had passed with no news from him, despite the multiple searches and numerous visits to various state agencies. "You think the world should stop but it doesn't," she said with a broken voice. "We've encountered such apathy and had to walk on our own for some time." The handkerchiefs she held in her hands are a means of telling the story of her son and the many other stories people ask her to embroider differently, more humanely (see figure 6.5). Monterrey is one of several cities in Mexico and abroad to have a local group of *bordadores* working on embroidering and displaying these handkerchiefs at public plazas and related human rights events as a means of creating awareness around these crimes (De la Fuente 2012; Martínez 2012). Like the *chismosas* described by Zubillaga, Llorens, and Souto in this volume, it is the mothers and other family members of victims of exacerbated violence who stepped up to organize new community responses to violence in the absence of adequate state measures. As with the Caravan for Peace, few people attended these public gatherings that began as weekly get-togethers in March 2012 and gradually shifted to monthly meetings by the end of the year.

Alternatively, a greater number of Monterrey residents and public officials sought to reclaim loss of public spaces through closing streets for bicycle and pedestrian use on Saturdays or Sundays. All mayors of the Monterrey Metropolitan Area elected for the 2013–2016 period implemented *vías recreativas*, a policy of closing streets for leisure practices during the weekend. For example, on March 10, 2013, the municipality

Figure 6.5
Embroidering peace in Nuevo León.
Men and women stop to watch members of FUNDENL hang rows of embroidered handkerchiefs at the *Macroplaza* in downtown Monterrey, Nuevo León. Picture taken by author on September 30, 2012.

Figure 6.6
"Guadalupe, Live Your City."
Guadalupe residents exercise on a main avenue blocked by traffic agents on a Sunday morning. Local police patrol the perimeter on the outer lanes. Picture taken by author on April 14, 2013.

of Guadalupe launched the initiative "Guadalupe, Live Your City" (see figure 6.6). In an online editorial, the mayor asserted:

> What we are aiming for is clear, to establish an attractive and safe urban space so that our families can go out on the streets again and mingle with each other and the rest of Guadalupe residents, through leisure, physical activities, culture and sports . . . we are beginning to reclaim public space. (Garza 2013)

I conducted observations of most of these sites during my fieldwork, documenting similar elements: free bike lending, painting activities for children, Zamba or similar aerobic dance lessons, and yoga, among others. Sparking conversation with multiple passersby, I learned many attended these programs regularly and would be at home otherwise as there was "nowhere else to go" (Field notes, April 14, 2013). A male resident in his sixties told me the *vía recreativa* in San Nicolás was located on an avenue people had avoided for some time as it was locally known that organized crime operated there and "it smelled like death" (Field notes, June 30, 2013). Dressed in a karate uniform after a martial arts display with his son, the man continued to explain:

> The problem was severe because different commandos were constantly driving through this avenue displaying their AK-47 . . . asking for, well, *derecho de piso* [extortion] . . . the one who sold *barbacoa* [shredded beef], the one who sold electric parts, the one who rented music, the one with the taco stand, the little store owner, the tamales guy, so it was a very serious problem . . . because behind these different flashing trucks with armed men you saw the local police, so it was all organized, until this whole [military] confrontation against them took place freeing things up. (Field notes, June 30, 2013)

Vías recreativas have been successful in different municipalities where hundreds, and in some cases thousands, of residents gather on the streets on a regular basis. For example, a woman began to practice yoga on a weekly basis at the *vía recreativa* in Escobedo:

> It's a healthy environment, I think this is what the city needs given the things we've been through and that seem to be calming down. It's good for the children. We were very scared. We didn't want to socialize with neighbors or friends and this does motivate me to come out and I've made new friends here [weekly yoga class]. This is a very positive action. (Field notes, October 8, 2013)

Like this woman, several residents referred to the "new friends" they've made, providing some evidence of the construction of new social ties at these sites. Moreover, a few dozen men and women reported running into old friends or work colleagues they had not seen in years. In some cases, these encounters lead to renewing those relationships. For example, a thirty-eight-year-old woman in Guadalupe said she ran into one of her mother's friends: "I hadn't seen her in ten years. Ironically, we live 2, 3 blocks away from each other" (Field notes, April 21, 2013). Following that encounter, they began to see each other more frequently. Thus, blocking streets on a regular basis with leisure activities provided a space and incentives for residents to gather. The regularity of these initiatives may foster the construction of new social ties at a neighborhood level and on some occasions, the renewal of old social ties as well.

In sum, embroidering handkerchiefs to publicly mourn the dead and disappeared in public plazas is the most outspoken critique of recent state security policies I documented in my fieldwork, while *vía recreativas* is a state effort to reorganize the sociability it has contributed to destroy. In this sense, I found violence and fear prompted not only the destruction but also the construction of new forms of public space.

FURTHER QUESTIONS ON FEAR, SOLIDARITY, AND SOCIABILITY

Much scholarly work on fear in the social sciences has focused on explaining variations in individual perceptions of "fear of crime" (Dammert 2012; Farrall, Jackson, and Gray 2009; Lee 2001) or the existence of "cultures of fear" (Furedi 2006; Glassner 2009). Although focused on explaining fear, this scholarship provides little evidence on what fear is or how it can reconfigure everyday spaces and practices. A sudden wave of spectacular drug violence (2009–2012) produced an unfortunate, ideal site to study these concrete aspects of fear as residents of the Monterrey Metropolitan Area reconfigured their everyday lives in response. In this chapter I sketched out four logistics of fear as a means of analytically organizing shifts in everyday life in response to increased violence. In the first section, I briefly traced armoring practices ranging from state policies closing streets and gating parks to individual initiatives raising higher walls and enforcing further security measures at home. In the second section, I turned to camouflaging techniques employed by residents seeking to become "invisible." Both armoring and camouflaging strategies reconfirmed what much scholarship on urban violence has documented: fear makes us stay at home, suspect our neighbors, and retreat from public space (Caldeira 2000; Rotker 2002). Yet I argued fear may not only isolate individuals but also bring people together. In the third section, I documented examples of caravanning practices by which individuals sought collective transportation strategies as a means of coping with a feared trajectory. In the final section, I presented two examples of new forms of public space where individuals regrouped for public mourning or for leisure. I argued these last two strategies attest to a less-examined dimension of fear.

Beyond the Monterrey Metropolitan Area, groups of *bordadores* have regrouped in plazas in Guadalajara, Tijuana, Aguascalientes, Torreón, and Xalapa, to mention a few cities in Mexico (M. P. Montero 2012). I witnessed these local groups stretch solidarity ties for the first time at a national scale in downtown Mexico City on December 1, 2012. Hundreds of handkerchiefs hung from light posts along the Avenida Juárez the day current president Enrique Peña Nieto took office, only to be quickly removed when protests took a violent turn. Solidarity ties stretched beyond national borders. Handkerchiefs were embroidered by sympathizers in Tokyo, Montréal, Santiago de Chile, Córdoba, and were exhibited in public plazas in Barcelona, Brussels, and New York, among others (Bosch 2014). The growing *Bordando por la paz* initiative evokes memories of mothers circling the Plaza de Mayo in Buenos Aires or women embroidering *arpilleras* in Santiago de Chile (Agosín 1996). Hence, just as there are patterns to how increased violence, crime, and fear have led to the abandonment of public space in Latin American cities (Caldeira 2000), might there also be patterns to how citizens have sought to reclaim or recreate public space?

Similarly, although the term *vías recreativas* was coined in Monterrey, the policy is not unique to this metropolitan area. Over two hundred cities around the world have adopted street closure programs as a "best practice" in the last decade (Montero, forthcoming). These initiatives are often implemented as a means of fostering physical health among city dwellers and promoting cycling as a means of transportation. Nevertheless, in contexts of high violence and crime, such policies may serve the main purpose of securing a safe space for collective leisure practices. Indeed, it is telling that the first *ciclovía* was inaugurated in the 1970s in Bogotá—a city with a history of high violence and crime. Although this first *ciclovía* has brought thousands of Bogotanos together over the past forty years, sociologists observing how sociability is organized along the *carrera séptima* attest to the reproduction of social inequalities within this space (Gomescásseres 2003). Indeed, such scholarship calls for further research on the extent to which these new forms of public space challenge social inequalities or contribute to reproducing, and perhaps accentuating, class and spatial segregation.

NOTES

1. This research was assisted by a grant from the Drugs, Security and Democracy Fellowship Program administered by the Social Science Research Council and the Universidad de los Andes in cooperation with funds provided by the Open Society Foundation and the International Development Research Centre, Ottawa, Canada; as well as a grant from the University of California Institute for Mexico and the United States. I thank Javier Auyero for inviting me to write this chapter, as well as Loïc Wacquant, Laura Enriquez, Teresa Caldeira, Claude Fischer, Verónica Zubillaga, and Reynaldo Rojo for their comments and suggestions. I thank Magdalena Guzmán and Rebeca Sandoval for their research assistance; Amanda Watkins and José López for use of their artwork; as well as José Manuel Prieto, Leticia Saucedo, and all other members of the urban violence seminar held at the Universidad Autónoma de Nuevo León (2012–2013).
2. Although I set 2012 as an end date to a period of escalating gruesome and spectacular drug violence, I do not wish to imply that it has ended. Building on the research of political scientists on patterns of drug violence, it is more likely that the *visibility* of drug violence declined as a fragmented state security apparatus became more cohesive (Durán-Martínez 2013). The adjective *spectacular* highlights the use of violence as a spectacle (D. Goldstein 2004) designed to instill fear.
3. The definitions of armoring, camouflaging, caravanning, and regrouping at the beginning of the following sections were taken from the online Merriam-Webster dictionary, 2013.

WORKS CITED

Agosín, Marjorie. 1996. *Tapestries of Hope, Threads of Love: The Arpillera Movement in Chile 1974–1994*. Albuquerque: University of New Mexico Press.

Altuna, Emiliano, Carlos Rossini, and Diego Osorno. 2012. *El Alcalde*. Bambú Audiovisual/ IMCINE-FOPROCINE.

Amnesty International. 2013. *Confronting A Nightmare: Disappearances in Mexico*. London: Amnesty International.

Astorga, Luis. 2005. *El siglo de las drogas*. Plaza & Janés.

Auyero, Javier, and Agustin B. D. Lara. 2012. "In Harm's Way at the Urban Margins." *Ethnography* 13(4): 531–577.

Baltazar, Elia, Lydiette Carrión, Thelma Goméz Durán, John Gibler, Luis Guillermo Hernández, Vanessa Job, and Alberto Nájar. 2012. *Entre las cenizas: historias de vida en tiempos de muerte*, edited by Marcela Turati and Daniela Rea. Oaxaca: Surplus Ediciones.

Bosch, Lolita. 2014. "Bordamos por la paz de México en Nueva York." *Nuestra Aparente Rendición*. Retrieved April 14, 2014, from http://nuestraaparenterendicion. com/index.php/biblioteca/cronicas-y-reportajes/item/2309-bordamos-por-la-paz-de-m%C3%A9xico-en-nueva-york.

Briceño-León, Ricardo. 2007. *Fractured Cities: Social Exclusion, Urban Violence and Contested Spaces in Latin America*. Caracas: Zed Books.

Burawoy, Michael. 2003. "Revisits: An Outline of a Theory of Reflexive Ethnography." *American Sociological Review* 68: 645-679.

Caldeira, Teresa. 2000. *City of Walls: Crime, Segregation, and Citizenship in São Paulo*. Berkeley: University of California Press.

Campbell, Howard. 2009. Drug War Zone: Frontal Dispatches from the Streets of El Paso and Juárez. Austin: University of Texas Press.

Campos Garza, Luciano. 2014. "Piden limpiar nombres de estudiantes del ITESM asesinados." *Proceso*, March 19. Retrieved from http://www.proceso.com.mx/?p=367661.

Campos, Isaac. 2012. *Home Grown: Marijuana and the Origins of Mexico's War on Drugs.* Chapel Hill: The University of North Carolina Press.

Capron, Guénola. 2006. *Quand la ville se ferme: Quartiers résidentiels sécurisés.* Bréal.

Cárdia, Nancy. 2002. "The Impact of Exposure to Violence in São Paulo: Accepting Violence or Continuing Horror?" In *Citizens of Fear: Urban Violence in Latin America*, edited by Susana Rotker. New Brunswick, NJ: Rutgers University Press.

Consejo Nacional de Población. 2013. Indicadores demográficos básicos 1990-2030. Retrieved from http://www.portal.conapo.gob.mx/index.php?option=com_conten t&view=article&id=125&Itemid=230.

Dammert, Lucia. 2012. *Fear and Crime in Latin America: Redefining State-Society Relations.* New York: Routledge.

De la Fuente, Daniel. 2012. "Bordando la esperanza." *El Norte*, August 26. Retrieved from http://www.elnorte.com.

Domínguez, Miguel. 2011. "Regresan vacacionistas; congestionan aduanas." *El Norte*, April 25. Retrieved from http://www.elnorte.com.

Dudley, Steven. 2012. *The Zetas and the Battle for Monterrey.* Retrieved from http://www. insightcrime.org/reports/zetas_monterrey.pdf.

Durin, Séverin. 2012. "Los que la guerra desplazó: familias del noreste de México en el exilio." *Desacatos* 38: 29–42.

Durkheim, Emile. [1893] 1998. *De la division du travail social.* Paris: Presses Universitaires de France.

Durkheim, Emile. [1912] 2008. *Les Formes élémentaires de la vie religieuse.* Paris: Presses Universitaires de France.

El Norte. 2011. "Protestan y se blindan." January 27. Retrieved from http://www.elnorte.com.

Elias, Norbert. [1939] 1989. *El proceso de la civilización: Investigaciones sociogenéticas y psicogenéticas.* Mexico City: Fondo de Cultura Económica.

Enciso, Froylán. 2014. "Prohibir las drogas, herencia carrancista." *Milenio,* April 6. Retrieved from http://www.milenio.com/cultura/Prohibir-drogas-herencia-carrancista-dominical- Venustiano_Carranza- iniciativa_0_274772746.html

Enciso, Froylán. n.d. *Made in Sinaloa: From the Regional to the Global History of the Mexican War on Drugs, 1909–1985.* State University of New York at Stony Brook.

Farrall, Stephen, Jonathan Jackson, and Emily Gray. 2009. *Social Order and the Fear of Crime in Contemporary Times.* Oxford: Oxford University Press.

Furedi, Frank. 2006. *Culture of Fear Revisited: Risk-taking and the Morality of Low-expectation.* London: Continuum.

Garza, César. 2013. " 'Vive tu ciudad' [1939] unirá a familias en Guadalupe." *Grupo Dominio,* March. Retrieved from http://dominio.fm/columns/view/99-"vive-tu-ciudad"-unira-a-familias-en-guadalupe.

Gibler, John. 2011. *To Die in Mexico: Dispatches from Inside the Drug War.* San Francisco: City Lights Bookstore.

Glassner, Barry. 2009. *The Culture of Fear: Why Americans Are Afraid of the Wrong Things.* New York: Basic Books.

Goffman, Alice. 2009. "On the Run: Wanted Men in a Philadelphia Ghetto." *American Sociological Review* 74: 339–357.

Goffman, Alice. 2014. *On The Run: Fugitive Life in an American City.* Chicago: University of Chicago Press.

Goldstein, Daniel. 2004. *The Spectacular City: Violence and Performance in Urban Bolivia*. Durham and London: Duke University Press.

Goldstein, Donna M. 2003. *Laughter Out of Place: Race, Class, Violence, and Sexuality in a Rio Shantytown*. Berkeley: University of California Press.

Gomescásseres, Tatiana. 2003. "Deporte, juego y paseo dominical: una aproximación a la ciclovía de Bogotá." *Revista Colombiana de Sociología* 21: 175–203.

Granados, Marco. 2011. "Lado B/Dos noticias." *El Norte*, September 3. Retrieved from http://www.elnorte.com.

Heinle, Kimberly, Octavio Rodríguez Ferreira, and David A. Shirk. 2014. *Drug Violence in Mexico: Data and Analysis Through 2013*. Justice in Mexico Project, University of San Diego. Retrieved from http://justiceinmexico.files.wordpress.com/2014/0 4/140415-dvm-2014-releasered1.pdf.

Human Rights Watch. 2013. *Mexico's Disappeared: The Enduring Costs of a Crisis Ignored*. Retrieved from http://www.hrw.org.

Instituto Nacional de Estadística y Geografía. 2013. Estadísticas de mortalidad. Retrieved from http://www.inegi.org.mx/lib/olap/consulta/general_ver4/MDXQueryDatos. asp?proy=mortgral_dh.

Kessler, Gabriel. 2009. *El sentimiento de inseguridad: Sociología del temor al delito*. Buenos Aires: Siglo XXI.

Lee, Murray. 2001. "The Genesis of 'Fear of Crime.' " *Theoretical Criminology* 5(4): 467–485.

Lessing, Benjamin. 2012. *The Logic of Violence in Criminal War: Cartel-State Conflict in Mexico, Colombia, and Brazil*. University of California at Berkeley.

Low, Setha. 2006. "Towards a Theory of Urban Fragmentation: A Cross-Cultural Analysis of Fear, Privatization, and the State." *Cybergeo: European Journal of Geography* (Online) 34. Retrieved from http://cybergeo.revues.org/3207.

Loyola, Bernardo, and Stefan Ruiz. 2011. "The Cholombians: Sticky Sideburns and Stoner Cumbia in Northern Mexico." *Vice* 18(3): 84-92.

Martínez, Sanjuana. 2012. "Madres de desaparecidos bordan pañuelos como una forma de resistir y aliviar el dolor." *La Jornada*, September 2. Retrieved from http://www.jornada.unam.mx/2012/09/02/politica/017n1pol.

Mauss, Marcel. [1905] 2006. "Essai sur les variations saisonnières des sociétés eskimos." *Sociologie et anthropologie*. Paris: Presses Universitaires de France.

McIlwaine, Cathy, and Caroline Moser. 2007. "Living in Fear: How the Urban Poor Perceive Violence, Fear and Insecurity." In *Fractured Cities: Social Exclusion, Urban Violence and Contested Spaces in Latin America*, edited by Kees Koonings and Dirk Krujit. London: Zed Books.

Menchaca, Andrea. 2010. "Cambian hábitos por miedo." *El Norte*, November 21. Retrieved from http://www.elnorte.com.

Montero, Martha P. 2012. " 'Bordar por la paz': la herida en un pañuelo." *Sinembargo*, December 5. Retrieved from http://www.sinembargo.mx/05-12-2012/449678.

Montero, Sergio. forthcoming. "Worlding Bogota's Ciclovia: From Urban Experiment to International 'Best Practice.' " *Latin American Perspectives*.

Montes de Oca, Violeta. 2009. Se cierran con todo. *El Norte*, October 18. Retrieved from http://www.elnorte.com.

Osorio, Javier. 2013. *Hobbes on Drugs: Understanding Drug Violence in Mexico*. University of Notre Dame.

Osorno, Diego E. 2012. *La guerra de los zetas: viaje por la frontera de la necropolítica*. Mexico City: Grijalbo.

Pain, Rachel. 2000. "Place, Social Relations and the Fear of Crime: A Review." *Progress in Human Geography* 24(3): 365–387.

Rebotier, Julien. 2011. "Security Practices and Inequalities in Caracas: New Drivers for an Old Logic?" *Spatial Justice* 4. Retrieved from http://www.jssj.org/.

Reguillo, Rossana. 2002. "The Social Construction of Fear: Urban Narratives and Practices." In *Citizens of Fear: Urban Violence in Latin America*, edited by Susana Rotker. New Brunswick, NJ: Rutgers University Press.

Rodríguez, Alberto. 2008a. "Mantienen vecinos debate por muro." *El Norte*, March 3. Retrieved from http://www.elnorte.com.

Rodríguez, Alberto. 2008b. "Rechazan rejas en colonia." *El Norte*, May 20. Retrieved from http://www.elnorte.com.

Rodríguez, Alberto, and Perla Martínez. 2011. "Logra violencia tumbar rechazo a 'muro' divisorio." *El Norte*, August 6. Retrieved from http://www.elnorte.com.

Rotker, Susana. 2002. "Cities Written by Violence: An Introduction." In *Citizens of Fear: Urban Violence in Latin America*, edited by Susana Rotker. New Brunswick, NJ: Rutgers University Press.

Simon, Jonathan. 2006. *Governing through Crime: How the War on Crime Transformed American Democracy and Created a Culture of Fear.* New York: Oxford University Press.

Snyder, Richard, and Angélica Durán-Martínez. 2009. "Does Illegality Breed Violence? Drug Trafficking and State-sponsored Protection Rackets." *Crime, Law and Social Change* 52(3): 253–273.

Villarreal, Ana. n.d. *Drug Violence, Fear of Crime and the Transformation of Everyday Life in the Mexican Metropolis.* University of California at Berkeley.

Villarreal, Ana. 2013. "Kidnappable: On the Normalization of Violence in Urban Mexico." *Global Dialogue* 3(3). Retrieved from http://www.isa-sociology.org/global-dialogue/2013/04/kidnappable-on-the-normalization-of-violence-in-urban-mexico/.

Villarreal, Andrés. 2002. "Political Competition and Violence in Mexico: Hierarchical Social Control in Local Patronage Structures." *American Sociological Review* 67(4): 477–498.

Villaséez, José, and Rodríguez, Alberto. 2011. "Libran paisanos las extorsiones al pasar por NL." *El Norte*, December 24. Retrieved from http://www.elnorte.com.

Vázquez, Abraham. 2013. "Cierran colonias a como pueden." *El Norte*, May 8. Retrieved from http://www.elnorte.com.

Wacquant, Loïc. 2004. "Decivilizing and demonizing: the remaking of the black American ghetto." In *The Sociology of Norbert Elias*, edited by Steven Loyal and Stephen Quilley. Cambridge: Cambridge University Press.

Watkins, Amanda. 2014. *Cholombianos.* Mexico City: Trilce.

Wilson, James, and George Kelling. 1982. "Broken Windows." *The Atlantic*, March 1982. Retrieved from http://www.theatlantic.com/doc/print/198203/broken-windows.

CHAPTER 7

Chismosas and Alcahuetas

Being the Mother of an Empistolado within the Everyday Armed Violence of a Caracas Barrio

VERÓNICA ZUBILLAGA, MANUEL LLORENS,
AND JOHN SOUTO

We met Doris[1] after hearing about a group of women from two historically marginalized sectors—La Quinta and Portillo—of a larger barrio known as Catuche, situated in the northern part of Caracas, not far from the Presidential Palace. These women had formed "peace commissions" and had negotiated a ceasefire pact with youth in their neighborhoods. Doris was the community coordinator appointed by the religious educational organization Fe y Alegría to support the daily functioning of the Comisiones de Paz de Catuche.

The peace commissions were formed after a long night of shooting confrontations between the youths from La Quinta and Portillo. In the past two decades, hundreds of young men had already been killed in this historic confrontation, and that night another young man was killed in Portillo. It was his mother, Ana, who took the initiative to call and gather her female neighbors to "do something to stop the killings." Every time we spoke about that night, Ana was visibly moved and her retelling of the event was always accompanied by her tears:

> It was horrible the death of my son. Because that night when he died, I saw the boys
> as they cried, shouted, and when we took him to the hospital, the boys were punching
> the wall. I stood, and seeing all this, being in all this pain, and seeing them crying,

screaming, I left. And then at the funeral, crying, I said: "This cannot continue! We have to fight! We ourselves! We cannot let another death happen over there!"

When word reached the young men of La Quinta that Ana, the mother of the young man murdered in Portillo, had called upon the women of her sector and pleaded not for revenge but that all of them, women, they go up to La Quinta to talk, they answered: "They don't need to talk to us, they need to talk to the *viejas chismosas*."[2] This phrase carries different meanings, but it was taken at face value and the petition to talk was delivered to the women of La Quinta and not to the men. It was then that the women, specifically the mothers, took on the challenge to listen, talk, and negotiate a series of agreements that led to the creation of the peace commissions—Comisiones de Paz—or Comisiones de Convivencia[3] de Catuche.

Ana and her fellow women called upon Doris and Janeth, both from Fe y Alegría, to mediate between the two communities, and after they each got together with both groups of neighbors, they decided to take the risk and call a meeting. "We were very scared, it was a huge responsibility!" remembered Doris. She continued:

> That night . . . what people from Portillo were saying, was the same as what the people from La Quinta were saying. The same needs: "We are tired of putting mattresses on our heads! We are tired of running away! We are tired of not being able to be outside! We are tired of having to call our families whenever we get to our homes! Stop it!" And at the end, they cried, they hugged each other, they talked. That meeting was overwhelmingly moving.

Following this meeting, they decided to create the Comisiones de Convivencia—made up of six women from Portillo and seven women from La Quinta—and they developed an agreement that was approved during an assembly. They summoned the young men, many of whom were their own sons and nephews, and they also committed to the pact, which obliged them to avoid challenges that could trigger armed confrontations. For example, they swore not to provoke their rivals with signs (flashlights or laser lights)[4] and to avoid mutual provocations, such as crossing the borders of their barrio at night, all which normally ended in shootouts. Residents regained freedom of movement across sectors. Women and young men agreed that all trouble among them should be channeled through the commissions, which would serve as containment groups. They also explicitly agreed that no one would display or threaten others with a gun. Anyone who failed to comply with the pact agreements would be confronted by the commission and ultimately would be reported by both committees to the police. Each commission started to meet every week in their own sector and once a month with their neighbor commission. They could also convoke emergency get-togethers whenever the youth threatened to break the pact, as they did many times.

As residents ourselves of Caracas, a city whose homicide rate is one of the highest in the world,[5] we felt compelled to research and analyze the web of social processes that made the pact possible.[6] But as our research advanced, we perceived among the women a constant state of uneasiness, a permanent grief, a subterranean grudge. These women were on the peace commissions and they had, indeed, succeeded in ending this unrelenting chain of deaths. However, we also observed that they were key agents in stoking the hateful linkages that reproduced an ever-present and contingent violence in the neighborhood. Thus we began to ask ourselves: how can we understand this feminine participation in the cycle of violence in the barrio?

What we report here is the experience of a group of women living in a Caracas barrio characterized by a state of warfare. In particular, we will discuss the experiences of mothers of armed youth in the context of Bolivarian Venezuela,[7] where 144,000 violent killings were officially registered as homicides between 1999 and 2012. Social alarm over the state of violence and the massive availability of handguns is high.

Through the daily experiences of these women, we highlight the contradictions of living in contemporary Bolivarian Venezuela. On the one hand, inequalities, poverty, and political exclusion are issues that are constantly raised and attacked in the Chávez government's political discourses and policies. On the other hand, social suffering generated by the deaths of young men—either by their peers or by the police in their neighborhoods—and the mourning that follows are tightly linked to the state's abandonment of its key pacifying role.

Given this context, we are interested in understanding how these structural factors shape and impact barrio residents' daily lives. We are especially interested in the lives of women: their experiences and their roles, specifically as mothers, in the dynamics of violence in Catuche; and the ways they are capable of both reducing and reproducing violence. With the lives of women in mind, we ask: How do structural factors emerge in the daily experiences of barrio residents, reproducing violence and generating conflict between families? How do these women deal with chronic violence and the constant presence of guns in their neighborhoods?

Social science research on urban violence has largely relied upon a male-centered reading (Gay 2005; Koonings and Veenstra 2007; but see Hume 2009 and Goffman's chapter in this book for exceptions). Robert Gay (2005), who provided a rare testimony of a woman linked with the drug world in Rio de Janeiro, underscores the need to understand the complexity of violence and inequality in Latin American cities from a point of view that is sensitive to female perspectives and experiences. Indeed, young males are not the only subjects of violence. There are also the mothers, sisters, and partners who are forced to live through the whirlwinds of violence. As Alice Goffman shows in her chapter in this book, women close to young men get chased, arrested, and jailed because the police view them as potential sources of information. Nevertheless, female participation in acts of violence is a topic that is scarcely treated in the literature. Understanding the complexities of violence implies being sensitive and understanding other logics of action that are associated with female participation—how women contribute to as well as challenge violence in their daily contexts.

First, we argue that the Bolivarian government's social investments and social programs have undoubtedly improved people's life conditions, as measured by Venezuela's life quality indicators in areas such as poverty and health. Yet, a close look from an ethnographic perspective reveals that in Bolivarian Venezuela, the barrios, like other poor urban conglomerations in Latin America, continue to represent urban spaces where residents experience the accumulation of structural disadvantages and conditions that generate tensions and social unrest among neighbors. In the second and third parts of this chapter, we discuss the everyday state of warfare that is perpetuated by a profusion of arms and a chronic lack of justice. In the fourth section, we focus on women's experiences as mothers and how they deal with the sense of helplessness and blame they carry with them. And finally, in the fifth part, we discuss how families, and especially mothers, participate in the transmission of hatred, unwittingly compelling their sons and nephews to take revenge, thus preventing an end to the armed conflicts.

The research on which this text is based was carried out between November 2009 and July 2012. In this period, we went every week to the neighboring sectors La Quinta and Portillo in the Catuche barrio. We also conducted eleven group discussions (five sessions in one neighborhood and six sessions in the other) with the thirteen women of the Comisiones de Paz. Two group discussions were also held with the youth of one neighborhood. In sum, on a weekly basis we discussed the events that took place in their community. Additionally, one of the researchers was permanently working in the community as a psychologist with Doris. We also carried out in-depth interviews with each of the thirteen women of the Commissions and with nine young men from one barrio and one from the other community. We had frequent conversations with Doris, who accompanied us in our reflections and provided validation for many of our interpretive insights. Also, we had several sessions of "sharings" (*compartires*) where we partook in meals with the women. Finally, as we

Figure 7.1
A view from Catuche

were preparing our analysis we presented our findings to each group of women in order to incorporate their concerns and suggestions.

STILL SEARCHING FOR A PLACE TO LIVE: HOW THE STRUCTURAL DISADVANTAGES IN THE BARRIO GENERATE SOCIAL UNREST AMONG FAMILIES

Even though the social programs known as *Misiones Sociales*[8] have improved people's life conditions considerably—mainly by increasing their income, consumption capacity, and health conditions—the *barrios,* like other poor urban areas in Latin America, continue to represent spaces where residents experience the accumulation of structural disadvantages and dereliction (see figure 7.2 and 7.3) (Auyero, Burbano de Lara, and Berti 2014). The right to be part of the city in terms of proper housing remains a social debt that the Bolivarian state holds with its citizens, implicating the state in the permanent tension and unrest that permeates social relations in Catuche (Auyero 2007; Wacquant 2007). Caracas, like many other Latin American cities, arose with notorious divisions between the *urbanizaciones* where the middle- and upper-class sectors are settled and the barrios where the poor reside. The latter represent spaces of self-construction and silent struggles where those excluded from wealthier areas attempt to improve infrastructural conditions in the midst of relegation (Bayat 2000) and where self-help strategies and favor exchanges among family groups remain paramount for dealing with adversity given the lack of support from private and public institutions (Adler de Lomnitz 1975; Gonzáles de la Rocha 1999). By 1990, barrio residents in Caracas made up 40 percent of the city's population; more recent estimations put this number at 50 percent (Cilento 2008).[9]

During the two and a half years that we visited these communities, regular tension and disputes related to lack of housing were particularly

Figure 7.2
Houses grow on top of houses and amid state's dereliction

Figure 7.3
La Ceiba, historic tree in Catuche

salient. Families continue to grow and face pressing need for housing. Land invasions and self-constructed homes continue to increase. In Catuche, a well-established barrio, invasions still generate a great deal of anxiety for older residents. Explosive situations often result due to the widespread use of guns in this area.

Virginia, a member of the peace commissions and the mother of a respected drug dealer in the barrio, was particularly frustrated: a group of land invasions were built next to her house, hindering the entrance of the garbage disposal trucks. During our conversation with her and her sister Maritza about this issue, they were talkative as usual but exhausted:

Maritza: 15 days ago, more or less, the issue of the garbage. We had an ugly quarrel down there, and we almost punched each other— *nos torteamos*—because we are not going to leave either. We had a meeting; everything was on hold because one of the women that was in the peace commission, was invading this area. They were invading everywhere, and then we had the problem of garbage, then we said, the boys here said: if they keep the garbage truck from coming in, we will throw the containers into the creek, and everything will explode! And we were in the peace commission meeting, and she [a woman that was part of the invasion] was saying that she felt attacked! And then Virginia said: "Well, look, I'm going to say one thing, if this mess cannot be solved, if the truck cannot go by, this is going to blow up!"

Virginia: I called my son. I will bring my son and he will start shooting everybody!

The invading family was comprised of *damnificados*, homeless victims of the massive rains and landslides that took place in the barrio in 2000. Thirteen years later, they were still waiting for the government to keep its promise to provide them with a place to resettle. In the meantime, the Tovares, another homeless family, decided to occupy a barrio building's party hall and build three houses on another piece of land. Orlando, the nephew of the woman in the peace commission that took part in the invasion, explained his point of view:

> We live here in the building's party hall, we borrow it because we are *damnificados*, and people are always attacking us so horribly. My aunt was the first to make the decision, because she could not keep waiting for the government to give her a home. Then people say: "The Tovares seized the land!" It is not like that, but my uncle is a *damnificado*, my aunt is a *damnificada*, my mother is a *damnificada*, and a cousin is a *damnificada*, so they built three houses that take up almost half of the land, so the Tovares are already in four houses, then they say "The Tovares took the land!," I was telling them [his family members involved in the invasion]: you ask for a letter from the neighborhood association, who are the ones that own the land, and say you are going to live there, because Chavez gave that spot to the damnificados, because the government has to find a place . . . but wow, there is already like a war, and everyone is saying: "Fuck! The party room! They have to get out!"

Maritza and Virginia were very insistent in their concerns:

Maritza: The same family all the time screwing around— *echando vaina*— screwing around here screwing around there, screwing themselves— *joden aquí, lo quieren joder a unos mismos*.

Virginia: They don't dare fuck with me, because if I tell my son, my son will stop everything! Here everyone is devoured, even the old! What bullshit is that! Because it is not fair, because they will build there, and they will not leave room for the garbage truck! Ahhh you will be comfortable here and all of us fucked!

The uneasiness was pervasive. Be it groups of families from their own barrio, or even worse, people foreign to the barrio, invasions were a constant menace, and with them came the possibility of armed interpersonal violence between residents. The social unrest was permanent because residents' ability to solve problems themselves was limited, putting the neighbors in a permanently vulnerable situation. In Catuche, each period of heavy rains destroyed houses built on unstable land, producing more and more *damnificados*. Also, as time passed by, the daughters and sons of the different neighbors founded their own families and needed a place to live nearby.

Due to the historic and continuing public neglect of urban dwellers, and an accumulation of adversities throughout the 1990s, some barrios like Catuche have become densely populated areas, where neighbors are forced to struggle among themselves to defend or gain territory due to the administration's abandonment or ineptitude in fulfilling old prom- ises and basic obligations. Events like this show once more how structural violence, particularly the action or inaction of privileged actors such as the state, contribute to a permanent state of animosity and competition between people in precarious living conditions who are just struggling for a basic right (Bayat 2000; Braun and McCarthy 2005; Bourgois 2009; Wacquant 2002).

But perhaps the domain where the state was even more connected— both directly and indirectly—to interpersonal armed violence in Catuche was through guns. For example, youth frequently accessed ammunition through police agents; moreover, the availability and rampant use of arms can be attributed to the lack of protection provided by the state and the absolute lack of control of arms and ammunition in the streets. The wide- spread use of guns in Catuche produced, from the women's perspective, a daily state of uneasiness (*zozobra*), a fundamental dimension of the every- day lethal violence experienced in Catuche.

LIVING AMID ABANDONMENT AND THE EXCESS OF ARMS

The armed antagonism between young men of La Quinta and Portillo has existed for at least two decades and has produced countless deaths.

When we first visited the Community Center at Catuche —*el Centro Comunitario de Catuche*—one of the images that struck us the most was a corkboard on the wall, where little cards with photos of the barrios' youth that had been killed were hung. There were three young men's photos, with their date of birth and death. All were between twenty and twenty-one years old when they were killed. Each of the little cards included small reminiscent texts about them that expressed their eternal presence in the memory of their loved ones.

But we were more astounded when we realized that every one of the thirteen women of the peace commissions we were interviewing had suffered a direct loss: their own young sons or other male relatives who had died due to gunshot wounds. Olivia had a brother who was killed; Victoria, an uncle; Marina's son and nephew were shot to death; Ana had lost two of her young sons; María lost two nephews; Julia lost her uncle and her best friend; Yabelis's son was killed, as well as five cousins, two uncles, and two brothers; Nadia and Antonia each lost a brother; Doris's son was killed; Xinia had lost her brother and three nephews; Virginia and Maritza, who were sisters, had a little nephew and a niece hit by a stray bullet (*bala perdida*).

In fact, the narratives we were collecting described the experience of living in contexts of cyclic, daily armed confrontation, where gunshots and crossfire were routinely experienced. The vocabulary used, such as "the first to fall," was one similar to that used by victims of war, which also coincides with Villarreal's analysis (this volume) of drug violence in Monterrey.

Virginia, who lived in one of the outermost houses of the barrio and hence was exposed to shootings that affected even kids of the family, told us:

> There are innocent people here who don't have any problems with the others. For instance, my niece was killed, and she was just a child. In my house there have never been problems, and look, my family was the first to fall. My sister was hit while she was inside, do you understand? But since we are here, the first house that was in front was ours, all the bullets came our way.

The widespread availability of guns makes a substantive difference in the resolution of disputes, or in traditional demonstrations of force that could, in the past, be seductively compelling for observers. Virginia explains nicely:

Virginia: I came here young, and it was zesty; it was pure fistfighting [*peleas de puños*] there were blows back and forth and back and forth.
Verónica: Zesty? How so?
Virginia: I tell you it was juicy because it was a clean fight. It was healthy. A fistfight never killed anyone. Not like now. It was healthy, healthy! (Laughter and several commented).
Manuel: You tell it as if it was something you could enjoy!
Virginia: Sure! We never saw dead people, it was like a cock fight. Action! You knew that there were not going to be deaths. Not like now, Boom! And the bodies we have.

The widespread presence of lethal weapons in youth's immediate environments and the dynamics of armed violence produce a sentiment of complete helplessness. Very early in their lives, youth incorporate the sense of living in a world of pure antagonism where the strongest rules. In order to survive in this context, it becomes necessary to arm themselves and become personal vigilantes in their territories (Zubillaga 2009). Youth are responding to the extremely inhospitable social conditions, where tens of thousands are involved in a dynamic of armed violence. They kill and die every year but are not a "band of deviants" (Wacquant 1992).

As the narratives of these youth suggest, once they have acquired a gun in order to protect themselves, new challenges and experiences emerge. We are not arguing that guns cause the interpersonal armed violence among the youngsters[10] but, as B. Latour invites us to reflect upon, it is pertinent to ask what differences these devices introduce. In what sense do these objects become participants in different courses of action? In what sense do they shape the actions of others? (Latour 2005, 72–79).

When we spoke with these women's sons and nephews—who share with youth from other cities the same realist nihilism vis-a-vis education and employment as channels to obtain recognition and respect (Bourgois 1995; Zubillaga 2009)—guns were particularly present in their vocabulary when accounting for their participation in armed confrontations. Enrique explained it this way:

> I hung out and fooled around with them sometimes, then I stopped studying, and started working. By that time I bought the gun and I kept spending time with them (laughter in the background) and suddenly we said: "Hey let's go take it out and around! Let's take it on a walk!" Because I can say one thing for sure, when one buys a gun, your mentality— *la mentalidad*—changes, you . . . seek the adrenaline, you look to grab and shoot.

Carrying a gun involves a state of *andar empistolado*. Especially for youth who had no job and were out of school, guns were an intensely compelling and seductive object. They were viewed as useful in the search for enemies and to solve disputes, but also to help one experience thrilling emotions in forging their masculine identities and seeking respect (Katz 1988; Zubillaga 2008; Baird in this volume). They usually called the guns *las bichas*, turning them into living animalized beings, but they also had more particular names: if they bought it from a girl the gun would have her name; or if it had a particular attribute, such as rust, it might be called *oxidado*.

Arms are a crucial object in the chain of death known as *la culebra*—a term applied to the enemy and the situation of conflict that is settled with death, and that is prolonged in a chain of revenge and more deaths. In this sense, *la culebra* has an undeniable moral character, given the fact that it is associated with an offense that requires an answer or the unsustainable degradation of the receiver. It has a salient collective character, because following commitments of solidarity and rules of reciprocity (Mauss 1997), it expands among members, establishing a web of endless affronts to young men living in close proximity (see Zubillaga 2008).

The notable role of guns in the arousal of a state of animosity between youngsters from Portillo and La Quinta and in the expansion of these deaths among the web of friends, was consistently highlighted by the young men. As Enrique puts it:

> Once in the midst of trouble, you think a lot of things, because one is always calm, but imagine that a bullet, for instance, hits you in one leg, or anywhere on the body . . . it makes you have *la mente*— *uno se crea la mente*—do you understand? It changes the mindset— *la mentalidad*. So you might stay calm, but you can also search for vengeance, and it generates more problems, because it is you, and it is also those who are with you, for instance Orlando, Fabricio, will be with me, and we are three . . . So the problem is not only that, but in the next generation, because the problem with the people that come before from other generations [is that they pass down vendettas] . . . it passes from one and goes and gets the other. At least for the commission of peace, the mentality of the new generation will change, I mean, they won't bring that mentality.

During several of the meetings with the youngsters of Portillo, it was evident, and so they said, that they hid their arms in order to not have them in front of us. Only once was there an exception: the young men had promised to keep a friend's gun while he had to do a short errand nearby. Ignacio, a part of our team who was with them that day, was a little afraid of an accident and offered his backpack to keep the gun safe.

LA ZOZOBRA: SURVIVING EVERYDAY ARMED VIOLENCE

Zozobra was the term often used by the women to describe the state of unrest that permeated their communities due to the regular armed confrontation. It expresses the anguish of the very real possibility of dying amid crossfire. This cyclical state of armed confrontation can be understood as an intermittent armed conflictivity, within which the state's lack of regulation allows and encourages an unending chain of deaths that devours young men and produces a strong sense of helplessness among the women. The youth, aware that one way to prevent attacks is by showing their own recklessness in order to discourage others' aggression, generates more aggression and violence (Bourgois 1995; Zubillaga 2009). These armed exchanges ultimately engulf their mothers, aunts, and sisters as well.

At the climax of the armed confrontation between the young men from Portillo and La Quinta, women reported how they provided material support to the youngsters involved in the confrontations.

Barbara: There were times when we all had to help them [everybody agrees]. You know what I mean? Because if not they would have come and killed us all. There were times when we had to help them, we bought bullets and all. I'm not ashamed to say it! If not we would all be dead, because there were too many of them. They'd stay up all night taking care of us and we'd give them food. I'm not telling lies, this is the reality of our life.

Elisa: At one point we had to make molotov bombs for them.

Barbara: Exactly!

Elisa: And we distributed them among the apartments, because they [the kids from the other sector] were going to enter everywhere.

Youngsters' rampant use of guns to deal with disputes —whether drug-related issues, the crossing of barrio boundaries, or stealing—brings about cyclical routine shootings and a daily state of uneasiness (*zozobra*) during periods when armed confrontations are at their peak —that is, when they are involved in *culebras*. For the women, the body is the site of the most intense emotions, as expressed in phrases like "*estado de nervios*," "we couldn't sleep, we couldn't live," and "I was going crazy."

When armed confrontations are at their peak, the women's narratives revealed that everyday journeys and errands were overwhelmed by the fear of dying. Antonia put it this way: "The one who was going out had to yell, to see if one could go in, if one could go in quickly. It was a great *zozobra*, it was a curfew for us. At all times."

During the *culebra* periods, women are forced to develop different strategies to protect themselves and their families. In the event of a late-night shooting, they hide themselves under their beds, turn off the lights, close their doors; if their houses are near the shootings, they take shelter in neighbors' homes. But the most painful temporary solution was to send their sons away:

Yenny: Everyone was taking their children out of this place, I sent mine to Ciudad Bolivar, I kept crying, they were afraid.

Marina: I sent mine away too, to Los Teques, because I was afraid.

Maritza: I sent him [her son] away for ten years, more or less, like ten years, he came back just recently, it will be a year and a half since he has been here, and yet I have to always keep moving him from here to there, moving him everywhere.

These women's actions can be understood as survival strategies deployed by disadvantaged groups (Adler de Lomnitz 1975; Cariola 1989; Gonzáles de la Rocha 1999). Traditionally, the concept of survival strategies has emphasized its economic dimension —the set of practices that the popular sectors engage in to ensure their biological and material reproduction in the absence of institutional sources of solidarity (Adler de Lomnitz 1975; Cariola 1989). However, in this case, vulnerability emerges from a direct menace to biological life through the armed conflictivity in the region due to the widespread selling of arms, the illegal drug economy, and lethal violence.[11]

In response to the new challenges posed by the widespread use of arms and state abandonment, these survival strategies operate to protect one's family and preserve biological life. They represent another layer in the process of cumulative disadvantages faced by the poor (Gonzáles de la Rocha 2004) that radiate from the traditional social and economic realm to the most basic political realm of life preservation.

Figure 7.4
Rests from the past in La Quinta

By underscoring the need to speak about political strategies of survival, we want to stress that in Latin America, specifically in Caracas, amid scarcity, the poor are obliged to privatize responses vis-à-vis the most basic individual, civil, and human right: the right to life (Caldeira 1996; Jelin 1996). For women, this state of abandonment, the profusion of arms, and the intensification of difficulties that threaten life itself, is experienced, above all, as a sense of daily emergency expressed in *zozobra*. Their responses to this state of intermittent armed conflictivity, as in a situation of war, stem from the need to take cover in their own dwellings during armed confrontations, the impulse to carefully manage information in order to complete everyday activities, the urge to displace their male children to avoid life-threatening circumstances, the obligation to form difficult and always fragile agreements with armed youth in an effort to regulate violence, and the necessity of providing ammunition or profiting from their sons' capacities to exert violence in order to prevent others' aggressions.

In other words, political strategies of survival in this context of armed conflictivity and abandonment range from covering to negotiating with the armed youth, to participating directly in the armed confrontations, to enacting violence themselves. These practices are linked to intense emotions such as fear, grief, and rage stemming from the sense of injustice and defenselessness they feel as a result of repeatedly losing their beloved sons and relatives. Thus—given the everyday urgency and structurally imposed forms of suffering (Bourgois 2009)—these women's practices are inseparably intertwined with subjectivities full of sorrow and rage.

BLAME IT ON THE MOTHERS: THE *ALCAHUETA* AND THE GENDERING OF CULPABILITY FOR VIOLENCE

As the literature on violence in Latin America has highlighted, the state's participation in lethal violence and its concomitant sensation of *zozobra* is not limited to its neglect or its withdrawal from the pacification of social relations but also includes its direct intervention (Pinheiro 1996; Caldeira 1996; Briceño-Leon and Zubillaga 2002; Auyero, Burbano de Lara, and Berti 2014). Its participation spans a continuum, from the involvement of police agents in the illicit trade of guns and ammunitions—which contribute directly to the daily armed confrontations—to the direct struggle with barrios' neighbors—which include the women—to their direct participation in extrajudicial killings.[12]

According to the young men's narratives, the police agents (*los pacos*, as they called) were one secure source for ammunition and bigger weapons—bigger than the common thirty-eight and nine millimeter ones. The young dark-skinned men had plenty of tales of being harassed by the police:

> The other day, my God! the cops came—*los pacos*—he put one in the knee ... imagine that mess ... and grabbed some kids—*chamos*—and then the kids said: "No no no we are not *malandros* we're coming from work!" And they took them to a wall there plam plam plam! They shot trying to kill them but they couldn't hit them ... just grazed here on the head ... *una vaina loca*!

One of the most painful experiences lived by Ana's son Kevin was having his best friend killed by the police.

The women also have terrible stories of their encounters with police agents. Olivia's narrative recounts a young man's execution perpetrated by a police agent that she witnessed in front of her window. Once we were speaking about the police she burst out:

> I say, for instance, the boy that was killed, he raised his hand, I saw it from my window. My window is facing the court, the boy raises his hand as if to say [STOP!] ... but no way! When the policemen shot him the first time and he ran to the court ... it looked like if he was going to lift his shirt to show he had nothing, he had no weapons, but when he does so ... it was pin, pin, pin! Horrible! We shouted from the window: Leave him murderer, murderer! Horrible, horrible, then they dragged him away as if he were a dog.

The brutality depicted in this narrative is not isolated. It is embedded in an entire machinery that calls for and justifies the death of young men of barrios by defining them as "pre-delinquents," as the vice minister of Citizen Security once publicly stated.[13]

If it is true that within the political transformation process known as the Bolivarian Revolution, political inclusion and recognition have been widely supported, it is also true that the increase in violent crimes has allowed state actors to utilize extremely stigmatizing expressions to justify police killings and the expansion of punitive repression, which principally affects those social sectors that have benefited from this recognition.[14]

These killings illustrate in all its crudeness how the state participates actively in creating a state of warfare. They reveal the establishment, over time, of what we could call a lethal stigmatization focused on young dark-skinned males from low-income areas. Such stigmatization is expressed, on the one hand, by the construction of extremely degrading categories used to classify youngsters who fit these features and, on the other hand, in the killing of those males by police officers, supported by the acquiescence of their supervisors and many sectors of society. Like Huggins, Haritos-Fatouros, and Zimbardo (2002) point out in the case of police torture and killings in Brazil, this is an "atrocity system." Beyond the perpetrators of killings exists a whole web of officials and their superiors who ignore, excuse, support, or even reward those killings.

A peculiarity of this lethal stigmatization lies in the fact that, by constructing the idea that young dark-skinned males from low-income areas are a biological hazard, the violence enacted upon their bodies results in a sense of asepsis; that is, the life of healthy and decent citizens depends on their elimination. These definitions—as Foucault (2003) pointed out when speaking about racism within the context of modern states—urge and justify their killing rather than their exclusion. Instead of arbitrary detention or imprisonment of youngsters from low-income areas, these definitions result in their deaths, thus resolving the contradictions for a political regime like Venezuela's which identifies itself with the deprived sectors. In this sense, even if this stigmatization has pervaded Venezuelan society, justifying arbitrary forms of subjection throughout our history, the extent of these killing practices and the loud silence that surrounds them among the general population now appears unprecedented. It speaks to a normalized violence, an invisible genocide, which, as Scheper-Hughes (2004) invites us to see, reveals itself in the social production of indifference.

Women, however, are not exempted from this struggle. The hostility and the moral struggle that characterizes the relationship between the women and the police agents are evident. Olivia told us:

> When the police came once, they told us: "You are the *malandros' alcahuetas*."[15] That's what they tell us: "you are *alcahuetas*." Because they [the police] are battering the boys, but if they are already holding them, why do they have to mistreat them? They're handing over their IDs . . . Why do they have to . . . why do they have to mistreat them? Then, we went out to defend them.

These women's stories about their relationship with the police emphasize the gendering of culpability that exists in the Venezuelan context. Being mother and slum dweller by definition also means being an *alcahueta*. This highly stigmatizing epithet signals the failure of the parental project, embodied in the (single) mother who is responsible for crime; it defines a mother as an accomplice, one who covers up her son's morally shameful actions. It epitomizes maternal failure, the failure of the mother's authority over the child.

Recently, this blame—an evident expression of what we call lethal stigmatization—was represented in the words of General David Benavides, responsible for military security operations in Caracas, who stated: "The final destination of every delinquent is either jail or under-ground."[16] The general continued his speech by drawing attention to families, asking that they "take care of their children" who are "disori-ented, using drugs or committing robberies . . . Sir, to keep your loved ones from their own demise, call upon them to reflect; remove them from this world of crime."

The state's astonishingly blatant failure to control crime is deposited entirely on the family, and more specifically on mothers: the *alcahuetas* are the ones to blame for the violence, not the chronic lack of justice, not the evident police corruption or the context of helplessness and lack of supports in parenting, not the lack of opportunities for the youth when they grow up, and certainly not the massive and uncontrolled availability of handguns. As Patricia Márquez (1999, 89) remarked in her ethnogra-phy of homeless children and violence in Caracas, the "intense focus on particular family forms and holding women responsible for youth trans-gressions and violence make it possible for the state to brush aside the all too real problems of public discontent and extreme socioeconomic inequality."

Instead, mothers are held responsible for instilling "proper values" in their young sons as well as supervising their behavior. And they are charged with these burdens in the harshest of contexts without any help. The pressure to manage these responsibilities produces in single moth-ers a sense of shame and guilt, which operates as a form of symbolic vio-lence (Campbell 1993; Warr 2005). In Catuche, the women regularly mentioned that they were perceived as *alcahuetas*, referring to the burden they carry because of this denigrating social categorization. The women we spoke with often said they felt overwhelmed and spoke with shame of losing control over their sons or nephews.

Finally, the peace commission has ended up being a responsibility added to the tasks of motherhood. Indeed, a big part of the commissions rests on the mothers' actions and dispositions to serve as supervisors, mediators, and punishers—actions that are responsibilities of the state. This leads back to a debate opened up by Scheper-Hughes (1992), who traced the experiences of Brazilian women living in extreme poverty and facing the frequent death of their infant children. She argues that the pre-occupation in psychological literature with mourning, attachment, and bonding tacitly implies that these are the duties of women, specifically mothers. She writes: "Emotion work is frequently gendered work. And we may want to consider whether the psychological theories on maternal love, attachment, grief and mourning are not a 'rhetoric of control' and a discourse of power 'by other means'" (Scheper-Hughes,1992, p. 427).

In Catuche, women are not only burdened with the responsibility of raising their sons alone under adverse circumstances; they also carry the burden of the pacification of social relations, a responsibility for which the state is not held accountable. This is on top of the emotional consequences of repeated violent losses.

MOURNING AND THE TRANSMISSION OF HATRED

While women made the ceasefire possible, they also contributed to the dynamics of violence in Catuche. In this section we discuss the emotions produced by mourning the loss of young men from their communities as well as the anger and hatred these losses produced.

In one conversation where women from both communities were present, we asked, "How many deaths have you all suffered?" One of the women answered, "Well I've lost five cousins, two uncles and two brothers." Immediately a woman from the other community responded, "Yes, and one of your cousins who died is the one who murdered my brother." In just one minute, two women had mentioned ten murders, and the entanglements of these victims surfaced.

In a conversation with the young men of one of the communities, the same issue came up. Again they hesitated and told different stories that they had heard: someone had stolen something from someone from the other sector; a man had borrowed a gun but had gotten drunk the night before he was supposed to return it and failed to appear on time. "A misunderstanding," Eduardo called it, "it was all a misunderstanding." Violence, revenge, and loss have escalated to such a degree that those implicated can't really remember what they were fighting about. In Doris's words:

> The same mothers without wanting to, pass the hate on to the kids. Why? Because they killed my son and in my pain I lose sight of what is around me and how I can influence others, and I start saying things like, "I saw the guy who killed my boy, I saw his sister and she did so and so to me" ... and the kid grows with hate and when he's at a certain age, the thought that's in his head is: "I am going to get revenge."

Paradoxically, the same men and women who have suffered the consequences of this armed violence and have waged an incredible mobilization to stop it are the ones that in other ways perpetuate it.

Traces of loss and trauma permeated our conversations. Dozens of exchanges concerned the violent events that led to someone's death or their personal close encounters with it.

Over and over again, when the women talked about traumatic episodes, numerous signs of emotional wounds became evident. For example, it was common for them to say afterward, "It's as if I was reliving it again right now, as if time had not passed." This traumatic reliving of the experience, along with a host of other symptoms, turned many of our encounters into moments to share and reflect back on sadness, fear, and rage. Much of what we found echoed what other researchers have described as the traumatic sequels common in social groups that have survived war or violent persecution. Numerous psychologically oriented theories and researchers have described a series of typical reactions when one's group is threatened (Apprey 2004; Pynoos et al. 2004; Volkan 1997; Volkan 2006). These include hyperarousal; increased group cohesion and increased identification with the in-group; fight or flight responses, which lead to *us* versus *them*; and polarized perceptions.

Some of the more intricate aspects of the emotional consequences of the violent deaths of loved ones are the rage and hate they produce and the fact that these emotions are too much to bear in the absence of justice or other modes of coping with grief (Rosaldo 2004). In one group interview, after a few mothers mentioned their empathy for women of the other sector, Virginia burst out:

> Maybe among us, ok. Because we knew each other, you knew my niece and my nephew, ok. But it's a lie that I cared that they killed that other kid! God forgive me, but they didn't care either! What did one of the thugs that killed Milagros [the woman's niece], a girl of only eight years old, say? He said that the kid shouldn't have been on the street waiting for bullets at that hour. That's what he said. Or am I wrong? They didn't care about our pain, so we don't care about their pain. Let's be clear about this, we're in this now because yeah, thank God, but this is bullshit, I don't kid myself, I see things as they are, because that's how they are!

Virginia's comment is notable because she dared to say what the other women might also have been struggling with but didn't express, at least to us. They preferred to talk about their work to eradicate violence and how the peace commissions had brought peace. But until then they had not talked about the grudges they continued to hold against those who had murdered their loved ones. Virginia emphasized the lines drawn to separate the sectors, describing the ways she taught the children of her sector to maintain an allegiance to their group and build antagonism toward the other one:

> Ok we have peace, we don't want any trouble, but it's not like we're going to get together with them because there are deaths on both sides. It's not like we're going to live together, right? That's what I've told the kids over and over again so they understand what is what. We don't want any more deaths, let them go out, pass through their sector, but it's not like we're going to live together.

The pain and unresolved loss was evident every time we talked about the past. As Virginia mentioned in the quote above, these feelings are passed on to the children, a form of transgenerational transmission which Volkan (1997) defines as "when an older person unconsciously externalizes his traumatized self onto a developing child's personality." He continues, "A child then becomes a reservoir for the unwanted, troublesome parts of an older generation. Because the elders have influence on the child, the child absorbs their wishes and expectations and is driven to act on them. It becomes the child's task to mourn, to reverse the humiliation and feelings of helplessness pertaining to the trauma of his forebears" (Volcan 1997, 43).

In our conversations, the women systematically pointed out how these wounds, the pain, the hatred, and the transmission of revenge passed "from generation to generation," within family groups in La Quinta and Portillo. This never-ending animosity among kinship was uttered in expressions such as: "It is like a chain, kids grow, they go with the same stuff in their heads: 'Because that guy killed my brother!' and there they have their enemies readymade, as they say." The length and temporal extension of this animosity was then put into words like Ana's: "It started many years ago and leaves behind a trail of repercussions, so it ends here and starts there. It began in a group and then goes from generation to generation."

"They don't forget their deaths and neither do we." Virginia insisted upon this impossibility in our conversations. The inability to forget these deaths turns these women into the bearers of their son's obligation for revenge. They become the figure of the "bereaved" (*el doliente*), a fundamental actor within the *culebra*, reproducing the chain of death and revenge implied by it. The place of women in the transmission of pain and grudges is portrayed in the description of "old gossipers" (*viejas chismosmas*), which these women complained about being called. *Viejas chismosmas* is a demeaning phrase that refers to the fact that women don't tend to be the main actors in the play of physical violence, but they do play a crucial role in the circulation of information and the building up or tearing down of a reputation in a place where reputation can mean life or death. *Viejas chismosmas* would then be a sort of social character defined by its

gender that expresses the ways social suffering is internalized and reproduced in the everyday subjective processes of "stocking" and transmitting
their bereavement onto their children.

In Catuche, women take actions that not only make ceasefires a possibility but also perpetuate the dynamics of violence. Thus these courageous
women find themselves in an ambivalent and sometimes paradoxical situation. They are both the protagonists of the pacification of a violent community and, at times, the catalysts of violence. This situation, we believe,
is a mark of the main paradox that engulfs women in the logic of violence
and armed confrontations in their neighborhood. Women suffer and con-
vey their pain. In consequence, their sons, the bereaved —*dolientes*—are
compelled to exert revenge and at the same time become sacrificed.

The creation of the commissions has brought on a new possibility of regulation, in which mothers bond together and pressure the young men in their
communities to abide by an agreed-upon set of rules. When one of them
breaks one of the rules, the commission acts to warn or punish the man. In
many cases this creates tensions between loyalties. The mother feels disloyal
to her son, because she is exposing him to public shame or punishment. But
at the same time, loyalty to the process of the commissions has grown and
she feels committed to this process. This helps to sustain the agreements.

The importance of mourning and trauma that we have underlined is
problematic, since, as stated earlier, it risks turning the women into the
main culprits or those responsible for dealing with the pain. But our
analysis does not reduce these cycles of violence to emotion. Rather, we
emphasize how structural conditions and cultural assumptions play out
in daily interactions. The experience of material deprivation, the excess
of guns, and rigid gender roles help to produce male confrontations that
result in a long string of violent losses. It is through the emotional impacts
of these experiences that the consequences of structural conditions are
encrypted in interpersonal relationships. The state's abandonment of
its pacifying role and the lack of an effective judicial system prolong the
sense of injustice and leave the community, with an unbearable grief, to
fend for itself and clamor for justice.

FINAL COMMENTS

The singular experience of Bolivarian Venezuela serves to illustrate the
darkness that can engulf Latin American societies and their hopes for
greater inclusion of the traditionally excluded majorities. Moves toward
social and economic inclusion expressed in social policies such as redistribution do not necessarily bring about a decrease in violence.

As we have seen in Catuche, the absence of justice and historical bitterness are intertwined with the pain of mourning. Pain, when left without reparation, transforms into anger and anger transforms into a search for revenge (Caldeira 2000; Rosaldo 2004). The pain is such that it cannot be forgotten, and one death results in yet another, producing unending violence amid the bereaved. Here, courageous women are the protagonists of the pacification of a community characterized by armed conflictivity. Yet, at the same time they can also be catalysts of violence: women in their mourning and narratives of grief compel their sons to exert revenge and at the same time become sacrificed.

The cyclical presence of armed confrontations and the resulting chain of deaths that we have discussed force us to think about an unprecedented condition of cyclical mourning. It compels us to coin a new condition of "anti-citizenship," a condition constituted through living the recurrent pain of a series of mournings, which do not allow for recovery before a new catastrophe arrives. Could we speak then of anti -citizenships in persistent mourning? Such a denied citizenship, would be characterized by the experience of structural violence, the lack of institutions to which one can appeal, no state to which one can call upon to institute justice, to attend to or make amends for losses, nor the least guarantee life preservation.

In the 1990s, Susana Rotker (2000, 16) spoke about citizenships of fear, referring to this "new citizenship condition" as that of "being a potential victim, that has been developing a new form of subjectivity . . . characterized by the generalized sensation of insecurity that permeates the Latin American capitals . . . that alludes to the urban sentiment of generalized helplessness and the risk of paralysis . . . which includes all the insecurity practices that redefine the relation with Power, with kindred, with space." Here we would argue that the condition of cyclical mourning for the deaths of relatives surpasses the threshold of fear and insecurity and places itself in the cracks of pain over the loss, in the grieving that is interlaced with the hijacked lives of the beloved, in the complete lack of a minimal guarantee for the preservation of life.

This condition of recurrent mourning emerges as a definitive example of anti-citizenship if we embrace the point of view of Elizabeth Jelin (1996) and Susana Rotker (2000), who evoke Hannah Arendt (1997). These writers invite us to think of citizenship in terms of the right to have rights, belonging to a community of rights and responsibilities. They explain that the ethics of citizenship rest primarily in nonviolence: where nobody suffers or is injured, protection is guaranteed, and it is possible to establish justice.

NOTES

1. The research on which this article is based was conducted with financial support from the Open Society Institute and the Consejo de Desarrollo Científico Humanístico y Tecnológico de la Universidad Católica Andrés Bello. During fieldwork we had the support of Gilda Núñezas well as Ignacio Lucart, Valentina Larrazabal, and Diana Castellanos. We are most grateful to participants of the workshop "Violence at the Urban Margins" for such stimulating discussions, and especially Javier Auyero for his insightful comments and for being such a wonderful editor. Many thanks to Jacinto Cuvi, our paper discussant, and to Katherine Jensen and Yana Stainova, for their readings and suggestions. We can't thank Rebecca Hanson enough for her precious English proofreading and her always illuminating comments, as well as David Smilde for his support of our research during all these years.

2. *Viejas chismosas*: the old women who gossip.

3. *Convivencia*: coexistence, and getting along. It is a coexistence that has a degree of agreement.

4. Curiously, many of the confrontations were set off by symbolic acts of defiance of one group to the other. For example, pointing flashlights toward the windows of their male rivals.

5. Caracas has become one of the most dangerous cities in Latin America. The homicide rate for 2011 was 95 per 100,000 inhabitants (Sanjuán 2011). When this rate is compared to that of other Latin American cities, the difference is obvious: Bogotá (23), Medellín (39), Río de Janeiro (39), Sao Paulo (14), San Salvador (150), Ciudad Juárez (150) (Briceño-León 2010). What is shocking about violence in Caracas is the relatively steep increase: in 1998, the homicide rate was 63 per 100,000 inhabitants and by 2008, it had already almost doubled (127 homicides per 100,000).

6. We have provided a thorough analysis of the peace commissions of Catuche in Verónica Zubillaga, Manuel Llorens, Gilda Núñez, and John Souto,. *Violencia armada y acuerdos de convivencia en una comunidad caraqueña: una larga marcha por la paz* (Caracas: Editorial Equinoccio, Universidad Simón Bolívar [in press]). For an abridged version, see *Acuerdos Comunitarios de Convivencia. Pistas para la acción* (Caracas: Amnistía Internacional).

7. 1998 marks the onset of a period of accelerated transformations and conflict escalation known in Venezuela as the Bolivarian Revolution under Hugo Chávez's government. Venezuela was subsequently renamed República Bolivariana de Venezuela and the term "Bolivarian" has been added to many institutions' names to highlight this "revolutionary" transformation and its novelty: Fuerza Armada Bolivariana, Gobierno Bolivariano, Policía Nacional Bolivariana.

8. In Bolivarian Venezuela, public policies intended to combat poverty and inequality are called *Misiones Sociales*. The misiones consist of a series of social programs created in 2003—a year of intense political confrontation after the coup of 2002—to meet the needs of the most vulnerable. Although Misiones Sociales have been criticized for being corrupt, since their implementation, poverty measured in terms of income has decreased significantly, dropping from 55 percent to 26 percent between 2003 and 2011 (Instituto Nacional de Estadística, consulted February 4, 2013, http://www.ine. gov.ve/index.php?option=com_content&view=category&id=104&Itemid=45#.)

9. The residents of Rio de Janeiro favelas make up about 18.6 percent of the city's population (Koonings and Veenstra 2007). Therefore, while Rio's favelas make up one-fifth of the population, one-half of Caracas's population lives in barrios.

10. Weapons cannot be considered a "cause" of urban violence (in general) nor in juvenile violence (in particular), but it is known that they are strongly present in the killings and ultimately contribute to the lethality of aggressions (see Cano 2001).

11. People's narratives in Villarreal's chapter (this volume) are also experiences of vulnerability in contexts of state abandonment and the rampant presence of armed actors. Indeed, we could say that Villarreal's logistics of fear constitute self-help strategies similar to those developed in warzones to manage exposure to the violence produced by the presence of armed actors. As Villareal points out: "The term *logistics*, a military term in its origins, is particularly adequate to encompass the new strategies documented here, given that these are military strategies down-scaled and extended into civilian life: armoring, camouflaging, caravanning, and regrouping."

12. We are thinking here of the continuum of violence posited by Scheper-Hughes and Bourgois (2004) that refers to "the ease with which humans are capable of reducing the socially vulnerable into expendable nonpersons and assuming the license— *even the duty—to kill, maim or soul-murder.*"

13. Belisario Landis, the Vice-Minister of Urban Security bemoaned that the police had executed 2000 pre-delinquents. According to his declaration: *This is a situation I regret, because we are talking here of young people that could have benefited from rehabilitation programs. But they leave us very few options when they start shooting each other or the police.* El Nacional, September 19, 2000. In 2010, More recently, the current Minister of Justice, Miguel Rodríguez Torres stated in a press interview: *I'll give you a number: out of every 100 homicides occurring in Venezuela, 76 are clashes between gangs or gangs and security forces. These 76 deaths are accounted for statistics, but they are not directly attributable to a lack of security, but rather to differences between gangs that have developed a culture of violence and weapons, so that the only solution to their differences is to kill each other.*

14. Military authorities responsible for citizen security policies have made tragically famous speeches defining crime as requiring a bellicose response. For example the category of "potential delinquent" or "pre-delinquent" outlined by Belisario Landis, the vice-minister of Urban Security, was used to justify the death of *two thousand* young men by the police (*Diario El Nacional*, September 19, 2000). Police abuse can be seen in the increasing cases recorded as "resistance to authority." This includes, to a large extent, deaths caused by an alleged police resistance [Personal conversation with the Chief of the Statistics Division of the Venezuelan Scientific Police (Cuerpo de Investigaciones Científicas, Penales y Criminalísticas), January 25, 2010]. In 1999, 607 cases were recorded; in 2003, the number of these cases quadrupled, reaching 2,305 deaths; and finally, in 2011, a record high: 3,492 [Source: División de Estadísticas, Cuerpo de Investigaciones Científicas Penales y Criminalísticas].

15. *Alcahueta* means a cover-up, a mother who conceals her son's actions

16. "El destino final de todo delincuente es la cárcel o bajo tierra." Statements from the Commander of Core 5 broadcasted through Venezolana de Televisión on September 6, 2010.

WORKS CITED

Adler de Lomnitz, Larissa. 1975. *Cómo sobreviven los marginados*. Mexico City: Siglo Veintiuno Editores.

Apprey, Maurice. 2004. "From the Events of History to a Sense of History: Aspects of Transgenerational Trauma and Brutality in the African-American Experience." In

Analysts in the Trenches: Streets, Schools, War Zones, edited by Bruce Sklarew, Stuart Twenlown, and Sallye Wilkinson. London: The Analytic Press.

Arendt, Hannah. 1997. *¿Qué es la Política?* Barcelona: Ediciones Paidós.

Auyero, Javier, Agustin Burbano de Lara, and Maria F. Berti. 2014. "Violence and the State at the Urban Margins." *Journal of Contemporary Ethnography.* Vol 43(1) 94–116.

Auyero, Javier. 2007. "Relatos etnográficos de violencias urbanas." In *Parias Urbanos. Marginalidad en la ciudada a comienzos del milenio,* edited by Loic Wacquant. Buenos Aires: Manantial.

Bayat, Asef. 2000. "From Dangerous Classes to Quiet Rebels: Politics of the Urban Subaltern in the Global South." *International Sociology* 15(3): 533–557.

Bourgois, Philippe. 1995. *In Search of Respect: Selling Crack in El Barrio.* New York: Cambridge University Press.

Bourgois, Philippe. 2009. "Treinta años de retrospectiva etnográfica sobre la violencia en las Américas." In *Guatemala. Violencias desbordadas,* edited by J. E. López García. Córdoba: Universidad de Córdoba.

Braun, Bruce, and James McCarthy. 2005. "Hurricane Katrina and Abandoned Being." *Environment and Planning* 23: 802–809.

Briceño-Leon, Roberto, and Veronica Zubillaga. 2002. "Violence and Globalisation in Latin America." *Current Sociology* 50 (1): 19–37.

Caldeira, Teresa. 2000. *Ciudad de Muros.* Barcelona: Editorial Gedisa.

Caldeira, Teresa. 1996. "Crime and Individual rights." In *Constructing Democracy. Human Rights, Citizenship and Society in Latina America,* edited by Elisabeth Jelin. Boulder, CO: Westview Press.

Campbell, Beatrix. 1993. *Goliath. Britain's Dangerous Places.* London: Methuen Publishing Ltd.

Cano, Ignacio. 2001. *La importancia del microdesarme en la prevención de la violencia.* Río de Janeiro: ISER y Universidad Estadual de Río de Janeiro.

Cariola, Cecilia. 1989. *Crisis, sobrevivencia y sector informal.* Caracas: Editorial Nueva Sociedad, ILDIS-CENDES.

Cilento, Alfredo. 2008. "Políticas de alojamiento en Venezuela: aciertos, errores y propuestas." *Tecnología y Construcción* 24 (2). Retrieved from http://www2.scielo.org.ve/scielo.php? script=sci_arttext&pid=S0798-96012008000200004&lng=en&nrm=iso.

Foucault, M. 2003. *Society Must Be Defended: Lectures at the Collège de France, 1975 – 1976.* New York: Picador

Gay, Robert. 2005. *Lucía. Testimonies of a Brazilian Drug Dealer's Woman.* Philadelphia: Temple University Press.

Gonzáles de la Rocha, Mercedes. 1999. "La reciprocidad amenazada: un costo más de la pobreza urbana." *Revista Latinoamericana de Estudios del Trabajo,* enero. 5 (9): 33-50

Huggins, Martha, Mika Haritos-Fatouros, and Philip Zimbardo. 2002. *Violence Workers: Police Torturers and Murderers Reconstruct Brazilian Atrocities.* Berkeley: University of California Press.

Hume, Mo. 2009. *The Politics of Violence: Gender, Conflict, and Community in El Salvador.* Malden, MA: Wiley-Blackwell.

Jelin, Elisabeth. 1996. "Citizenship Revisited." In *Constructing Democracy. Human Rights, Citizenship and Society in Latina America,* edited by Elisabeth Jelin and Eric Hershberg. Boulder, CO: Westview Press.

Katz, Jack. 1988. *Seductions of Crime.* New York: Basic Books.

Koonings, Kees, and Sjoerd Veenstra. 2007. "Exclusión social, actores armados y violencia." *Foro Internacional* 47(3): 616–636.

Latour, Bruno. 2005. *Reassembling the Social. An Introduction to Actor Network Theory.* New York: Oxford University Press.

Márquez, Patricia. 1999. *The Street is my Home. Youth and Violence in Caracas.* Stanford, CA: Stanford University Press.

Mauss, Marcel. 1997 [1950]. "Essaie sur le don. Forme et Raison de l'Echange dans les sociétés archaïques." In *Sociologie et Anthropologie.* Paris: Presses Universitaires de France, 145–284.

Pinheiro, Paulo. S. 1996. "Democracy without Citizenship: Democratization and Human Rights." Paper presented at the International Conference Democratic Transitions in Latina America and Eastern Europe. Paris, March 4–6.

Pynoos, Robert, Alan Steinberg, Grete Dyb, Armen Goenjian, Sue-Huei Chen, and Melissa Brymer. 2004. "Reverberations of Danger, Trauma and PTSD on Group Dynamics." In *Analysts in the Trenches: Streets, Schools, War Zones,* edited by Bruce Sklarew, Stuart Twenlown, and Sallye Wilkinson. London: The Analytic Press.

Rosaldo, Renato. 2004. "Grief and a Headhunter's Rage." In *Death, Mourning, and Burial. A Cross-cultural Reader,* edited by Antonius C. Robben. Malden: Blackwell Publishing Ltd.

Rotker, Susana. 2000. *Ciudadanías del Miedo.* Caracas: Nueva Sociedad.

Scheper-Hugues, N. (1992). *Death Without Weeping: The Violence of Everyday Life in Brazil.* Berkeley: University of California Press.

Scheper-Hughes, Nancy, and Philippe Bourgois. 2004. *Violence in War and Peace. An Anthology.* Oxford: Blackwell Publishing.

Volkan, Vamik. 2006. *Killing in the Name of Identity: A Study of Bloody Convicts.* Charlottesville, VA: Pitchstone Publishing.

Volkan, Vamik. 1997. *Bloodlines: From Ethnic Pride to Ethnic Terrorism.* Boulder, CO: Westview Press.

Wacquant, Loïc. 1992. "The Zone." *Actes de la Recherche en Sciences Sociales* 93: 39–59.

Wacquant, Loïc. 2002. "Scrutinizing the Street: Poverty, Morality, and the Pitfalls of Urban Ethnography." *American Journal of Sociology* 107(6):1468–1532.

Wacquant, Loïc. 2007. *Parias Urbanos. Marginalidad en la ciudada a comienzos del milenio.* Buenos Aires: Manantial.

Warr, Deborah. 2005. "Social Networks in a 'Discredited' Neighbourhood." *Journal of Sociology* 41(3): 285–308.

Zubillaga, Veronica. 2008. "La culebra: una mirada etnográfica a la trama de antagonismo masculino entre jóvenes de vida violenta en Caracas." *AKADEMOS* 10(1): 179–207.

Zubillaga, Veronica. 2009. "Gaining Respect": The Logic of Violence among Young Men in the Barrios of Caracas, Venezuela." In *Youth Violence in Latin America. Gangs and Juvenile Justice in Perspective,* edited by Gareth Jones and Dennis Rodgers. New York: Palgrave Macmillan.

CHAPTER 8

Managing in the Midst of Social Disaster

Poor People's Responses to Urban Violence

JAVIER AUYERO *AND* KRISTINE KILANSKI

INTRODUCTION

While political violence—once a defining feature of Latin America—has receded significantly over the course of the past two decades, street violence, drug-related violence, domestic abuse, child abuse, and sexual assault have risen dramatically in its stead (Arias and Goldstein 2010; Briceño-León 1999; Caldiera 2000; Goldstein 2012; Imbusch et al. 2011; Jones and Rodgers 2009; Koonings 2001; Koonings and Kruijt 2007; Pearce 2010). Rather than being distributed equally throughout the region, this "new urban violence" is concentrated within slums and shantytowns (Rodgers et al. 2013), disproportionately impacting the most disadvantaged populations, particularly adolescents and youth (Brinks 2008; CELS 2009; Gay 2005).[1]

The proliferation of interpersonal violence in poor urban communities has been devastating. On an individual level, exposure to chronic violence not only increases the risk of physical harm, or even death, but also contributes to a host of negative developmental, emotional, and behavioral outcomes (Farrell et al. 2007; Friday 1995; Holton 1995; Osofsky 1999; Popkin et al. 2010). At the aggregate level, chronic exposure to violence creates something akin to "social disaster" (Garbarino 1993), making communities at the urban margins hostile places to grow up and live (Guerra et al. 2003).

Those occupying the urban margins have not responded passively to the growing levels of violence in their communities. While journalistic, ethnographic, and other accounts of life at the urban margins point to a number of ways in which individuals and communities respond to violence—for example, through direct retaliation (Papachristos 2009), collective action (Hume 2009), and lynchings (Goldstein 2012; Snodgrass Godoy 2002)—the "specializ[ation] and balkaniz[ation]" of research on violence in the social sciences (Jackman 2002, 387) has prevented a full and nuanced account of community and individual responses to increased interpersonal violence at the urban margins from forming. Drawing on three years of collective ethnographic research in the violence-plagued community of Ingeniero Budge, we have developed a typology of "poor people's responses to urban violence" in an effort to fill this gap.

Our decision to present social action—which in practice is rich, complex, and boundary-blurring—in the form of a typology is twofold. First, we aim to break through the disciplinary and subject-area boundaries, noted by Jackman (2002) above, that have operated to obscure (1) a full understanding of the mechanisms through which violence is produced and reproduced, and (2) the widespread impact of violence on people living at the urban margins. Researchers of "family violence" (Gelles 1985; Kurst, Swanger, and Petcosky 2003; Tolan et al. 2006) rarely engage with research on street or gang violence (Harding 2010; Venkatesh 2008; McCart et al. 2007; Bourgois 1995) and vice versa. However, the community violence studied by Harding, Venkatesh, and others co-occurs with the family violence studied by Tolan, Gelles, and colleagues in the lives of many poor people, and as ethnographic accounts at the urban margins attest, there is no clear-cut boundary between violence occurring inside and outside the home (Bourgois 1995; Kotlowitz 1991; LeBlanc 2004; see Hume and Wilding, this volume). Indeed, different forms of violence tend to be positively correlated (Garbarino 1993; Guerra et al. 2003; Hume 2009; Korbin 2003; Margolin and Gordis 2000; Walton et al. 2009) and can feed into each other, and even morph types, forming what Philippe Bourgois and Nancy Scheper-Hughes have entitled the "continuum of violence" (Bourgois 2009; Scheper-Hughes and Bourgois 2004).

Our current work is heavily influenced by recent research that has attempted to shift the conversation from individual types of violence to an examination of the co-presence of, and relationship between, violence(s) in the lives of the poor (Hume 2009; Jones 2009; Richie 2012; Wilding 2010). For example, our typology sheds light on those occasions in which strategies to cope with interpersonal violence evoke even more violence (e.g., when the community engages in vigilante justice to punish a rapist; see Zubillaga et al., this volume).

Second, we offer this typology to expose a myth—a myth that has currency first and foremost among those living at the urban margins, and a myth that is often reproduced unquestioningly by researchers of violence. This myth is that when confronted with widespread interpersonal violence, people living at the urban margins are too paralyzed by fear to respond. By capturing the many things that people *do* to cope with violence, we hope to draw attention to the active efforts of those living in the urban periphery to construct meaningful lives for themselves *despite* their exposure to hostile conditions. We undertake this effort with the recognition that at least some of these responses contribute to the amplification, rather than the reduction or destabilization, of "new urban violence."

The focus of this chapter is on responses to widespread *interpersonal* violence. Importantly, interpersonal violence only comes into full relief when it is understood within a particular historical, political, economic, and cultural context, allowing researchers to consider how and why particular formations of violence have emerged within a given social space. Interpersonal violence, in many ways, can be considered a response in itself to the economic, political, structural, and symbolic forms of violence that contribute to the very creation of the urban margins (Scheper-Hughes and Bourgois 2004). These same forces produce hierarchies *within* the urban margins, which make some individuals and groups in inner cities, favelas, or barrios more vulnerable to certain forms of violence, or more likely to take certain steps in reaction to violence, than others. The typology we put forth is designed as a blueprint that can be usefully applied to help make sense of the manifestations of and responses to interpersonal violence operating in other field sites across the Americas; it cannot, given the reasons above, replace the practice of conducting careful ethnographic research to unearth the nuances of how violence shapes the lives of individuals within particular social spaces.

Below, we provide further context on Ingeniero Budge and detail the methods we used to gather insights into poor people's multiple and varied responses to widespread interpersonal violence. Drawing on field notes and interviews, we lay out our four-part typology of poor people's responses to violence, detailing responses that are violent and nonviolent as well as individual and collective in nature.

SITE AND METHODS

Ingeniero Budge (pop. 170,000) sits in the southern part of metropolitan Buenos Aires. Located adjacent to the banks of the highly polluted Riachuelo River, extreme levels of infrastructural deprivation—or what Braun and McCarthy (2005) would term the "material dimension of state abandonment"—characterize the area: unpaved streets, open-air sewers, broken sidewalks, scarce lighting, and random garbage collection.

But the state has not entirely deserted Ingeniero Budge. One public hospital, several public schools, the Asignación Universal por Hijo (AUH) (the Argentine conditional cash transfer program effective since 2008), and other welfare programs (e.g., Argentina Trabaja, Plan Vida) mark the state presence in the area and provide assistance to most of the area's residents. Patronage networks linked to the governing party and soup kitchens funded by Catholic charities are also sources of assistance for those in need in the area, providing crucial resources such as food and medicine. These public and charitable sources of income and aid are supplemented in most homes by work in the informal labor market, most typically in construction, domestic service, and scavenging.

In addition, many of the residents of Ingeniero Budge rely on the largest street fair in the country, located at the neighborhood's northern limit, to earn additional income. Known by the name La Salada, the fair consists of three different markets (Urkupiña, Ocean, and Punta Mogote) where, twice a week, thousands of shoppers converge to buy counterfeit apparel and small electronics as well as food.[2] According to the Economic Commission of the European Union (*La Nación*, March 10, 2009), La Salada is the "world's emblem of the production and commercialization of falsified brand merchandise." Either as owners or employees of one of the fair's thousands of stalls or as workers in one of the hundreds of sweatshops that manufacture the goods sold there, many residents from the neighborhood benefit from the presence of this vast street fair (D'Angiolillo et al. 2010).

This chapter is based on twenty-five formal, in-depth interviews with residents of Ingeniero Budge as well as—perhaps more importantly—innumerable informal conversations and direct observations carried out over a three-year period (June 2009–June 2012) by a team of collaborating ethnographers. During this period, one of the research collaborators for this project also worked in the area as an elementary school teacher in two public schools (Auyero and Berti 2013). The article draws on the detailed ethnographic notes this research collaborator took based on her students' activities inside and outside of the school and on dozens of conversations with school teachers and parents. This chapter also draws upon one hundred short interviews (lasting between thirty minutes and an hour) with residents of Ingeniero Budge designed to catalogue the most common problems in the community from the perspective of those who live there. Interviewees were selected via snowball sampling. In addition, the first author conducted interviews with five doctors working at the local hospital and the local health center, and accessed hard-to-find data on homicides in the area through personal contacts at the Defensoría Municipal, the office that collects death records from the local morgue.

Fieldwork continued more sporadically throughout the second half of 2012 and the first three months of 2013. During this time, the first author interviewed "expert" informants, including doctors at the main local hospital (who provided data on injuries and deaths in the area), seven police agents who work in the area, and a social worker at the local public school. Auyero also attended a community meeting and a protest rally to address neighborhood violence, both held in February 2013. Finally, Auyero conducted archival research on local newspapers (all of them accessible online), focusing on instances of interpersonal violence (injuries in interpersonal disputes and homicides) between 2009 and 2012 in order to pinpoint the geographic location of this violence, information not recorded by the Defensoría.

Auyero tape-recorded, transcribed, and systematically analyzed the in-depth interviews for their content. Field notes were coded and analyzed using open and focused coding (Emerson et al. 1995). Applying the evidentiary criteria normally used for ethnographic research (Becker 1958, 1970; Katz 1982, 2001, 2002), higher evidentiary value was assigned to individual acts or patterns of conduct recounted by many observers than to those recounted by only one observer. Although particular in their details, the testimonies, field notes, and vignettes selected below represent behavior observed or heard about with consistent regularity during the course of our fieldwork.[3]

VIOLENCE ON THE GROUND

For the purposes of this chapter, we adopt a modified version of the World Health Organization's (WHO) definition of violence as "the intentional use of physical force or power, threatened or actual, against oneself, another person, or against a group or community, that either results in or has a high likelihood of resulting in injury, death, [or] psychological harm" (Krug et al. 2002, 4). In this paper, we focus attention on *interpersonal* and *collective* violence. The first includes family and intimate partner violence (i.e., physical aggression "between family members and intimate partners, usually, though not exclusively, taking place in the home" [Krug et al 2002, 5]) and community violence (i.e., physical aggression "between individuals who are unrelated, and who may or may not know each other, generally taking place outside the home" [Krug et al. 2002, 5]). Our definition of collective violence departs from the one provided by Krug et al in that it refers to any "episodic social interaction that immediately inflicts physical damage on persons and/or objects ("damage" includes forcible seizure of persons or objects over restraint or resistance), involves at least two perpetrators of damage, and results at least in part from coordination among persons who perform the damaging acts" (Tilly 2003, 12). By contrast, the WHO's definition confines collective violence to that inflicted "by larger groups such as states, organized political groups, militia groups and terrorist organizations" (Krug et al. 2002, 4).[4]

Using a restricted definition of violence, and drawing upon official figures, we can assert that over the past twenty years, violence has increased substantially in Argentina's most populous state—in line with trends in other urban areas of Latin America. Official data for Buenos Aires show a doubling of crime rates between 1995 and 2008, from 1,114 to 2,010 criminal episodes per 100,000 residents and from 206 crimes against persons (e.g., homicide, assault, and battery) to 535 per 100,000 residents. Reports of sexual and domestic abuse have also risen during the last two decades (*La Nación*, February 24, 2008). This violence does not uniformly affect all neighborhoods. For example, the intensification in violence is even more pronounced in poverty-stricken Ingeniero Budge. According to the municipal Defensoría General, homicides in Ingeniero Budge have increased 180 percent since 2007—from seventeen to forty-eight between January and October of 2012 (meanwhile the population of the municipality where Ingeniero Budge is located grew only 4.2 percent between 2001 and 2010). The murder rate in Ingeniero Budge is thus 28.4 per 100,000 residents—four times that of the state of Buenos Aires.

In-depth interviews with five physicians who work in the emergency rooms at the local hospital and health center, and with a social worker at the local school, confirm that interpersonal violence has skyrocketed. "Today," says a doctor with fifteen years of experience in the district, "it is much more common to attend to patients with injuries provoked by gunshots or knives . . . at least one per day." The director of the emergency room at the local hospital seconds this general impression; he says that the number of people wounded by gunshots or knives (*heridos por armas de fuego y arma blanca*) has increased 10 percent each year throughout the last decade. All five of the physicians agree that the number of patients injured in street fights increases during the two days a week in which La Salada is open. As one emergency room doctor puts it: "The fair is a source of conflict. There's an increase in interpersonal aggression during the days its markets open to the public. Thousands of people come with cash to buy [goods] or with merchandise to sell. There are many robberies, lots of them at gunpoint."[5] Unsurprisingly, criminal activity and the violence that often accompanies such activity preoccupy residents. Most of our one hundred interviewees cited delinquency, insecurity, robberies, and drug dealing as their main concerns regarding life in Ingeniero Budge.

Small "bands" (e.g., "La banda del gordo Mario," "La banda de los Guille," and "Los corsarios") devoted to the storage, preparation, and distribution of drugs in Ingeniero Budge and surrounding areas have helped to fuel this rise in interpersonal violence (see Sain 2009). For example, shots between police and drug dealers were exchanged several times throughout the course of our fieldwork in response to police operations to seize the stashes of cocaine and *paco* (the local name for free-base cocaine) held by bands operating in the area.[6]

During our fieldwork with third, fourth, and sixth graders, aged eight to thirteen, shootouts, armed robberies, rapes or attempted rapes, and street fights were routine topics of conversation (for a description of violence among children in the neighborhood, see Auyero and Berti 2013). Hardly a week went by without one or more of the sixty children describing episodes involving violence that they had heard about, witnessed, or experienced firsthand.

Although no official figures exist, interviews with social workers and teachers at the local school suggest that physical aggression between family members and intimate partners, sexual violence, and child abuse have also intensified. As one counselor puts it, "violence inside the family has reached unsuspected levels." Our field notes, plagued with instances of children talking about their parents fighting and/or beating them, attest to the generalized character of this type of violence: "My dad fights with my mother all the time . . . Last time, he nearly killed her," Jonathan (age thirteen) told us. "[Excerpt from field diary, March 17, 2010] Several red spots dot Joana's (age eight) notebook. 'Sauce,' I think. 'She has been eating while doing homework.' But I'm wrong. It's blood. 'My dad beats me so that I do the homework,' she states matter-of-factly when I innocently ask her about the red spots." Sexual violence inside and outside the home (in the form of rapes or attempted rapes) is also quite widespread, impacting—as elsewhere—girls more than boys.

Life in Ingeniero Budge, as it should be clear by now, is anything but peaceful. Violence is experienced, witnessed, or deliberated over by residents in their homes, schools, and streets. What do residents do about this wide-spread violence? How do they individually or collectively respond to what they describe as the "general insecurity" produced through chronic exposure to violence?

During the course of fieldwork, many residents told us that "there's nothing you can do" about the violence that puts them and their children in harm's way. "People here are scared," said one long-term resident named Laura (age fifty-one). "If you do something, they [the perpetrators] might get you and hit you or your family. They may retaliate," she continued. Verónica (age thirty-four), added, "People do not report it to the police because they are scared." At a community meeting held in Ingeniero Budge, most residents agreed that fear has a demobilizing effect: "There are a lot of people who are angry about all this insecurity, but they are afraid to come to the meetings . . . they don't want to report anything because they are afraid they won't be able to go back to their homes." "People here are afraid," they said, "because they think that the drug dealers are in cahoots with the authorities." Fear, the residents concluded, "paralyzes us all."

Although the residents of Ingeniero Budge described themselves and their neighbors as too paralyzed by fear to confront violence in their community, our field notes capture a multitude of strategies utilized by residents to cope with or counteract their hostile surroundings. As a matter of fact, at the same community meeting in which people expressed paralyzing fear, a public rally was organized to claim police protection (more below), offering a welcome reminder of the contradiction between what people say and what people do (Khan and Jerolmack 2013). Despite their expressions of fear, impotence, and (perceived) "futility" (Bandura 1982), our field notes from Ingeniero Budge show that individuals and communities do not stand by passively in the face of widespread violence.

Our goal in this chapter is to draw attention to the many and varied ways in which individuals and communities respond to violence. Careful analysis of interviews, informal conversations, and field notes gathered during three years of research in Ingeniero Budge reveal four categories of responses that locals have devised to combat the threat of, or exposure to, interpersonal violence:

1. Individualized nonviolent responses, as when residents seclude themselves inside their homes, increase the supervision of their children, bolster their own precautions when venturing into public space, fortify their homes, and (occasionally) report incidents to the police.
2. Individualized violent responses, as when residents forcibly confine their children when they perceive they are "getting in trouble," or beat

(actual or potential) perpetrators of violence (including their own children) and/or those who are thought to be "bad influences."
3. Collective nonviolent responses, as when residents come together in meetings and public rallies to protest police inaction (and complicity with crime) and demand state protection, or when they organize a public shaming of known drug dealers.
4. Collective violent responses, as when residents attack the homes of rapists, beat perpetrators, and physically punish thieves.

These are analytical distinctions that get blurred in daily practice. The same people who seclude their families to protect themselves and their loved ones from street violence (category 1, above) may also rely on physical constraint or violence to keep children from "falling in with the wrong crowd" (*las malas compañías*, as they put it) (category 2, above). Violence overlaps and bleeds (Hume 2009). The victim of violence in one setting may be the perpetrator of violence in another, such as when women who have experienced long-term domestic abuse kill their partners (Richie 1996), or when a father beats his son after the family home is ransacked by drug dealers looking for money that the son owes them.

The following ethnographic reconstructions illustrate the variety of responses to actual or potential violence (individualized and collective, violent and nonviolent) captured in our field notes with regularity, as they evolve in and interpenetrate the lives of poor residents.

Individual Nonviolent Responses

Many of the adult residents we interviewed reported coping with widespread violence by secluding themselves and their loved ones inside their homes. Residents explained: "I stay in my room, watch TV, I don't get involved with anybody." "Right after dinner, we all get inside, and we padlock our door—When the street market is open, there are many robberies, and there's always some crazy kid with a gun, and they might shoot at each other, and a stray bullet might hit my kids . . . So, we stay inside. We try to keep the same schedule every day."

Residents have not only secluded themselves in their homes, but have also made physical modifications to their homes that increased their (perceived) level of safety. Like middle-class families in other parts of the Americas (Caldeira 2000), many residents in Ingeniero Budge have built higher walls around their properties, installed stronger doors ("so they can't kick it down and break in"), and added padlocks to their windows.

Not surprisingly, these residents reported exercising caution when entering public spaces, for example, by avoiding travel in certain neighborhoods at night or altogether and by devising practices that increased their level of perceived safety, such as walking in pairs or groups. Residents say: "You can't go to work in peace. I'm always looking around to see if someone is following me, always watching my back . . . We can't live like this." "I don't walk around . . . I always take a car service when it gets dark." "I always make sure someone waits for me at the bus stop."

In addition to engaging in self-monitoring in public spaces, parents closely supervise the activities of their children, for example, through limiting their children's mobility and regulating their interactions with outsiders. One resident explained: "I take care of my kids by talking to them, by checking with whom they get together, by not letting them out after certain hours." A second resident added: "I try to be with them, close to them, to avoid something bad happening to them, I don't want them to be far from me . . . Anything can happen to them, these days there are many daring men (atrevidos). There are men who abuse young girls. I try to get them to stay inside, to not to leave the house." "You have to be with them all the time, they have to call me often if they are outside," explained a third resident.

Residents clearly go to great lengths to avoid violence. But given the chronic nature of violence in the community, residents are unable to protect themselves fully, despite their best efforts. Some residents report the violence they experience and/or witness to authorities—though this is an infrequent individual-level response to violence. One neighbor clearly articulates the reasons that residents of Ingeniero Budge are hesitant to call the police in response to a violent episode: "The cops are always late, to collect the body if someone was killed, or to stitch you up if you've been raped." What Kirk and Papachristos (2011) call "legal cynicism,"—the shared belief that law enforcement agents are "illegitimate, unresponsive, and ill equipped to ensure public safety"—is quite generalized in Ingeniero Budge. Legal cynicism emerges out of the perceived unavailability or bias of law enforcement agents, but it is also reinforced by the suspected complicity between cops and criminals (more below).

Despite a generalized distrust of the state police (an institution that residents perceive as highly corrupt and brutal),[7] some residents resort to the police in a last ditch attempt to (re)gain control over sons or daughters involved in drug use and perceived to be at physical risk. Mothers and fathers turn to the state out of impotence and fear: impotence in the face of the lure of highly addictive substances (such as paco) and fear of having a child either murdered by a drug gang or killed from an overdose. Parents' dread and helplessness in response to drug-addicted children was palpable throughout our fieldwork. For example, one parent explained: "You can't do anything against drugs . . . I die if he dies . . . you have no idea how I anguish every time I think that he can die because of the drugs." Without access to other forms of support such as drug treatment facilities, parents in Ingeniero Budge summon the punitive arm of a state they distrust to control and discipline the lives of their sons or daughters.[8] From this perspective, the police force has the same "sociological ambivalence" that the prison system has for many inmates' relatives in the United States (Comfort 2008).

Individualized Violence

Individuals may also respond to violence (directly or indirectly experienced violence and/or prospective violence) with more violence. For example, women may respond to attacks or abuse perpetrated by intimate partners with violence in self-defense, in retaliation, and/or to preempt further incidents of abuse. (We recorded multiple testimonies of women who punched or knifed their spouses in response to physical and/or sexual assault).

Parents may engage in physical aggression against sons and daughters in an attempt to keep their children safe. Fists, kicks, sticks, and chains are deployed to convince children to stay away from "*malas compañías*" (friends deemed bad influences). If children have "already [fallen]," parents may engage in physical violence in an attempt to control their children's addiction to drugs or alcohol and the violent behavior that sometimes accompanies habitual drug use. Parents say things like: "Next time I see you with a joint, I'll break your fingers"; "He came home so drugged up, I punched him in the face until blood came out of my fingers"; and "I chained her to the bed so that she couldn't go out and smoke."

After a particularly difficult week with her son Leonardo (age sixteen), who is addicted to free-base cocaine, Ana (age forty-five) told us: "I hit him with the broom. I hit him everywhere, arms, legs . . . I lost it . . . I swear to you, I lost it, I didn't want to stop beating him until I could see blood coming out." Her voice trembling, her eyes filled with tears, she then adds: "Leonardo has stolen many things from me. The first time I beat him was when he sold a cellphone he stole from us . . . I beat him really bad; I grabbed his fingers, and told him that if he did that again, I was going to break his fingers, one by one so that he couldn't steal again. He never took a cellphone again, but he stole sneakers, t-shirts, socks . . . He steals stuff from me and resells it for 20 pesos so that he can buy his drugs."

Ana is afraid her son will be killed. Violent deaths of young people occur with some regularity in Ingeniero Budge, meaning parents' fear for their children's safety is often justified. Leonardo's half-brother, Matías, was killed in an attempted robbery a few months before we met (his half-dead body was abandoned in front of the local hospital, presumably by his partners in crime, and his killer is still unknown). Ana portrays her efforts to control Leonardo through physical force as justified because they help, in her mind, to protect him from being killed: "Last night, he came back home high, drugged up, aggressive. He still obeys me and he has not tried to hit me yet, but the friend with whom he does drugs, does not even respect his mother, he is out of control . . . What if [Leonardo] is the next one to die? I'm really anguished. When he comes back drugged, I can't do anything else other than beat him, because he doesn't understand me, because I've spoken to him and he never listens. And I don't want to hit him anymore, for him, for me, for my daughters who see everything."

The use of force in an effort to prevent children from further harm is also illustrated in the case of Alicia (55), her son Victor (27), and her friend's son Ezequiel (17). "When Ezequiel came back to the house," recalls Alicia, "he was about to smoke another pipe [of *paco*]. I struck him across his face. 'Son of a bitch,' I told him, 'Don't you see that you are making your mother suffer? She is very worried about you. And don't you even think about hurting her, because I'll strike you harder next time.'" According to Alicia, Ezequiel needs to "respect" his mother, a respect that is attained, if need be, through the use of physical force. As Alicia puts it: "When my kid [Victor] disrespected me . . . he still has the marks of the metal chain with which I hit him on the head." Alicia not only hit her son with that chain but also used it to tie him up. As she recollects: "When he was drugged, he would not obey me. He escaped from the house. I chained him to his bed so that he couldn't leave his room. I cried so many times for him. I told him I didn't like to hit him, and that I only did that because he was high on drugs." All the violence didn't "cure him," she admits; he was "rescued" in prison: "He stopped taking drugs when he did time for a robbery . . . those three years behind bars did him good. Now he is cured."

Importantly, drug treatment facilities, mental health facilities, and other institutional supports that middle-class parents may turn to for assistance in dealing with at-risk children are not accessible to most parents living in this region. Thus, most parents perceive only two available alternatives for protecting at-risk children from harm: physical control (that sometimes involves physical violence and other times involves only monitoring of whereabouts) and turning children over to the authorities.

Collective Violence

Over the course of our fieldwork, we heard dozens of stories about the rape or attempted rape of girls by their acquaintances or family members. In most cases, the perpetrators were uncles or stepfathers. While acknowledging its widespread character, a social worker at the local school states matter-of-factly that "nobody reports those cases because the police laugh at them." Police authorities, however, state that reports of sexual violence inside the home have been steadily growing. We also heard many stories about sexual violence that took place outside the home and were perpetrated by people unrelated to the victim. Over the course of individual interviews, parents articulate their fear of allowing their daughters to roam alone or freely in public spaces: "I can't let her go alone . . . what if they rape her? It's frightening." Despite this panic—a panic with a very real basis—neighbors do not trust the police to address these kinds of cases when they occur. They think cops are slow in reacting against sexual violence and/or complicit in it (rumors about the existence of what a neighbor calls "the blowjob police"—i.e., cops who demand sexual favors from neighborhood adolescents—run rampant).[9] As a result, neighbors rarely rely on legal charges (and a possible arrest) to punish perpetrators of sexual violence. Instead they deploy targeted collective violence. "My cousin was almost raped yesterday [a few blocks from the school]. My neighbors went to the home of one of those *violines*, and kicked his door down," explained one resident. *Violines*, Josiana (8) matter-of-factly informs us, are "those who make you [have] babies."

Melanie's mother explains the origins of the bullet that her daughter has lodged in her leg, an explanation that demonstrates how collective violent retaliation may be utilized as a strategy to respond to interpersonal violence.

> See, that son of a bitch wanted to rape her. It was on December 24 (Christmas Eve). We have a big family, so we had asked a neighbor to roast some meat for us. This is a neighbor I've known all my life. My brother-in-law brought home some of the food, but not all, so I sent Melanie and my niece to pick up the rest. When they got to our neighbor's house, he was drunk, and he had a knife in his hand. He wanted to rape them. He told Melanie and my niece that if they didn't suck his dick, he was going to kill one, and then rape and kill the other. Luckily, they were able to push him aside— maybe because he was really drunk—and they escaped. They ran home and told us what had just happened. My husband, my brothers-in-law, my brother and some other neighbors went to his house and beat the shit out of him (*lo recagaron a palos*). They beat his face to a pulp; he was full of blood. They left him there, lying on the floor, and came back home. After dinner, around midnight, that son of a bitch came

to my house and shot at Melanie. Luckily, the bullet hit her in the leg. All the men in
my house went back to his house and beat the shit out of him again. I had to run to the
Gandulfo [local hospital thirty minutes away]. I spent the night of the 24th and the
25th there. They checked her out very well, to see if she had been raped. Luckily, the
guy didn't get to do anything to her.

In the absence of a state institution that is deemed responsive and fair when
dealing with crime and/or violence, people have long taken collective
steps to protect community norms about appropriate behavior. Although
lynching became a racialized practice in the United States—employed by
whites against blacks (typically based on flimsy evidence of black men's
predation of white women and often directed at those in positions of economic and political power in the black community, suggesting alternative
motives for punishment [Wells 1997; Feimster 2009; Freedman 2011])—
prior to the turn of the twentieth century, both blacks and whites living in
the South utilized lynchings to police members of their own racial groups
in the absence of a strong state presence (Hill 2010).

Collective violence is not only utilized in response to acts of sexual
violence. During our fieldwork we were informed of several instances
in which residents had joined together against people victimizing their
neighborhood through burglaries or robberies. Occasionally this type of
reaction has lethal consequences, such as when a twenty-three-year-old
man was killed by a group of neighbors who had caught him by surprise when he was trying to break into a home (*Crónica*, April 13, 2011).
A few weeks before the incident, a neighbor from the area had told us
that, after repeated break-ins, residents were "organizing to defend"
themselves.

Collective Nonviolent Responses

People in Ingeniero Budge also gathered together to take collective nonviolent action in an attempt to counteract violence in their communities. The organization Mothers Against Paco is comprised of a small
but active group of mothers whose sons and daughters are addicted to
free-base cocaine. They have been active in the neighborhood since 2004
when, according to one of its founding members, Isabel, they began to
"notice these kids, all dirty, without much clothing, walking like zom-
bies." At the time, Isabel was the coordinator of a soup kitchen and was
unfamiliar with the physical and psychological effects of *paco*, the drug
to which many of these zombie-like kids were addicted. Through basic
research and meetings with authorities and physicians, Isabel and her

neighbors, in a kind of grassroots collective action that resembled those organized around environmental pollutants, quickly became skilled at absorbing scientific knowledge (Brown 1991; Brown et al. 2000; Cable and Walsh 1991).

The violence triggered by drug dealing and consumption did not escape Isabel's and her neighbors' notice, and the group soon began to organize protests against the presence of dealers in their neighborhoods. In an innovative move, the members of Mothers Against Paco began engaging in public shaming (locally known as *escraches*) of drug dealers by marching around dealers' houses, denouncing the deleterious effects of the product that dealers were selling, and demanding court action. "At the beginning," Isabel remembered, "it was just three or four of us . . . but then, we grew . . . in the last *escrache*, we were more than one hundred . . . the judge took notice and issued a search warrant."

Peaceful collective action is also directed against the authorities, particularly the police, who are seen as complicit with the violence that impacts the area. On February 13, 2013, a group of two dozen residents of Ingeniero Budge attended a meeting called by community organizers and Mothers Against Paco. The meeting was called after the murder of sixty-three-year-old resident Luciano Tolaba. Tolaba resisted a robbery—believed to have been initiated by three young adults under the influence of drugs and/or alcohol—and was punched and stoned to death as a result.

The explicit purpose of the meeting was to demand greater protection from the local police precinct. But the meeting also served as an arena for residents to vent their frustrations with police complicity with drug dealers and police inaction in the face of increasing violence in the neighborhood. What was said there (and screamed and chanted at the rally two days later) shows that overwhelming violence has the potential to unite residents as it becomes collectively defined as a contentious political issue. The following field note is representative of the sorts of conversations that took place at the community meeting, and later, at the rally:

> February 13, 2013. Nerina, a grassroots activist, opens the meeting and attempts to summarize the impetus for the gathering: "There have been many deaths in the neighborhood recently, and the police is nowhere to be found . . . there are a lot of kids who are consuming *paco*, and lots of *transas* (drug dealers)." Isabel, the most outspoken leader of Mothers Against Paco, shares: "Things are quite messed up. I do not want more police, or *mano dura* . . . I want the police to do their job. We all know where the *transas* are . . . we have insecurity because the kids who are on drugs, steal in order to buy." Alicia, another leader of Mothers Against Paco, begins to speak

about police complicity with dealers: "They know where they are but they don't do anything." It is then the turn of Elisa, a 50-year-old woman whose son has recently been murdered. In a low, trembling voice, she clearly elaborates the problem they are all facing: "My son was killed because of a fight between two bands that wanted to control the area. We all know who killed him but the state prosecutor wants witnesses. And who is going to be a witness? The kids [who know] are afraid because they know that the cops are complicit with the dealers. Nobody wants to talk, nobody wants to report. Everybody knows who killed my son, but nobody talks."

For about an hour, those at the meeting shared stories about their concerns with sons or daughters who are addicted to *paco*, pills, and/or alcohol ("Many, many times, I gave him money so that he could buy drugs . . . because I don't want him to be around stealing. I never told him the money was for drugs, but I knew . . . I just don't want him to be killed trying to get money to buy."), and about police protection or complicity ("I asked one of the dealers if he wasn't afraid of the cops . . . and he looked at me and said that you just have to bribe them."). The phrase "liberated zone" (*zona liberada*) was repeatedly uttered, conveying both widespread knowledge about police complicity and also a generalized feeling of being "unprotected." As the meeting came to a close, attendees agreed upon the main claim they would make in the rally that would proceed two days later: "We want the police and the courts to fulfill their role. No more liberated zones. Those who consume should not go to jail, dealers should be imprisoned." The flyers calling residents to the rally summarized their point of view: "Enough drugs and deaths in our community. No more liberated zones."

> Friday, February 18. Approximately 80 residents march through the streets of Budge carrying placards that read "No more liberated zones" and chant songs that claim "Justice for Tolaba." Residents gather peacefully in front of the local precinct demanding protection and police action against drug dealers. An eight year old carries a sign that, I believe, encapsulates the fear and impotence that overwhelms Budge's residents: "I'm growing up in a neighborhood full of drugs and criminals. What do I do?"

Two weeks later, partially in response to this collective mobilization (and partially, due to internal disputes within the police), five agents from Budge's police station were indicted, accused of illegal detentions, fabricating reports (falsely accusing neighbors of drug dealing), planting evidence, and (possibly) distributing drugs. The chief of the station was removed when forty bags of marijuana were found inside the precinct, presumably used to plant evidence and/or to distribute in the area. This incident shows that through joining together neighbors can and do make their communities safer.

DISCUSSION AND CONCLUSIONS

Our ethnographic research in Ingeniero Budge reveals the multiple ways in which residents at the urban periphery seek to cope with the "generalized insecurity" of living in neighborhoods plagued by chronic interpersonal violence. Despite residents' claims that the "fear" produced through exposure to chronic violence "paralyzes us all," they are proactive in protecting themselves and their loved ones from violence (for example, by secluding themselves in their homes, or acting with great care in public spaces) and coping with the violence perpetrated against them when it, almost inevitably, occurs.

Sometimes residents respond to interpersonal violence individually; other times they join together with family, friends, and/or neighbors to take collective action. Most of the residents' actions are aimed toward avoiding or reducing their exposure to violence. However, sometimes their responses end up perpetuating violence—for example, when residents lynch a neighbor suspected of rape or child molestation, or when a parent physically assaults a child in an attempt to intimidate him or her from engaging in dangerous activities, such as drug use.

The typology we have laid out based on our findings in Ingeniero Budge can be applied to other sites to help make sense of the active efforts of residents coping with the "social disaster" produced through widespread chronic violence (Garbarino 1993) to make safer and more meaningful lives for themselves and their loved ones. Context, as always, matters.

The residents of Ingeniero Budge (like residents in many communities at the urban peripheries) largely lack access to trusted state and/or private institutions. When sons and daughters fall in with *las malas compañías*, parents in Ingeniero Budge draw on the limited array of resources that they *do have* to keep their children safe—one of which includes their fists. When parents turn to the state for help with their children, it is evidence of their desperation rather than a vote of confidence in their local government agencies, which they largely view as corrupt, debased, and ineffectual. An understanding of the local institutional context, then, is necessary for understanding the shape that violence and negotiations with violence take within a community or neighborhood (Harding 2010). Further research should examine when, how, and the effect to which the state polices poor peoples' disputes and how state presence impacts the character and course of local responses to violence.

Access to institutional resources is typically stratified along the lines of gender, race, age, sexuality, and other such group affiliations. Groups who have more access to police protection will likely respond to violence in different ways than their neighbors, for example, through reporting violence to authorities rather than taking punishment into their own hands. Thus, a better understanding of how responses to violence are shaped by these socially constituted categories (which have different meanings attached to them depending on local context) is needed. Gender is an especially important analytical tool for understanding how communities and individuals work to mitigate chronic violence. In Ingeniero Budge, as in communities all across the Americas, care for children falls mainly to mothers, many of whom are the sole or main providers for their families. The everyday responses to violence noted in our typology are a key part of the practice of mothering in communities along the urban periphery. Mothers, our research suggests, are key in teaching children how to cope with *and* how to use violence (see also Wilding 2010).

Finally, future research needs to examine when, how, and why some responses to violence become part of individuals' toolkits for coping with their hostile surroundings rather than others. We need to scrutinize what people seek to accomplish when they use, threaten to use, or refuse to use physical force (whether it is to gain respect [Bourgois 1995; Penglase 2010; Zubillaga 2009], to seek retaliation [Jacobs 2004; Jacobs and Wright 2006; Mullins, Wright, and Jacobs 2004; Papachristos 2009], or something else), and what they learn in their repeated attempts to deal with violence. Doing so will allow us to grapple with one of the most difficult open questions in violence studies: does, and under what conditions does, violence become "normalized" (Bourgois 1995; Scheper-Hughes 1992)?

NOTES

1. Funds for this project were provided by the National Science Foundation (NSF Award SES-1153230), the Harry Frank Guggenheim Foundation, and by a grant from the Office of the Vice President for Research at the University of Texas at Austin. Funds were also provided by the Joe R. and Teresa Lozano Long Professorship and the Andrew W. Mellon Foundation Faculty Travel Grant given by the Teresa Lozano Long Institute of Latin American Studies (LLILAS).
2. Although La Salada remains largely unregulated, the state makes impromptu appearances at the market, demanding property taxes, investigating violations of international copyright laws, and/or demanding sewage systems that do not pollute the (adjacent) Riachuelo (Scarfi and Di Peco 2011). For insightful accounts of the history and workings of these markets, see Hacher 2011 and Girón 2011.
3. Our study was approved by the University of Texas at Austin IRB (protocol # 2011-05-0126).
4. We are aware of more encompassing definitions of violence (Bourgois 2009; Farmer 2004; Jackman 2002), but for analytical purposes in this paper we restrict the definition of violence to the "behavior by persons against persons that intentionally threatens, attempts, or actually inflicts physical harm" (Reiss and Roth 1993, 35). On the advantages of a circumscribed definition of violence, see Tilly 2003.

5. Out of the twenty-seven homicides reported between 2009 and 2013 in local newspapers, eight took place adjacent to the street fair—most of them in relation to a robbery attempt. Newspapers underreport homicides (note the discrepancy between number of homicides reported by local media and the number of homicides recorded by the Defensoría General). We include newspaper information in order to pinpoint the geographic location of the homicides as this information is not recorded by the Defensoría.

6. For journalistic reports on the effects of this drug among the marginalized youth, see "Lost in an Abyss of Drugs, and Entangled by Poverty," *New York Times*, July 29, 2009; "Perderse en la garras de la muerte," *La Nación*, September 20, 2008; "A New Scourge Sweeps through Argentine Ghettos: 'Paco,'" *Christian Science Monitor*, April 5, 2006. For an ethnographic account, see Epele 2010.

7. Police brutality is part of the standard operating procedure of the state police in Buenos Aires—especially when poor youth from shantytowns and squatter settlements are involved (CELS 2012; Daroqui et al. 2009). In Ingeniero Budge, this "violent and arbitrary penalization of poverty" (Müller 2012, 16) took the form of an infamous "massacre" in 1987 in which three youngsters from the neighborhood were brutally murdered by the local police. The locale also suffered five cases of lethal police violence between 2005 and 2011 (CORREPI 2012).

8. Adults' reliance on a corrupt and brutal state in an effort to protect children and young adults is not without historical precedence. Cheryl Hicks (2010) found multiple examples of black working-class families voluntarily submitting their daughters to the criminal justice system in an effort to keep them safe from the perceived moral and physical dangers presented by early twentieth-century urban life. Hicks writes: "Working-class families' concern about their daughters and young female kin was shaped by their specific perceptions of their neighborhood's reputation. When young black women rejected their family's attempts to protect and guide them by establishing clear rules, some elders made their private concern about these young women public and sought to utilize the wayward minor laws" (188).

9. See newspaper report "Deseos Urgentes," published in *Página/12*, March 19, 2012 (www.pagina12.com.ar). Similarly, multiple US scholars have drawn attention to the role of the police in the sexual victimization of poor women, queer youth of color, and other marginalized groups (Mogul, Ritchie, and Whitlock 2011; Richie 2012).

WORKS CITED

Arias, Desmond, and Daniel Goldstein, eds. 2010. *Violent Democracies in Latin America*. Durham, NC: Duke University Press.

Auyero, Javier, and Maria Fernanda Berti. 2013. *La violencia en los márgenes*. Buenos Aires: Katz Ediciones.

Bandura, Albert. 1982. "Self-efficacy Mechanism in Human Agency." *American Psychologist* 37(2): 122–147.

Becker, Howard. 1958. "Problems of Inference and Proof in Participant Observation." *American Sociological Review* 23: 652–60.

Becker, Howard. 1970. *Sociological Work: Methods and Substance*. Chicago: Aldine.

Bourgois, Philippe. 2009. "Recognizing Invisible Violence: A Thirty-year Ethnographic Retrospective." In *Global Health in Times of Violence*, edited by Barbara Rylko-Bauer, Linda Whiteford, and Paul Farmer. Santa Fe, NM: School of Advanced Research Press, 18–40.

Bourgois, Philippe. 1995 (2003). *In Search of Respect: Selling Crack in el Barrio.* 2nd ed. Cambridge: Cambridge University Press.

Braun, Bruce, and James McCarthy. 2005. "Hurricane Katrina and Abandoned Being." *Environment and Planning D: Society and Space* 23(6): 802–809.

Briceño-León, Roberto. 1999. "Violencia y desesperanza." *Nueva Sociedad* 164: 122–132.

Brinks, Daniel. 2008. *The Judicial Response to Police Violence in Latin America: Inequality and the Rule of Law.* New York: Cambridge University Press.

Brown, Phillip, Stephen Kroll-Smith, and Valerie J. Gunter. 2000. "Knowledge, Citizens, and Organizations: An Overview of Environments, Diseases, and Social Conflict." In *Illness and the Environment: A Reader in Contested Medicine,* edited by Stephen Kroll-Smith, Phillip Brown, and Valerie J. Gunter. New York: New York University Press, 9–25.

Brown, Phil. 1991. "The Popular Epidemiology Approach to Toxic Waste Contamination." In *Communities at Risk: Collective Responses to Technological Hazards,* edited by Stephen R. Couch and J. Stephen Kroll-Smith. New York: Peter Lang Publishing, 133–155.

Cable, Sherry, and Edward J. Walsh. 1991. "The Emergence of Environmental Protest: Yellow Creek and Three Mile Island Compared." In *Communities at Risk: Collective Responses to Technological Hazards,* edited by Stephen R. Couch and J. Stephen Kroll-Smith. New York: Peter Lang Publishing, 113–132.

Caldeira, Teresa do Rio. 2000. *City of Walls: Crime, Segregation, and Citizenship in São Paulo.* Berkeley: University of California Press.

Centro de Estudios Legales y Sociales (CELS). 2012. *Derechos humanos en Argentina.* Informe 2012. Buenos Aires: Siglo XXI.

Centro de Estudios Legales y Sociales (CELS). 2009. *Derechos humanos en Argentina.* Informe 2009. Buenos Aires: Siglo XXI.

Comfort, Megan. 2008. *Doing Time Together: Love and Family in the Shadow of the Prison.* Chicago: University of Chicago Press.

CORREPI (Coordinadora contra la Represión Political e Institucional). 2012. Archivo de casos. Buenos Aires: CORREPI.

Crónica. 2011. "Lincharon a un delincuente en Ingeniero Budge." April 13. http://www. cronica.com.ar/imprimir/?n=3124.

D'Angiolillo, Julián, Marcelo Dimentstein, Martín Di Peco, Ana Guerin, Adriana Massidda, Constanza Molíns, Natalia Muñoa, Juan Pablo Scarfi, and Pío Torroja. 2010. "Feria La Salada: Una centralidad periférica intermitente en el Gran Buenos Aires." In *Argentina: Persistencia y diversificación, contrastes e imaginarios en las centralidades urbanas,* edited by Margarita Gutman. Quito: Olacchi, 182–193.

Daroqui, Alcira, ed. 2009. *Muertes silenciadas.* Buenos Aires: Centro Cultural de la Cooperación.

Emerson, Robert, Rachel Fretz, and Linda Shaw. 1995. *Writing Ethnographic Fieldnotes.* Chicago: University of Chicago Press.

Epele, Maria. 2010. *Sujetar por la herida: Una etnografía sobre drogas, pobreza y salud.* Buenos Aires: Paidós.

Farmer, Paul. 2004. "An Anthropology of Structural Violence." *Current Anthropology* 45(3): 305–25.

Farrell, Albert, Elizabeth H. Erwin, Kevin W. Allison, Aleta Meyer, Terri Sullivan, Suzanne Camou, Wendy Kliewer, and Layla Esposito. 2007. "Problematic Situations in the Lives of Urban African American Middle School Students: A Qualitative Study." *Journal of Research on Adolescence* 17(2): 413–454.

Feimster, Crystal N. 2009. *Southern Horrors: Women and the Politics of Rape and Lynching.* Cambridge, MA: Harvard University Press.

Freedman, Estelle B. 2011. "'Crimes which Startle and Horrify': Gender, Age, and the Racialization of Sexual Violence in White American Newspapers, 1870–1900." *History of Sexuality* 20(3): 465–497.

Friday, Jennifer. 1995. "The Psychological Impact of Violence in Underserved Communities." *Journal of Health Care for the Poor and Underserved* 6(4): 403–409.

Garbarino, James. 1993. "Children's Response to Community Violence: What do we Know?" *Infant Mental Health Journal* 14(2): 103–115.

Gay, Robert. 2005. *Lucia: Testimonies of a Brazilian Drug Dealer's Woman*. Philadelphia: Temple University Press.

Gelles, Richard. 1985. "Family Violence." *Annual Review of Sociology* 11:347–367.

Girón, Nacho. 2011. *La salada: Radiografía de la Feria más Polémica de Latinoamérica*. Buenos Aires: Ediciones B.

Goldstein, Daniel. 2012. *Outlawed: Between Security and Rights in a Bolivian City*. Durham, NC: Duke University Press.

Guerra, Nancy L., Rowell Huesmann, and Anja Spindler. 2003. "Community Violence Exposure, Social Cognition and Aggression among Urban Elementary School Children." *Child Development* 74(5): 1561–1576.

Hacher, Sebastian. 2011. *Sangre salada*. Buenos Aires: Marea Editorial.

Harding, David. 2010. *Living the Drama: Community, Conflict, and Culture among Inner-city Boys*. Chicago: University of Chicago Press.

Hicks, Cheryl D. 2010. *Talk with You Like a Woman: African American Women, Justice, and Reform in New York, 1890–1935*. Chapel Hill, NC: University of North Carolina Press.

Hill, Karlos. 2010. "Black Vigilantism: The Rise and Decline of African American Lynch Mob Activity in the Mississippi and Arkansas Deltas, 1883–1923." *The Journal of African American History* 95(1): 26–43.

Holton, John K. 1995. "Witnessing Violence: Making the Invisible Visible." *Journal of Health Care for the Poor and Underserved* 6(2): 152–159.

Hume, Mo. 2009. *The Politics of Violence: Gender, Conflict, and Community in El Salvador*. Malden, MA: Wiley-Blackwell.

Imbusch, Peter, Michel Misse, and Fernando Carrión. 2011. "Violence Research in Latin America and the Caribbean: A Literature Review." *International Journal of Conflict and Violence* 5(1): 87–154.

Jackman, Mary. 2002. "Violence in Social Life." *Annual Review of Sociology* 28: 387–415.

Jacobs, Bruce, and Richard Wright. 2006. *Street Justice: Retaliation in the Criminal World*. New York: Cambridge University Press.

Jacobs, Bruce. 2004. "A Typology of Street Criminal Retaliation." *Journal of Research in Crime and Delinquency* 41(3): 295–323.

Jones, Gareth, and Dennis Rodgers, eds. 2009. *Youth Violence in Latin America: Gangs and Juvenile Justice in Perspective*. New York: Palgrave.

Jones, Nikki. 2009. *Between Good and Ghetto: African American Girls and Inner-city Violence*. Rutgers, NJ: Rutgers University Press.

Katz, Jack. 1982. "A Theory of Qualitative Methodology: The Social System of Analytic Fieldwork." In *Contemporary Field Research*, edited by Robert M. Emerson. Boston: Little, Brown and Company, 127–148.

Katz, Jack. 2001. "From How to Why: On Luminous Description and Causal Inference in Ethnography (Part I)." *Ethnography* 2(4): 443–73.

Katz, Jack. 2002. "From How to Why: On Luminous Description and Causal Inference in Ethnography (Part II)." *Ethnography* 3(1): 73–90.

Khan, Shamus, and Colin Jerolmack. 2013. "Saying Meritocracy and Doing Privilege." *The Sociological Quarterly* 54(1): 9–19.

Kirk, David, and Andrew Papachristos. 2011. "Cultural Mechanisms and the Persistence of Neighborhood Violence." *American Journal of Sociology* 116(4): 1190–1233.

Koonings, Kees, and Dirk Kruijt, eds. 2007. *Fractured Cities: Social Exclusion, Urban Violence and Contested Spaces in Latin America.* London: Zed Books.

Koonings, Kees. 2001. "Armed Actors, Violence and Democracy in Latin America in the 1990s." *Bulletin of Latin American research* 20(4): 401–408.

Korbin, Jill. 2003. "Children, Childhoods, and Violence." *Annual Review of Anthropology* 32: 431–446.

Kotlowitz, Alex. 1991. *There are no Children Here: The Story of Two Boys Growing Up in the Other America.* New York: Anchor Books.

Krug, Etienne G., L. L. Dahlberg, James A. Mercy, Anthony B. Zwi, and Rafael Lozano, eds. 2002. *World Report on Violence and Health.* Geneva: World Health Organization.

Kurst-Swanger, Karel, and Jacqueline Petcosky, eds. 2003. *Violence in the Home: Multidisciplinary Perspectives.* New York: Oxford University Press.

La Nación. 2008. "Creció 50% el abuso sexual de menores." February 24. http://www. lanacion.com.ar/990034-crecio-50-el-abuso-sexual-de-menores.

La Nación. 2009. "Un "emblema mundial" de lo ilegal." March 10. http://www.lanacion. com.ar/1107045-un-emblema-mundial-de-lo-ilegal.

LeBlanc, Adrian. 2004. *Random Family: Love, Drugs, Trouble, and Coming of Age in the Bronx.* New York: Scribner.

Margolin, Gayla, and Elana Gordis. 2000. "The Effects of Family and Community Violence on Children." *Annual Review of Psychology* 51: 445–479.

McCart, Michael, Daniel Smith, Benjamin Saunders, Dean Kilpatrick, Heidi Resnick, and Kenneth Ruggiero. 2007. "Do Urban Adolescents Become Desensitized to Community Violence? Data from National Survey." *American Journal of Orthopsychiatry* 77(3): 434–442.

Mogul, Joey L., Andrea J. Ritchie, and Kay Whitlock. 2011. *Queer (In)justice: The Criminalization of LGBT People in the United States.* Boston: Beacon Press.

Müller, Markus-Michael. 2012. "The Rise of the Penal state in Latin America." *Contemporary Justice Review* 15(1): 57–76.

Mullins, Christopher, Richard Wright, and Bruce Jacobs. 2004. "Gender, Street Life and Criminal Retaliation." *Criminology* 42(4): 911–940.

Osofsky, Joy D. 1999. "The Impact of Violence on Children." *The Future of Children* 9(3): 33–49.

Papachristos, Andrew. 2009. "Murder by Structure: Dominance Relations and the Social Structure of Gang Homicide." *American Journal of Sociology* 115(1): 74–128.

Pearce, Jenny. 2010. "Perverse State Formation and Securitized Democracy in Latin America." *Democratization* 17(2): 286–386.

Penglase, Ben. 2010. "The Owner of the Hill: Masculinity and Drug-trafficking in Rio de Janeiro, Brazil." *The Journal of Latin American and Caribbean Anthropology* 15(2): 317–337.

Popkin, Susan, Tama Leventhal, and Gretchen Weismann. 2010. "Girls in the 'Hood: How Safety Affects the Life Chances of Low-income Girls." *Urban Affairs Review* 45(6): 715–744.

Reiss, Albert, and Jeffrey A. Roth. 1993. *Understanding and Preventing Violence.* Washington, DC: National Academic Press.

Richie, Beth. 1996. *Compelled to Crime: The Gender Entrapment of Black Battered Women.* New York: Routledge.

Richie, Beth. 2012. *Arrested Justice: Black women, Violence, and America's Prison Nation.* New York: New York University Press.

Rodgers, Dennis, Jo Beall, and Ravi Kanbur, eds. 2013. *Latin American Urban Development into the Twenty First Century: Towards a Renewed Perspective on the City.* New York: Palgrave.

Sain, Marcelo. 2009. "El fracaso del control de la drogas ilegales en Argentina." *Nueva Sociedad* 222: 132–146.

Scarfi, Juan Pablo, and Martin Di Peco. 2011. *Assessing the Current Challenges of La Salada Fair in Greater Buenos Aires: Towards a New Agenda for Urban and Political Design.* Unpublished manuscript.

Scheper-Hughes, Nancy. 1992. *Death without Weeping: The Violence of Everyday Life in Brazil.* Berkeley: University of California Press.

Scheper-Hughes, Nancy, and Philippe Bourgois. 2004. *Violence in War and Peace: An Anthology.* Malden, MA: Blackwell Publishing Ltd.

Snodgrass Godoy, Angelina. 2002. "Lynchings and the Democratization of Terror in Postwar Guatemala: Implications for Human Rights." *Human Rights Quarterly* 24(3): 640–661.

Tilly, Charles, ed. 2003. *The Politics of Collective Violence.* Cambridge: Cambridge University Press.

Tolan, Patrick, Deborah Gorman-Smith, and David Henry. 2006. "Family Violence." *Annual Review of Psychology* 57: 557–583.

Venkatesh, Sudhir. 2008. *Gang Leader for a Day: A Rogue Sociologist Takes to the Streets.* New York: Penguin.

Walton, Marsha, Alexis Harris, and Alice Davidson. 2009. "'It Makes Me a Man from the Beating I Took': Gender and Aggression in Children's Narratives about Conflict." *Sex Roles* 61: 383–398.

Wells, I. B. 1997. *Southern Horrors and Other Writings: The Anti-lynching Campaign of Ida B. Wells, 1892–1900,* edited by Jacqueline Jones Royster. Boston: Bedford.

Wilding, Polly. 2010. "'New Violence': Silencing Women's Experiences in the Favelas of Brazil." *Journal of Latin American Studies* 42: 719–747.

Zubillaga, Veronica. 2009. "'Gaining Respect': The Logic of Violence among Young Men in the Barrios of Caracas, Venezuela." In *Youth Violence in Latin America: Gangs and Juvenile Justice in Perspective,* edited by Gareth A. Jones and Dennis Rodgers. New York: Palgrave MacMillan, 84–104.

CHAPTER 9

When the Police Knock
Your Door In

ALICE GOFFMAN

The number of people imprisoned in the United States remained fairly stable for most of the twentieth century, at about one person for every thousand in the population (US Department of Justice 1982, 3). In the 1970s, this rate began to rise and continued a steep upward climb for the next thirty years (Uggen, Manza, and Thompson 2006, 285, 287–288). Today, roughly 3 percent of adults in the nation are under correctional supervision: 2.2 million people in prisons and jails, and an additional 4.8 million on probation or parole (US Department of Justice 2012, 3). These rates are five to nine times higher than western European nations and significantly higher than China and Russia (Walmsley 2011, 3, 5). In modern history, only the forced labor camps of the former USSR under Stalin approached these levels of penal confinement (Solzhenitsyn 1973).

The fivefold increase in the number of people sitting in US jails and prisons over the last forty years has prompted little public outcry. In fact, many people scarcely notice this shift, because the growing numbers of prisoners are drawn disproportionately from poor and segregated Black communities. Black people make up 13 percent of the US population but account for 37 percent of the prison population.[1] Among Black young men, one in nine are in prison, compared with less than 2 percent of white young men (The Pew Center on the States 2008, 6). These racial differences are reinforced by class differences. It is poor, Black young men who are being sent to prison at truly astounding rates: approximately 60 percent of those who did not finish high school will go to prison by their mid-thirties (Pettit and Western 2004, 151, 164).

Sociologist David Garland (2001, 1–2) has termed this phenomenon *mass imprisonment*: a level of incarceration markedly above the historical and comparative norm, and concentrated among certain segments of the population such that it "ceases to be the incarceration of individual offenders and becomes the systematic imprisonment of whole groups."

For six years I lived in a segregated and relatively poor Black neighborhood in Philadelphia and endeavored to learn firsthand how unprecedented levels of imprisonment and the more hidden systems of policing and supervision that have accompanied them were changing everyday life there. After a number of years, I expanded the study from the young men who are the main targets of the police and the courts to partners, family members, and neighbors.

The families described here agreed to let me take notes for the purpose of one day publishing the material, and we discussed the project at length many times. I generally did not ask formal, interview-style questions, and most of what I recount here comes from firsthand observations of people, events, and conversations. People's names and identifying characteristics have been changed, along with the name of the neighborhood.

The central finding of this research is that historically high imprisonment rates and the intensive policing and surveillance that have accompanied them are transforming poor Black neighborhoods into communities of suspects and fugitives.

In Ana Villarreal's chapter, we see that the drug war in Mexico has caused an escalation of drug-related murder in cities like Monterrey, creating a culture of fear and suspicion and leading people to develop coping strategies for an unprecedented level of violence in their everyday lives. In Philadelphia we also see how the war on drugs has created a culture of fear and suspicion, in this case through intense policing and imprisonment. A climate of fear and suspicion pervades everyday life, and many residents live with the daily concern that the authorities will seize them and take them away. Indeed, the fear of capture and confinement has seeped into the basic activities of daily living—work, family, romance, friendship, and even obtaining much-needed medical care. A new social fabric is emerging under the threat of confinement: one woven in suspicion, distrust, and the paranoiac practices of secrecy, evasion, and unpredictability.

This chapter considers the particular situation of women linked by love or family to the men the police are in the business of arresting. Because the police turn to girlfriends, mothers, and relatives for information about these young men's whereabouts and activities, women face a special kind of difficulty: that of being turned, against their will, into informants on the men they hold dear.

THE SIXTH STREET NEIGHBORHOOD AND
THE POLICE

When I first came to the neighborhood of Sixth Street in 2002, 93 percent of its residents were Black. Men and boys stood at its busiest intersection, offering bootleg CDs and DVDs, stolen goods, and food to drivers and passersby. The main commercial street included a bulletproofed Chinese takeout store that sold fried chicken wings, single cigarettes called "loosies," condoms, baby food, and glassines for smoking crack. The street also included a check-cashing store, a hair salon, a payday loan store, a Crown Fried Chicken restaurant, and a pawnshop. On the next block, a Puerto Rican family ran a corner grocery. Roughly one-fourth of the neighborhood's households received housing vouchers, and in all but two households, families received some type of government assistance.[2]

Sixth Street is not the poorest or the most dangerous neighborhood in the large Black section of Philadelphia of which it is a part—far from it. In interviews with police officers, I discovered that it was hardly a top priority of theirs, nor did they consider the neighborhood particularly dangerous or crime ridden. Residents in adjacent neighborhoods spoke about Sixth Street as quiet and peaceful—a neighborhood they would gladly move to if they ever had enough money.

Still, Sixth Street has not escaped three decades of punitive drug and crime policy. By 2002, police curfews had been established around the area for those under age eighteen, and police video cameras had been placed on major streets. In the first eighteen months that I spent in the neighborhood, at least once a day I watched the police stop pedestrians or people in cars, search them, run their names for warrants, ask them to come in for questioning, or make an arrest.[3] In that same eighteen-month period, I watched the police break down doors; search houses; and question, arrest, or chase people through houses fifty-two times. Nine times, police helicopters circled overhead and beamed searchlights onto local streets. I noted blocks taped off and traffic redirected as police searched for evidence—or, in police language, "secured a crime scene"—seventeen times. Fourteen times during my first eighteen months of near daily observation, I watched the police punch, choke, kick, stomp on, or beat young men with their nightsticks.

WOMEN CAUGHT BETWEEN

To understand the situation of women close to young men getting chased, arrested, and jailed, we must first understand the way the police view such women: as potential sources of information. The reliance on intimates as informants is not the dirty dealing of a few rogue cops, nor the purview of a few specialized officers. Police don't reserve this treatment for the families of those few men who make their most-wanted list. In our 2007 household survey of the Sixth Street neighborhood, 139 of the 146 women reported that in the past three years, a partner, neighbor, or close male relative was either wanted by the police, serving a probation or parole sentence, going through a trial, living in a halfway house, or on house arrest. Sixty-seven percent of the women we interviewed said that during that same period, the police had pressured them to provide information about that person.

As the police lean on women to help round up their partners, brothers, and sons, women face a crisis in their relationship and their self-image. Most help the police locate and convict the young men in their lives, and they must find a way to cope publicly and privately with their betrayals. A rare few manage to resist police pressure outright, garnering significant local acclaim. A greater number work to rebuild themselves and their relationships after they have informed, which is sometimes successful and sometimes not.

GETTING THE NEWS

The journey from intimate to informant (or, in rarer cases, from intimate to resister) often begins when a woman discovers that the man in her life has become wanted by the police, or has become more legally precarious than he had been.[4]

On an unusually warm Sunday afternoon in March, Aisha and I sat on the wide cement steps of her four-story subsidized apartment building. Her boyfriend, Tommy, leaned on the railing beside her, chatting with a neighbor who had stopped on his way home. Aisha's aunt and neighbor sat farther up the steps, waiting for their clothes to finish at the Laundromat across the street. We passed around a bag of jalapeño sunflower seeds and kept our eye out for Aisha's cousin, who was supposed to be coming back with a six-pack from the corner store. Time dragged on, and Tommy remarked that she'd probably taken our pooled money and gone to the bar.

As we sat watching the kids play and spitting the shells into little piles beside us, Tommy unfolded a notice he had received that day from family court, a notice that he must appear before a judge because the mother of his two-year-old son was asking for back payments in child support. If he came to court empty-handed, he told us, the judge might take him into custody on the spot. If he didn't show up, a warrant may be issued for his arrest for contempt.

"She just mad you don't mess with her no more," Aisha said. "She knows you pay for all his clothes, all his sneaks. Everybody knows you take care of your son."

"When is the court date?," I asked.

"Next month," Tommy answered, without looking up.

"Are you going to go?"

"He don't have six hundred dollars!" Aisha cried.

We tried to calculate how many days in jail it would take to work off this amount, but we couldn't remember if they subtract five dollars or ten dollars for each day served. Aisha's aunt said she thought it was less than that. Aisha concluded that Tommy would lose his job at the hospital whether he spent two weeks or two years in jail, so the exact amount he would work off per day was of little consequence.

Tommy looked at Aisha somberly and said, "If I run, is you riding?"

"Yeah, I'm riding."

A neighbor's five-year-old son started to cry, claiming that an older boy had pushed him. Aisha yelled at him to get back onto the sidewalk.

"If they come for me, you better not tell them where I'm at," Tommy said quietly.

"I'm not talking to no cops!"

"They probably don't even have your address. They definitely coming to my mom's, though, and my baby-mom's. But if they do come, don't tell them nothing."

"Shoot," Aisha said. "Let them come. I'll sic Bo right on them."

"Yeah?" Tommy grinned appreciatively and nudged Aisha with his shoulder.

Aisha's aunt turned and eyed her skeptically, shaking her head.

"I'm not letting them take him," Aisha fired back. "For what? So he can just sit in jail for four months and lose his job? And don't see his son?"

Aisha and Tommy began dating shortly after I first met her, when she was a high-school freshman. What she liked about him then was that he was gorgeous and dark skinned, even darker than she was. Tommy, she said later, was not only her first, he was also her first love. They kept in touch for years afterward, though Tommy had a child with another woman, and Aisha began seriously seeing someone else. When Aisha turned twenty-one, this second man was sentenced to fifteen years in a federal penitentiary in Ohio. About six months later, Aisha and Tommy got back together. Soon after that, Tommy began working as a custodian at the Hospital of the University of Pennsylvania. When he got the call for the job, they cried and hugged in the living room. Aisha had never dated a guy with a real job before, and she became the only woman in her extended family with this distinction.

"If they lock me up, you going to come see me?," Tommy asked her.

"Yeah, I'ma come see you. I'ma be up there every week."

"I know that's right," Aisha's neighbor said. "Them guards up there going to know your name. They going to be like, 'You *always* coming up here, Aisha!'"[5]

We laughed quietly.

Later that evening, two of Aisha's girlfriends came by. She told them about her conversation with Tommy: "He talking about, 'if I run, is you riding?' Shoot, they ain't taking him! They're going to have to kill me first."

For Aisha, the news that Tommy might be taken came as a crushing personal blow. But it was also an opportunity to express her devotion, meditate on their relationship, and contemplate the lengths she would go in the future to hold it together.

Other women considered their family member's pending imprisonment in more political terms. Mike's mother, Miss Regina, was in her late thirties when we met. A reserved and proper person, she had made good grades in high school and got accepted to a local college. She became pregnant with Mike that summer. The way she told it, Mike's father was the first person she had ever slept with, and she hoped they would get married. But the man became a heavy crack user and was in and out of jail during Mike's early years. By the time Mike was ten, Miss Regina told his father to stop coming around.[6]

By all accounts, Miss Regina worked two and sometimes three jobs while Mike was growing up, and she raised him with little help from her own parents. Mike got into a lot of trouble during his high-school years but managed to get his diploma by taking night classes.

By the time Mike came of age, the drama with the mother of his two children and his frequent brushes with the authorities had caused Miss Regina "a lifetime of grief." By twenty-two, Mike had been in and out of the county jail and the state prison over the previous few years, mostly on drug charges.

When we met, Miss Regina was working for the Salvation Army as a caretaker to four elderly men and women whose homes she visited for twelve- or eighteen-hour shifts three times a week. She had moved to Northeast Philadelphia a few months before we met, noting that the Sixth Street neighborhood had become too dangerous and dilapidated.

The house she was renting was spotless; she even had a special machine to clear away the smoke from her cigarettes.

Miss Regina had just gotten home from work, and had started a load of laundry in the basement. Her mother and I were watching the soap opera *Guiding Light* on the plush loveseat in the living room when the phone rang. From the kitchen Miss Regina yelled, "I don't believe this." She passed me the phone; it was Mike, who told me his PO (probation officer) had issued him a warrant for breaking curfew at the halfway house last night. He had come home from prison less than a month ago; this violation would send him back for the remainder of his sentence, pending the judge's decision. When we hung up, Miss Regina lit a cigarette and paced around the living room, wiping down the surfaces of the banister and TV stand with a damp rag.

"He's going to spend two years in prison for breaking curfew? I'm not going to let them. They are taking all our sons, Alice. Our young men. And it's getting younger and younger."

Miss Regina's mother, a quiet, churchgoing woman in her sixties, nodded and mumbled that it is indeed unfair to send a man to prison for coming home late to a halfway house. Miss Regina continued to pace, now spraying cleaning solvent on the glass table.

> Let me ask you something, Alice. When you go up the F [local slang for the Curran-Fromhold Correctional Facility (CFCF), the county jail], why do you see nothing but Black men in jumpsuits sitting there in the visiting room? When you go to the halfway house, why is it nothing but Black faces staring out the glass? They are taking our *children*, Alice. I am a law-abiding woman; my uncle was a cop. They can't do that.

On seventy-one occasions between 2002 and 2010, I witnessed a woman discovering that a partner or family member had become wanted by the police. Sometimes this notice came in the form of a battering ram knocking her door in at three in the morning. But oftentimes there was a gap between the identification of a man as wanted and the police's attempts to apprehend him. Before the authorities came knocking, a letter would arrive from the courts explaining that a woman's fiancé has either missed too many payments on his court fees or failed to appear in court, and that a bench warrant was out for his arrest. Or a woman would phone her son's PO and learn that he did indeed miss his piss test again or had failed to return to the halfway house in time for curfew, and an arrest warrant would likely be issued, pending the judge's decision. At other times, women would find out that the man in their lives was wanted because the police had tried and failed to apprehend him at another location.

In fifty-eight of the seventy-two times I watched women receive this news, they reacted with promises to shield their loved one from arrest. In local language, this is called "riding."

Broadly defined, to ride is to protect or avenge oneself or someone dear against assaults to person or property. In this context, to ride means to shield a loved one from the police and to support him through his trial and confinement if one fails in the first goal of keeping him free.[7]

It may come as a surprise that the majority of women I met who learned that a spouse or family member was wanted by the police initially expressed anger at the authorities, not the man, and promised to support him and protect him while he was hunted. In part, I think these women understood how easy it was to get a warrant when you are a Black young man in neighborhoods like Sixth Street; they understood that warrants are issued not only for serious crimes but for technical violations of probation or parole, for failure to pay steep court fines and fees, or for failure to appear for one of the many court dates a man may have in a given month.[8] A second and related reason for women's anger is that the police have lost considerable legitimacy in the community: they are seen searching, questioning, beating, and rounding up young men all over the neighborhood. As Miss Regina often put it, the police are "an occupying force." A third reason is more basic: no matter what a woman's opinion of the police or of the man's actions, she loves him and does not want to part with him or see him subjected to what has been referred to as the "pains of imprisonment" (Sykes 2007, 63–83).

Riding is easy to do in the abstract. If the authorities never come looking, a woman can believe that she will hold up under police pressure and do her utmost to hide the man and protect him. So long as the threats of police pressure and prison are real but unrealized, a woman can believe in the most idealized version of herself. The man, too, can believe in this ideal version of her and of their relationship.

A few days after Tommy received the notice from family court, he went to the police station and turned himself in. The police never came to question Aisha. They did come for Miss Regina's son, Mike.

WHEN THE POLICE COME

I'd spent the night at Miss Regina's house watching *Gangs of New York* with Mike and Chuck for maybe the hundredth time. I had fallen asleep on the living room couch and so heard the banging in my dream, mixed in with the title-page music, which the DVD played over and over.

The door busting open brought me fully awake. I pushed myself into the couch to get away from it, thinking it might hit me on the way down if it broke all the way off its hinges. Two officers then came through the door, both of them white, in SWAT gear, with guns strapped to the sides of their legs. The first officer pointed a gun at me and asked who was in the house; he continued to point the gun toward me as he went up the stairs. I wondered if Mike and Chuck were in the house somewhere, and hoped they had gone.

The second officer pulled me out of the cushions and, gripping my wrists, brought me up off the couch and onto the floor, so that my shoulders and spine hit first and my legs came down after. He quickly turned me over, and my face hit the floor. I couldn't brace myself, because he was still holding one of my wrists, which was now pinned behind me. I wondered if he'd broken my nose or cheek. (Can you break a cheek?) His boot pressed into my back, right at the spot where it had hit the floor, and I cried for him to stop. He put my wrists in plastic cuffs behind my back; I knew this because metal ones feel cold. My shoulder throbbed, and the handcuffs pinched. I tried to wriggle my arms, and the cop moved his boot down to cover my hands, crushing my fingers together. I yelled, but it came out quiet and raspy, like I had given up. My hipbones began to ache—his weight was pushing them into the thin carpet.

A third cop, taller and skinnier, with blond hair cut close to his head, entered the house and walked into the kitchen. I could hear china breaking and watched him pull the fridge away from the wall. Then he came into the living room and pulled a small knife from its sheath on his lower leg. He cut the fabric off the couch, revealing the foam inside. Then he moved to the closet and pulled board games and photo albums and old shoes out onto the floor. He climbed on top of the TV stand and pushed the squares of the drop ceiling out, letting them hit the floor one on top of the other.

I could hear banging and clattering from upstairs, and then Miss Regina screaming at the cop not to shoot her, pleading with him to let her get dressed. All the while, the cop with his foot on me yelled for me to say where Mike was hiding. It would be my fault when Miss Regina's house got destroyed, he said. "And I can tell she takes pride in her house."

TECHNIQUES OF PERSUASION

If the police decide to go after a man, chances are they will ask his relatives and partner where he is. Because these intimates are immersed in the lives of their legally precarious family members and partners, they tend to have considerable knowledge about their activities and routines. They know where a young man shops and sleeps, where he keeps his possessions, and with whom he is connected.

These days it isn't difficult, expensive, or time-consuming for the police to identify family members who may have information about the whereabouts or incriminating activities of wanted man. Nor does it require direct knowledge of the neighborhood or its inhabitants gained through close association. Rather, information about a man's relatives, children, partner, and relationship history can now be easily retrieved with a few keystrokes.

When the police arrest and process a man, they ask him to provide a good deal of information about his friends and relatives—where they live and where he lives, what names they go by, how to reach them. The more information he provides, the lower his bail will be, so he has a significant incentive to do this. By the time a man has been arrested a number of times, the police have substantial information about where his girlfriend works, where his mother lives, where his child goes to school.

Once a man has become wanted, the police visit his mother or girlfriend and try to persuade her to give him up. In the words of one former Warrant Unit officer, "We might be able to track people with their cell phones or see every guy with a warrant in the neighborhood up on the computer screen, but when it comes down to it, you always go through the girlfriend, the grandmother, because she knows where he is, and she knows what he's done."[9]

After the police locate a family member or partner, they employ a series of techniques to gain the woman's cooperation. These begin when the police are searching for a man or arresting him, but may continue through his trial and sentencing as they attempt to gather information that will facilitate a conviction.[10]

The most direct pressure the police apply to women to get them to talk is physical force: the destruction of their property and, in some cases, bodily injury. From what I have seen around Sixth Street and nearby neighborhoods, police violence toward women occurs most frequently during raids. During these raids and also during interrogations, police deploy a number of less-physical tactics to get uncooperative women to talk. The major three are threats of arrest, eviction, and loss of child custody.

Threats of Arrest

During raids and interrogations, the police threaten to arrest women for an array of crimes. First, they explain to a woman that her efforts to protect the man in her life constitute crimes in their own right. When

Chuck's mother, Miss Linda, blocked the police's entrance to her home and waved an officer away as he pulled up her carpet and opened up her ceiling, the officers explained that they could charge her with assault on an officer, aiding and abetting a fugitive, and interfering with an arrest. They also told her that she would face charges for the gun they found in her house, since she didn't have a permit for it. (In fact, in Philadelphia a permit is required only for carrying.) When Aisha's neighbor said she would refuse to testify against her son, officers told her that she would go to jail for contempt. Once she agreed to cooperate, they informed her that if she changed her statement she would be jailed for lying under oath.

The police also make it clear to a woman that, in addition to her efforts to protect the man in question, many of her routine practices and everyday behaviors are grounds for arrest. Over the course of raids and interrogations, the officers make women realize that their daily lives are full of crimes, crimes the police are well aware of and crimes that carry high punishments, should the authorities feel inclined to pursue them. When the police came for Mike's cousin, they told his aunt that the property taxes she hadn't paid and some long overdue traffic fines constituted tax evasion and contempt of court. The electricity that she was getting from her neighbor two doors down, via three joined extension cords trailed through the back alley (because her own electricity had been long cut off, and for the use of which she was babysitting her neighbor's two children three times a week), constituted theft, a public hazard, and a violation of city code.

The police also explain to a woman that she can be charged for the man's crimes. Mike's girlfriend told me she was sure she would be charged for possessing the gun or the drugs if she didn't give Mike up, since the police found them in her house and car. The police also threatened to bring her up on conspiracy charges, claiming that they had placed a tap on her cell phone and so had proof that she was aware of Mike's activities.

Police raids also place a woman's other male relatives in jeopardy. When Mike had a warrant out for his arrest and the police were showing up at his mother's house, she became very worried that her fiancé, who was driving without a license and selling small quantities of marijuana as a supplement to his job at the hospital, would come under scrutiny. Because it is very likely that the other men in a woman's life are also facing some violation or pending legal action (or engaged in the drug trade or other illegal work), the police's pursuit of one man represents a fairly direct threat to the other men a woman holds dear.

Finally, the police tell a woman that if her present and past behavior is insufficient grounds for arrest, they will use every technology at their disposal to monitor her future activities. Any new crimes she commits will be quickly identified and prosecuted, along with any future crimes committed by her nearest and dearest. If she drives after she has been drinking, if she smokes marijuana, if her son steals candy from the store—they will know, and she or he will go to jail.

The threat of arrest and imprisonment is a powerful technique of persuasion, perhaps more so when deployed on women. Fewer women than men go to prison or jail, making it a scarier prospect. Women prisoners don't receive the same degree of familial support available to men, as visiting people in prison is considered women's work, done for men by their partners and female kin, and men are less able to visit.[11] In the Sixth Street neighborhood, people tend to regard imprisonment as more of an indictment of a woman's character and lifestyle than a man's, partly on the grounds that police routinely stop and search men, while women must do something more extreme to get the police's attention.

Threats of Eviction

In addition to threatening arrest and imprisonment, the police also threaten women who do not cooperate with eviction.[12] They told my next-door neighbor that if she didn't give up her nephew, they would call Licensing and Inspection and get her dilapidated house condemned. And when the police came to Steve's grandmother's house looking for him, they noted that the electricity and gas weren't on, the water wasn't running, and the bathtub was being used as an outhouse. These violations of the municipal health and building codes would easily constitute grounds for the city to repossess her property. The officers also informed her that the infestation of roaches, mice, and fleas in the house were sufficient grounds for the landlord to revoke her lease. Further, since she had placed the bail for Steve in her name, his running meant that the city could go after her for the entire bail amount—not just the 10 percent she put up—which meant the city could also take her car and her future earnings. When the police came to Aisha's neighbor's house looking for the neighbor's on-again, off-again boyfriend, they informed her that if she didn't give him up, they would come back late at night in a full raid. Since her apartment was subsidized, she could be immediately evicted for harboring a fugitive and putting her neighbors at risk. She would lose her present accommodations and all rights to obtain subsidized housing in the future.

Child Custody Threats

Another tactic that the police use to persuade women to talk is threatening to take away their children. When the police raided Mike's neighbor's house, they told his wife that if she didn't explain where to find him, they'd call Child Protective Services and report that the windows were taped up with trash bags, that the heat had been cut off and the open stove was being used as a furnace, and that her children were discovered sleeping on the sofa. Officers also found marijuana and a crack pipe in the house. If she continued to be uncooperative, this evidence would build a powerful case for child neglect and unfit living conditions. That evening, the woman packed up her three children and drove them to Delaware to stay with an aunt until the police activity died down.

Most of the threats police make to women over the course of a raid, a stop, or an interrogation are never realized. Consequently, when a woman attempting to protect a man from the authorities does get arrested or evicted, or loses custody of her children, the news spreads quickly. Anthony had a cousin who lived in Virginia; he was sentenced to five years in prison for conspiracy to sell drugs and possession of an illegal firearm after the cousin refused to serve as a witness for the case against the father of her child. With both her parents in prison, the four-year-old daughter was sent to Philadelphia, where she was passed from relative to relative. Two of Miss Linda's neighbors got evicted from their government-subsidized housing for harboring a fugitive and interfering with an arrest when the police entered their home searching for a man who had robbed a bank. Families around Sixth Street often recalled such stories when they anticipated a raid, or after some interaction with the police.

Presenting Disparaging Evidence

In order to get her to provide information, the police may injure a woman or destroy her property. If she persists in protecting the man, they threaten to arrest her, publicly denounce her, confiscate and appropriate her possessions, evict her, or take her children away. We might call such violence and threats *external forces of attack*, as they operate from the outside to weaken the bond between the woman and the man the police are after.

The authorities also work within the relationship, by presenting the woman with information about the man that shatters her high opinion of him and destroys the positive image she has of their relationship. We might call this an *internal attack*, as it works to break the bond between a man and woman from the inside.

The police's presentation of disparaging evidence operates as a complex, two-way maneuver. First, they demonstrate to the woman that the man she is trying to protect has cheated on her. They show her his cell phone records, text messages, and statements from women in the neighborhood. The improvement of tracking technologies means that no large effort need be made to furnish these pieces of evidence: they can be quickly gathered at a computer. If the police have no concrete evidence, they suggest and insinuate that the man has been unfaithful, or at least that he doesn't truly care about the woman but is simply using her. At this point, the officers explain that at the first opportunity, this man who does not love her will give her up to save his own skin; he will allow her to be blamed for his crimes. Perhaps he has already done so.

Just as the officers are explaining to the woman how her partner has been unfaithful and duplicitous, and would easily let her hang for his crimes, so they present the man with evidence of *her* betrayals. They show him statements she signed down at the precinct detailing his activities, or the call sheet filled out at the Warrant Unit, where, after repeated raids on her house, she phoned to tell authorities where he was hiding. They may also show him evidence that she has cheated on him, which they collect from statements given by other men and women in the couple's circle or by tracking the woman's cell phone, bills, and purchases.

In short, the police denigrate the man and the relationship to the point that a woman cannot protect him and continue to think of herself as a person of worth. In anger and hurt, and saddled with the new fear that this man who doesn't love her may try to blame her for his misdeeds, leaving her to rot in prison, a woman becomes increasingly eager to help the police.

Moral Appeals

The previous techniques work by weakening the bonds between the woman and the man the police are pursuing. Moral appeals to the value of imprisonment operate on the opposite principle: they rely on the strength of the woman's attachment and play on her resolve to help and protect the man. Specifically, moral appeals involve adjusting what the woman believes to be the right thing to do concerning the man she loves.

Before the police's intervention, a woman may believe that it is best for the man in her life to stay out of prison. He will go crazy in his cell, get stabbed, get AIDS, or have an unhealthy diet. The prison won't see to his medical needs, like his diabetes or the worrisome bullets lodged in his body.[13] He will lose his job if he has one, or find it more difficult to find work once he comes home. Being in a cell day after day, cut off from society, with guards barking orders at him, he will become dehumanized, and normal life will become unfamiliar to him. To keep him from this fate, sacrifices must be made.

The police explain to the woman that this logic is flawed. In fact, the man would benefit from a stay in prison. He needs to make a clean break from his bad associates. It is not safe for him on the streets. He might be killed if he continues to sell drugs, or he may overdose, if his proclivities run that way. He is spiraling deeper and deeper into dangerous behavior; jail will be a safe haven for him. Going to prison will teach him a lesson; he will emerge a better man, one more capable of caring for her and the children. The drama must end, they tell her, his drama and the drama that comes because of all the police activity. He has too many legal entanglements, too many court cases, warrants, probation sentences. He will be better able to find work without the warrants. It would be better if the man simply got it over with and began his life afresh. She can help him; she can save him before it is too late. He will thank her one day for this tough love.

A variant on this line of persuasion is that while it may not be best for the man to go to prison, it will be best for the family as a whole. Protecting the man means that she risks losing her children and her home; the bail in her name means that she could go into debt to the city and be jailed if she cannot pay it. His actions also expose her children to bad people and bad things. As a responsible mother, sister, or daughter, she should save her family and turn him in.

Promises of Confidentiality and Other Protections

The police's persuasion techniques are often bolstered by promises that no information she provides will be shared with the man or with anyone else among her acquaintance. In twenty-one of the twenty-four raids that I witnessed, officers told family members that the man would never be made aware that they had given him up. During the two questionings I was involved in, the police assured me of my confidentiality, and when women recounted their own interrogations, they mentioned that the same promise was made to them the majority of the time.

The Multipronged Approach

Violence, threats, disparaging evidence, moral appeals, and promises of protection are analytically separable, but the police often deploy these techniques in tandem, each serving to strengthen and reinforce the others.

It was difficult for me to observe women's interrogations, because they were conducted behind closed doors at the police department, and women were reluctant to recount their experience once they got back home. For these reasons, I have used my own interrogation as an example.

This interrogation is notable because the police made use of many of the techniques described above, despite having very little to work with: they did not know what my relationship was to the men they were interested in; I was not living in public housing; I had no children; and neither I nor anyone in my immediate family had an arrest history or pending legal problems.

I had dropped Mike and Chuck off on Sixth Street and was heading toward the airport to pick up a friend. Two unmarked cars come up behind me, a portable siren on top of the first one, and I pulled over. A cop walked over to my window and shone a flashlight in my face; he ordered me to step out of the car and show him my license. Then one of the cops told me I was going with them.

I left the car on Second Street and got into the backseat of their car, a green Lincoln. The white cop in the back with me would have been skinny if not for the bulletproof vest, holster, gun, nightstick, and whatever else he had in his belt. He cracked his bubble-gum hard and smelled like the stuff Mike and Chuck use to clean their guns. On the way to the precinct, the white cop who was driving told me that if I was looking for some Black dick, I didn't have to go to Sixth Street; I could come right to the precinct at Eighth and Vine. The Black cop in the passenger side grinned and shook his head, saying something about how he didn't want any of me; he would probably catch some shit.

At the precinct, another white guy patted me down. He was smirking at me as he touched my hips and thighs. There is a certain look of disdain, or perhaps disgust, that white men sometimes give to white women whom they believe to be having sex with Black men—Black men who get arrested, especially.

They took me up the stairs to the second floor, the Detective Unit. I sat in a little room for a while, and then the two white cops came in, dark-green cargo pants and big black combat boots, and big guns strapped onto their legs. They removed the guns and put them on the table facing me. One cop leafed through a folder and put pictures in front of me of Mike, then Chuck, then Reggie. Most of the pictures were of Sixth Street, some taken right in front of my apartment. Some mug shots. Of the forty or so pictures he showed me, I knew about ten men by name and recognized another ten. They questioned me for about an hour and a half. From what I remembered many hours later:

Is Mike the supplier? Do you think he'll protect you when we bring him in? He won't protect you! Who has the best stuff, between Mike and Steve, in your expert opinion? We know you were around here last week when all that shit went down. (What shit?) We saw you on Second Street, and we know you're up on Fourth Street. What business do you have up Fourth Street? I hate to see a pretty young girl get passed around so much. Do your parents know that you're fucking a different nigger every night? The good cop countered with: All we want to do is protect you. We are trying to help you. We're not going to tell him you gave us any information. This is between us. No paper trail. Did you sign anything when you came in? No. Nobody knows you are even here. The bad cop: If you can't work with us, then who will you call when he's sticking a gun to your head? You can't call us! He'll kill you over a couple of grams. You know that, right? You better hope whoever you're fucking isn't in one of the pictures you're looking at here, because all of these boys, see them? Each and every one of them will be in jail by Monday morning. And he'll be the first one to drop your name when he's sitting in this chair. And then it's conspiracy, obstruction of justice, harboring a fugitive, concealing narcotics, firearms. How do you think we picked you up in the first place? Who do you think is the snitch? What is your Daddy going to say when you call him from the station and ask him to post your bail? Bet he'd love to hear what you are doing. Do you kiss him with that mouth?

To fully grasp the effect of these techniques of persuasion on women, we must understand the broader context of police violence in which they occur.

Between November 2002 and April 2003, I spent a large part of every day with Aisha and her friends and relatives, who lived about fifteen blocks from Sixth Street. From the steps of her building or walking around the adjacent blocks, on fourteen occasions, a little more than twice a month, we watched the police beat up people while they were arresting them. Here is one account from the fall of 2007:

It is late afternoon, and Aisha and I are sitting on the stoop, chatting with her aunt and her older cousin. Aisha's mother sits next to us, waiting for her boyfriend to come with five dollars so that she can finish her laundry.

A white police officer jogs by, his torso weaving awkwardly, and his breath coming loud enough for us to hear. Then I notice a young man running a little ahead of him, also out of breath, as if he had been running for a long time. The man slows to a walk, and leans down with his hands on his knees. The cop approaches him, running in this stilted way, and grabs the back of his neck with one hand, pushing him down to the ground. Drawing his nightstick, he straddles the man in a half crouch, and begins hitting him in the back and neck with it.

Two of Aisha's neighbors get up off the steps and quietly approach the scene, keeping some yards away. Aisha makes no move to get up; nor does her aunt or cousin. But we lean over to see.

Police cars pull up to the corner with sirens and lights on, first one then another, then another, blocking the street off. They handcuff the young man, whose face is now covered in blood, especially the side that had been scraped across the cement.

The police move the man to the cop car, and one cop places his hand on top of the man's head to guide him into the backseat. Then they look around on the ground, apparently searching the area for something. Two of the cops speak into walkie-talkies.

"He must have had a gun or drugs on him," Aisha's aunt says.

"I didn't see nothing," a neighbor replies.

When the police cars begin to pull off, a neighbor says that she saw one cop punch the man in the face after he was already cuffed.

Aisha's cousin, a stout young man of nineteen, gets up off the steps.

"Yo, I'm out, Aisha. It's too hot on your block."

"Okay," she laughs. "Tell your mom I said hi."

An elderly woman comes out after a few minutes with a bucket of bleach and water and pours it over the sidewalk, to clean the blood. Aisha and I go back to talking about her boyfriend, who has just received a sentence of fifteen years in federal prison. As the day goes on, I notice that Aisha and her family make no mention of what we have seen. Perhaps because they don't know the man personally, this event is not important enough to recount to those not present when it occurred.

That summer was punctuated by more severe police action. On a hot afternoon in July, Aisha and I stood on a crowded corner of a major commercial street and watched four officers chase down her older sister's boyfriend and strangle him. He was unarmed and did not fight back. The newspapers reported his death as heart failure. In August, we visited an old boyfriend of Aisha's shortly after he got to county jail. Deep lacerations covered his cheeks, and his eyes had swollen to tiny slits. The beating he took while being arrested, and the subsequent infection left untreated while he sat in quarantine, took most of the vision from his right eye.

In interviews, Warrant Unit officers explained to me that this violence represents official (if unpublicized) policy, rather than a few cops taking things too far. The Philadelphia police I interviewed have a liberal understanding of what constitutes reasonable force, and a number of officers told me that they have orders from their captains that any person who so much as touches a cop "better be going to the hospital."

In sum, the police apply a certain amount of violence to women to get them to talk, but substantially more to men as they chase them down and arrest them. The violence that women witness and hear about fixes what the police are capable of doing firmly in their minds. This knowledge likely spurs their cooperation, should the police desire it.

BECOMING A SNITCH OR AN ABANDONER

As the police roll out their methods, as they raid a woman's house and pull her in for questioning, the woman's public reckoning commences. Relatives, neighbors, and friends watch to see how she will hold up as the police threaten to arrest her, evict her, or take her children away

When the raids and interrogations begin, many women find that they cannot live up to the hopes they and others had for their conduct. Rather than be the man's "ride-or-die chick," they implore him to turn himself in. Rather than hide him and help him survive, they kick him out of the house and cut off all contact, perhaps leaving him without food or shelter. Rather than remain silent in the face of police questioning, they give up all the information they can.

Shortly after Mike's baby-mom, Marie, had given birth to their second child, the police came to his mother's house looking for him on a gun charge. When Marie heard this news, she called me on the phone to discuss it and, in between her screams and cries, explained her concerns for him:

> You remember last time? He stopped eating! And then they put him in the hole [solitary confinement] for no reason. Remember how he was in the hole? I can't take those calls no more. He was really losing it. No sunlight. Nobody to talk to. Plus, he could get stabbed up, or get AIDS. How I'm supposed to take care of the baby? They don't care he got a bullet in his hip. Won't none of them guards pay attention to that, and I can tell it's getting ready to come out [push through the skin].

Firm in her conviction that Mike would suffer in jail, and determined to keep her growing family together, Marie promised to do whatever she could to protect him from the authorities.

Then the police paid a visit to Marie's house. They came early in the morning, waking up the baby. They didn't search the house, but sat and talked with her about the necessity of turning Mike in.

I came over that afternoon. Visibly shaken, Marie seemed to have adopted quite a different view of things:

Marie: He needs to get away from these nut-ass niggas out here, Alice. It's not safe for him on the streets; he could get killed out here. He needs to go in there, get his mind right, and come out here—

Marie's mother: —and act like a man.

Marie: Yes. Because the drama has to stop, Alice. He has too much stuff [legal entanglements]. He needs to go in and get all that taken care of. How he supposed to get a job when he got two warrants on him? He needs a fresh start. He ain't going to like it, but he going. Soon as I see him [I'm calling the number on the card the police gave me].

In fact, Marie did not call the police on Mike right away; she tried to persuade him to turn himself in. Mike refused, and Marie continued to try to "talk some sense into him" over the next few days. She called the number on the card on the fifth day, after a second visit from the police. As they drove him off in handcuffs, we sat on the stoop and talked.

Marie: I know he not going to take my visits right away but I don't care, like, it had to be done. It's too much drama, Alice. He can call me a snitch, I don't care. I know in my heart—
Marie's mom: —that was the right thing to do.

After Marie got Mike taken away, he castigated her daily from jail and spread the word that she had snitched. This, she said, was nothing compared to the internal anguish she felt over betraying the father of her two children, and her most trusted friend. The pains of his confinement, she explained, rested on her shoulders:

> Every time he hungry in there, or he lonely, or the guards is talking shit to him, that's on my head. Every time he miss his son—I did that to him.

THE "TRUE RIDER"

Overwhelmingly, women who come under police pressure cave: they cut off ties to the men they had promised to protect, or they work with the police to get these men arrested and convicted. When this happens, women suffer public humiliation and private shame, and face the difficult task of salvaging their moral worth in the wake of their betrayals. Most often, the relationships are permanently ruined; to salvage her dignity, the woman may start over with a new man in a new social scene—perhaps a few blocks away or, better yet, in another neighborhood. Four times I observed women pack up and move after being publicly labeled a snitch.

I witnessed a number of situations in which the police pressure never materialized. The man turned himself in, or wasn't pursued after all, or the police caught up to him quickly and so didn't get around to putting pressure on his girlfriend or relatives. In these cases, the woman doesn't have to manage her spoiled identity or reconstruct her relationship, because she didn't have to resort to betraying her boyfriend, brother, or son.

In other cases, a woman is able to support and protect the man because the police don't connect her to him and therefore don't put pressure on her or her family directly. Because a man's main girlfriend and close relatives tend to be known to the police and targeted for information, he often finds his inner circle untrustworthy, while someone with whom he has a weaker connection—a new friend, an old girlfriend, or a more distant cousin—turns out to be the "true rider."

A few women around Sixth Street showed remarkable strength in resisting police pressure. Miss Linda's ability to stand firm was widely recognized in the Sixth Street community. As Mike once proclaimed to a small crowd assembled on her steps after a raid, "She might be a thief and her house might be dirty as shit, but Miss L ain't talking. She don't care if they bang her door in, she don't *give* a fuck!"

Miss Linda would often say that she rode hard for her three sons because she had more heart than other women, but the truth of the matter was that she also had more practice. Chuck, Reggie, Tim, and their friends and associates brought the law to her house on at least twenty-three occasions during my six years on Sixth Street.[14]

When her middle son, Reggie, was seventeen, the police stopped him for loitering on the corner, and he allowed them to search him. An officer discovered three small bags of crack in the lining of his jeans, and Reggie started running. The cops lost him in the chase, and an arrest warrant was issued for possession of drugs with intent to distribute.

That evening, Miss Linda prepared her house for the raid she seemed sure was coming. She located the two guns that Reggie and his older brother, Chuck, had hidden in the ceiling, and stashed them at a neighbor's. She did the same with Chuck's bulletproof vest, his bullets, and the tiny plastic baggies he used to hold the small amounts of crack he was selling at the time. She took her marijuana stash, along with her various crack-smoking paraphernalia, to her boyfriend's house three blocks up. And after some effort, she secured accommodations for Chuck's close friend Anthony, who had been sleeping in their basement and had a bench warrant out for failure to appear. She let her neighbors know that the police were coming so that their sons and cousins could go elsewhere for the night. (This was in case the police got the wrong house, which had happened before, or in case they decided to search the houses nearby.) She dug out the sixty dollars Reggie had hidden in the wall, as the police typically take whatever cash they find. She persuaded her father, Mr. George, to sleep at his girlfriend's place that night, in case "the law gives him a coronary."

Though Miss Linda had instructed Reggie to leave the house before midnight, he fell asleep by accident, and was still there when a three-man SWAT team busted the door in at about four in the morning. (The door remains broken and unlocked to this day.) Miss Linda had slept on the couch in preparation and, unsure if Reggie was still in the house, launched into a heated argument with the officers to delay their going upstairs. This ruse proved successful. According to Reggie, he was able to leave through a window in his bedroom and run through the alley before they could catch him.

The next night, three officers returned and ordered Reggie's younger brother, Tim, and Mr. George to lie facedown on the floor with their hands on their heads while they searched the house. According to Tim, an officer promised Miss Linda that if she gave Reggie up, they would not tell him that she was the one who had betrayed him. If she did not give her son up, the officer said he'd call Child Protective Services and have her youngest son taken away, because the house was infested with roaches, covered in cat shit, and unfit to live in. On this night, she again refused to tell the police where Reggie was.

Shaken but triumphant, Miss Linda came out early the next morning to tell her friends and neighbors the story. We sat on her iron back-porch steps that look out onto the shared alleyway.

> I do my dirt, I'm the first to admit it. Some people say I'm a bad mother. You can say what you want about me, but everybody knows I protect my sons. All three of them. These girls out here can talk all they want, but watch when the fucking law comes BAM! knocks they door in. Don't none of these girls know about that. They can talk, but won't none of them ride like me. Only some females is true riders, and I'm one of them females. [Takes a drag from her cigarette, nods her head confidently. Grins.] They can come back every night.

When her cousin came to sit with us, Miss Linda repeated the story, adding that she had deliberately worn her sexiest lingerie for the raid and had proudly stuck out her chest and butt when the officer was cuffing her against the wall. She acted this out to shrieks of laughter. She said that she told a particularly good-looking officer, "Honey, you so fine, you can search me anytime!"

Later in the day, more police officers came to search the house, and while they were pulling it apart once again, Reggie phoned to see if they were still there and if his mother was alright. Sitting not two feet from one of the officers, she coolly replied, "Yeah, Mom-Mom. I got to call you back later, because the police are here looking for Reggie. You haven't seen him, have you? Okay, alright. I'll call you back later. I'll pick up the Pampers when I go food shopping."

When the police left, Miss Linda told me: "Big George [her father] is going to tell me to clean this shit up as soon as he comes in. But I'm not cleaning till next week. They're going to keep coming, and I'm not putting this house back together every fucking morning."

I was there two nights later when the police raided Miss Linda's house for the third time. On this night, three officers put plastic cuffs on us and laid us face down on the living room floor while they searched the house. Despite her previous boasts of telling off the police and propositioning them with "I got three holes, pick one," Miss Linda cried and screamed when they dropped her to the floor. An officer mentioned that the family was lucky that Mr. George owned the house: if it were a Section 8-subsidized building, Miss Linda and her sons could be immediately evicted for endangering their neighbors and harboring a fugitive. (Indeed, I had seen this happen recently to two other families.) Upstairs, the police found a gun that Miss Linda couldn't produce a permit for; they arrested her and took her to the police station. When Tim and I picked her up that afternoon, she said she was told that she would face gun charges unless she told the police where to find Reggie. They also promised her anonymity, though she said she didn't believe them for a second.

Though by her own and Tim's accounts Miss Linda had been quite stalwart up until this point, the third raid and the lengthy interrogation seemed to weaken her resolve. When Reggie came around later to pick up the spaghetti she had prepared for him, she begged him to turn himself in. He refused.

A week later, Miss Linda was coming home from her boyfriend's house and found her TV and clothing dumped in the alleyway. Her father, Mr. George, told her that he would no longer allow her to live there with Tim if she continued to hide Reggie from the police:

> This ain't no damn carnival. I don't care *who* he is, I'm not letting nobody run through this house with the cops chasing him, breaking shit, spilling shit, waking me up out of my sleep. I'm not with the late-night screaming and running. I open my eyes and I see a nigga hopping over my bed trying to crawl out the window. *Hell*, no! Like I told Reggie, if the law run up in here one more time I be done had a stroke. Reggie is a grown-ass man [he was seventeen]. He ain't hiding out in my damn house. We going to fuck around and wind up in jail with this shit. They keep coming, they going to find some reason to book my Black ass.

Mr. George began calling the police whenever he saw Reggie in the house, and Miss Linda told her son that he could no longer stay there. For two months, Reggie lived in an abandoned Buick LeSabre parked in a nearby alleyway.

Though under extreme duress, Miss Linda nonetheless refused to tell the police where to find Reggie. And while she ultimately begged him to turn himself in, and then kicked him out of the house when her father threatened to evict her, she never gave her son up to the police. While Reggie was sleeping in the Buick, she kept in close touch with him, supplying him with food almost every evening. Her neighbors and family, and Reggie himself, seemed to believe that she had done the best she could, better than anyone else could have done. The evening the cops took Reggie in, I sat with Miss Linda and some of her neighbors. She poured Red Irish Rose wine into small plastic cups for us.

> Well, at least he don't have to look over his shoulder anymore, always worried that the law was going to come to the house. He was getting real sick of sleeping in the car. It was getting cold outside, you know, and plus, Reggie is a big boy and his neck was all cramped up. And he used to come to the back like: "Ma, make me a plate," and then he'd come back in twenty minutes and I'd pass him the food from out the window.

Brianna, Chuck's girlfriend, responded, "You ride harder than any bitch out here, and Reggie knows that."

THE RIDER REBORN

Veronica was eighteen when she met Reggie, who was nineteen. She had been dating one of Reggie's friends, though not seriously, and this man never had much time for her. He would leave her with Reggie while he was busy, and as Reggie put it, one thing led to another. Soon Veronica was spending most evenings at Reggie's. Chuck and Tim were starting to call her Sis.

"At first I couldn't fall asleep," she told me a few weeks into this relationship. "I was scared the bugs would crawl on me at night. You really have to love a Taylor brother to sleep in that house." Indeed, the kitchen crawled with roaches, ants, and flies; the floors themselves looked like they were moving, as if you were in some psychedelic bug dream.

One night, Veronica woke up thinking that the roaches were crawling on the bed again, only to see Reggie scrambling to make it out the window while yelling at her to push him through. This was not easy, as Reggie is a young man of substantial girth. Then two cops busted through the bedroom door and threw Veronica out of the bed. They cuffed her to the bed frame for an hour while they searched the house, she told me the next day, even though it should have been plain to them that Reggie had fled through the still-open window, which naturally would have been shut in February. She said they told her they'd find out every illegal thing she did, every time she smoked weed or drove drunk, and they'd pick her up every time they came across her. They would put a special star in her file and run her name, and search her and whoever she was with whenever they saw her. They told her they had tapped her cell phone and could bring her up on conspiracy charges. Despite these threats, Veronica couldn't tell them where Reggie had run, because she simply did not know.

Later that day, Reggie called her from a pay phone in South Philly. Veronica pleaded with him to turn himself in. He refused, and she told him then and there that they were through.

Reggie put Veronica "on blast," telling his friends, relatives, and neighbors that she had cut him loose when the police started looking for him. He then began seeing Shakira, a woman he had dated in high school.

The next day, Veronica called me in tears: Reggie had told everyone on the block that she wasn't riding right, that she didn't really give a fuck about him, and that she was out as soon as shit got out of hand. He told her he would never have expected it, thought she was better than that.

As Veronica retreated from Sixth Street, Shakira stepped up to help Reggie hide. She met him at his friend's house and spent the next few days holed up in the basement with him. She arranged for a friend to bring them food. In the meantime, the police raided Miss Linda's house, Veronica's house, and Reggie's uncle's house. But they didn't visit Shakira's house or question her family, which seemed to allow her to preserve her role as a brave and loyal person. I went to see her and Reggie on the third day.

Shakira: I been here the whole time, A. When they [the police] came to his mom's we was both there, and he went out the back and I been here this whole time.
Reggie: She riding hard as shit.
Alice: That's what's up [that's good].
Reggie: Remember Veronica? When she found out the boys [the police] was looking for me, she was like: click [the sound of a phone hanging up]. She'd be like, "I see you when I see you." Shakira ain't like that, though; she riding like a mug [motherfucker, i.e., very hard]. She worried about me, too.

We didn't hear from Veronica for a few weeks, and then the police found Reggie hiding in another shed nearby. They came in cars and helicopters, shutting down the block and busting open the shed with a battering ram.

When Reggie could make a phone call, he let Veronica know that he wasn't seeing Shakira anymore. Veronica wrote him a letter, and then she started visiting him. Because the bus routes don't line up well, it takes three hours to get to Northeast Philadelphia, where the county jails are.

Veronica had never visited a guy in jail before, and we'd often discuss what outfit she could wear to look her best while complying with the jail's regulations.

As Veronica made the weekly trek to the county jail on State Road, Reggie's friends stayed home. They didn't write; they didn't put any money on his books.

Every day, Reggie voiced his frustration with his boys over the phone to me:

> Niggas ain't riding right! Niggas ain't got no respect. G probably going to do it [put money on his books], but Steve be flajing [bullshitting, lying]. When I come home, man, I'm not fucking with *none* of these niggas. Where the fuck they at? They think it's going to be all love when I come home, like, what's up, Reggie, welcome back and shit . . . But *fuck* those niggas, man. They ain't riding for me, I got no rap for them when I touch [get home]. On my word, A, I ain't fucking with *none* of them when I get home. I would be a fucking nut for that. Brandon especially, A. I was with this nigga *every day*. And now he's on some: "My bad, I'm fucked up [broke]." Nigga, you wasn't fucked up when I was out there! I banged on that nigga, A [hung up on him].

Despite their continued promises to visit and to send money, not one of Reggie's boys had made the trip after three months. Only Veronica came. She wrote him about two letters every week, with him writing two or maybe three letters back. Sometimes she and I would go together to visit him. On Reggie's birthday, Veronica wrapped a tiny bag of marijuana in a twenty-dollar bill and smuggled it to him in the visiting room.

One afternoon, Veronica and I were sitting on Miss Linda's second-floor porch playing spades with her. Though usually quiet, Veronica spoke for the longest I'd heard:

> Ain't none of his boys go visit him, none of them . . . The only people that visit is me and Alice. Like, that should tell him something. Your homies ain't really your homies—I'm the only one that's riding. I'm the only real friend he got. Who's putting money on your books? They said they was going to put some on there, but they ain't do it. The only money he got on his books is from me and you.

It seemed that Veronica, who had dropped Reggie while he was on the run, who was humiliated as a weak and disloyal person, was now, through the work of visiting and writing letters, reborn a faithful and stalwart companion.

Women can also salvage their relationships and self-worth by gradually letting the details of a man's confinement fade and joining with him to paint her conduct in a more positive light. Eight times I noted that a woman visiting a man in custody would join with him to revise the events leading up to his arrest and trial in ways that downplayed her role in his confinement.

When Mike was twenty-four and his children were three and six years old, he began dating a woman from North Philly named Michelle. Within a month they had become very close: Michelle's three-year-old son started calling Mike "Daddy," and Michelle's picture went up on Mike's mother's mantelpiece next to his graduation picture and the school photos of his son and daughter. He started spending most nights at her apartment.

Michelle was the first Puerto Rican woman Mike had ever dated, and he had high hopes that her ethnic background would signify strong loyalty. "With Spanish chicks," he said, "it's all about family. Family is everything to them. Black chicks ain't like that. They love the cops."

Michelle and Mike explained to me separately that Michelle was nothing like the mother of Mike's children, Marie, who so frequently called the police on him. Since Michelle's father and brothers sold drugs, she was used to the police and the courts, and wouldn't cave under their pressure. With strong memories of her mother struggling with her father's legal troubles all through her childhood, Michelle told me that she was a second-generation rider. She also expressed that she loved Mike more than any man she had ever met, including her son's father, who was currently serving ten years in federal prison.

Michelle's loyalty would be tested three months into their relationship. Mike missed a court appearance, and a bench warrant was issued for his arrest. Upon hearing the news, Michelle assured me that nothing—not the cops, not the judge, not the nut-ass prison guards—would break them apart.

At around four o'clock the following Friday morning, she phoned me sobbing: the cops had knocked her door down and taken Mike. He tried to run, and they beat him out on the sidewalk with batons. She said they beat him so badly that she couldn't stop screaming. Why did they have to do that? They had already put him in handcuffs.

At the precinct, the police kept Mike cuffed to a desk for eighteen hours in the underwear they had found him in. The next morning, they brought Michelle down to the station and questioned her for three hours. Then they showed Mike Michelle's statement, which detailed his activities, his associates, and the locations of his drug-selling business. When he got to county jail, he wrote her a letter, which she showed me:

> Don't come up here, don't write, don't send no money. Take all your shit from my
> mom's, matter of fact, I'll get her to drop that shit off. You thought I wasn't going to
> find out that you a rat? They showed me everything. Fuck it. I never gave a fuck about
> you anyway. You was just some pussy to me, and your pussy not even that good!

Mike spread the word that Michelle was a snitch, and this news was the hot topic for a few days between his boys on the block and those locked up.

Incensed and humiliated, Michelle explained to me that Mike had no right to be angry with her. He clearly didn't care about her. In fact, despite all his claims to the contrary, the police had shown her the text messages and phone calls that proved he was still seeing Marie. Not only that, but Mike had tried to pin the drugs on her and claimed that the gun in the apartment belonged to her father. Michelle wrote him a scathing letter back:

> I should have known that you were still messing with your baby-mom. I felt like a fool when they showed me your cell phone calls and texts at 2 and 3 in the morning. And don't even try to tell me that you were calling your kids, 'cause no 7 year old is up at 2 a.m. Did you think I wasn't going to find out you tried to put that shit on me? I read every word. That bitch can have you.

With concrete evidence of Mike's infidelity, Michelle came to see that Mike did not value or respect her: their relationship had been a sham. She began to regard her past association with him as sordid and shameful, and her present efforts to protect him humiliating. At the same time, the police were showing Mike that she had betrayed him. Injured and humiliated, he rebuffed and belittled her just as she faced indisputable evidence of his duplicity and confronted the possibility that this man who didn't love her might let her hang for his crimes.

Two days later, the cops took Michelle out to the suburbs where Mike had been selling. According to the police report, she gave up his stash spot, his runner, and all the customers she knew about.[15]

A friend of Mike's explained it like this:

> The girl said, "Fuck it, I've only known him for three months, I want to keep my kid." Plus, her mom is in a nursing home, and she has custody of her two little sisters, so you know they told her they was going to kick her out the spot [the Section-8 building] and take her son and her sisters and shit. She has too much on the line. That bitch ain't think twice. She was like: What do you want to know?

After Mike's mother and grandmother and I attended his court dates and saw Michelle's statement, Mike declared that she was a snitch and stopped talking to her for a while. The news spread quickly to Mike's boys—both those on the block and those locked up.

Though at first Michelle was able to justify her actions by noting that the police had threatened to take her children away and that Mike had in fact been cheating on her, these details seemed to have been forgotten in the neighborhood's collective memory as the weeks dragged on, and she increasingly came to feel that she had betrayed a good man. As his trial dates came and went, she began visiting him more often, and sending money and letters. Slowly, Michelle and Mike began to reconcile.

Some months later, Mike and I were chatting in the visiting room. He mentioned that the girlfriend of one of his friends had recently testified against that man in court. "She's a fucking rat," Mike said. "She don't give a fuck about him." We debated the circumstances of this, and I commented on how difficult it is to remain silent when the police threaten to evict you or take your kids. As an example, I noted that while Michelle clearly loved Mike, she had informed on him under just this kind of police pressure.

At this point our weekly gossip turned into a heated argument. Other visitors in the room began to stare as Mike forcefully explained to me that Michelle had not snitched. In fact, it was the woman in whose house he had been renting a room that had given the statement against him.

"You supposed to be keeping tabs! Like, that's your *job*. You're getting stu-
    pid. You used to remember every fucking thing."
"I really thought it was Michelle," I replied limply.
"What the fuck good are you if you can't even get basic shit right?"

My confidence as the group's chronicler quite shaken, I apologized profusely. At his next court date a month later, I asked Mike's lawyer to show me the statement again. Checking over the lengthy police report, I realized that my notes were accurate. Michelle had informed on Mike, on three separate occasions. I wasn't sure whether she had convinced Mike that she had remained silent, or they were both simply trying to put it behind them, but I decided it would be best not to bring it up again.

On our next visit, Mike lamented that one of his boys was continuing to call Michelle a snitch. "Niggas is gonna hate," he said. "That's been my whole life, since middle school. Everybody wants what I got."

I nodded my head in solidarity.

THE DIZZYING JOURNEY FROM RIDER
TO SNITCH

Many women in the Sixth Street neighborhood view the forcible and unexpected removal of a boyfriend, brother, or son to be, as Mike's girl-friend once put it, "the end of everything." When a woman gets the news that the police may be after the man in her life, she may take it as her obli-gation to help him hide from the authorities. Through protecting him, she makes a claim for herself as a loyal girlfriend or a good mother, an honorable and moral human being.

If the police never come looking for the man, she can continue to believe that she would do her utmost to shield him from the authorities, should the occasion for bravery and sacrifice arise. But if the police do come, they typically put pressure on her to provide information.

For the police and the district attorney, the task of turning intimates into informants is mostly a technical problem, one of many that arises in the work of rounding up and processing enough young men to meet informal arrest quotas and satisfy their superiors. But the role the police ask women to play in the identification, arrest, and conviction of the men they love presents deeper problems for women: problems for their sense of self.

To be sure, some of the women I came to know on 6th Street didn't seem to care very much whether their legally entangled family members or neighbors were in jail or not. Some even considered the confinement of these troublesome young men a far preferable alternative to dealing with them on the outside. But those who took these positions generally keep their distance from the men the police were after, and consequently tended not to know enough about their whereabouts to be very useful to the authorities. It is the women actively involved in the daily affairs of legally precarious men who prove most helpful in bringing about their arrest, so those women who consider the possible confinement of a son or boyfriend a grave event, a wrenching apart of their daily life, are the ones that the police enlist to capture and confine them.

When the police begin their pressure, when they raid a woman's house or pull her in for questioning, a woman faces a crisis in her relationship and in the image she has of herself: the police ask her to help imprison the very man she has taken it as a sacred duty to protect. Not only do the police ask her, they make her choose between her own security and his freedom. For many of the women I have come to know on Sixth Street, this choice is one they are asked to make again and again. It is part of what enduring the police and the prisons is about.

Relatives and neighbors looking in on this crisis from the outside may see a woman's options in stark terms: she can prove herself strong in the face of threats and violence and protect the man, or she can cave under the pressure and betray him. If she withstands the police, she will garner public acclaim as a rider. If she caves, she will suffer humiliation as an abandoner or an informant.

But as the pressure increases, a woman's perspective on right and wrong begins to shift. As the police roll out their techniques of persuasion, she finds herself increasingly cut off from the man she loves, and interacting more and more with the authorities. The techniques they use to gain her cooperation turn her basic understandings about herself and her significant others upside down. She learns that her children and her home aren't safe, nor are the other people she holds dear. She begins to see her daily life as an almost endless series of crimes, for which she may be arrested at any moment the police see fit. She learns that the man she loves doesn't care about her, and comes to see her involvement with him as sordid, shameful, and pathetic.

As the police show the woman that her boyfriend has cheated, or that her son may try to blame her for his crimes, she comes to realize that protecting him from the authorities may not be such a good idea after all. Threatened with eviction, the loss of her children, her car, or all future housing benefits, her resolve to shield him weakens. By the time the police assure her of confidentiality, she begins to see the merits of working with the authorities.

CONCLUSION

There is an excitement surrounding wanted men. They are, in a certain way, where the action is.[16] But wanted men also stop coming around as much or as routinely. Their contributions to the household, though perhaps meager to begin with, may cease altogether. Their life on the run may be exciting, but it is a holding pattern; it has no forward motion. To some degree, a man's wanted status demands that a woman live in the present, and this present is a dizzying and uncertain one.

Out of this morass, the police offer the woman a dubious path: she can turn against the man; she can come over to their side. As she begins to orient herself to their way of thinking, she finds a way out of the dizzying holding pattern created by the man's evasion and the police's pressure. She is now able to chart some forward path and leave the upside-down world the raids and interrogations have created. Maybe he will hate her and she will hate herself, but at least she is moving forward.

As the police make it harder for her to remain on the man's side, they construct a vision of what life would be like without him, independent of the involvement with crime and with the police that he requires. They create a distinctive path for the woman that involves a change in how she judges herself and others.

A woman who contemplates changing sides discovers that a number of lines of action become available to her. She may urge the man to turn himself in or, if pressure persists, she may give him an ultimatum: give yourself up or I will. She may openly call the police on the man, in plain view of their mutual family and friends. She may turn him in secretly and attempt to conceal that she has cooperated with the authorities. Alternately, she may cut off ties with him, refuse to speak to him anymore, or kick him out of the house.

During this process, the pressure imposed by the police allows the woman to reconcile herself to her behavior, and the police's techniques come in handy as justifications for her actions. But when the man is taken into custody and the pressure from the police ceases, it becomes increasingly difficult for the woman and the rest of the community to accept what she did. She must now deal head-on with the public humiliation and private shame that come with abandoning or informing on the man she professed to care about.

It is in the nature of policing that officers tend to interact most with those in whose behavior they find fault, such that the woman's encounters with the police begin when she refuses to comply and end when she comes over to their side. That is, her intense and intimate association with the authorities lasts only for the duration of their denigration and her resistance. Once she cooperates and gives the man up, the police abandon their interest in her. At the moment she changes sides, she finds herself surrounded by neighbors and family who mock and disdain her, who consider her actions immoral and betraying.

Throughout this process, the woman takes a journey rife with emotional contradictions. The news that the man in her life has become wanted prompts a renewal of her attachment, such that she strengthens her commitment to him just as he ceases to play an active role in her daily life, to furnish her with any concrete future, or to assist her financially. When the man is taken into custody and the pressure to inform on him lifts, a woman can pledge her devotion once more and make amends. Unlike life on the run, his sentence or trial has a clear end point. She can coordinate her life around the visiting hours, and the phone calls in the morning and evening. She can make plans for his return.[17] But since she has contributed to his confinement, her attempts to repair the relationship coincide with his most heated anger against her. Even if he forgives her, a woman can renew her commitment to him and return to regarding him as good and honorable only after he has left her daily life most completely, as he sits in jail or prison.

Once a woman's son or partner is incarcerated, she may come full circle. As she did when she first got the news that the authorities might come looking, she returns to thinking that the police, the courts, and the prisons are unjust, and she will do just about anything to protect and support the man she loves.

A few skilled intimates do not travel the path the police put forward, as they are able to resist the pressure in the first place. They learn to anticipate raids and to mitigate the damage that a raid may cause. They learn to make a scene and become a problem for police by vocally demanding their rights, by attracting a large audience, or by threatening to sue or go to the newspapers. They practice concerted silence, learning how to reveal as little as possible. They distract the officers from the direction the man ran, or the box in which incriminating evidence may be found. They also make counteroffers, such as sexual favors, or provide information about someone else the police might be interested in. Their refusal to cave under pressure means that their conduct calls for little explanation, and their relationships need few repairs.

Though some women manage to salvage their relationships, their reputations, and their sense of self after they cooperate, and a rare few are able to withstand police pressure and garner some honor and acclaim, it must be said that the police's strategy of arresting large numbers of young men by turning their mothers and girlfriends against them goes far in creating a culture of fear and suspicion, overturning women's basic understandings of themselves as good people and their lives as reasonably secure, and destroying familial and romantic relationships that are often quite fragile to begin with.

NOTES

1. On the first page of his landmark study of social conditions in Philadelphia's seventh ward, W. E. B. DuBois (1899, 1) included the footnote, "I shall throughout this study use the term 'Negro,' to designate all persons of Negro descent, although the appellation is to some extent illogical. I shall, moreover, capitalize the word, because I believe that eight million Americans are entitled to a capital letter." I have capitalized the word *Black* in this work for the same reasons, and to follow him.
2. Of the 217 households surveyed by Chuck and me in 2007.
3. In eighteen months of daily fieldwork, there were only five days in which I observed no police activity.
4. While conducting fieldwork, I became attentive to the particular moment that women discover a partner or son is wanted by the police by reading studies of people receiving life-altering news in hospitals and doctors' offices. There, family members learn that a loved one has a disease, not a warrant for arrest, but the shock and confusion are common to both, and the news may have a similarly transformative effect on relationships. For two excellent studies of hospital patients and their families receiving life-altering news, see Sudnow (1967, chapter 5) and Maynard (2003, 9).
5. This conversation was recorded with permission on my iPhone. Some off-topic pieces of the discussion were omitted.
6. The way others tell it, Mike's mother didn't exactly tell his father to stop coming around—he did that all on his own.
7. The term *rider* has been discussed by Jeff Duncan-Andrade (2007, 623), who uses the spelling *rida*. He defines it as a "popular cultural term that refers to people who can be counted on in extreme duress."
8. There are few systematic studies of the legal and financial obligations incurred by people moving through the courts. In a unique study, Harris, Evans, and Beckett (2010) quantify the financial burden for a sample of people in Washington State. They find

that those who have been convicted of misdemeanor or felony charges will owe on average more than $11,000 to the courts over their life span, and likely will pay significantly more than that because of the interest accruing on their legal debts.

9. From a taped interview with two former members of the Philadelphia Warrant Unit, 2010.
10. These techniques as I describe them represent the women's perspective on the police's efforts to secure their cooperation. For a contemporary treatment of police work from the officers' perspective, see Moskos 2008.
11. In Philadelphia, a man cannot visit a jail where he has been an inmate for six months after his release. In practice, this paperwork takes quite a while to go through, so that men who have ever been an inmate at a county jail are often denied visitation rights to any of the local jails. Prisons also run the names of visitors, making it dangerous for men with warrants or other legal entanglements to go there for visits. A third barrier to visitation is the canine unit, which is occasionally stationed in the prison or jail parking lot. Though visitors can refuse to allow the dogs to search their vehicles, they will be denied entrance to the facility.
12. For a detailed account of evictions among poor families in the United States, see Desmond 2012a and 2012b.
13. Research suggests these are quite realistic fears. Incarceration increases the likelihood of infectious disease and stress-related illnesses, according to Michael Massoglia (2008a). The same researcher has shown that incarceration causes long-term negative health effects (Massoglia 2008b).
14. Of course, that Miss Linda was good at protecting Chuck, Reggie, and Tim from the police may also have contributed to the frequency of police raids, as her firm protectionist stance likely encouraged her sons' continued residency in the house. Other neighbors explained her ability to ride by the fact that in comparison with other women, Miss Linda had little to lose. Since her father owned the house, it wasn't as easy to evict her. Since the house was already in quite poor condition, she didn't fear the destruction caused by the raid as much as other women did. And since she held no job, the police couldn't threaten to notify her employer.
15. Michelle never admitted to this; Mike's lawyer showed his mother and me the statement at the arraignment.
16. For a nuanced account of the many excitements and pleasures to be found in breaking the law, see Katz 1990.
17. For an illuminating account of the complex ways in which women view the confinement of a loved one, including some surprising upsides to romantic involvement with a man sitting in prison, see Comfort 2007, 127–127, 174.

WORKS CITED

Comfort, Megan. 2007. *Doing Time Together: Love and Family in the Shadow of the Prison.* Chicago: University of Chicago Press.

Desmond, Matthew. 2012a. "Disposable Ties and the Urban Poor." *American Journal of Sociology* 117: 1295–1335.

Desmond, Matthew. 2012b. "Eviction and the Reproduction of Urban Poverty," *American Journal of Sociology* 118: 88–133.

DuBois, W. E. B. 1899. *The Philadelphia Negro*. Philadelphia: University of Pennsylvania Press.

Duncan-Andrade, Jeff. 2007. "Gangstas, Wankstas, and Ridas: Defining, Developing, and Supporting Effective Teachers in Urban Schools." *International Journal of Qualitative Studies in Education* 20(6): 617–638.

Garland, David. 2001. "Introduction: The Meaning of Mass Imprisonment." In *Mass Imprisonment: Social Causes and Consequences*, edited by David Garland. London: Sage.

Harris, Alexes, Heather Evans, and Katherine Beckett. 2010. "Drawing Blood from Stones: Monetary Sanctions, Punishment and Inequality in the Contemporary United States." *American Journal of Sociology* 115: 1753–1799.

Katz, Jack. 1990. *Seductions of Crime: Moral and Sensual Attractions in Doing Evil.* New York: Basic Books.

Massoglia, Michael. 2008a. "Incarceration as Exposure: The Prison, Infectious Disease, and Other Stress-Related Illnesses." *Journal of Health and Social Behavior* 49: 56–71.

Massoglia, Michael 2008b. "Incarceration, Health, and Racial Disparities in Health." *Law and Society Review* 42: 275–306.

Maynard, Doug. 2003. *Bad News, Good News: Conversational Order in Everyday Talk and Clinical Settings.* Chicago: University of Chicago Press.

Moskos, Peter. 2008. *Cop in the Hood: My Year Policing Baltimore's Eastern District.* Princeton, NJ: Princeton University Press.

Pettit, Becky, and Bruce Western. 2004. "Mass Imprisonment and the Life-Course: Race and Class Inequality in U.S. Incarceration." *American Sociological Review* 69: 151–169.

The Pew Center on the States. 2008. "One in 100: Behind Bars in America 2008." Washington, DC: Pew Charitable Trusts.

Solzhenitsyn, Aleksandr. 1973. *The Gulag Archipelago.* New York: Harper and Row.

Sudnow, David. 1967. *Passing On: The Social Organization of Dying.* Englewood Cliffs, NJ: Prentice-Hall.

Sykes, Gresham. 2007 [1958]. *Society of Captives.* Princeton, NJ: Princeton University Press.

Uggen, Christopher, Jeff Manza, and Melissa Thompson. 2006. "Democracy and the Civil Reintegration of Criminal Offenders." *Annals of the American Academy of Political and Social Science* 605: 281–310.

US Department of Justice. 1982. "Prisoners 1925–81." Washington, DC: Government Printing Office.

US Department of Justice. 2012. "Correctional Populations in the United States, 2011." Washington, DC: Government Printing Office.

Walmsley, Roy. 2011. "World Prison Population List," 9th ed. London: International Centre for Prison Studies.

PART 4

Ethnographic Positions and the Politics of Violence

CHAPTER 10

Standpoint Purgatorio

Liminal Fear and Danger in Studying the "Black and Brown" Tension in Los Angeles

RANDOL CONTRERAS

INTRODUCTION

In the United States, urban ethnographers of violence sometimes provide fascinating accounts of how they enter field sites. There are the "outsiders," like Philippe Bourgois (2003) and Timothy Black (2009), who grapple with racial, class, educational, and cultural differences between themselves and study participants. There are the "insiders," like Robert Durán (2013), Victor Rios (2011), and myself (Contreras 2013), whose biographies ease the research access, but make us grapple with our new status as academics. In all, we learn that "insider" and "outsider" statuses are fluid, or as Dwyer and Buckle (2009) note, there is always "the space between."[1] In other words, a researcher's different statuses (such as race, class, and gender) can change their relationship to a group under different situations.

Yet before gaining group access, both insider and outsider ethnographers experience moments of "liminality" (Turner 1969), moments where they occupy an ambiguous and lonely space—moments where they belong neither to their world nor the world they wish to enter. Anthropologist Norris Johnson (1984) likens this liminal experience to one of Arnold Van Gennep's (1960) *rite de passage* typologies: first the target group *stops* a researcher from gaining access; then the group makes the researcher *wait* for access; then the group provides the researcher with an opportunity to *transition* into access; and then the group finally allows the researcher *entry* into its world. Johnson also adds that an ethnographer's race and gender complicate the sequence. Racial and gender similarities can smooth entry, while racial and gender differences can make it a rough, bumpy ride.

But what happens when an Afro-Latino ethnographer is studying two groups—a Black one and a Latino one—and their liminal status is in relationship not to one group but to two groups instead? What space does such a researcher occupy when those groups oppose each other, hate each other, and do violence against each other based on racial hatred? Where does a researcher sit as he or she makes sense of this dangerous position? How does a researcher feel when in a state of double liminality, or a double state of an extended *stop* or *wait*?

That researcher occupies what I call a *standpoint purgatorio*. This is a tormenting positional space that results from being both insider and outsider to two or more conflicting groups. In Los Angeles (LA), I occupy that torturous, liminal space as I try to examine the ethnoracial tension between Mexicans and African Americans. As a child of Dominican immigrants, I share cultural and racial spaces with both ethnoracial groups. Yet there are spaces we do not share, which put me in a unique, but dangerous position. Below, I describe my standpoint ordeals, ones that I am still trying to overcome.

Let me start at the beginning.

THE DREAM AND NIGHTMARE OF LA

It was just like the movies. Driving down Santa Monica Boulevard, I marveled at the soft, giant palm trees, the cool breeze, the outdoor eateries and restaurants, the people standing or strolling, the bright lights, the cool cars, the boulevard watching, the cruising—all that made me believe in sunny southern California. I had just arrived from Baltimore, a gloomy city of rain, pain, abandonment, and thriving heroin markets. As a South Bronx native, I searched for something new, out of my box, like beaches, waves, and endless sunny days. My new tenure-track job at Cal State Fullerton (Orange County) would give me this chance. Also, I was reuniting with *mi compañera*, who started her tenure-track job a year earlier at Cal State Northridge (San Fernando Valley). *Ay, que perfecto.*

The next sunny morning, *mi compañera* and I ran some errands, which required driving out of her middle-class Sherman Oaks neighborhood. As we neared our first destination, my dream LA faded away. Potholed roads. Empty sidewalks. Worn-out strip malls. Beat-up cars. Dingy two- and three-story apartment buildings. Scarred boulevards and streets. Dilapidation—everywhere. *Coño, qué pasó?*

The ride rattled me back into LA's other realities, which I had already known existed. LA was dire poverty and the loss of manufacturing jobs. LA was Mexican, Salvadorian, Asian, and African American gangs. LA was immigrant scapegoating and immigrant exploitation. LA was Black residents making up too much of California's prison population. LA was police brutality and ethnoracial uprisings. LA wasn't all rolling hills or beach condos and surf and movie star smiles.

LA, for the poor, was hell, a cruel existence.

In the coming months, I observed another reality: LA was ethnoracial tension. Possibly hate. When African Americans, Asians, and Latina/ os neared each other, they often tensed up, got quiet, got serious, stared straight ahead. This differed from the east coast, where folks didn't necessarily like each other but publically tolerated ethnoracial differences. They rode crowded public transportation together, walked crowded sidewalks together, and just seemed at ease together in crowds. But in LA, people seemed uneasy around ethnic "Others." And African Americans and Latina(os) tensed up around each other the most.

Fascinated (and disturbed), I wanted to examine this "Black and Brown" tension. So I decided on a three-pronged field research approach: spend a year or so in a Mexican-dominated community, spend a year or so in an African American-dominated community, and spend a year or so in a community with about an equal makeup of Mexicans and African Americans. In this way, I would cover it all.

But *un tremendo problema* would complicate my plans.

STANDPOINT PURGATORIO

Whenever I came near Mexicans in public, they tensed up, looked away, or left the area. At first, I thought my younger looks fit me into the general profile of the stereotypical threatening minority male. *Pero cómo?* I wore Sketcher shoes, prescription eye glasses, and regular fitting jeans with only a *slight* sag. Yet Mexicans avoided me, sometimes treating me as invisible or as carrying the plague. In department stores, Mexican employees secretly (or so they thought) followed me. In authentic Mexican restaurants, Mexican cashiers and servers rarely smiled or looked me in the eye. It happened so much that I felt self-conscious. Sometimes, I didn't want to go out to eat or run errands. I no longer wanted to explore LA. I saw myself as a problem.

Then one day I got the answer. I was holding an elevator door for an elderly Latina, who struggled to make it in on time. After getting inside, she thanked me in heavily accented English. "*A su orden,*" I responded, implicitly letting her know that she could speak Spanish if she wished. Her head snapped in surprise and she gave me a curious look. She hadn't thought that I was Latino or Dominican. Many of my Mexican students later revealed that I looked like a light-skinned Black at first sight. *The hair,* they said, made them think that. They also rarely saw Caribbean Latina/os, who have salient African features. Now it hit me: most LA Mexicans categorized me as African American. This explained their avoidance, their treating me like the Other.

I actually thought it would be easy to do field research in a Mexican neighborhood. Its residents spoke Spanish; I spoke Spanish. Cool LA radio stations played *bachata* music; I could kill it on the dance floor. Mexicans ate rice and beans; I could eat rice and beans *for life.* I was a child of immigrants; they were a community of immigrants with US-born children. We shared some history and culture, I thought.

On the other hand, I believed that it would be hard to access African Americans in LA. In New York City, Latina/os and African Americans generally got along, but mostly in sharing urban culture: they listened to the same hip hop music, spoke the same street lingo, followed the same fashions, shared the same hairstyles, and even walked and gestured alike. And with similar phenotypes and skin color, they were sometimes hard to tell apart.

However, Latina/os made sure to state differences: they were tied to a distant homeland, knew a second language (Spanish), ate different foods, and claimed a link to White Spain (at least in the Dominican community). These distinctions raised their status and avoided the social stigma put on US Blacks. It also created resentment on both sides, with one hearing an occasional "stupid Spanish motherfucker" here, and a "*maldito Negro sucio*" there. So, for research in New York City, I always thought it easier to enter a Latina/o community than a Black one.

In LA, a different dynamic existed. In malls, shops, and restaurants, I walked around African Americans without feeling unwanted or shunned. I made friendly eye contact with them and they returned it with a nod. I stood in line behind them, and they didn't shift uneasily or look uncomfortable. I asked them questions, and they looked straight into my eyes. They engaged me. They embraced me. They made me feel at home in LA. Soon I sought Black faces and spaces whenever I went out. I felt a bond with them.

In LA, I was Black.

Clearly, a few African Americans knew that I wasn't an LA African American. They thought that I was Belizean, or as one African American barber told me, "some type of Black, like from New Orleans." Yet they never saw me as Latino, or Mexican. Sometimes, I stopped seeing myself as a Latino too. Not that I no longer felt *entirely* Latina/o, or Dominican. At home, I still ate my favorite Dominican dishes, searched YouTube for the latest Dominican events, and polished my bachata dance moves with *mi compañera*. And in my car, I sometimes blasted merengue, bachata, and salsa music to ease the freeway monotony that is LA. But as soon as I stepped out of those spaces—my home, my car—I identified with how most of LA saw me.

As Black.

In a sense, I identified easily with African Americans. I shared the urban culture—the music, the fashion, the hairstyles, the language—that they continuously recreated. I also shared the psychological and social traumas that resulted from larger historical oppression at the hands of European Whites. In LA, I shared the terrible everyday experience of being a Black pariah, which shaped and influenced our movements, feelings, and thoughts.

At the same time, I did not fully identify with LA African Americans. I was brought up under a different context and culture. Though my world was urban, cool, and endangered, it was also urban-island code-switching, it was *platanos, arroz, gandules,* with broccoli, oatmeal, and French Fries; it was fast-paced merengue— *poom-poom-poom-poom-poom*—with hip hop coolness— *dime habe', que lo que, dame lu', come e'*—that was a fusion of experiences: the Black experience, the immigrant experience, the inner-city experience with a slice of the Caribbean.

I was also unsure of the outcome if my Dominican-ness surfaced while interacting with African Americans. Because it was a two-way street: LA Latina/os generally avoided Blacks, and Blacks generally avoided them. Blacks felt most uncomfortable around Mexicans and sometimes voiced their resentment (they took away jobs, they said). So I worried about them seeing me hang out in public with Mexicans or hearing my Spanish slang when I relaxed after a few drinks. How would a Black passenger react if after turning on my car, they immediately heard:

♪

Ay, recházame – es que no puedo aceptar tu am-o-o-o-r
Ay, olvidame – áunque nos duela hay que aceptar ese dol-o-o-o-r

♪

Would they question our friendship and trust? Would they question my Blackness? Would they ask that dangerous question: "Whose side is he on?"

In LA, my positionality put me in a limbo, one that spun me round and round and round. I was partially inside and outside both groups. So I was neither here nor there, I was here and there, I was understood and misunderstood, I was accepted and unaccepted, I went in and went out, I had direction, but was misdirected, I got lost, but I was found, I was confused, confused, confused, about which path to take at the fork in this torturous road!

I suffered tremendously in this halfway house of positionality, or what I call *standpoint purgatorio*. This refers to the tormenting positional space occupied by a field researcher who is partially insider and outsider to two or more groups under observation. This unique positionality haunts them, torments them, and tears them apart as they are unsure of where they stand in the eyes of all groups involved. It has no resemblance to the Catholic notion of purgatory; it is the furthest thing away from purification or a state of grace. It is a space of pain, of hurt, of *puro dolor.*

Yet it is also a space of fear. Fear of being threatened and hurt. Fear of ultimately being *un muerto* in the field. My fear came from wanting to understand the ethnoracial tension through the eyes of the drama's main actors. They were the marginalized young Mexicans and African Americans who shared school cafeterias, classrooms, and yards. They were the young and old returning from jail and prison, the most likely to be in violent gangs. They were the most likely to question and distrust me, to put me in danger. *Peligro!*

STUDYING THE MEXICAN COMMUNITY

Eventually, I bracketed my public interactions with Mexicans and created a wonderful fieldwork fantasy. It went as follows:

I would walk around a Mexican neighborhood often. I would become so familiar that in time I could strike up a conversation at a restaurant or grocery store, where people surely hung out. We would talk about anything, about food, sports, or politics. Soon I would walk down streets where everyone knew me: *"Llegó El Profe!"* they would call out upon my arrival. I would play cards and dominoes with them. I would drink tequila and beers with them. I would attend birthday parties and *quinceañeras* with them. I would even be asked to be a child's godfather or *padrino*, forever cementing my communal ties. *Olvidate*, this fieldwork would be a breeze.

Excited, I asked my Mexican students if they knew anyone in an LA Mexican community. Unfortunately, most of them were from Santa Ana and Anaheim, two poverty-ridden cities in Orange County. One Mexican student, though, advised me after class not to enter certain LA neighborhoods. You look Black, she told me, and Mexican gangbangers don't like Blacks. She then warned me to avoid her hometown of Hawaiian Gardens, a small city about fifteen miles southeast of LA. Over there, Mexican gangbangers beat up Black people, she said. I asked her if they only targeted Black gang members. It didn't matter, she replied; they targeted any Black person, regardless.

I was shocked. I knew that ethnoracial tension sometimes resulted in violence. But here the violence seemed extreme, based on pure racial hatred alone. I later learned that as early as 1993, Mexican gangs in Hawaiian Gardens harassed, attacked, and shot Black residents, and fire-bombed and spray-painted racial slurs on Black-owned homes (Adams 1993). In 2009, LA county sheriffs indicted over one hundred members of Hawaiian Garden's Mexican Varrio 13 gang. The charges ranged from murder and extortion, to illegal weapons and drugs—and to attacks on Black residents, like the beating of a Black male with a rake and the shooting of a Black male doing yard work, just for being Black (Glover and Winton 2009). According to law enforcement, HG Varrio 13 proudly referred to itself as the "Hate Gang," whose goal was to rid the city of Blacks.

Chilling. The gang's alleged racial cleansing goal not only disturbed me but also put fear in me. Now I worried about Mexican gangs targeting me as a Black man. But this occurred in Hawaiian Gardens, I reasoned, not LA. I still had a chance.

Since I eventually moved to Burbank (in the southeast corner of the San Fernando Valley), I became interested in the nearby Mexican communities: Eagle Rock and Highland Park. Eagle Rock, though, had gentrified too much for my research tastes. Young white professionals and hipsters dominated its scene. But Highland Park still kept a strong Mexican cultural presence. Once again, I dreamed up a fieldwork fantasy: I would often visit Highland Park and walk around its beautiful hills, bungalows, and craftsman-style homes. I would slowly get to know its residents and eventually become a community celebrity" "*Llegó El Profe!*" they would call out upon my arrival.

However, Highland Park was home to the Avenues, a Mexican gang that had been around for about fifty years. They controlled the area's violent drug market and were loyal to *La Eme*, or the Mexican Mafia, which dominated southern California's Latino gangs in state prisons.[2] By the mid-1990s and early 2000s, they had also become more than a drug-dealing gang. They became a racist gang that wanted to cleanse the area of Blacks (Mock 2006; Pelisek 2005).

In 1999, the murder of Kenneth Wilson: while parking his car to visit a friend, Avenue members driving in a stolen van saw him, threw a racial slur, and shot him several times.

In 2000, the murder of Christopher Bowser: after filing police reports for being racially harassed and chased by Avenue members, they shot him repeatedly while he waited at a bus stop.

In 2000, the murder of Anthony Prudhomme: two months after renting a basement room in Highland Park, Avenue members broke in and shot him in the face (he was actually bi-racial, half-white, half-Black).

Federal indictments later claimed that Avenues members had attacked some Black men playing basketball in a public park; beat up a Black man using a public pay phone; beat up another Black man walking with a Latina; harassed a Black woman with racial slurs in a supermarket; pistol-whipped a Black jogger; and drew chalk outlines of human bodies (resembling a murder scene) in the driveway of a Black family's home (Mock 2005; Pelisek 2006). In 2006, several Avenues members were convicted of murdering Wilson and Bowser, and for conspiring to violate the civil rights of African Americans (US Department of Justice 2006).

I felt as though I were in a bad dream, that at some point I would awaken. The ethnoracial tension I could sociologically understand: ethnoracial groups saw themselves in competition for scarce social and economic resources. It was the racial cleansing component that I could not fathom. This was not the Jim Crow South. This was not the Ku Klux Klan. We lived in an era where such racist violence was largely condemned. How, then, could some members of the Mexican community commit such horrific acts against Blacks?

Clearly, I did not believe that Mexican residents as a whole accepted or encouraged such violence. It was unfair and wrong to generalize the beliefs and behavior of a few individuals to an entire population. Also, newspaper accounts voiced the reaction of some Mexican residents, who were shocked and saddened by those race-based attacks. Yet my fear of researching a Mexican-dominated community increased. Would Mexican gang members allow me in their public spaces? Would they view my frequent visits as a bothersome Black presence? Would they see me as the start of a great Black "infestation"?

I was unsure.

EL MAYATE

Conversations with my son heightened my concerns. He has a deep brown skin color and roughly textured hair, obvious African physical traits. And though he strongly identified as Dominican, he only hung out with African American classmates. According to him, the Black students (who made up less than 2 percent of the high school's population) had befriended him on the first day of school. The Hispanic students (who were mostly Mexican and about 25 percent of the school's population) stayed away from him, acknowledging him for occasional greetings.

One day, a male Mexican student heard my son speak Spanish to a Mexican girl. His reaction: "Fool, I thought you were a Mayate! I didn't know you were cool." Afterward, he introduced him to other Mexican students by saying, "Fool, you'll never guess what this fool is." Then my son would speak Spanish to instant shouts of: "Oh shit, this fool looks just like a Mayate! He speaks Spanish! What is this fool?" My son would then explain that he was Dominican. Then they would laugh and slap him fives. Now he was cool with Mexican students. He wasn't Black.

But he never felt comfortable hanging out with Mexicans. When some of them greeted him, they jokingly said, "Hey, Mayate!" Or they called him over by saying, "Mayate, come over here, fool." Or they made racist Black jokes in his presence. When he got a part-time job at Kmart, the same happened. After a few Mexican co-workers found out that he was Dominican, they referred to him as *El Mayate*. They also made him the brunt of their racist Black jokes. When he got angry, they told him: "Fool, we know you're not really a Mayate."

He also recalled one night when he hung out with a Mexican classmate in North Hollywood. There, they met up with some of his friend's gang-banger homeboys. The Mexican gangbangers, though, refused to shake my son's hand, giving him "mad dog" looks instead. His friend then said, "Nah fool, he's not a Mayate. He's Dominican. The fool speaks Spanish." Then they relaxed and gave him their hand. "We thought you were a fuck-ing Mayate," they told him and smiled when he spoke Spanish. Afterward, they talked about shooting people, which made him feel uncomfortable. He reasoned that by the mad dog looks he had first gotten, they probably would've shot him because he looked Black.

After hearing the story, I asked him if he really knew what *Mayate* meant. "It's just the Mexican word for Black people," he responded, inno-cently. We looked it up online and found variations of the following (I'm paraphrasing from urbandictionary.com):

> A derogatory word used by Mexicans and Mexican-Americans to refer to a Black per-
> son. Its literal definition is dung beetle, which is dark and eats shit.

My son looked deflated, confused. I suspected that he pondered how he was actually being called the lowest form of life, an insect that feeds on feces. "So that's what it really means," I finally said, breaking the silence. He didn't say anything, looking as if in a daze. He then received a text message on his cell phone, read it, and said that he had to go. *Ay, mi hijo.*

Clearly, most of his Mexican friends would never commit hate crimes against Blacks. Yet the foundation for this possibility existed. It was in that nasty, ugly reference, *Mayate*, which made dark-skinned people sub-human, worthless, less than wild beasts. If taken too far, the word allowed for a bracketing of morality. This opened the space for violence, violence based on racial hatred alone.

I became more concerned about my planned research. But I tried to create an upbeat side to my son's experience. As long as Mexican gang-bangers knew I was Dominican, the coast was clear. Spanish seemed to be a racial signifier, a language that linked Dominicans and Mexicans to a common colonizer, Spain. So I needed to highlight this connection. But how does one appear "Spanish" when they first pass for Black in LA? Perhaps wear T-shirts with big, bold Spanish words:

LATINO POR SIEMPRE!

Perhaps roll down my windows and let out loud cumbia music from my car:

> ♪
>
> *Carmen, se me perdió la cadenita,*
> *con el pito de Nasareno,*
> *que tu me regalaste Carmen . . .*
>
> ♪

Perhaps just address everyone and everything in my Spanish, which I purposely mixed with English to make up for my shortcomings:

Yo, bro, *imaginate eso!*

Even if Mexican gangbangers accepted me as a "Latino" or "Hispanic," I could still be *likened* to the Other. So they could take me in, but still keep me out through framing me as kin to Mayates. They might have less respect for me. They might be more impatient with me. They might hold a double-standard toward me. They (the men) might feel uncomfortable when I neared their women and children. In all, I expected to enter at the bottom of the Mexican community's racial ranking system. I became even more uncomfortable. Harassment. Intimidation. Violence. All of these could be wielded at me.

THE ROLE OF THE STATE

My fears worsened after I learned about official practices within California state prisons. As official policy, inmates are separated on the basis of race (Goodman 2008). At reception centers, Black inmates are coerced into housing with other Blacks; Whites with other Whites; Hispanics with other Hispanics—regardless of racial identification or national origin! Only when inmates enter prisons can they choose the category of "Other" (Ibid.). But in prison, inmates encounter racial segregation at its worst. For instance, amenities, like certain showers, are reserved for particular ethnoracial groups (Ibid.). Also, ethnoracial groups refuse to share common hair instruments and clippers with other groups. If forced to, each group cleanses them with chemicals, making sacred what they see as racially profane (Walker 2013). Thus, the California correctional system hurts inmates in three ways: it imposes its own rigid race definitions; it heightens racial tension through segregation; and it treats racial differences as "fact."

Intrigued (and disturbed), I wondered how I would fair racially in jail or prison. So I met with Reggie, a former African American gang member from South Central. He had spent much time incarcerated and prided himself on knowing prison politics. I asked him how I would be racially categorized.

"You would go with the Blacks, homie," Reggie answered, "'cause you look Black. You would go with us and get down with us fo'[r] sure."

"But what if I don't want to [gang]bang," I asked, "and just want to do my time? Would I still go with Blacks?"

"Yeah, you would still go with the Blacks," he responded, "but you could also go with the Other. That's for people that aren't Black or Hispanic, like Asians and people like that. Those people there don't usually bang [affiliate with gangs]. But you might have some Black homies wondering why you're there. So you better off coming with us [Blacks]."

"Could I go with the Hispanics?," I asked. "I do have a Spanish last name."

"Nah, I don't know about that, homie," he responded. "You might be able to go with the Norteños (an alliance of Hispanic gangs from northern California). They got some Black homies. But then you gotta bang [do gang activity] for them. I know fo' sure that Sureños (an alliance of Hispanic gangs southern California) ain't gonna take you in. You look too Black."

For Reggie, I was Black. I was concerned again about my research. I knew that the Sureños, through the Mexican Mafia, had a loose alliance with the Aryan Brotherhood against the Black Guerilla Family. And LA was the bastion for Sureño gangs. So if prison politics hit the streets, I would be around Mexican gangbangers who hated Blacks with a passion. It helped little that in Canoga Park, on the western end of the San Fernando Valley, a Mexican gang randomly attacked Black residents (Coca 2007; LA Times 2011). They had shot Black football players from Pierce College, harassed and assaulted Black students in grade schools, and murdered Black residents—all of whom were non-gang affiliated.

And the anti-Black violence by Sureño gangs went beyond LA. It crossed deep into the eastern portion of LA county, into cities such as Monrovia and Azusa.[3] But there, Black gangs would retaliate, shooting and killing random Mexicans too. Police authorities claimed that the racial violence originated from racial hatred in jails and prisons. Whether this was true, I did not know. I still hadn't spoken to enough former inmates.

Yet I suspected that prison segregation played a role. It made Mexicans and African Americans deepen the boundaries between insiders and outsiders. This could hurt me. Though I passed for Black, African Americans might focus on our language and cultural differences. Though I spoke Spanish, Mexicans might focus on physical appearance. Now both communities might consider me less "in" than "out." Both communities could close the racial and cultural spaces that made my field research possible.

HOOD HOPPING IN COMPTON

Eventually, I started exploratory fieldwork in Compton, the infamous city below LA. A third of its population was African American, with a growing Hispanic population making up most of the rest. Given the population dynamics, I thought I could drive down its streets, walk in its strip malls, eat in its restaurants, and just hang around without seeming out of place. My initial trips to Compton confirmed this hunch. However, I observed that Mexicans still seemed uncomfortable around me. Mexican women avoided eye contact or slightly turned their heads as they walked past me. Mexican men stiffened up or became stoic in my presence. On the other hand, African Americans acknowledged me and examined me out of curiosity. Except for the gangbangers, who just seemed hypervigilant in all public spaces, African Americans acted as though I belonged.

In Compton, I was Black.

Through a colleague, I met two Mexican Compton residents, both men in their early twenties. In our first meeting, we drove through Compton at night and observed its eerie dilapidation. Later, we ate at a local McDonald's and discussed the city's schools and gangs. Once they got comfortable, they admitted that they thought I was African American at first sight. (They had never seen a Dominican before, so I just didn't look Latino.) Again I worried about doing field research in a Mexican community.

About a month later, I complained to one of the guys, whom I call Miguel, about the lack of good, affordable barbershops in the San Fernando Valley. He then invited me to his local barbershop, telling me that it was cheap and gave fresh "taper fades." Later that week, I joined him for a haircut and saw that all of the barbers and clients were Mexican. Some of them looked at me with surprise and others immediately looked away. After I sat, some took side peeks at me and others stared at me with blank expressions (I saw this through a large mirror that went from wall to wall).

When it was my turn, my barber, who was friendly, began a conversation with me. He wished I knew Spanish, he said, since the barbers joked or made fun of each other a lot in Spanish. I did know Spanish, I told him. Puzzled, he asked, "Wow, you're African American and know Spanish? How did you learn?" I then explained that I was Dominican and learned Spanish at home. I then spoke some Spanish, which made most of the clients turn toward me. Now they seemed to relax and no longer looked tense. Now they looked at me out of curiosity. I felt relieved.

However, my later visits resembled the first. When I entered, everyone looked surprised or tense, took peeks or stared. And since I no longer spoke Spanish to my barber (he only spoke English to me), the tension stayed. The conversations between barbers, however, were great for fieldwork. I learned what it was like to be a young Mexican male in a marginalized and stigmatized community. Many of them were school dropouts, drank lots of alcohol, consumed heavy drugs, and experienced violence firsthand. I also heard underlying racial tension in their stories. If they criticized gangs, it was only African American ones. Not a word on Mexican gangs.

Despite the great barbershop stories, I often could not wait to get done and leave. It was hard to sit and wait two or three hours for a haircut when people seemed uncomfortable with me. (That wouldn't stop me from going, though. A great, affordable haircut is hard to come by in LA.)

I also spent time with a few African American residents in Compton. They complained about how Mexican immigrants took away jobs, only spoke Spanish, lived in overcrowded conditions, and kept farm animals in their yards. As they told their stories—which terribly resembled the narratives of gun-toting, border-patrol-supporting, anti-immigrant Whites—they associated me with Blackness. However, once I revealed that my parents where Dominican immigrants who only spoke Spanish, they tensed up and shut down.

"But you're still half-Black, right?," a Black female resident once asked me. "What do you mean?," I responded.
"Like your mom or dad is African American," she clarified.
"I mean, I have African ancestry," I responded, "but both of my parents were born in the Dominican Republic. And I speak Spanish and practice Dominican culture. So I see myself as Dominican."

Suddenly, she got quiet. She had just spent the last half hour bitterly attacking Mexican immigrants for not learning English and for "stealing" African American jobs. After a few moments, she smiled sheepishly and then avoided eye contact as she cleared the dining room table. From the kitchen, she asked me if I wanted to know anything else. I then realized that she now linked me to Mexican immigrants. I took her last question as my cue to exit her home.

Such incidents made me take seriously the warning of some Black residents, who advised me not to study both African Americans and Mexicans in the same city. If so, both groups might label me a "hood hopper," which had a bad connotation.

Derek, an African American in his late twenties, explained:

> Like if people see you hanging out in different hoods, they'll start saying, "Man, this homie is a hood hopper. This homie hangs out with us, he hangs out with them, he got no loyalty, he's probably telling them stuff about us." That's what they're gonna say. You don't want that to happen. The [gang] bangers could kill you for that. And I'm talking about the Black gang bangers! You stick to one hood, homie. Don't study Blacks here [Compton] if you gonna study Mexicans here [too]. Like don't act like you all cool with Blacks, then be all cool with the Mexicans. Nobody likes that shit. The Cholos [Mexican gang members] definitely don't like that shit. Just be careful, homie.

Coño. I had just started to relax, feel comfortable with the Compton field site. True, Mexican residents still seemed uneasy around me. But I was determined to get them used to me—to one day say *"Llego El Profe!"* when they saw me. However, now I could be perceived as a "hood hopper," who claimed to be down for one clique, one gang, one hood, one people— one race—while claiming the same for all others. I could then be framed as a traitor, a backstabber, a Judas, a two-faced, a liar, a hypocrite, someone lacking honor, dignity, and respect. Someone worthy of *muerte*, worthy of death. *Ay, mi madre!*

I once asked Miguel if he identified with the city of Compton. "Yeah, I identify with Compton," he answered, "with Mexican Compton, at least." Here, he drew a line, creating two sides to Compton, a Black one and a Brown one.

I stood in between.

Fear arose within me. Anger too. And tension. I felt torn. My loyalty was to both communities, not just one. It seemed like I had to choose sides.

Back and forth I rocked . . . up and down I bounced . . . round and round I spun . . . Ay, the agony! This standpoint purgatorio tormented me in LA.

I didn't know what to do.

CONCLUSION: *MI FAMILIA*, MY SON

LA's freeway traffic (a tormenting purgatory on its own) has slowed my research. During the teaching semester, I travel forty miles from my Burbank home to Fullerton, my campus job. From both places I travel to Compton, which is twenty-five miles from home and twenty miles from campus. The freeway congestion lengthens the commute to well over an hour each way (unless I head out before dawn, which I do now for teaching). I can only spend lots of time in Compton during the winter and summer breaks.

To make life easier, I can move to Compton or South LA. But I think of my family, especially my son. His experiences, along with the recent hate crimes, make me fear for him. The dividing line between Black and Brown is too solid, too strong. He may have to choose a side. Or a side may be chosen for him. I cannot put him in that position; I do not want him to see the world through a racist, hateful lens.

A recent racial attack in Compton reinforced my decision.[4] A Black family (a mom and three teenage children) moved into a Compton home during the past Christmas break. Their family friend stood on the sidewalk as four Mexican gang members drove by him in an SUV. They stopped their car and yelled "nigger" at him. Then they threatened him with a gun. Then they beat him with metal pipes. Later, over a dozen people (it is unclear if they were gang members) stood in front of the home yelling threats. Someone threw a beer bottle, shattering the living room window. For the next several weeks, the racial harassment continued: the gang drove by the home daily, yelling racial slurs and threats. Afraid, the family eventually left.

I cannot risk my son experiencing the same pain.

Still, such race-driven violence requires understanding. Though it seems senseless, to the actors it makes sense. This violence is also tied to urban marginality, a condition linked to the larger segregationist policies of the state. I must put together the pieces of this troubling, disturbing puzzle. I must understand the Black and Brown tension that is now LA.

In all, whether one is inside or out, a tension exists between the researcher and participants. There is always liminality and "the space between." Studying two or more conflicting groups amplifies the ambiguity and tension. In my case, both groups can view me as not standing alone, as the opposing group's extension. This space torments me since I am unsure of where I stand in their perspectives. I am also unsure if this increases my risk for injury or, in the worst case scenario, for death. This is what puts me in a standpoint purgatorio. This is what shapes and influences my research movements and apprehensions.

NOTES

1. Banks (1998) created a typology of four categories: indigenous-insider, indigenous-outsider, external-insider, and external-outsider. These categories stand for the different ethnic, race, class, and cultural values and knowledge brought by researchers to a field site. For an early discussion of "insiders" and "outsiders," see Merton 1972.
2. For a fascinating look into *La Eme*, see Blatchford 2008.
3. See Audi 2011; Quinones and Winton 2011; Quinones, Esquivel, and Hennessy-Fiske 2008.
4. See Quinones, Winton, and Mozingo 2013.

WORKS CITED

Adams, Emily. 1993. "Series of Hate Crimes Shakes up Residents of Hawaiian Gardens." *Los Angeles Times*, March 13: 1.

Audi, Tamara. 2011. "Latino Gang Targeted Blacks, U.S. Says." *Wall Street Journal*, June 8: A.2

Banks, James. 1998. "The Lives and Values of Researchers: Implications for Educating Citizens in a Multicultural Society." *Educational Researcher* 27(7): 4–17.

Black, Timothy. 2009. *When a Heart Turns Rock Solid: The Lives of Three Puerto Rican Brothers on and Off the Streets.* New York: Pantheon Books.

Blatchford, Chris. 2008. *The Black Hand: The Bloody Rise and Redemption of "Boxer" Enriquez, a Mexican Mob Killer.* New York: HarperCollins.

Bourgois, Philippe. 2003. *In Search of Respect: Selling Crack in El Barrio.* 2nd ed. New York: Cambridge University Press.

Coca, Rick. 2007. "Latino Gang Makes Blacks Its Target." *LA Daily News*, August 6: N.1

Contreras, Randol. 2013. *The Stickup Kids: Race, Drugs, Violence, and the American Dream.* Berkeley: University of California Press.

Durán, Robert. 2013. *Gang Life in Two Cities: An Insider's Journey.* New York: Columbia University Press.

Dwyer, Sonia, and Jennifer L. Buckle. 2009. "The Space Between: On Being an Insider-Outsider in Qualitative Research." *International Journal of Qualitative Methods* 8: 54–63.

Glover, Scott, and Richard Winton. 2009. "Massive Raids Target Hawaiian Gardens Gang." *Los Angeles Times*, May 22: A.1

Goodman, Philip. 2008. ""It's Just Black, White, or Hispanic": An Observational Study of Racializing Moves in California's Segregated Prison Reception Centers." *Law & Society Review* 42(4): 735–770.

Johnson, Norris B. 1984. "Sex, Color, and Rites of Passage in Ethnographic Research." *Human Organization* 43(2): 108–120.

Los Angeles Times. 2011. "Gang Member Sentenced to Life in Racially Motivated Killing of Bowling Alley Worker." June 9.

Merton, Robert. 1972. "Insiders and Outsiders: A Chapter in the Sociology of Knowledge." *American Journal of Sociology* 78: 9–47.

Mock, Brentin. 2006. "Latino Gang Members in Southern California Are Terrorizing and Killing Blacks." In *Intelligence Report*. Montgomery, AL: Southern Poverty Law Center.

Pelisek, Christine. 2005. "Avenues of Death: How Highland Park's Latino Gang Targets African-Americans." LA Weekly, July 14 – 20, 27(4): . (or Retreived from: http://www.laweekly.com/2005-07-14/news/avenues-of-death/

Quinones, Sam, Paloma Esquivel, and Hennessy-Fiske. 2008. "Cross-racial Shootings Spark Fear in Monrovia." *Los Angeles Times*, January 31: B.1

Quinones, Sam, and Richard Winton. 2011. "Azusa Gang Terrorized Blacks, Indictment Says." *Los Angeles Times*, June 8: A.1

Quinones, Sam, Richard Winton, and Joe Mozingo. 2013. "Wave of Violene as Compton Changes; A Latino Gang is Intimidating Blacks to Leave What was Once And African American Enclave." *Los Angeles Times*, January 25: A.1.

Rios, Victor. 2011. *Punished: Policing the Lives of Black and Latino Boys*. New York: New York University Press.

Turner, Victor. 1969. *The Ritual Process: Structure and Antistructure*. Chicago: Aldine Publishing Company.

US Department of Justice. 2006. "Gang Members Convicted of Federal Hate Crimes for Murders and Assaults of African Americans." Accessed at www.usdoj.gov.

Van Gennep, Arnold. 1960. *The Rites of Passage*, translated by Monika B. Vizedom and Gabrielle L. Caffee. Chicago: University of Chicago Press.

Walker, Michael. 2013. "Jim Crow in Jail: Race Codes in Inmate Society." *American Journal of Sociology* (Revised and Resubmitted).

CHAPTER 11

Death Squads and Vigilante Politics in Democratic Northeast Brazil

NANCY SCHEPER-HUGHES

PREFACE

There is little to celebrate in these amazing chapters about the return of vigilantes and social banditry, the new and deadly codes of the street, gangs and guns, moral economies of addiction, the politics of death itself, and revolutionary nostalgia, in the short and violent lives on the urban peripheries of the Americas. One is both intrigued and horrified by the description of "liberation theology" deployed in the post-Catholic, Pentecostal/ Penitential world of crack, Christ, and captivity in Guatemalan drug rehabilitation centers. Kevin O'Neill's (this volume) opening scene of a kidnapped drug addict, tied up and wrapped inside a thin mattress, trussed up with twine and lying on the floor of a Pentecostal center reminds me of Taussig's vignette-turned-into-monograph about the passing scene of a poor Colombian woman (or man) sewing her husband (or partner) into a cocoon under a highway in his book, *I Swear I Saw This* (Taussig 2011). The image of addicts begging for freedom—including freedom from their addictive selves—in the private, unregulated *anexos* (drug rehabilitation programs) found in Mexico and California (Anderson and Garcia 2013) is a script that elsewhere in the world, especially among Native American youth, leads to suicide. How are these Christian "rehabilitation" centers allowed to exist as parallel prisons, and how do they captivate the imaginations of addicts and their kin? Something that has haunted me throughout my career as an anthropologist is the problem of how and why people become willing executioners of others as well as of themselves; how do they become complicit in their own undoing?

But somehow, neither habitus, nor bare life/bare death, nor moral economy are sufficient. The ethnographies of violence presented here are extremely rich but historically and politically decontextualized. I assume it is because all of that context is to be presumed. But we are talking about lives without livelihoods, histories of terror, small wars and invisible genocides, and massive internal dispossessions and displacements. The role of the United States and other more distant superpowers in the pro- duction and reproduction of ganglands and gang wars is sidelined, at best a footnote. Gang violence is a transnational phenomenon and the result of the political repressions of the 1980s that prompted a wave of forced migrations from Central America to the United States. People seeking sanctuary and jobs ended up in Los Angeles and other major cities with large Latino communities and long-established gang traditions. When US authorities began, in the 1990s, deporting large numbers of detained or arrested young men suspected of being gang members, these men brought the US gang culture back into their countries of origin. From there, things began to deteriorate very rapidly.

There are hints, but no full analysis, of the dramaturgical, performa- tive, and theatrical aspects of violence, the staging of violent episodes that can be as orchestrated as an Italian opera. This is not to say that the per- formances don't get out of hand or that the actors don't stray from their intended scripts from time to time. Violence is like drugs and it is often addictive. When Albie Sachs refers to his "addiction" to the excitement of waging the anti-apartheid struggle in South Africa—one that resulted in his loss of limb and near death—or when anthropologist Meira Weiss says that in Jerusalem, following a spate of bombings, people grow bored, they speak of violent events with a blend of horror and exultation. The immedi- ate experience of violent trauma can produce altered states that are not dissimilar from states of ecstasy or what William James called "varieties of religious experience." There is a transcendental aspect to violence as well.

Finally, what is the role of violence in the construction of new or tran- sitional democracies? Democracy as based on the extension of citizen- ship to the broader "masses" is one of the hallmarks of modernity. But classical theories of democracy have rarely considered that violence among citizens is a condition of its development, one that is character- istic of democracies rather than simply episodic. Classic democratic theory proceeds as if the problem of internal violence has already been solved either by the "civilizing process" (in Norbert Elias's sense) or in the modern disciplines and self-disciplines (in Foucault's sense) or in the theory of the modern nation-state that combines the rule of law with the monopoly on violence. In new democracies or in transitional democracies—or in the interregnum between what Carolyn Nordstrom called war/not war—extremely high levels of everyday violence by police and marginal populations is emblematic. This mix is especially potent in those societies in the Americas—North, Central, and South—when drug cartels and death squads (some of these police driven) both use a language of democratic rights and "rule of law" to justify their brutality and their sanction to kill.

LIVES WORTH LIVING AND DEATHS NOT WORTH GRIEVING

Judith Butler has tried to disentangle "what counts as a livable life and a grievable death" (2004, xv) in relation to the role of American foreign policy in determining the way that different lives are valued or devalued. Donna Haraway (2007) observed that certain lives (animal lives, in particular) are "made killable" by their vulnerable position in social hierarchies of dominance. Grief, sacrifice, lives worth saving, and lives that are better dead than alive are defined and governed by moral economies. In this final chapter I will explore the amoral economies and political frameworks that define expendable and dispensable lives versus lives worth saving, be they supernumerary infants (Scheper-Hughes 1993), loose and dangerous street children (Scheper-Hughes and Hoffman 2005) or "troublesome" Black men in Brazilian shantytowns.

A persistent theme that has defined my life's work, derived from a tradition of critical theory, is a concern with the violence of everyday life, the "small wars and invisible genocides" (Scheper-Hughes 1998) that took place without recognition or acknowledgment of the mass deaths hidden in the well-kept books of the civil registry office in Timbaúba, Pernambuco, Brazil. In *Death without Weeping: the Violence of Everyday Life in Brazil*, I used the concept of "everyday violence" to refer to the routinization and normalization of violence through bureaucracies and institutions by "agents of the social consensus" (Basaglia 1987), be they politicians, teachers, agronomic engineers, urban planners, sugar plantation managers, directors of medical forensic institutes, morgues, civil servants, doctors, or traditional Catholic priests and nuns. The everyday violence of infant mortality, slow starvation, infectious disease, or despair and humiliation that destroys humans with even greater frequency is invisible or misrecognized. When plywood coffins were produced in great number and distributed freely to afflicted families on the Alto do Cruzeiro, structural violence was amplified by symbolic violence: "Here, the coffins for your children are ready and waiting." When doctors in the municipal clinic prescribed tranquilizers and appetite stimulants for hungry babies, we entered the ethical gray zone shared by the mothers who were desirous of the drugs and the doctors who were more than happy to supply them.

Although the primary thesis of *Death without Weeping* concerned the overproduction of angel babies, amid the "letting go" of infants lacking "a talent for life" were other narratives that evoked such terror that they were transmitted in coded language, gesture, mime, piercing side glances, hard stares, and fragments of sentences that concealed more than they revealed. These strange communiqués from the Alto do Cruzeiro concerned the existence of an extermination group that was holding "court" and deciding who would be the next to die. Without warning, and occasionally in plain view, these avenging angels would swoop down on their prey, killing them in a rat-a-tat-tat of semiautomatic rifle shots or more silently with knives or by throwing them under speeding cars and trucks, making them disappear. All this was taking place during the rebirth of democracy in Brazil.

Chapter 6 of *Death without Weeping*, "Bodies, Death, and Silence," was a first attempt to situate the strange accounts somewhere between the real, the surreal, and the uncanny. Life in Timbaúba and on the hillside shantytown of Alto do Cruzeiro has a literary quality not in spite of but because the majority of my informants were illiterate and what constituted evidence for them required reflection and imagination. The violence of illiteracy resides in its power to stupefy, to amaze, to frighten, to confuse, and to terrorize those who know that something is terribly amiss, but they don't have a word or a name for it, nor a way to negate or verify the state of affairs.

Thus, I began to follow the rumors by following the [dead] bodies from the IML, the Medical-Legal Institute, (the state morgue of the capital city, Recife), into the Timbaúba cemetery. I searched slowly through the musty and heavy old-fashioned ledger books kept in plastic or in brown paper wrapping tied with string in the private office of the scrupulous and protective notary and official registrar of the *município*, Dona Amantina. Here, I will bring the story up to date based on several short field trips to Timbaúba (also known as Bom Jesus da Mata) between 1992 and May 2014, some lasting a few months, others a few weeks. I will expose and explore the paradoxes, but I cannot solve them.

Figure 11.1
Long-term research. Alto do Cruzeiro, 2014

1964-THE MILITARY COUP AND FEAR OF COMMUNIST SUBVERSION

It was fifty years ago that I first walked up to the top of the Alto do Cruzeiro, in Timbaúba, Pernambuco, with a hammock and a plastic suitcase. I was looking for a small mud hut nestled in a cliff where I was to live with Nailza da Silva, a recent migrant from Mato Grosso, and her husband, Ze Antonio, an itinerant railroad worker. It was December 1964, four months after a military coup toppled the left-leaning presidency of João Goulart amid headlines in the *New York Times* warning of peasant insurgency in Pernambuco, aided by misinformed reports of Marxist insurgency (Horowitz 1964; Martinis 1966). The junta, with US support, was especially concerned about a peasant organization, the Ligas Camponeses, led by a poor lawyer from Recife named Francisco Juliao. The Ligas made some headway with landless peasants and sugarcane cutters who worked on large plantations and sugar mills, including some of my neighbors on the Alto do Cruzeiro. But the group advocated for burial rights under the slogan "Six Feet Under and a Coffin" (De Castro 1969). To be fair, land rights were likely to come next.

It was the beginning of an anthropologist's life's work, somewhere between an obsession, a trauma, and a romance with the shantytown, home to five thousand displaced sugarcane cutters expulsed from one of a dozen plantations and *usinas* (industrialized sugar mills) where they had lived and worked. Now they were seasonal contract workers, earning roughly a dollar a day to cut and sack cane. Poor, hungry, disoriented, they threw together homes made of straw, mud and sticks, and—in the worst instances—scrap material. They threw together families in the same bowdlerized fashion, taking whatever was available and making do, like the *bricoleurs* of Claude Levi-Strauss (1966). For these people, who lacked water, electricity, and sanitation, and faced daily food scarcities, epidemics, and military police violence, premature death was an everyday occurrence. Former members of the demobilized peasant leagues explained that their goal was not to overthrow the government but to claim the right to a grave of one's own rather than being shoved into a common grave in a borrowed municipal pauper's tin coffin, known as the "chin-chopper" (*batendo queixo*). That was the extent of the Marxist threat in rural Pernambuco in 1964.

The confusion in Timbaúba was great at that time. In trying to reconstruct the effect of the Ligas in Timbaúba, I spoke in 2014 with a sympathetic progressive woman now in her late seventies from a respected family who owned a small cooperative bank and a pharmacy. Dona Ruth spoke about the confusion in 1963 when rural workers, members of the Ligas, marched to the center of Timbaúba waving their hoes and shovels in front of the Catholic church and the sport club. But both Ruth and D. Irene, a domestic worker from the Alto do Cruzeiro, were n n unclear about the agenda. "We did not know what they were after or what they wanted." D. Irene said. Ruth said, "They said that they were Communists but everyone who cared about the poor were called Communists." Irene added, "We knew that the labor union was threatened by them, and that those who joined the Ligas would be beaten up. So we all tried to look the other way, to not get too involved. People were killed for being members."

My assignment for the Pernambucan Health Department was to immunize children, educate midwives, attend births in an emergency, treat infections, bind up wounds, and visit mothers and newborns at home to monitor their health and refer them as needed to the district health post or to the emergency room of a private hospital owned by the mayor's brother, where charity cases were—depending on local patron-client relations—sometimes attended.

The first birth and one of the first infant deaths I witnessed was one in which I was implicated, summoned in the middle of the night to attend the labor of a fifteen-year-old neighbor on the Alto do Cruzeiro. Lourdes gave birth in her hammock to a scrawny little mottled infant, barely alive, who died a few hours later and was buried in the back-yard next to an open-pit latrine by the putative father, an older and scary Black man named Valdimar. He frightened me because his face was paralyzed into a menacing grin, but a gentler human being I have not encountered since. Valdimar hung himself a few months later, after Lourdes ended the relationship, blaming Valdimar for the infant's pathetic and misbegotten, if not cursed, birth. I don't remember who cut him down, but I do remember the barking puppy at his dangling feet, a little bitch named Lika after the Sputnik space dog. So perhaps they were Marxists after all.

I spent several months cycling through the miserable huts on the Alto with a little brown medical kit officially equipped with a bar of soap, a glass syringe, several needles, scissors, antiseptics, aspirin, bandages, and a pumice stone to sharpen the needles that were used over and over again to immunize hundreds of Alto babies and children against diphtheria, whooping cough, tetanus, small pox, and tuberculosis.

But what haunted me then, in addition to my own incompetence, was something I did not comprehend and had neither the skill nor the wits to understand: why the women of the Alto did not grieve the deaths of their infants and babies.

Sixteen years elapsed before I was able to return to Timbaúba, and to the Alto do Cruzeiro, this time as a medical anthropologist. It was 1982, the beginning of the end of twenty years of the military dictatorship. This was my first of four anthropological field trips to the shantytown of Alto do Cruzeiro to study love and death, specifically mother love and child death under conditions so dire that life there resembled a refugee camp or the emergency room of an inner-city hospital.

Eduardo Galeano (1975) described Northeast Brazil as a concentra-tion camp for more than forty million people. This was not a gross exag-geration, as decades of nutritional studies of sugarcane cutters and their families in the *zona da mata* of Pernambuco demonstrated evidence of slow starvation and stunting. These Brazilian *nanicos*, nutritional dwarfs, were surviving on a daily caloric intake—"camp rations," you might say—similar to the inmates of the Buchenwald death camp. The concentration camp analogy was a subtext in my account of mother love and child death on the Alto do Cruzeiro. Life on the Alto resembled prison camp culture with a moral-ethic based triage and an ethics of survival. But what did mother love mean to shantytown women who have given birth eleven times and buried nine infants? Under the murderous economic, environ-mental, and political conditions of the Alto do Cruzeiro, especially during the military years (1964–1984) and the early and uneven transition to democracy (1985–1992), many infants did not survive the first year of life.

What were casual and forgivable lapses of maternal attention and care under ordinary circumstances in the first world were lethal in the precarious context of shantytown life where hyper-vigilance of fragile and vulnerable infants was required of mothers who were themselves struggling for survival. Mothers and infants could be rivals for scarce resources. Thus, Alto mothers renounced breastfeeding as impossible, as sapping too much strength from their own "wrecked" bodies. I was once scolded by my Alto neighbor and *comadre*, Dalina: "Why grieve the death of infants who barely landed in this world, who were not even conscious of their existence? Weep for us, Nanci, for their mothers who are condemned to live in order to care for those who do survive."

"Good-enough mothering" was problematic in a place where it was *easy enough for anyone to die*. Scarcity made mother love a fragile emotion, postponed until the newborn displayed a will to live, a taste (*gusto*) and a knack (*jeito*) or a talent for life. A high expectancy of death prepared mothers to "let go of" and to hasten the deaths of deselected babies by reducing the already insufficient food, water, and care. Infants died, mothers said, because they had no desire to live. They were elusive creatures, more like birds—here today, gone tomorrow; it was all the same to them, I was told. It was best to help them "go" quickly.

The angel babies of the Alto were "transitional objects," neither of this earth nor yet fully spirits. In appearance they were ghostlike: pale, wispy haired, their arms and legs stripped of flesh, their bellies grossly extended, their eyes blank and staring, their faces wizened, a cross between startled primate and wise old sorcerer. These babies were kept at arm's length by their mothers. Primo Levi (1988) might have called them miniature "*Musselman*," a reference to the cadaverous "living dead" in Auschwitz known in camp argot as "Muslims." These were victims whose state of exhaustion was so great, whose despair was so palpable, whose collapse so complete, that they looked and behaved like walking mummies. Sometimes unable to stand on two feet, these "given-up" inmates were said to resemble Muslims at prayer. Their lethal passivity and indifference seemed to announce an availability for execution. Thus, they were isolated and reviled by those in the camps who still clung, however absurdly, to hope and to life itself.

The given up and given-up-on babies of the Alto were described as "ready" for death. "Dead or alive," one Alto mother said. "It's all the same to them." Thus were infants transformed into transitional or sacrificial objects. One mother, Luiza Gomes, explained: "The first nine of mine had to die to open the way so that the last five could live." "I think," said her neighbor Edite Cosmos, "that these deaths are sent to punish us for the sins of the world. But the babies don't deserve this since we are the sinners, but the punishment falls on them." "Be quiet," said Beatrice. "They die, like Jesus did, to save us from suffering." This paradox of the death of some serving the lives of others, in this case the lives of the mothers, was hard to take. When I dared to question this brutal ethos, I was chided: "Don't cry for our babies who are allowed to die; cry for us who are forced to live to take care of the others."

The experience of too much loss, too much death, led to a kind of patient resignation that some clinical psychologists might label as "postpartum depression" or an "accommodation syndrome." But I argued that this particular constellation of motherhood was neither pathological nor abnormal. It was a moral code. Not only had a continual exposure to trauma obliterated rage and protest, it had also minimized attachment by the sage overprediction of loss and premature death so as to diminish sorrow. No tears were wasted at an infant burial, a task often left in the hands of older children. Children buried children on the Alto do Cruzeiro. The practice killed two birds with one stone: it allowed mothers to absent themselves from the burial rites, and it forced children to face and accept the death of their siblings as a commonplace fact of life.

I recall a birthday party for a three year old on the Alto do Cruzeiro in which the birthday cake, decorated with candles, was placed on the kitchen table next to the tiny blue cardboard coffin of the child's nine-month-old sibling who had died during the night. Next to the coffin a single vigil candle was lit. Despite the tragedy, the child's mother wanted to go ahead with the party. "*Parabéns para voce,*" we sang to the three year old, clapping our hands. In the Alto, the Brazilian birthday song has special resonance: "You survivor, you—you lived to see another year!"

When Alto mothers cried, they cried for themselves, for those left behind to continue the *luta*, the daily struggle that was life. But they cried the hardest for their children who almost died but surprised everyone by surviving against the odds. Wiping a stray tear from her eye, an Alto mother would speak with deep emotion of the child who, given up for dead—"the candle already burning 'round his little hammock"—suddenly beat death back, displaying a *desejo* (fierce desire) and a *gusto* (a real taste)—for life. Ah, these tough and stubborn children were loved above all others. And they were raised to be fierce and wild (*brabo*), to spit in the eye of the willing executioner, whoever that was.

I sometimes thought of the angel babies more in terms of René Girard's (1987a, 1987b) idea of sacrificial violence. The given-up, offered-up angel babies of Bom Jesus seemed to me to be prototypical generative scapegoats, sacrificed in the face of terrible domestic conflicts about scarcity and survival. And that is, in fact, just how their mothers sometimes spoke of them. And these Catholic women often said that their infants died just as Jesus died, so that others—especially they themselves—could live. "Better the child should die," Alto women say to each other, "than either you or I." The question that lingered, unresolved, in my mind was whether this Kierkegaardian "leap of faith" entailed a certain Marxist "bad faith" as well. It was never my intention to cast blame on shantytown mothers for putting their own survival over and above that of their infants and small babies, for these were moral choices that no person should be forced to make. But infants themselves were viewed as an unlimited, indeed limitless, supply of souls that could be constantly recirculated. This allowed the die-outs of shantytown babies—in some particularly "bad" years, as many as 40 percent of all the infants born in the Alto do Cruzeiro—to pass without comment, surprise, or grief. "Well, it's just a baby," women would say. Here we reach the most deeply protected of all public secrets: the violence of everyday life.

In Northeast Brazil, "acceptable death" took the form of holy indifference and a faith in a kind of "magical replaceability" that emphasized the interchangeability of persons. One more, one less . . . there are always more from where they come from. "Don't grieve, Dona Maria, it's only a baby. You'll soon have another." And it was here that maternal thinking and military thinking converged. When mothers greet their frail and untrustworthy (because they might disappoint the mother) newborns as strangers to be excluded or aliens and invading enemies whose lives are a threat to personal or family stability, they are expressing a dangerous—though all too human—sentiment that is essential to military recruitment and thinking: the idea of "acceptable death." When angels (or martyrs) are fashioned from the dead bodies of those who die young, maternal thinking most resembles military, especially wartime, thinking. On the battlefield as in the shantytown, triage, thinking in sets, and a belief in the magical replaceability of the dead predominate. Above all, ideas of acceptable death and of meaningful (rather than useless) suffering extinguish rage and grief for those whose lives are taken and allow for the recruitment of new lives and new bodies into the struggle.

The gray zone is populated by a thousand little betrayals in the desperate, covert, and continuous struggle to survive. Like Primo Levi, Brazilian peasants from the drought- and famine-plagued Northeast are keenly aware that the "good" die young and that the ability to survive disaster requires "a knack for life" and a willingness to cheat death. Survival tactics are not always the most morally edifying. Survivors of the camps, like drought survivors in Northeast Brazil, comment on their own complicity: "None of us here is innocent."

There was a kind of magical replaceability about infants, similar to what one might find on a battlefield. As one soldier falls, another takes his place. This kind of detached maternal thinking allowed the die-outs of shanty-town babies—in some years, as many as 40 percent of all the infants born in the Alto do Cruzeiro died—to pass without shock or profound grief. "Well, it's just a baby," Alto women would say. A woman who had lost half her babies told me, "Who could bear it, Nanci, if we are mistaken in believing that God takes our infants to save us from pain? If that is not true, then God is a cannibal. And if our little angels are not in heaven flying around the throne of Our Lady, then where are they, and who is to blame for their deaths?" If mothers allowed themselves to be attached to each newborn, how could they ever live through their short lives and deaths and still have the stamina to get pregnant and give birth again and again? It wasn't that Alto mothers did not experience mother love at all. They did, and with great intensity. Mother love emerged as their children developed strength and vitality. The apex of mother love was not the image of Mary and her infant son, but a mature Mary, grieving the death of her young adult son. The Pietà, not the young mother at the crèche, was the symbol of mother-hood and mother love on the Alto do Cruzeiro. And in the meantime, a veritable maternal reproductive revolution has transformed the meaning of motherhood, childhood, and fertility.

DEATH SQUADS AND DEMOCRACY

Meanwhile, another crisis in the politics of death was brewing. In 1984 the Brazilian military called it quits and decided to allow for a gradual return to democracy, a shift that brought some anxiety to a community accustomed to military rule. It began with rumors of a death squad, *un grupo de exter-mínio*, operating in the Alto do Cruzeiro, a phenomenon that should not have accompanied the peaceful transition to democracy after twenty years of the military dictatorship, a dictatorship that never reached the horror of Pinochet's Chile, or the "Dirty War" in Argentina, or the genocide in Guatemala, but which had a savagery and a specificity of its own. In 1987, democracy was being rebuilt by robust civil society. The new constitution guaranteed rights to the disenfranchised—to rural workers, to the urban poor, to illiterates, to mothers, and to street children. But then while I was in the field, several young men of the Alto do Cruzeiro—each of them Black, young, and in trouble with the law for petty theft, drunkenness, vagrancy, glue-sniffing, and other infractions—were seized from their homes by unidentified men "in uniform" and were "disappeared." A few days later two of the bodies were found, slashed, mutilated, and dumped between rows of sugarcane. The police arrived with graphic photos for family members. "How do you expect me to recognize *meu homem*—my man—in this picture?," Dona Elena screamed hysterically. The same story was repeated in 1988 and 1989. Finally, they came late one night for the teenage son of Irene, known as Irene Preto (Black Irene), the boy everyone on the Alto knew with some affection as "Nêgo De."

The existence of a paramilitary "death squad" with close ties to the local police force was suspected, but on this topic people were silent, speaking, when they did at all, in a rapid and complicated form of sign language. No one wanted to be marked. The disappearances and murders began to include street children, several of whom lived in the open-air marketplace, taking shelter at night in between the stalls and under canvas awnings and helping themselves to bits of produce from crates and baskets. While many of the shop owners were tolerant of the street urchins, others enlisted in a local campaign, a *limpeza*, to clear the city of its pests. The complicity of the populace, especially the middle classes, with the death squads had a logical consistency. The complicity of the poor community of Alto do Cruzeiro was more difficult to understand, but for both there was a residue of the military years and a kind of "shock" with the opening of democratic processes. For twenty years, the military state had kept the social classes segregated and the "hordes" of "dangerous" street youths contained to the favelas or in detention. When the old military policing structures loosened following the new dispensation, the shantytowns ruptured and poor people, especially unemployed young men and street children, descended from the hillsides and climbed up from the river banks and seemed at once to be everywhere, flooding downtown streets and public *praças* once the normal preserve of *gente fina* (the cultivated people). The presence of the poor and working classes flaunting their misery and their "criminalized" needs "in broad daylight" and "in public" (of all places!) was seen as an assault on the social order. Excluded and reviled, the loose and abandoned street kids of Timbaúba were easily recruited to work for local small-time mafia (as they are locally called), especially as drug messengers (*aviões*).

Death squads and vigilante justice are not new in Northeast Brazil. During the colonial period up through the postcolonial years of the Republic, hired guns worked for sugar plantation and sugar mill owners to keep their slaves and then, after abolition, their debt slaves cutting and milling sugarcane at the same levels of human misery. During the military years, death squads returned in the employ of the state to deal with political dissidents. In the democratic 1990s, vigilantes and *justiceiros* arose within a policing vacuum, an excessively weak state, and in the wake of a new transnational, transregional traffic in arms, drugs, and children for commercialized international adoption (Scheper-Hughes and Hoffman 1998).

These extrajudicial executions represented an unofficial death penalty, one carried out with chilling cruelty. Official statistics identified the state of Pernambuco as the "champion" of violence in Brazil, and Timbaúba, with a population of 57,000, as the crime capital of the state between 1995 and 2000. The homicide rate was estimated to be 40 per 100,000. During this period, the Legal Medical Institute (the police mortuary and forensic lab) in Recife, the state capital of Pernambuco, received the bodies of approximately fifteen children a month. Black and brown (mixed race) bodies outnumbered white bodies twelve to one, and boys outnumbered girls at a ratio of seven to one.

According to a report in 2012, "A cor dos homicidios no Brasil,"[1] more than one million people were murdered in Brazil between 1980 and 2011, making Brazil the world's seventh most violent country, following El Salvador, the US Virgin Islands, Trinidad and Tobago, Venezuela, Colombia, and Guatemala. Among those between fourteen and twenty-five, homicides skyrocketed 326 percent to reach 53 per 100,000 inhabitants, said the study published by the Latin American Studies Center (Cebela). Violence in Brazil, once concentrated in major cities in the south spread over the past ten years to the interior and to the north and northeast of the country. The vast majority of murder victims are men and Blacks. Almost two-thirds (77 percent) of all young people murdered are Afro-Brazilians in a country where half the population claims African descent.

In Timbaúba, the state of political anarchy peaked in 2000, when a turn of events led to an aggressive pursuit and arrest of fourteen local men associated with the death squad (*grupo de extermínio*) that had been terrorizing the city and its surrounding rural areas. A small group of local activists, some of them constitutionally empowered as human rights and child rights advocates, joined forces with a judge, indifferent to death threats, and an idealistic and tough-minded public prosecutor in a battle to wrest the *município* from its murderous vigilantes.

2001: AN UNEXPECTED AND UNWANTED INVITATION TO RETURN TO TIMBAÚBA

In 2001, I received a fax in Kroeber Hall, the Department of Anthropology at Berkeley, from Dr. Marisa Borges, a judge in Timbaúba and Dr. Humberto Da Silva Graça, a state-appointed public prosecutor in Timbaúba. The fax included a twelve-page indictment against a man named Abdoral Gonçalves Queiroz, and twenty-three accomplices who had been—depending on one's class position and politics—either "protecting" or "terrorizing" this economically strapped interior town for the latter half of the 1990s. The fax caused considerable consternation in my household, for it included a request for me to return to Timbaúba to put my anthropological skills to work in supporting a human rights vanguard in its efforts to recapture the *município* from the vigilantes. As Judge Borges explained: "We are trying to restore 'the rule of law' and to extend basic rights to all the people of Timbaúba, including the shantytowns and the peripheral rural districts." The choice of words—rule of law, basic rights, etc.—was unexpected. It sounded almost like promotional materials from Amnesty International or the Open Society Institute. But then came the question: "Will you join us in the struggle?"

Specifically, the judge and prosecutor wanted my help in identifying the many unknown and unidentified victims of the death squad. The relatives of victims and survivors were afraid to come forward and testify. They did not trust the police or the courts. Only a fraction of the death-squad executions had come to the attention of the prosecutor and the judge. There were problems identifying and locating the bodies of the victims, as some were buried in unofficial, unregistered, and unmarked graves. Others were duly registered and shelved at the civil registry office. Many deaths had never been reported by the police or never left the police station. During the reign of Abdoral, the police were either complicit or simply utterly passive, leaving the policing of the *município* in the hands of the vigilantes who were known in Timbaúba as "Police 2," but many said that was a modest way to label their power and monopoly on violence in the *município*.

The question was put to me bluntly: could I identify the hidden victims of the death squads by using the same skills I had employed in uncovering previously invisible infant and child mortalities? I hesitated. Was this an appropriate role? At what point does the anthropologist leave anthropology behind and join a frankly political struggle? Or was this a false dichotomy, as Pierre Bourdieu argued when he called for a scholarship *with*, rather than opposed to, commitment? (Bourdieu 2010). In the end I really did not have a choice, as my published work was implicated in the legal proceedings against Abdoral and his band. A Spanish translation of *Death without Weeping* (1997) had reached members of the local intelligentsia and human rights "communities" in Timbaúba. A high-school teacher produced a rough translation of chapter 6, "Bodies, Death and Silence," which was copied and distributed to the judge, prosecutor, and the local police force of Timbaúba. The police, civil and military, had been involved in earlier death squad activities, and the thought that police in Timbaúba knew what I had to say about them filled me with foreboding.

A decade after I had identified the existence of an incipient death squad, which I described as restricted to the marginal and shantytown neighborhoods where the executions were protected by a "law of silence" and a political culture of impunity, the death squad had grown and become a semiofficial arm of the local government. The death squad was not a "parallel force"; it *was* the government of Timbaúba. How had this come about?

The social bandits arose initially to fight against an earlier death squad. Abdoral was a known and familiar actor in Timbaúba. As the expected effects of drug trafficking in Timbaúba created public insecurity, the people of Timbaúba accepted Abdoral and his hired guards as a legitimate public security operation to interrupt the gangs and organized drug and arms traffickers, and to solve the problem of dangerous street children and "vagrant" young men who were hired as *pistoleiros* and then executed by the same bandits who had hired them.

By 2000, violent crime and homicides in Pernambuco reached 50.3 per 100,000 (Nóbrega Zaverucha and Rocha 2011), a statistic suggesting that the people of the Alto do Cruzeiro were correct in saying that they were caught in a war, a "revolution" that was killing their young men, especially young men of color. But few of the victim's families would share information with the new prosecutor, Humberto Graça, and Judge Mariza Borges, making them complicit in their own executions. Accustomed to vigilante justice, strong men, and social bandits (see Hobsbawm 2000; Scheper-Hughes 1996), they were not yet willing to trust the fragile new democracy and its promise of "order and progress," the elusive dream of the Brazilian Republic.

A MODERN-DAY LAMPIÃO OF TIMBAÚBA: "HE STEALS BUT HE GETS THINGS DONE"

Abdoral Gonçalves Queiroz was the head of a private "public security" operation known as the Guardian Angels, described in Prosecutor Graça's brief as "a hyper-active death squad of hired killers—a *grupo de extermínio*" charged with the executions of more than one hundred people, most of them former street kids and young men—poor, uneducated, unemployed, and Black. Prominent figures in Timbaúba society, such as well-known businessmen and local politicians, applauded the work of the death squad, also known as "Police 2," and were allegedly active in the extrajudicial "courts" that were deciding who in Timbaúba should be the next to die. None of these prominent citizens were indicted or brought to trial. Their fingerprints were not found on the smoking guns, and they were safe even if they had commissioned the deaths, which could be purchased for as little as R$500.

When a "job" was agreed upon, the vigilantes, dressed in black and armed with guns and automatic weapons, walked together in formation to their appointed destination. Doors and windows were quickly shut and soon thereafter shots were heard. Everyone in the Alto do Cruzeiro knew their assigned script: "I didn't see! I didn't hear! I don't know anything!" The accused victims might receive warnings, or might simply be "rubbed out" without knowing of what they were accused. Abdoral's gang was also involved in the traffic and distribution of drugs and small arms (rifles, twelve-caliber guns, and pistols) throughout the Brazilian Northeast. The prosecutor spoke of a "peaceful coexistence" between the parallel traffic in murder, arms, and drugs. Children and adolescents who delivered stolen merchandise were protected by Abdoral as long as they obeyed orders. Those who strayed from his control were executed. Between 1995 and 2000, Abdoral's gang had eliminated the cohort of Timbaúba's male street kids.

A few of the murdered street children were noted in the prosecutor's brief:

Jose Roberto de lima ("Nau Jabau") 18; Leonardo ("Nego Leo") 21; carlos Fernando da silva ("Nando Malaquia") 18; geraldo (Coxinha) 17; ANTÔNIO belarmino ("Tonho da Irmã") 18; ANTÔNIO ("Tonho Pampa") 20; raimundo ("Mifiu") 17; Isaias (Cabeleireiro) 20; Marconi Farias 19 [assassinated with his two older brothers]; "pinana," 20, brother de "Tonho Pampa"; edson josé da silva (Fofão) 13; "Peu" 22; "Rui" 16; Luciano ("Matuto") 17; Severino 15; Cláudio júnior 18; Pedrinho 22; Gilvam (Biu's son) 19; Marcos fernandes ("Marcos Malaquia") 16; severino gomes da silva ("guru") 17; Edilson 17 (murdered in front of his common law wife and children.)

The precise identification of the hired guns and their victims was difficult because most street kids and poor young men who were associated with Abdoral's gang were known only by their nicknames. And truth be told, a great many adults from the poor hillsides of Timbaúba do not know their own registered legal names or those of their spouse and children. It is no wonder that Judge Borges confused one victim, Givam, for another street kid, Edivaldo, who was still alive. The web of loose personal identities in Timbaúba often resembled a tragicomic Shakespearean drama. Help came in the form of local citizens who were appointed or elected or volunteered as official child rights advocates under the Brazilian Constitution of 1987, which established the role of *conselhos tutelares* (similar to our term of *guardiam ad litem*) in each of Brazil's *municípios*. These advocates were often the first to be called upon to mediate and investigate as well as to protect minors accused of crime or illegally imprisoned. One of Timbaúba's child advocates, Gildete, herself a former street child, was fearless and relentless in her attempts to protect street kids from summary execution at the hands of Abdoral and his backers. In the following excerpt of an audiotaped closed meeting that I attended at the office of Prosecutor Humberto Graça in 2001, Gildete summarized the situation:

> The *limpeza*, "street cleaning," was ordered by local business leaders, the *empresarios* of Timbaúba. The idea was to rub out, to remove, all the street urchins [*molekes*] who spent their days sniffing glue (*cheirando cola*), stealing, and getting into trouble. The commercial class wanted them gone because they were hurting business, keeping people away from shopping in Timbaúba. They complained that business was declining because there were too many "dirty flies" in the marketplace. So, they paid Abdoral's group to take care of them, but only *after* they used them for their dirty work. Abdoral and his gang were actually recruiting street kids to steal for them and to serve as runners (*aviões*) in regional drug deals. Whenever the kids got caught, rather than implicate Abdoral, they provided a pretext to justify his clean-up operation and to demonstrate to the car salesmen and the other shopkeepers that he was representing *their* interests and to show how much they needed the protection he was selling.

Abdoral was a classic double agent.

Dr. Mariza Borges related her feelings of helplessness over a complicated case that was in her dock: "Here is a case I am dealing with right now having to do with two minors who were convicted of highway robbery, an infraction of article 155, paragraph 4, inciso 4 of the Brazilian Penal Code." The young boys were rescued once from Abdoral and placed in custody in a prison in a distant city for their own protection against the death squads. But they managed to escape. One was killed within the week. The judge pointed to the death certificate of Edmilson Felix da Silva. His partner, an adolescent named Givaldo Andre da Silva, was promised a fair defense. In court, however, he readily implicated himself in the work of Abdoral's gang. He said that he was in the street with two buddies, Edmilson and Ronaldo, when a truck arrived that circled behind them, opened the cargo door, and took out three boxes of merchandise. The three knew where and to whom they could deliver the stolen goods. But he said that he had heard stories that minors who committed thefts were killed. He said he knew that he could die and that he was afraid of death, but he reminded himself that he had committed other thefts and not been caught. So they grabbed the cargo and ran for it. But Givaldo longed for a different life. He had studied for a couple of years and wanted to know how to read and write. He wanted to have a job and a family. His social welfare report suggested that he get protective and rehabilitative care. That was the spirit of the new law, Borges said. She continued, with deep hints of disappointment and sarcasm:

In this great "Lion of the North" state of Pernambuco, where is this boy Givaldo going to get the social and educational measures he needs? Givaldo needs safe shelter with treatment for drug and alcohol addiction and to provide the basic education he needs. There are no places in the state to help juveniles like him who wander the streets, the fruit of broken homes, lacking any financial means to support himself. I am revealing the extremely embarrassing situation of the Judge of the Child and Adolescent Branch. One feels totally powerless, because *I know how* these young people should be taken care of. Givaldo needs to be put in a special boarding school with a strict regime, where you wake up at 6 in the morning, exercise, take your bath, have a meal, attend class for four hours, then lunch, you have a rest, you have some leisure, some sports or other games. Then he should have a "professionalization" class until 6 p.m. and then everything begins again the next day. And then there is also the question of prayers, to get him involved in some kind of religion.

I could not help but think what my graduate students honed on the wheel of Foucault and his powerful critique of the soft glove of the state hidden in governmentality and bio-power might think about Judge Borges's solution to the problem of street kids and crime. Borges continued:

The rehabilitative structures are absent. So as it is now when a judge like me in the Child and Adolescent Division gets one of these minors, it will go as it did with Edmilson [who was murdered]. We tried to take the steps . . . Here in the hearing we made our pleas for him [ruffling papers]. I spent all night worried about these children. The problem is that the social problem is embedded, and what we need is to prevent the problem and to implement public policy in this direction. As for the minor Edmilson, who was assassinated, he stated in his [earlier] deposition that he had sniffed glue but that he had stopped and that he was a friend of Givaldo, for about a year. He lived for a couple of years in FEBEM, a federal institution for delinquent children, where he worked in the bakery. He confessed to having taken things that did not belong to him. Then he went to Rio to live with an aunt for a while, but she sent him back to Pernambuco. Here, he worked as a stone mason's assistant until the day his brother, Severino Felix da Silva, was murdered in his bedroom, in the bed next to Givaldo, strangled by four men under orders from Abdoral. It was the day before Givaldo's eighteenth birthday. He said he lived in fear of his brother's killers, but he did not know where to hide. He ended his deposition, "I am afraid that I will be killed just like my brother."

And so he was.

"Here's a living portrait of Timbaúba" Judge Borges concluded for the moment. I asked Dr. Graça, the prosecutor, how Abdoral managed to escape from justice for so many years. Dr. Graça explained that the

(284)   *Violence at the Urban Margins*

problem was structural: "What you call structural violence," he said to my surprise. When he began his work with a state CPI (a congressional investigation) on "Violence and Drug Trafficking" in 2000, everything indicated that Timbaúba was a central location for drug and stolen cargo trafficking and for summary executions. He summoned Abdoral to the investigation and explained the charges against him. Abdoral either was or pretended to be amazed. He asked how could he be a vigilante when he was a hired official by the mayor of Timbaúba and he was paid by the state. The answer was that Timbaúba was a vigilante state, but I had to keep my silence. Graça later reflected:

> It's true, that Abdoral doesn't seem like a very hardened criminal or a particularly cruel man. When I spoke to him about the legal process, and I asked him whether he understood why I was prosecuting him, he said he was not sure. I explained that it was my obligation to investigate and prosecute crimes such as the ones he was involved in. Otherwise, the one who would go to jail would be me. He told me he understood that it was my job and he even said: "Do your job, that's the correct thing to do." I was taken aback. But once I came across the reports of his victims and the testimony of the mothers . . . then it's completely absurd. The reports indicated that he was not always present at every single execution or crime scene, but he was present for a great *many of them*. He did not even hide himself.

However, very much like Lampião (Lewin 1979; Singelmann 1975), the notorious folk hero of the backlands, Abdoral could be charming, generous, and courtly, as well as brutal. He collected weekly tribute, a tax to terrorize and eliminate "problematic" individuals, from the large and small businessmen in Timbaúba. Most of his victims at first were street children in Timbaúba, individuals that a great many people believed were better off dead. Abdoral's gang used intimidation, kidnappings, beatings, torture, and public executions. They staged train and car accidents and drownings, and they hid the bodies in clandestine graves in sugar planta-tions and in forest undergrowth. So, during the 1990s, Timbaúba, a place where the majority of the people lived in deep poverty, became a primary transit point for the new regional traffic in drugs, arms, and stolen mer-chandise (motorcycles, cars, and trucks). At the same time, markets in babies for foreign adoption also preyed on and terrorized young, poor, and mentally fragile shantytown mothers. The town's outlaw status had become so legendary that young boys took to wearing baseball caps with "#1 Mafia" sewn across the front. "What does 'Mafia' mean?," I asked a cute little street urchin. "I don't know—beautiful, right?" he replied.

Timbaúba fell into the hands of Abdoral Queiroz in the dangerous interregnum in the democratic transition, a time when trust in the new and fragile democracy was weak, and belief in the traditional rural politics of populism, paternalism, and clientelism (Kenny 2002) filled the void that the military dictatorship had filled for two decades. Abdoral may have been a crook and a butcher, but he was able to deliver what the police could no longer provide: popular justice in the form of protection to local businesses, the settling of bad debts, vendettas, and running drug and arms markets throughout the region. Abdoral and his men, they could be "gentlemanly," as when they provided around-the-clock surveillance of a small cornmeal factory owned by the neurotic aunt of a town council member. And they could be ruthless, as when they accepted commissions to kidnap, torture, and humiliate young women caught in extramarital relations. Most of the gang's activities fell under neighborhood surveillance, "street-cleaning," and ridding the *município* of vagrants, drifters, chicken thieves, trouble makers, sexual deviants, and, eventually, just plain poor people. The small business community of Timbaúba was grateful for the activities of the Guardian Angels, which they saw as a gift to their social class.

As the band grew stronger, public institutions, from the mayor's office to the town council to the police to some members of the Catholic clergy, fell under its control. Those who refused to pay for Abdoral's protection were added to the hit list. Between 1995 and 2000, the squad killed most of Timbaúba's older male street children. Abdoral and his men grew bolder. They began to conduct their activities in public, appearing in the company of high-profile citizens, members of the commercial and landed classes. Eventually, the town capitulated to the extermination squad. It was not a parallel form of governance—it was the municipal government. Thus, no one protested when Abdoral's gunmen showed up at the town hall to collect their tribute from the city council or when Abdoral was seen in public bars and restaurants hobnobbing with the mayor. Indeed, by the late 1990s, no one in Timbaúba knew exactly where the local government began and where the *grupos de extermínio* ended. Things veered so out of control that Abdoral and a dozen of his men led the national holiday marchers, with the mayor and town council members in tow. They usurped the civil police, announcing their semiofficial role as a paramilitary unit. In short, the death squad became official.

Before the reign of terror was interrupted, more than 150 people had been murdered, execution style. In a small town like Timbaúba, it was spoken of as a "revolution," one that would never be covered by the national, let alone international, media. Similar events were occurring elsewhere in Brazil, but mostly in urban favelas. That a large old *município* of sixty thousand people known regionally for its small sugar plantations, its shoe factories, its hand-woven hammocks, and its weekly open-air markets that brought people from all around to purchase the food, clothing, furniture, refrigerators, stoves, television sets, and cars they needed, could simply collapse under the control of a sociopathological death squad was something very unique.

But Abdoral made a few errors. When he and his band, dressed in black with insignia armbands, were observed in public providing an armed entourage to protect truckloads of stolen and contraband merchandise, they began to be perceived as dangerous robber barons. The vigilantes began to demonstrate their fascist tendencies in attacks on white working- and middle-class people, in addition to the more socially acceptable targets of hatred: poor Blacks, the illiterate, the vagrants, and poor sick people. Attacks against sexual transgressors—known homosexuals, *travesti* [cross-dressers], and cross-racial and cross-class lovers—exposed a code of puritanical morality that was not embraced by most people even in this corner of rural Northeast Brazil. Had Abdoral and his gang kept their activities contained to the favelas, shantytowns, and rural "villas of misery" around Timbaúba, they might still be in control today.

I had not anticipated the openings initiated by the new constitution and its vision of "human rights" and the institutions it allowed to flourish, including the official roles created to protect the rights of children and other vulnerable people. In Timbaúba, those appointed to fill the roles of child rights counselors and human rights advocates were largely working-class intellectuals lacking professional credentials, resources, or symbolic capital. However, these rights workers mobilized around the constitution to rescue the endangered population of street children and unemployed young men of the shantytowns, the main targets of Abdoral's "hygienic exterminations."

They were joined by progressive teachers and lawyers, Catholic nuns, Marxist intellectuals, and ordinary working- and middle-class individuals who could no longer stand the egregious violations of justice and human rights. One was a local pharmacist in her early seventies. Another was a *farinha* (manioc flour) salesman before he became a poor people's lawyer. Another was the son of a failed shoe factory owner. One grew up with local street kids and talked rough and wore low-cut dresses. One was a German nun who collaborated with a Black educator and rights activist. The activists are Black, White, and in-between. It is politics, not race, that runs in their veins. They are married, single, celibate . . . and in-between. They include devout Catholics, skeptical agnostics, and quiet atheists. They have met over the years in small rooms sharing dog-eared paperbacks and pamphlets. They read and passionately debate Marx, Gramsci, Leonardo Boff, the Scriptures, Paulo Freire, Celso Furtado, and Cristovan Buarque. They are critical thinkers and astute strategists who use the techniques of the *bricoleur*, taking advantage of every possibility, every theoretical or practical opening at hand. They make political alliances and just as quickly break them. They do not have reliable access to email or the Internet.

Undaunted, they took to the streets to gather up Timbaúba's most threatened street children into a safe house run in large part by the older children themselves and following the philosophy of empowerment espoused by the MNMMR (*Movimento Nacional de Meninos e Meninas de Rua*) and the new child and adolescent statutes. They exposed a corrupt judge linked to commercial international child-trafficking adoption networks that preyed upon the poorest and weakest women of the community.

Nonetheless, on my return to Timbaúba in the summer of 2001, I found that there was also resistance to the intervention prosecutor's and the local human rights activists' efforts. Many ordinary local citizens were complicit with the death squad whom they identified as *justiceiros*, representatives of popular justice. The group was supported by the commercial class of landowners, car dealers, and distributors of merchandise. Names of powerful "strong men" who were the "owners" of Timbaúba's wealth were whispered to be backers of the death squads. Abdoral was seen in public with them in restaurants and bars and even in the zona, the red light district.

Abdoral's frequent visits to the Alto do Cruzeiro were largely unwelcome except by his clients and kingpins of heroin trafficking in the community. His presence was feared and turned residents into shut-ins, living under self-imposed curfews. Many recalled with horror a night in 1999, when six people were murdered on the Rua do Cruzeiro, the principal street leading up to the top of the Alto do Cruzeiro. "During the revolution," Irene said, using the local idiom to describe the terror as a revolution against the poor, "we all went underground. The streets were deserted; we kept our doors locked and our wooden shutters closed tight. We would slide in and out our back doors to go to work or to the fields, or to the market."

Biu, my fifty-six-year-old friend and key informant of many years, was among the last in Timbaúba to lose a family member to Abdoral's extermination group. Biu explained how her twenty-four-year-old son had met his untimely end walking home along the main road leading up to the top of Alto do Cruzeiro. Neighbors heard the shots and screams, but they were too frightened to leave their homes. The next morning it was left to Gilvan's older sister, Pelzinha, to discover what was left of his body, sprawled over a mound of uncollected garbage. A crowd of greasy winged vultures had discovered Gilvan first, and Pelzinha could barely recognize her brother. Well seasoned by a lifetime of traumatic events, Biu was stoic and ambivalent about the murder of her son.

> Gilvan was no angel. My family had turned against him, saying he was no good, a
> brawler, a drinker, and a thief who was always getting into trouble. In one fight he
> even lost an eye. But when they say to me that Gilvan really had to be killed, I feel
> dead inside. He was still my son! But I can't tell anyone, except you, how much I miss
> that boy. My own niece said, "Be grateful, Tia, for the little bit of tranquility that
> Gilvan's death has brought into your life." What does *she* understand?

I made my way to the civil registry office located in the municipal courthouse of Timbaúba where I reviewed all the dully and officially registered deaths from 1995 to 2000, the height of Abdoral's reign of terror. Officially recorded homicides represented, of course, only the tip of the iceberg, as most extrajudicial killings were disguised as accidents, suicides, and train- and car-related deaths. Many homicides were not registered at all and the bodies were hidden in small, clandestine graves in the rural surrounds. In all, our search through death records led to the identification of an additional thirty-one homicides that appeared to be linked *specifically* to Abdoral's exterminations.

In most cases, the police were not even alerted. The relative of the deceased would arrive at the registry office and report the name, age, and cause of death to Amantina, the easily irritated bureaucratic record keeper. No questions asked, the death certificates would be signed and stamped with the municipal seal and the information was shelved. The only reason for reporting the deaths was so that the deceased could be buried in a free plot at the municipal graveyard. No one wanted any trouble with the law—which at that time happened to be the death squad itself.

I pretended to be looking for infant and child mortalities according to my familiar role in the civil registry office. After a few weeks, however, I had to explain to the clerk of the records what I was looking for. Though she expressed no emotion, Amantina began to facilitate my search in subtle ways. "Here, look at this," she would say, shoving a book toward me with a particular page open. A total of ninety-three homicides were recorded via handwritten entries in the monthly ledgers of the Timbaúba civil registry between 1995 and 2000, roughly nineteen per year. Few of these murders were investigated, which is hardly surprising considering both the "social invisibility" of the victim population, on the one hand, and the likely involvement of civil and military police linked to Abdoral's extermination squad, on the other.

The majority of recorded homicides were of young men between the ages of fifteen and thirty. The youngest homicide victim was a boy

Figure 11.2
Amantina and Nancy

of twelve years, and the oldest a man of forty-one. The average victim, a subset of all homicides in Timbaúba, was a twenty-six-year-old Black (*Negro*) or mulatto (*Moreno*) male, unemployed, or casually employed, and residing in one of the poor hillside slums or peripheral rural villas of Timbaúba. In the 1990s, the vast majority of homicides were of street kids, unemployed Black men, petty criminals, and vagrants. We presented our report on "likely" death squad victims to Dr. Graça and the Ministry of the Public in Timbaúba to be used in their prosecutions and continuing investigations. In the end, Abdoral and twenty-three of his associates were arrested, prosecuted, and convicted of murder, conspiracy, intimidation, and extortion.

CAMANHADA CONTRA MORTE: THE MARCH AGAINST DEATH SQUADS

The time seemed ripe for a public denunciation of the death squad. A meeting, called by the rights activists, brought together a larger group of political leaders, teachers, and officials from the local Ministries of Education, Justice, and Public Security, to plan a public demonstration, a *camanhada*

Figure 11.3
March against death squads

or march, against death-squad violence, and to declare a truce and a time of peace. The event was held on July 19, 2001, one year after the arrest of Abdoral and his accomplices. While most residents were still too fearful of, or complicit with, the death squads (some of whom were still at large) to join the march, the municipal secretary of education declared the day a public-school holiday and fearlessly led the town's grade-school children and adult-school youths in the march down the main streets of Timbaúba.

She was joined by a few brave citizens, including José Carlos Araújo, a bold radio journalist well known in the region for his popular free-wheeling daily talk show on "community radio" (poor people's public radio), and his wife, Maria do Carmel. Although the day was miserably cold and rainy, hundreds of local residents came out of their homes to watch the unheard-of event from the sidewalk, registering their amazement and their excitement that it could be happening in Timbaúba. A sound truck accompanied the procession with Marcelo, the people's lawyer, doing his best to animate the event and to call others from the sidelines to join the march against death. His broadly accented Nordestino voice, announcing an "end to the reign of terror" and declaring a "cease-fire in the war against the poor" in Timbaúba, made him particularly vulnerable.

But none were more vulnerable than the front lines of the demonstration, which were reserved for the surviving cadre of local street children, who were dressed in white, each carrying a wooden cross bearing the name of a sibling or a friend who had been executed by Abdoral's gang. Following immediately behind them were about two dozen women—the mothers, older sisters, aunts, and wives of the men and boys who had been murdered—making public for the first time what had happened to them. My closest friends on the Alto do Cruzeiro were among them. Irene was laughing and shaking her head in disbelief that she could be so brave as to protest "in front of the world" the execution-murders of her husband and two young adult sons. Biu was a more reluctant protester, and she shyly hid herself in the midst of the mothers, refusing at first to carry the cross with the name of her murdered son, Gilvam. Thus, we took turns carrying the sign for her to honor her executed son.

Suddenly, two heavily armed police jeeps appeared at the front of the march as though intending to interrupt it. Stifled cries of warning split the protesters down the center, with the front lines of street children and human rights workers taking one street and the teachers and public-school children taking another. There was a moment of panic. Would the newly installed and human rights-trained police force show their true colors and turn on the demonstrators and open fire? Instead—to our relief, amazement, and delight—the police were going to accompany and protect the marchers. Moreover, inside the cab of one of the jeeps was the shackled figure of Abdoral Gonçalves Queiroz himself, whom the police put on view before the marchers, forcing the leader of the death squad, his head initially bowed, to snap to attention and witness the spectacle of raised crosses bearing the names of the victims that he and his gang had brutally murdered. Later, we learned that Judge Borges had arranged this dramatic confrontation as a display of the power of the law and a visible sign that the new police force were representing all the people of Timbaúba, even street kids and "marginals" from the favelas and peripheral, informal settlements of Timbaúba.

The march terminated in front of the city hall and spontaneous, if somewhat nervous, speeches were made by the new mayor, Galvaozinho, who had replaced the corrupt former mayor and his henchmen, who were allies of Abdoral and his gang. The current mayor and his staff were presented with a large brass plaque memorializing the end of the most recent reign of death squad terror in Timbaúba. The organizers of the march requested that the plaque be placed on the wall of a small public square facing the city hall, which they hoped could be renamed the Praça de Paz. The plaque read:

> With the Gratitude of the People of Timbaúba for All Those who Fought Against Violence and for Human Rights. Commemorating One Year of Peace, July 19, 2001.

That evening people gathered in front of their TV sets and on the Alto in groups at the few homes with operable television sets, to observe the media interviews and the wrenching profile of an emotionally overwrought woman, the adoptive mother of a teenage girl who had been kidnapped and tortured by Abdoral's gang.

As James Holston (2009) has noted, citizenship includes the right to be visible and to be heard, the freedom to participate openly in politics and social movements in the public sphere. The claiming of these rights by "disgraced" and stigmatized populations residing in peripheral neighborhoods is new, and Holston's term *insurgent citizenship* captures the revolutionary feeling of those participating for the first time in public protest. Among other things, citizenship is about the right of *public* self-representation, self-expression, the right to be seen, to be visible, which entails the notion of "public-ness" and the acknowledgment of being seen. The television coverage represented a "coming out" (to the public) and "the public eye," underscoring the importance of seeing and being seen in the affirmation of the citizen-subject. For the mothers and wives of the death-squad victims, the *camanhada* was their "coming-out" party. It made them feel strong and courageous, which of course they were.

A DEATH FORETOLD

Violent deaths did not cease in Timbaúba, but at least for a period they were not organized by roving bands of paramilitary death squads. On a return to Recife in February 2004 to give testimony at a parliamentary investigation on international organs trafficking, a contingent of human rights workers from Timbaúba arrived at the open session to relay discouraging stories of Abdoral and his henchmen re-arming themselves in prison and communicating with local bandits via cell phones. They feared that new death squads were forming, and without the help and protection of Prosecutor Graça, who had been re-assigned to another *município*, they would be in danger. Without Graça's moderating presence, Judge Marisa Borges was becoming a liability, brave but sometimes belligerent and ill informed. Some human rights activists were receiving death threats, and all feared betrayal at the hands of local double agents, powerful citizens (the "commercial class," as they put it) who, while appearing to support the rule of law and the rights of the poor, were actively supporting hired guns and arms traffickers behind the scenes. A large cache of arms, including illegal and restricted automatic weapons, had been discovered in the warehouse of a local shopkeeper, an affable fellow who sold children's toys, party favors, and cheap sports equipment. Stockpiles of illegal weapons and bullets were found in the garages of his friends and neighbors.

A few months later, word reached me of the cold-blooded murder of the popular working-class hero and community radio talk host, José Carlos Araújo. He was shot in the chest by two young gunmen on motorbikes on April, 24, 2004 outside his home in Timbaúba and in view of his wife, Maria do Carmel, and his three children. The thirty-seven-year-old folk musician—he and his wife and children performed *forró* music for dance parties throughout the region—turned truth teller and "voice of the poor" had made enemies in Timbaúba after denouncing the continued existence of death squads, even revealing the involvement of well-known local figures and businessmen in wanton murders in the region. The local police captured one of the suspected assassins, nineteen-year-old Elton Jonas Gonçalves, who confessed to killing Araújo because the journalist had accused him on the air of being a bandit.

On my next return to Timbaúba, my friend and local research assistant Marcelo brought me to the home of Maria do Carmel and her grieving family. There, I had to confront the role of the rights activists and our march against silence in inciting Maria's husband to name and disclaim Timbaúba's deadly killers. Carmel gave me copies of his taped radio programs leading up to his death. In one of these, José Carlos announced angrily over the radio waves that he was now ready and willing to inform the new police force so that they could take appropriate action:

> People from Alto do Cruzeiro are calling us and giving us details about the murder of a young man from the Alto. I'll pass this information along to the police, to the sheriff and his team. People are outraged! The boy was shot and killed last Saturday, about 7:30 in the morning and in public in the open market! No kidding! ... People are not yet ready to reveal the name of the assassin, but this guy knew what he was

doing. The police patrol begins at 8 a.m. and he did his business at 7:30 a.m.! In other words, he is very smart. He uses his intelligence to do evil, to commit crimes. He could use these same skills for good deeds . . . Evil begets evil, and the police won't be demoralized forever. The [common] people will put pressure on the police, and they won't eat dust forever. They will lose their patience and use the power they have, within the law, to catch him . . . I don't give a damn about bandits or bums. They should all go to hell to smoke Satan's pipe. If the police don't arrest him, even better. I hope they [the people] send him off [kill him]! If he had respected fathers and good citizens, I would shut up. But this guy does evil in his own community, he kills a father from his own neighborhood. To reign in a community of poor people is not bravery, it's cowardly!

By now one can begin to see the continuing danger of political populism and the lure of vigilantism in Northeast Brazil where, as José Carlos noted, evil begets evil and violence begets violence. The desire for peacemaking is double-crossed by the lack of basic trust in the state and its institutions. José Carlos was willing to hand over crucial information to the local police, but deep down he did not believe that the police were willing to end, or capable of ending, the law of misrule, of secret collaborations, of deals cut and lives sacrificed. If the police can't do it, he said, let the people do it for themselves.

A few days later José Carlos became more belligerent: "So, beware Pio, beware Jonas, and Antonio de Joana, you are all in big trouble. I always say that bandits and outlaws don't have much time to live, you either end up in jail or in hell! Any day now! Today's show is over, but I'll be back tomorrow to talk more about this violence."

In one of his final radio programs before the popular voice of the people was silenced forever, José Carlos seemed to be bidding farewell to the people of Timbaúba and the surrounding areas. It is an uncanny performance as if the popular radio journalist knew he could not go on in this manner without suffering retaliation. In a calm voice he said his goodbyes:

My friends, I do my duty with a clear conscience. But now it's time to return to reality, to the world of God, a world where I will never be betrayed. At the end of my program I always say that life is very good, but it also has difficult times. The way out of hard times is never to bow your head—quite the opposite—it is time to rise up and to keep going. Victory cannot be bought or stolen. The sorrow and tears of being vanquished are more valuable than the shame of not participating in this arduous journey and this struggle. And it is constantly fighting for victory where you will find me later, anywhere, anytime, at any corner, and you will say, "José Carlos, you were right." From the bottom of my heart I wish that God would be your main guide and give you reason to live through difficult times.

Figure 11.4
Another homicide on the Alto do Cruzeiro

Face to Face with Abdoral Queiroz

During fieldwork in 2007 among a cohort of thirty young men from the slums of Recife who had been recruited as kidney sellers to supply the needs of international transplant tourists from South Africa (Scheper-Hughes 2011), I spent many Sundays in a military prison where the Israeli organs broker, Gadalya ("Gaddy") Tauber, was serving an eleven-year sentence. He had rejected my overtures on previous field trips to Recife since his arrest in 2004, but now he had enough time on his hands to explain to me the ethics and political logic of his international human trafficking for kidneys scheme (Scheper-Hughes 2009). While there, I used the military prison guards to contact the superintendent of Hannibal Bruno prison, Brazil's largest state penitentiary, where Abdoral was serving his considerably longer thirty-year sentence.

"No, of course, the prisoner does not want to speak with a stranger," said the superintendent after several failed attempts to reach him by cell phone. With the clang-clang of banging cells and yelling men—some four thousand prisoners under one roof—any cell phone conversation was nearly impossible. "But I'm not a stranger," I yelled over the din. "Tell Abdoral that I am the *Americana*, Nanci, who lived for a long time on the Alto do Cruzeiro, and who used to travel by bicycle and *burro* through the main street of Timbaúba, when he was a kid. He knows who I am." "OK, OK," said the superintendent. "I can convince him to show you his face, but I can't force him to talk to you. Abdoral is very popular here, he is a 'message boy' for us [implying a kind of step-and-fetch-it]. He is very pliant, very cordial, very likable."

So, this is what I thought I wanted: to gaze at the face of the *mata-gente*. I had in mind images of commando leaders, and I imagined Abdoral as a dark, brooding young man, full of energy, native intelligence, and rage, spewing rap and hip-hop couplets praising freedom, money, death, and power. But the small man who was brought in front of me, pulled by a prison warden, was a Nordestino peasant, and he refused the meeting in a high-pitched nasal vernacular whine. "I don't have to talk to the United Nations. I have my rights." In Abdoral's four-square field-worker hands was a black felt bowler hat which he kept turning around, rubbing the brim nervously. He was dressed in a cheap, wrinkled white shirt and thick black pants, and on his feet were a pair of rubber-tire-soled sandals. Abdoral was mollified by a friend of mine who accompanied me, and she used the patronizing intimate "tu," the privilege of the patron to his poor client—Tu, Tu, Tu, Abdoral.

Of course, he was innocent (he said). How could he be prosecuted for being the chief (*chefe*) of an illegal death squad when he was an officially paid civil servant, employed by the previous mayor, Gilson Queroiz? The accusations and arrests were all politics as usual, the handiwork of the political enemies of *Prefeito* Gilson. OK, I agreed. "You were hired to clean up the city and some people in Timbaúba are still grateful for what you did. But you were convicted of receiving tribute and cash to kill young men who never had a chance to stand before a judge or to be represented by a lawyer. So who protected you? Besides Gilson, who else paid you? Was it 'Totinho' [a wealthy businessman and entrepreneur who was widely held to have financially backed the death squad]?" Abdoral's eyes rolled to the back of his head. "If I was the chief of the *bandidos*, tell me, have the deaths ended in Timbaúba?" "No," I replied. "They say that your son has taken over for you." "What business is it of yours? The only ones who are erased, are worthless dope fiends, drug addicts, thieves. The trouble is if you kill one or two, they blame every murder on you! I don't have to talk to you. Who sent you? The priest? The nuns? Give me your cell phone number—I will call you tomorrow." I declined, of course. I could see that Abdoral already had my number. "Excuse me, Dona Nanci, but I am taking my leave now," Abdoral said as he turned his back on me.

THE EPILOGUE: A STORY WITHOUT A MORAL
AND WITHOUT AN END

Following what Erich Fromm terms the "utopianism of the awake" (Pekkola 2010), one principle for all ethnographers is that "happy endings are premature." As in the ballad of "Frankie and Jonnie," this story about banditry and death squads in democratic Brazil is a story that has no moral, and a story that has no end—at least not in the sight of this chastened anthropologist-*companheira*. But other things have changed for the better. The value of long-term research—multiple returns between 1964 and 2014—is the ability to engage in a history of the present.

Despite the strong interventions against Abdoral's death squad in 2001, homicides in Timbaúba and especially in the former shantytowns have not ended. There are new strongmen and new populist political leaders with links to Abdoral and his protégés. The senseless violence against petty criminals, drug dealers, and their clients continues to put a damper on public life. For the past two years, I made my rounds on the Alto do Cruzeiro with "protection" provided by the *município*. No one speaks of death squads or extermination groups today, but the homicides hover around 38 per 100,000 people, most of them concentrated in the hills and working-class poor neighborhoods. Rather than organized crime, there is "disorganized" crime with young men from the three hillside rural slums of Timbaúba shooting each other in an absurd series of turf wars. A young man of seventeen was murdered on the Rua dos Indios at the top of the Alto do Cruzeiro a few days before I left the field. When I returned in May of 2014, more than twenty homicides had already been reported for the first four months of the year. Today some of these victims are adolescent girls and children under fourteen years old who have joined street gangs.

In a May 2014 exit meeting in Recife with Dr. Humberto Graça, the courageous prosecutor explained why he had never returned to Timbaúba after the convictions of Abdoral and his band. He feared retaliation and he grieved the loss of a critical group of local human rights advocates, our mutual *companheiros* and *companheiras*, who have been intimidated, punished, isolated, or chased away from Timbaúba. Graça's mood was somber and depressed. He recounted the things that he was able to accomplish and he grieved the inability to continue the struggle and to complete what was begun: the long walk to freedom from a history and tradition of violence, clientelism, fatalism, and terror that affected every major institution of the *município*. He denounced the ease with which police handed over their badges to vigilantes and public officials' falsification of birth and death certificates to hide crimes and protect murder suspects by issuing death certificates to living people so as to end legal proceedings. It was an absurdity, he said.

> Timbaúba has a long history of violence, because of its entrenched poverty, drug-related crimes, and lack of infrastructure and the basic resources of survival. Before Abdoral there was an extermination group known as the "Aureliano brothers." Abdoral was hired by the local government to get rid of them. And after Abdoral, who started out as a hero, a Zorro figure and who turned into an anti-Christ, an Exterminator, will come, as night follows the day, other *bandidos* and *mata-gentes* (hit men) backed by their wealthy supporters and hungry populist politicians who will fill their niche. They are already in place. What is needed not only in Timbaúba but in Brazil, is a moral as well as a political and economic, revolution—a total revolution.

NO MORE ANGEL BABIES

As for the promised good news, it began during the 2001 death-squad field research expedition. As I played cat-and-mouse with the manager of the public records office, trying to assemble a body count of suspicious homicides of young men that might be linked to the death squad, I tried

Figure 11.5
No more angel babies

Figure 11.6
Proud to nurse her baby

to conceal what I was doing by pretending to be counting infant and child deaths, as I had so many years before. Finally, I had to admit, with the registrar looking over my shoulder, that I was looking into youth homicides. She nodded her head. "Yes, it's very sad. But," she asked with a sly smile, "haven't you noticed the changes in infant and child deaths?" Once I began to scan the record books, I was wearing a smile, too. Could it be true? From hundreds to a few dozen infant deaths?

A single afternoon going over infant and toddler death certificates in the registry office was enough to document that something radical had taken place—a revolution in child survival that had begun in the 1990s. By 2001, available records showed a completed birth rate of 3.2 children per woman, and a mortality rate of 35 per 1,000 births—a drop from 110 per 1,000 in the 1960s. Subsequent field trips showed even further reductions. By 2009, data from the Brazilian Institute of Geography and Statistics recorded a rate of 25.2 child deaths per 1,000 births for Timbaúba. This could not have happened without a radical transformation of their mothers. Timbaúba had experienced what population experts call the demographic or epidemiologic transition. Births and infant deaths declined so rapidly and precipitously that it looked like a reproductive workers' strike.

The numbers—though incomplete—were amazing. Rather than three hundred plus mortalities in the mid to late 1960s and two hundred plus mortalities in the early 1980s, there were less than fifty childhood deaths per year recorded by the late 1990s. The women I spoke with—some of them first-time mothers, others expecting a second or third child—were confident in their ability to give birth to a healthy baby and to see that child live to adulthood. No one wanted to have more than two children, a pair—that was the goal. Although the Alto do Cruzeiro was still a dangerous place, and gangs, drugs, and the death squads were still in operation, women visiting the state-run clinic spoke of having control over their reproductive lives in ways that I could not have imagined. What was happening in Timbaúba was part of a national trend. Since the 1960s, birth rates and child death rates have plummeted. Over the past decade alone, Brazil's fertility rate decreased from 2.36 children per family to a national average of 1.9, which is below replacement level and lower than the two-children-per-woman fertility rate of the United States.

Many factors came together in producing this crucial reproductive transition. In Brazil, this reproductive revolution is linked to democracy and the coming into political power of President Enrique Cardoso (aided by his formidable wife, the anthropologist and women's advocate Ruth Cardoso), followed by *Companheiro-Presidente* Lula da Silva, and—since 2011—his hand-picked successor, Dilma Rousseff. President Fernando Henrique Cardoso (1995–2003) fortified the national health care system (Serviço Único de Saúde) with a program of local health agents who today visit at-risk households door to door, identifying crises, diagnosing common symptoms, and intervening to rescue vulnerable infants, toddlers, (and their mothers, let it be said) from premature death.

President Lula's Zero Hunger campaign, though much criticized in the popular media as a kind of political publicity stunt, in fact and on the ground supplied basic food stuffs (*cestas basicas*) to the most vulnerable households. The policy of dispensing monthly stipends (called student grants) to poor and single mothers for keeping their children in school turned elementary-school pupils into valuable household "workers." Literacy increased for both the children and their mothers, who often studied at home alongside their children. Women's literacy is the best predictor of lowered birth rates and reduced infant mortality.

What about the role of the Catholic Church? Despite the laws against abortion (except to save a mother's life or in the case of rape), Brazilian Catholics are independent and they have been going their own way for many years when it comes to women's health and reproductive culture (Caetano and Potter 2004). On the other hand, the teachings of liberation theology (while condemned by the late Pope John Paul II) dislodged a baroque folk Catholicism that saw God and the saints as "authorizing" infant deaths of angel babies. During one fieldtrip to Timbaúba, I was asked by Padre Orlando, who refused to continue the baroque custom of blessing the bodies of dead infants as they were being carried to the municipal graveyard, to give an orientation to poor women in the Casa Paroquial, the church hall. When I asked what form of contraception I could teach, the good priest replied, "I'm a celibate priest, how should I know? Teach it all, everything you know." I reminded him that only the Billings Method, the very unpredictable rhythm method, was approved by the Vatican, and he replied: "Just teach it all, everything you know, and then say, but the Pope only approves the not-so-safe rhythm method."

There is no doubt that when poor women begin to think of themselves as capable of deciding how many pregnancies they will have, their sentiments and practices around birth and infant care are radically transformed. Hope and optimism replace a sense of fate, destiny, and God's will. With hope in their hearts, they can depend on their infants to be few and healthy, and maternal attachment and affections can be released at birth rather than after a year or more of distanced and apprehensive waiting.

But the primary cause of the decline in infant mortality in the shantytowns of Northeast Brazil was the result of a basic municipal public health program, the installation of water pipes reaching almost all the homes in the shantytown with sufficient and clean water. Water equals life! It is amazing to observe how culture, beliefs, maternal sentiments and infant and child care practices are transformed, even revolutionized, following basic changes in the material conditions and therefore the possibilities of everyday life.

There are still many problems faced by the people of the Alto do Cruzeiro. As we have seen, drugs, gangs, and death squads have left their ugly mark on the community. These new features of antisocial life take some of the pleasure away, as one sees adolescents and young men of the shantytowns who survived that dangerous first year of life only to be cut down by bullets and knives at the age of fifteen or seventeen by local gangs, "strong men," *bandidos*, and local police in almost equal measure. But at least women on the Alto today do not lose their infants, children go to school rather than to the cane fields, and social cooperatives have taken the place of shadow economies. When they are sick or pregnant or a child is ill, they will not be turned away from cynical private clinics. There is a safety net for women and their infants, and it is strong, large, and deep. This allows me to hope that the reproductive revolution can be followed by the total revolution that Dr. Humberto Graça imagined, a revolution against senseless youth mortalities, vigilante politics, fatalism and fear, and death squads in democratic Brazil.

NOTE

1. See http://www.mapadaviolencia.org.br/mapa2012_cor.php.

WORKS CITED

Adorno, Sergio. 1995. "A Violencia na Sociedade Brasileira: um panel inconcluso em uma democracia nao consolidada." *Revista Sociedade e Estado* 10(2): 299–342.

Alvim, R. ed. 1991. *Da Violência Contra o Menor ao Extermínio de Crianças e Adolescentes.* Rio de Janeiro: NEPI-CBIA.

Alves, Maria Helena Moreira. 1985. *State and Oppression in Military Brazil.* Austin: University of Texas Press.

Amaral e Silva, A. F. 1991. "O Estatuto da Criança e do Adolescente e a Justiça Infância e da Juventude." *Cadernos Populares* 6. São Paulo: Sindicato dosTrabalhadores (SITRAEMFA); Centro Brasileiro para a Infância e Adolesência (CBIA)

Amnesty International. 1992. *Brazil, Impunity and the Law: The Killing of Street Children in Rio de Janeiro State.* London: Amnesty International

Anderson, Brian, and Angela Garcia. 2013. "Anonymous and Punitive: Mutual Aid Addiction Therapies in Mexico City." Paper presented at the Critical Psychiatry Workshop, Medical Anthropology Doctoral Program, University of California, Berkeley, April 2013.

Basaglia, Franco. 1987. "Institutions of Violence." In *Psychiatry Inside Out: Selected Writings of Franco Basaglia*, edited by Nancy Scheper-Hughes and Anne M. Lovell. New York: Columbia University Press, 59–86.

Bourdieu, Pierre. 2010. "For a Scholarship with Commitment." In *Sociology is a Martial Art. Political Writings by Pierre Bourdieu*, edited by Gisele Sapiro. New York: The New Press 179-85.

Butler, Judith. 2004. *Undoing Gender.* New York: Routledge.

Caetano, Andre, and Joseph Potter. 2004. "Politics and Female Sterilization in Northeast Brazil." *Population and Development Review* 30(1): 79–108.

Caldeira, Teresa Pires do Rio. 2000. *City of Walls.* Berkeley: University of California Press

Caldeira, T. 2002. "The Paradox of Police Violence in Democratic Brazil." *Ethnography* 3(3): 235–263.

da Costa, Antônio Carlos Gomes. "O novo direito da criança e do adolescente no Brasil: O conteúdo e o processo das mudanças no panorama legal." *A criança, o adolescente, o município: Entendendo e implementando a Lei No. 8069/90.*

de Carvalho, Maria do Carmo Brant. 1991. "O Estatuto da Criança e do adolescente e a política de assistência social." *Cadernos Populares* 9. São Paulo: Sindicato dos Trabalhadores em Entidades de Assistência ao Menor e à Familia (SITRAEMFA); Centro Brasileiro para a Infância e Adolesência

De Castro, Josué. 1969. *Death in the Northeast.* New York: Random House

de Souza, Herbert. 1992. "As crianças de rua." Carta Semanal do IBASE (Instituto Brasileiro de Analises Sociais e Económicas) No. 89.

Dimenstein, Gilberto. 1991. *Brazil: War on Children*, translated by Chris Whitehouse. London: Latin America Bureau.

dos Santos, Benedito Rodrigues. 1992. "A implantação do Estatuto da Criança e do Adolescente." *Os impasses da cidadania: Infância e adolescência no Brasil*, edited by Almir Pereira Júnior, Jaerson Lucas Bezerra, and Rosana Heringer. Rio de Janeiro: IBASE, 66–79.

Ferreira, Joao Marcelo Gomes. 2001. "Relatorios Referente as Irregularidades Atuais, Existentes nos Cemiterios, Sede, Distritos e Vilas de Timbaúba." Prefeitural Municipal de Timbaúba, April 19. (in author's possession)

GAJOP (Gabinete de Assessoria Jurídica às Organizações Populares/Centro Luiz Freire). 1992. "Minors and the Death Squad in Pernambuco."

Galeano, Eduardo. 1975. *Open Veins of Latin America: Five Centuries of Pillage of a Continent*. New York: Monthly Review.

Girard, René. 1987a. "Generative Scapegoating." In *Violent Origins: Ritual Killing and Cultural Formation*, edited by Robert Hamerton-Kelly. Stanford, CA: Stanford University Press, 73–105.

Girard, René. 1987b "A Non-Sacrificial Reading of the Gospel Text." In *Things Hidden Since the Foundation of the World*. Stanford, CA: Stanford University Press, 180–223.

Kenny, Mary Lorena. 2002. "Drought, Clientism, Fatalism and Fear in Northeast Brazil." *Ethics, Place, and Environment* 5(2): 123–134.

Vera Mello, Joscelyne. 1991. *Grupos de extermínio: A banalização da vida e da morte em Pernambuco*. Olinda: GAJOP.

Graça, Humberto da Silva. 2000. "(In)Sueguranca Publica em Timbaúba." Timbaúba, March 30. (unpublished public document, in author's possession)

Haraway, Donna. 2007. *When Species Meet*. Minneapolis: University of Minnesota Press.

Hobsbawm, Eric. 2000. *Bandits*. New York: The New Press.

Holston, James. 2009. *Insurgent Citizenship: Disjunctions of Democracy and Modernity in Brazil*. Princeton, NJ: Princeton University Press.

Holston, James, and Teresa Caldeira. 1997. "Democracy, Law, and Violence: Disjunctions of Brazilian Citizenship." In *Fault Lines of Democratic Governance in the Americas*, edited by F. Aguero and J. Stark. Miami: North-South Center and Lynne Rienner.

Horowitz, Irving Lewis. 1964. Revolution in Brazil: Politics and Society in a Developing Nation. New York: Dutton.

Huggins, Martha. 1997. "From Bureaucratic Consolidation to Structural Devolution: Police Death Squads in Brazil." *Policing and Society* 7: 207–234.

Levi, Primo. 1988. *The Drowned and the Saved*. New York: Vintage.

Levi-Strauss, Claude. 1966. *The Savage Mind*. Chicago: The University of Chicago Press.

Lewin, Linda. 1979. "The Oligarchical Limitations of Social Banditry in Brazil: The Case of the 'Good' Thief Antonio Silvino." *Past & Present Society* 82 (Feb): 116–146, available at http://www.jstor.org/stable/650595.

Louzeiro, José. 1990. "Genocide in the Baixada: Children are Being Murdered." In *The Killing of Children and Adolescents in Brazil*, edited by André Papi, Marisa Brandão, and Jorge L. C. Jardineiro.. Rio de Janeiro: Center for the Mobilization of Marginalized Populations (CEAP), 18–19.

Mbembe, Achille. 2003. Necropolitics. *Public Culture* 15(1): 11–40.

MNMMR (Movimento Nacional de Meninos e Meninas de Rua). 1991. "Guerra no centro da cidade." *O grito dos meninos e meninas de rua* 5(20): 4. (newsletter of the MNMMR, Pernambuco)

MNMMR. 1999. *Vidas em risco: assassinatos de crianças e adolescentes no Brasil*. Rio de Janeiro: IBASE.

Nascimento, Maria das Graças. 1990. "Street Children, the Right to Become a Citizen." In *The Killing of Children and Adolescents in Brazil*, edited by André Papi, Marisa Brandão, and Jorge L. C. Jardineiro. Rio de Janeiro: Center for the Mobilization of Marginalized Populations (CEAP).

Nobrega, Jose Maria, Jorge Zaverucha, Enivaldo Rocha. 2011. "Morete por Agressao em Pernambuco e No Brasil." *Rev. Sociol. Politic.*, Curitiba 19(40): 103–114, available athttp://www.uff.br/ineac/sites/default/files/artigo_zaverucha_nobrega_e_rocha.pdf.

Pachico, Elyssa. 2013. Northeast Brazil Suffers High Gun Deaths: Study. *In Sight Crime: Organized Crime in the Americas*. Available at http://www.insightcrime.org/news-briefs/northeast-brazil-suffers-highest-gun-deaths-study.

Pekkola, Mika. 2010. *Prophet of Radicalism:Erich Fromm and the Figurative Constitution of the Crisis of Modernity*. Jyväskylä, Finland: University of Jyväskylä.

Penglase, Ben. 1993. *Final Justice: Police and Death Squad Homicides of Adolescents in Brazil.* New York: Human Rights Watch/Americas.

Piva, Rodrigo. 2014. "Lugares Mais Violentos do Brasil." Available at http://curiosando.com.br/mais-violentas-brasil/.

Scheper-Hughes, Nancy. 1992. *Death without Weeping: The Violence of Everyday Life in Brazil.* Berkeley: University of California Press.

Scheper-Hughes, Nancy. 1996. "Small Wars and Invisible Genocides." *Social Science & Medicine* 43(5): 889–900.

Scheper-Hughes, Nancy. 1997. *La Muerte Sin Llanto: Violencia y Vida Cotidiana en Brasil.* Barcelona: Editorial Ariel.

Scheper-Hughes, Nancy, and Daniel Hoffman. 1998, "Brazilian Apartheid: Street Kids and the Search for Citizenship in Brazil." In *Small Wars; the Cultural Politics of Childhood*, edited by Nancy Scheper-Hughes and C. Sargent. Berkeley and Los Angeles: University of California Press.

Scheper-Hughes, Nancy. 2004. "Dangerous and Endangered Youth: Social Structures and Determinants of Violence," *Annals of the New York Academy of Science* 1036: 13–46. Special Issue of Youth Violence, edited by John Devine and James Gilligan. New York: Academy of Sciences.

Scheper-Hughes, Nancy. 2009. "The Ethics of Engaged Ethnography: Applying a Militant Anthropology in Organs-Trafficking Research." *Anthropology News* 50 (6): 13-14.

Scheper-Hughes, Nancy. 2011. "Mr Tati's Holiday and João's Safari - Seeing the World through Transplant Tourism." *Body and Society* 17 (2-3): 55-92.

Singelmann, Peter. 1975. "Political Structure and Social Banditry in Northeast Brazil." *Journal of Latin American Studies* 7(1): 59–83.

Soares, Leontina Célia. 1990. "Homicide: Author Unknown." In *The Killing of Children and Adolescents in Brazil*, edited by André Papi, Marisa Brandão, and Jorge L. C. Jardineiro. Rio de Janeiro: CEAP, 22–23.

Taussig, Michael. 2011. *I Swear I Saw This: Drawings in Fieldwork Notebooks.* Chicago: University of Chicago Press.

Timbaúba Agora. 2013. "Mulheres Ajudam na Coleta de Armas na Capanha do Desarmamento." *Quinta Feira*, December 12.

Weber, Demetrio. "Mapa da Violencia 2014: Taxa de Homicidos e a maior desde 1980." http://oglobo.globo.com/brasil/mapa-da-violencia-2014-taxa-de-homicidios-a-maior-desde-1980-12613765.

Zaluar, Alba. 1995. "Crime, medo e politica." *Sociedade e Estado* 10: 391–416.

Zaluar, Alba. 2004. *Integraçao Perversa: Pobreza e Trafico de Drogas.* Rio de Janeiro: Editora FGF.

Postface

Insecurity, the War on Drugs, and Crimes of the State: Symbolic Violence in the Americas

PHILIPPE BOURGOIS

¡Pobre México! ¡Tan lejos de Dios y tan cerca de los Estados Unidos!"
Nineteenth-century Mexican aphorism

How did Latin America emerge from the turmoil of political violence (both revolutionary and reactionary) in the 1950s through the early 1990s only to plunge into a cauldron of delinquent, criminal, interpersonal (and organized state and para-state) violence from the late 1980s to the mid-2010s? Building on a conceptualization of violence as operating along an overlapping continuum of physical, structural, symbolic and normalized-routinized modalities (Scheper-Hughes and Bourgois 2004; Bourgois 2010), it should come as no surprise that the nations from the region of the world with the highest levels of income inequality and the greatest historical levels of repeated US military, political, and economic interventions (bracketing the special case of the Middle East) also have the seven highest per-capita rates of homicide in the world. Nor should it be shocking that seventeen Latin American countries find themselves in the ignominious United Nations tally of the twenty most murderous states on earth (United Nations Office on Drugs and Crime [UNODOC] 2013; see Figures 1 and 2).

As the chapters in this book illustrate so well, there is extraordinary diversity across Latin American countries as well as within them—and even more diversity if we expand our understanding of the region to span all of the Americas from Canada, to Tierra del Fuego, and if we include the outer limits of the Caribbean islands, as well as the North American Latino diasporas, Native American homelands, and colonized possessions.

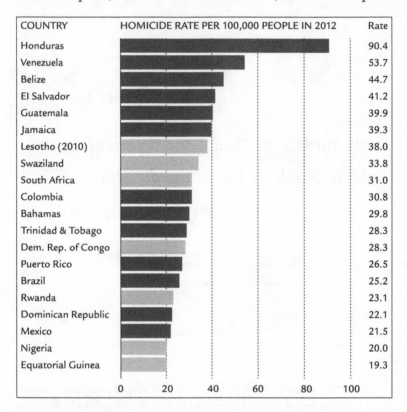

COUNTRY	HOMICIDE RATE PER 100,000 PEOPLE IN 2012	Rate
Honduras		90.4
Venezuela		53.7
Belize		44.7
El Salvador		41.2
Guatemala		39.9
Jamaica		39.3
Lesotho (2010)		38.0
Swaziland		33.8
South Africa		31.0
Colombia		30.8
Bahamas		29.8
Trinidad & Tobago		28.3
Dem. Rep. of Congo		28.3
Puerto Rico		26.5
Brazil		25.2
Rwanda		23.1
Dominican Republic		22.1
Mexico		21.5
Nigeria		20.0
Equatorial Guinea		19.3

Figure 1
Twenty Highest National Homicide Rates (U.N Office on Drugs and Crime 2013)

Nevertheless, with a broad brush, we can point to some major historical and contemporary political-economic structural factors, as well as cultural and colonial/neocolonial conditions, that promote violence and are shared throughout much of the Americas. Their modern history began with bloody colonial divide-and-conquer conquests and genocides, followed by pre-capitalist forms of enslavement of native peoples, and then two more centuries of proto-feudal bondage and peonage. Latin America's brutal history was one of the incubators of a globalized primitive accumulation process crucial to jump-starting British, French, Dutch, Danish, and US capitalism with the transatlantic African slave trade in the Caribbean and the southern United States. It was precisely the brutality of Caribbean and US plantation slavery production that rendered it so extraordinarily profitable, ultimately enabling the transition from merchant to industrial capitalism (Beckert 2014). Arguably, this post-genocide transatlantic

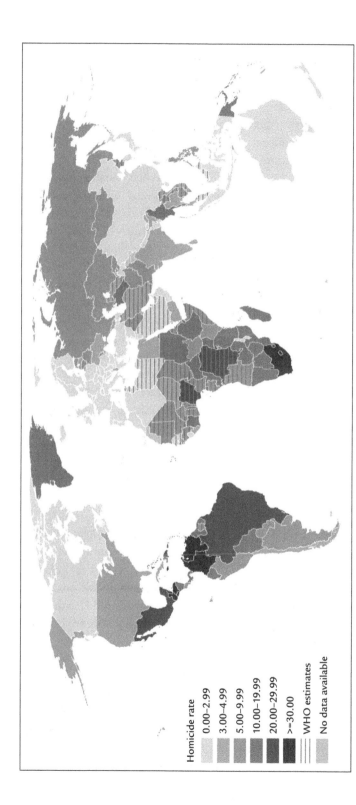

Figure 2
Global Murder Rates (U.N Office on Drugs and Crime 2013).

triangle trade created the foundation for the unequal terms of exchange and the monopoly control of capital and technology that have plagued North-South trans-hemispheric economic relations ever since the conquest of the Americas.

But let us fast forward through that violent colonial history of North/South resource extraction interrupted only temporarily by periodic indigenous and slave rebellions, and independence struggles and focus on the rise of US military and economic interventionism with the emergence of modern multinational corporations. Most notably the US transnational banana companies first cut their teeth making and breaking governments and redrawing national boundaries in Central America and the Caribbean to become the prototype for the corporate monopolies that have reshaped the history of social inequality across the entire globe. In this whirlwind history of violent accumulation, the countrysides of Latin America were denuded. Most nations tilted demographically to a precarious form of overly centralized mega-urbanization out of sync with available employment opportunities and natural resouces.

By the 1990s, Latin American nations found themselves deindustrialized without ever having been industrialized. The linchpin of this debacle has been the ongoing consolidation since the late 1980s of a US- and British-led neoliberal economic model that was pioneered in Chile after a bloody military coup, supported by the United States, overthrew a democratically elected socialist president. University of Chicago economists were invited to Chile to experiment with a free market resturcturing of the market, ironically in the context of massive state investment in violent political repression. By the 1980s, similar neoliberal structural adjustment reforms were being imposed routinely across the globe by the World Bank and the International Monetary Fund as a precondition for access to international finance aid and development funding (Harvey 2005). By the mid-2010s, privatization of public companies and services, global economic inequality, and multinational corporate power had risen to unprecedented levels, with the 85 richest individuals in the world holding as much wealth as the poorest 3.5 billion humans on earth (Moreno 2014). Unsustainable corporate depredations of natural resources and unequal terms of rural/urban trade propelled mass migrations of native and peasant semi-subsistence populations to capital cities and also to the United States.

Throughout this post-World War II Cold War history, Latin America also bore a disproportional brunt of direct US military invasions as well as subtler indirect political/military/diplomatic interventions, including dozens of military coup d'état sponsorships (Quigley 1992; Loveman 2010). This process of militarization and political-economic interventionism by the United States continues in the post-Cold War era in the name of combatting drugs and terrorism rather than communism.

THE GLOBALIZED NARCOTICS INDUSTRY

Perhaps the most nefarious, political outcome of the history of unequal economic development has been the symbolic violence effects of the globalized narcotics economy that filled the void of the dysfunctional legal economy. The hypervisibility of the delinquent violence that narcotics and organized crime generate is particularly confusing to people surviving precariously on the margins of the legal economy in poor, insecure neighborhoods. The virulence of petty criminal violence legitimates repressive responses and obscures political awareness that the Latin American addiction and violence epidemics are the fallout of political economic development policies imposed by international finance institutions, multinational corporate greed and opportunistic local elites. Overwhelmed by a genuine fear of physical insecurity and economic scarcity, both the rich and the poor find themselves blaming their local cultures, their neighbors, their politicians, and themselves for the proliferation of intimate cruelties and corruption that are, in fact, produced structurally by their nation's location in the northward flow of narcotics. Ironically, the global narcotics trade represents one of the few dramatic southward flows of capital in exchange for a primary agricultural product that has been rendered—by US and to a lesser extent European domestic policies—more valuable than oil and precious metals.

Since at least the late 1990s, almost all the heroin consumed in the United States has come from Latin America, primarily Mexico and Colombia (Rosenblum, Unick, and Ciccarone 2014). For even longer, cocaine has been an exclusively South American product. No significant amount of Asian and Middle Eastern heroin or hashish reached the United States between the late 1990s and the mid 2010s.

The production and processing of the primary raw materials for the narcotics trade—opiate poppies, coca leaves, cannabis plants—requires relatively low capital but high labor inputs. Unlike other agricultural products such as coffee, sugar, chocolate, grains, fruits, flowers, and vegetables that are also produced for export in Latin America with relatively low capital inputs and large amounts of labor, the profit margins for the export of heroin, cocaine, and marijuana are astronomical. Methamphetamine, a synthetic narcotic, offers equally high profits. Its monopolization by a few Mexican cartels for export to the United States began as an incidental supplement to their psychoactive products in the early 1990s. Methamphetamine trafficking boomed by the early 2010s as the Mexican cartels diversified their products and opened new markets in response to political shifts in United States law-enforcement priorities.

The irrational market value of psychoactive substances is an artificial product of their illegality, further exacerbated by their pharmacological potential to generate physical or psychological dependency. Illegal addiction markets also have the profitable advantage of imposing an inelastic demand on chronic consumers. Most importantly, however, zero-tolerance wars on drugs prevent heroin, cocaine, and marijuana prices from behaving like normal competitively-marketed legal products. If narcotics were decriminalized or legalized, their retail price would probably fall within the range of other popular addictive/semi-euphoric consumption items—coffee, tea, sugar, chocolate—or more likely within the range of more addictive and health-damaging psychoactive substances such as tobacco and alcohol.

The easy cash of illegal narcotics, like any excessively profitable primary resource export—most notably oil in the case of a country like Venezuela—distorts national patterns of economic development in producer nations. It curtails investment in human capital and stymies opportunities for employment in more diversified economic sectors that are not linked to narcotics production and consumption circuits. These disjointed economies, dependent on an extractive resource, lumpenize a disproportionately large sector of their populations. Furthermore, the influx of US narco-dollars distorts the consumption patterns of narco-elites. They squander their cash on the conspicuous consumption of foreign import luxuries and impose often humiliating patron-client relations on local personal service providers, from bodyguards and chauffeurs to sex workers and butlers. More importantly, the easy flow of illegal narcotics money corrupts politicians and spawns warlord-controlled fiefdoms. Entire nations morph into narco-states, institutionalizing the interface between the state and organized crime, imbricating it into the administrative bureaucracy. In the most affected nations (Bolivia in 1980–1982 and Honduras, Guatemala, and northern Mexico in the 2000s–2010s), the justice apparatus and some of the highest executive politicians and ministers—not to mention governors, mayors, judges, etc.—can be bought for an insignificant fraction of the narco-dollars accumulated by nouveau riche local drug bosses.

THE COLLATERAL DAMAGE OF LOCAL
ADDICTION MARKETS

The replacement of the Cold War with the War on Terror in the opening decades of the 2000s inevitably caused even greater seismic shifts in the transshipment routes used by the cartels to transport heroin and cocaine into the United States. The post-9/11 intensification of airspace monitoring by the United States diversified smuggling trails, making the globalized industry even more difficult to repress. Multiple short-legged transport layovers mushroomed throughout Central America and the Caribbean along airborne, overland, underground, and aquatic routes. Simultaneously, almost half a dozen Caribbean island nations, including the British Virgin Islands, emerged as mini-outlaw economies dedicated to international narcotics and fraud money laundering (US Department of State 2014).

Few nations have been entirely spared the scourge of narcotics passing through their territories northward, and most have developed bona-fide drug epidemics of their own among their urban poor. This scourge of local addiction is simply the collateral damage of the bad luck of being located along the latest smuggling paths leading to the United States (Bourgois 2013). Initially narcotics were not purposefully imported into most Latin American countries to supply local demands. The explosion of the drug consumption problem in so many large and small cities throughout Central America, the Caribbean, and northern Mexico is simply the geographical logistical accident of a few crumbs of the larger narcotics trade spilling over en route to a more profitable final destination in the United States. To lower transport costs, Local purveyors at transit points are paid in kind with a small sample of the product rather than in cash. To make money, these purveyors had to create new local markets for the drug. They flooded their communities with cheap narcotics—primarily cocaine in the form of crack ("roca," "piedra," "patraseado") or its precursor substances ("basuco" in Colombia, "paco" in Argentina, "base" in Ecuador). Relatively few Latin American countries—Venezuela, Argentina, and Brazil, for example—initially had a high-enough standard of living to represent an endpoint market for smugglers. As we see in most of the chapters in this volume, by the early 2000s cocaine derivatives had become a routinized scourge of the urban poor in most Latin American countries from the Andes to the US border.

COLD WAR CONTINUITIES IN THE US WAR ON DRUGS

Delinquent violence is the most visible harm of the global narcotics trade. A perverse—but in retrospect, predictable—continuity exists in what can be called the techniques of brutality that were at the core of the political violence and methods of domination during the Cold War era and the post-1990s not-so-new forms of criminal violence committed by both the delinquents and the state and para-state forces that repress delinquency (Taussig 2003; Carter 2014). During the Cold War, these techniques were disproportionately pioneered by military officers trained on US military bases and sometimes advised by US personnel or by US proxies (Gill 2004; Menjívar and Rodriguez 2005). Repression under the Cold War dictatorships was purposefully traumatic and visible, to demobilize popular political resistance. These same techniques resurfaced in the era of narco-delinquency. They include kidnappings, disappearances, public executions, public display of tortured and mutilated corpses, publication of death threats in the press, *limpiezas sociales* [social cleansings], mass graves, scorched-earth campaigns, assassinations of journalists, and the mobilization of rightwing evangelical redemption churches (Smilde 2007; Pine 2008).

Drawing, again, on the notion of the continuum of violence, we can unravel hypervisible physical violence from invisible violence (Bourgois 2010). The continuitiesof physical brutalities from the 1980s in the 2010s generate a post-Cold War symbolic violence—what Wacquant calls a "dictatorship over the poor" (Wacquant 2003)—that foments national- and international-level punitive policies. The impoverished infrastructures of most Latin American nations prevent them from adopting the US model of mass incarceration. Instead, intermittent popular support emerges for micro-genocidal massacres of youth in poor neighborhoods for the crimes of having tattoos on their body or baggy blue jeans. Euphemized as social cleansings or *ajusticiamentos* [administration of justice], entire generations have repeatedly been wiped out of poor neighborhoods in Honduras (Pine 2008, Carter 2014) Colombia (Taussig 2003), Guatemala (Godoy 2002), and Brazil (Caldeira 2000, Scheper-Hughes, this volume; see also critique by Penglase 2013), just to name a few of the nations where this particularly tragic form of internal bloodletting and surplus population disposal has been most well documented. An understanding of the symbolic violence of insecurity in the face of delinquent violence and its repression helps explain support for *mano dura* [hard-fisted] politicians, many of whom, not coincidentally, hail from nefarious Cold War military pasts (Rodgers 2009). In the case of Guatemala and El Salvador, for example, military officers infamous for their participation in rural genocides and death-squad coordination have been elected by popular majorities. These continuities of hypervisible, terrifying violence also help explain the popularity of evangelical conversion in many nations, as well as support for free-trade agreements—desperate responses to physical insecurity and economic destitution.

Consistently, the United States has been a global bully when it comes to drug policy. This began with the International Opium Convention of 1912 and continues through the early 2010s with the United States pressuring the UN Office on Drugs and Crime to take a zero-tolerance hard line against decriminalization/medicalization. Repeatedly, Latin American leaders have called for decriminalization of drugs in order to reduce the violence and corruption generated by their excessive profitability. The enormous all-cash drug economy relies on violence rather than state mechanisms to enforce contracts because of its illegality and regulate monopolies. Illegal drug markets, consequently, spawn illegal and legal small arms trade, primarily supplied by the United States where lax gun-control laws and a Cold War infrastructure of military aid have propelled deadly weapons southwards since the late 1990s (Geneva Small Arms Survey 2012; Tate 2013). Attempts by Latin American governments to decriminalize and regulate the negative violence and health effects of drug markets, not to mention to capture their extraordinary tax revenue potential, have been consistently sabotaged by the United States. On multiple occasions, the United States has even forced the repeal of newly passed laws decriminalize or medicalize drug use in Latin American nations.

Predictably, the repressive supply-oriented drug interdiction efforts of the United States have exacerbated the problem of global narcotics trafficking, exporting the harms of the US population's demand for narcotics to greater numbers of Latin American nations. For example, the flooding of high-quality, low-cost cocaine into the Florida Keys by the Colombian cartels during the early 1980s at the initiation of Reagan's war on drugs is thought to have been an unintended consequence of the Drug Enforcement Agency's crackdown on bulky and smelly marijuana. The valuable Colombian white powder's higher value per volume, and its minimal smell, was better adapted to small aircraft and speedboat transport, as well as to other diversified forms of smuggling (from keestering in anuses to false paneling to camouflaging inside shipping containers full of the legal products promoted by the proliferation of free trade agreements). In any case, soon after the US crackdown in the Florida Keys, the kilo wholesale price fell by half in 1983. By 1989, kilo prices had dropped another threefold (United Nations 2006), igniting the infamous US crack epidemic of the mid-1980s through early 1990s (Bourgois 1995, fn.77, 362–363; see also Golub and Johnson 1999.). Worse yet, during that Cold War era, the US Congress documented that the Central Intelligence Agency had facilitated the trans-shipment of cocaine to Los Angeles-based street gangs to fund the Nicaraguan counter revolution (Scott 1991). In the process, they jumpstarted what became Central America's uber-violent network of gangs in the 1990s (Zilberg 2007). Simultaneously, the Colombian cartels continued to diversify into heroin, outcompeting with a purer product the Asian and European cartels who formerly supplied the US heroin market (Rosenblum, Unick, and Ciccarone 2014).

Just as the United States treated many Latin America nations as mere pawns in its Cold War obsession for control of the hemisphere in the post-World War II period through the early 1990s, it has reproduced that same subordinated proxy-warrior role for many of its closest Latin American allies through the war on drugs. Nations become hyper-militarized, death squads and paramilitaries technified, and human rights abuses legitimized or rendered invisible when the priority becomes the enforcing the new US-led wars on drugs and terror (Carter 2014) . Arguably there is a disruptive cultural mismatch between the Anglo-puritanical prohibitionist moral violence that drives US drug policy and the more tolerant and forgiving Catholic approaches to substance use in Latin America. The global takeover of drug treatment initiatives throughout Latin America by often for-profit and rightwing evangelical Christian churches with roots in the United States throws a further wrench into this mismatched cultural-ideological stew with distinctly political effects (See O'Neill 2015).

PUNITIVE NEOLIBERALISM AND US DOMESTIC DEMAND AND SUPPLY

The US demand for narcotics is unique by the standards of wealthy industrialized nations because the United States has the highest levels of income inequality of any wealthy nation in the world compounded by a peculiarly phenotypically racialized pattern of urban segregation and economic exclusion. Huge reservoirs of desperately poor urban and rural populations, shunted into geographic wastelands with no useful participation in the legal economy, produce inelastic demands for heroin, cocaine, methamphetamine, and—to a lesser extent—marijuana. Ironically, these consumption demands are as transmutable as is the ability of organized crime to alter supply chains in the face of law-enforcement effects. Historically, one generation after another of mostly poor US citizens has shifted their addiction preferences, en masse, from one substance to another (Mars et al. 2014; Bourgois and Schonberg 2000; Golub and Johnson 1999).

The punitive US war on drugs and its neoliberal retrenchment of services and subsidies for the poor combined with unemployment ensures the persistence of an artificially large pool of desperate consumers condemned to cycle through a hostile deskilling carceral system that produces delinquent subjectivities (Foucault 1995) and eradicates the cultural or symbolic capital necessary to access legal employment (Bourdieu 2000). In contrast, other wealthy industrialized nations with more social democratic policies channel these same vulnerable populations toward medical treatment, job training, or vocational education programs. More simply, they also subsidize the survival costs of the indigent, removing the primary imperative for participation in the underground economies. The anguish of incarceration to both prisoners and their kin in poor communities in the United States further broadens the dislocation and alienation of entire inner-city segregated neighborhoods cross-generationally. The second- and third-generation children of incarcerated addicts become yet more collateral victims of the war on drugs, disproportionately propelled into subjectivies of outlaw poverty in one of the wealthiest nations in the world. Drugs fill their neighborhoods, propelling ever more desabilizing US narco-dollars to Latin America.

The same neoliberal punitive economic policy dynamics that swell the demand for drugs in the United States also render the endpoint retail markets of the global narcotics industry in the ghettos and rural wastelands of the United States resilient to police repression. The war on drugs reproduces its own Hydra-headed problem. Dozens of teenage dropouts—many of them the children of chronically incarcerated addicts—vie for time on drug-sales shifts in the shadows of abandoned urban factories that formerly employed their grandparents. As soon as sellers are arrested in zero-tolerance sweeps, others step up to replace them and narcotics distribution resumes sometimes before the police vans have driven away. No other wealthy industrialized nation on earth socializes such a large proportion of its native-born population into being ready, willing, and obliged to cycle through chronic incarceration—not to mention the risk of death or maiming on a daily basis and chronic exposure to the occupational hazard of narcotics addiction. US-born Latinos—especially those with a colonial relationship, such as Puerto Ricans or a proto-colonial relationship such as Chicanos, Mexican Americans and Native Americans—are, unsurprisingly, overrepresented in these most vulnerable endpoint rungs of the global narcotics labor force.

THE NEOLIBERALIZATION OF THE NARCOTICS INDUSTRY

On a structural historical level as well as a practical logistical one, the resilience of both drug demand and supply thrives in the shadow of the free-trade agreements imposed on Latin America by the United States. This occurred with the Caribbean Basin initiative in 1980, followed in 1994 in Mexico by NAFTA (North American Free Trade Agreement), and expanded by CAFTA (Central American Free Trade Agreement) in 2005. The negative effects of free trade will be even more massively expanded to South America if a version of the FTAA (Pacific-Latin America Free Trade Agreement of the Americas) is passed in the late 2010s. The massive crisscrossing container traffic of legal goods, dynamized by these international political economic subsidies to multinational corporations in the name of free trade, ensures ample space for the ongoing movement of heroin, cocaine, marijuana and methamphetamine. Free-market globalization also accelerates the destruction of local artisanal and peasant economies that are wiped out by the flooding of cheaper, industrially produced imports, thereby guaranteeing even more fodder for the foot soldiers of the narcotics transshipment economies as well as local customers for the narcotics markets that spill over en route.

In short, The cartels follow the logic of neoliberal globalized production. Like the legal corporations that dominate free trade, the cartels operate out of mobile, undercapitalized, just-in-time flexible production sites capable of shifting across national borders at a moment's notice. They carve out enclaves of control in isolated production locations—not unlike the phenomenon of the plantation and mining enclaves that also dot Latin America and the Caribbean and undermine nation-state sovereignty. In some countries, most notably Colombia, former revolutionary political movements have devolved into warlord-controlled narcotics cartels as socialist guerrilla fighters have morphed into greedy, power-hungry gangsters. Simultaneously, the traditional class of landlord oligarchs in Colombia also seized the opportunity for narco-profits and organized rural paramilitaries and urban death squads that have further distorted political processes and national sovereignty.

At the other end of the continuum, at the site of consumption in the United States, the front-line foot soldiers in the retail narcotics labor market have become nothing more than disposable workers (Rosenblum et al. 2014). Recreating a contemporary version of primitive accumulation, the street sellers bear the lion's share of the risk and human cost of the war on drugs (incarceration, premature death and/or maiming, and untreated addiction). Their addiction, incarceration, or early death creates profits for their local bosses as well as for Latin American organized crime, corrupt politicians, and money-laundering international banks—not to mention the treatment centers and prison services industries that fail to rehabilitate them.

Undocumented immigration to the United States for many countries (especially Central America, Mexico, and the Caribbean) has represented a stabilizing and a depoliticizing escape route for desperately poor surplus rural populations as well as for the newly urbanized shantytown dwellers throughout the hemisphere—more collateral damage from neoliberal globalization. Ironically, stripped of legal rights, they become yet another source of post-industrial primitive accumulation for the US economy, forced to work as underpaid day laborers and service workers because of their fear of deportation. These migrants, however, have also become a valuable source of desperately needed US-dollar remittances that reach the poorest of the poor in their home countries. Their villages and marginal urban neighborhoods become crèches for the production of more cheap docile labor, as well as reservoirs for superannuated and occupationally injured formerly undocumented laborers, much like the South African homelands in the apartheidera (Walter, Bourgois, and Loinaz 2004; Holmes 2013; Burawoy 1976). Almost a third of the population of El Salvador, for example, many of them former guerilla fighters, live in the United States.

The same undocumented emigration escape valve that normally depoliticizes and stabilizes poor communities, boomeranged in the 1990s with the deportation of gang members from the United States to Central America and Mexico, during the ramping up of US zero-tolerance crackdowns on delinquency. These crackdowns became yet another US-originated source of hyper-violence and criminalization. The cultural forms of the US street gang and the "righteous dopefiend" have been exported—or rather imposed—by the ups and downs of the US economy and its immigration and delinquency-repression policies. Since the late 2000s, northern Mexico has developed an HIV and injection-drug epidemic from deportees who were introduced to crack, heroin, and hypodermic syringes in US ghettos (Strathdee et al. 2008).

Hollywood and the music industry have also more hegemonically exported cultural archetypes of fantastical delinquent criminality that mimetically achieve a nightmare reality in the dirt-poor insecure urban margins (Gunst 2003, see critique by Thomas 2011) and in the post-Cold War overcrowded prisons of Latin America. The "Free Associated Commonwealth" of Puerto Rico—an actually existing colony of the United States—is a particularly poignant case in point. The United States has the highest gun ownership rate in the world, and this has condemned Puerto Rico in the 2010s to having the highest proportion of homicides committed with firearms of any nation in Latin America. The island of Puerto Rico's overall murder rate is also over 500 percent higher than that of the continental United States (Geneva Small Arms Survey 2012). Puerto Ricans, furthermore, suffer from exceptionally high HIV, depression, diabetes, asthma, addiction, obesity, cardiovascular diseases and internecine murder rates compared to other US ethnic groups (Canino et al. 2008, Deren et al. 2014, Ho et al. 2006, Tucker et al. 2010).

THE NON-LINEAR POLITICS OF VIOLENCE

In the 2010s the Mexican curse cited in the epigram may have been most violently visible in the blood-drenched no-go borderland zones of northern Mexico and it may have been most unhealthily reproduced in Puerto Rico, but the curse of being located in the US force-field applies as well to Central America, most of the Caribbean and much of South America. US economic and political domination, however, has been almost as violently resisted throughout the history of the Americas as it has been violently imposed. Symbolic violence is rarely omnipotent. It often bifurcates into a political violence of resistance, or, at least, a mimetic outpouring of nationalist or cultural-nationalist oppositional mobilization. Not coincidentally, on a policy level, many Latin American countries have bucked or slowed the international trend toward the neoliberal reorganization of their polities. Avowed leftists, socialists, former revolutionary guerilla fighters, and left-of-center populists or social democrats were elected and re-elected in several Latin American nations at the turn of the 21st century. Even more practically with respect to the harms of the narcotics industry, Latin American leaders—from across the political spectrum, including presidents and former presidents—have called for decriminalization/legalization/taxation of their drug industries to regulate the violence and to capitalize the profits for social redistribution. More apocalyptically, however, the capacity for violence to reproduce and morph itself along its structural/normalized-routinized/symbolic continuum (Bourgois 2010) cannot be controlled by political means in a linear, predictable manner. The potential for violence to destroy and brutalize as well as to expose inequalities or contradictorily to obscure true vectors of power can unpredictably change—for better or usually for worse—the courses of local and even global histories.

ACKNOWLEDGMENTS

Research funding provided by National Institutes of Health (NIH) grants DA 010164, as well as the John Simon Guggenheim Foundation, the American Council on Learned Societies, the School for Advanced Research in Santa Fe, and the National Endowment for the Humanities. Comparative and background data supported by NIH grants DA027204, DA027689, DA27599, and AA020331. Editorial assistance by Jeff Ondocsin.

WORKS CITED

Auyero, Javier, and María Fernanda Berti. 2015. *In Harm's Way*. Princeton, NJ: Princeton University Press.

Beckert, Sven. 2014. *Empire of Cotton: A Global History*. New York: Alfred A. Knopf.

Bourdieu, Pierre. 2000. *Pascalian Meditations*, translated by Richard Nice. Stanford, CA: Stanford University Press.

Bourgois, Philippe. 1995. *In Search of Respect: Selling Crack in El Barrio*. New York: Cambridge University Press.

Bourgois, Philippe. 2010. "Recognizing Invisible Violence: A 30-Year Ethnographic Retrospective." In *Global Health in Times of Violence*, edited by Barbara Rylko-Bauer, Paul Farmer, and Linda Whiteford. Santa Fe: School for Advanced Research Press, 17–40.

Bourgois, Philippe. 2013. "Preface à la nouvelle édition francaise." In *En quête de respect: le crack à New York* 2nd ed. Translated by Lou Aubert and Amín Pérez. Paris: Seuil.

Bourgois, Philippe, Fernando Montero Castrillo, Laurie Hart, and George Karandinos 2013. Habitus furibundo en el gueto estadounidense. *Espacio abierto* 22(2): 201.

Bourgois, Philippe, and Jeff Schonberg. 2000. "Explaining Drug Preferences: Heroin, Crack and Fortified Wine in a Social Network of Homeless African-American and White Injectors." *Proceedings of the Community Epidemiological Working Group: Trends in Drug Preferences*, 411–418.

Burawoy, Michael. 1976. "The Functions and Reproduction of Migrant Labor: Comparative Material from Southern Africa and the United States." *American Journal of Sociology* 81(5): 1050–1087.

Caldeira, Teresa Pires do Rio. 2000. *City of Walls: Crime, Segregation, and Citizenship in São Paulo*. Berkeley: University of California Press.

Canino, Glorisa, Doryliz Vila, Sharon-Lise T. Normand, et al. 2008. Reducing Asthma Health Disparities in Poor Puerto Rican Children: The Effectiveness of a Culturally Tailored Family Intervention. *Journal of Allergy and Clinical Immunology* 121(3): 665–670.

Cardoso, Fernando Henrique, César Gaviria, and Ernesto Zedillo. 2009. The War on Drugs Is a Failure. *Wall Street Journal*, February 23.

Carter, Jon Horne. 2014. Gothic Sovereignty: Gangs and Criminal Community in a Honduran Prison. *South Atlantic Quarterly* 113(3): 475–502.

Foucault, Michel. 1995. *Discipline and Punish: The Birth of the Prison*. 2nd ed. New York: Vintage Books.

Geneva Small Arms Survey. 2012. *Small Arms Survey 2012: Moving Targets*. Cambridge: Cambridge University Press.

Gill, Lesley. 2004. *The School of the Americas: Military Training and Political Violence in the Americas*. Durham, NC: Duke University Press.

Godoy, Angelina Snodgrass. 2002. "Lynchings and the Democratization of Terror in Postwar Guatemala: Implications for Human Rights." *Human Rights Quarterly* 24(3): 640–661.

Golub, Andrew, and Bruce Johnson. 1999. "Cohort Changes in Illegal Drug Use among Arrestees in Manhattan: From the Heroin Injection Generation to the Blunts Generation." *Substance Use and Misuse* 34(13): 1733–1763.

Gunst, Laurie 2003. *Born Fi' Dead A Journey through the Yardie Underworld*. Edinburgh: Canongate Books.

Harvey, David. 2005. *A Brief History of Neoliberalism*. Oxford: Oxford University Press.

Ho, Gloria YF, Hong Qian, Mimi Y. Kim, et al. 2006. Health Disparities between Island and Mainland Puerto Ricans. *Revista Panamericana de Salud Pública* 19(5): 331–339.

Holmes, Seth M. 2013. *Fresh Fruit, Broken Bodies: Migrant Farmworkers in the United States.* Berkeley: University of California Press.

Loveman, Brian. 2010. *No Higher Law: American Foreign Policy and the Western Hemisphere since 1776.* Chapel Hill: University of North Carolina Press.

Mars, Sarah G., Philippe Bourgois, George Karandinos, Fernando Montero, and Daniel Ciccarone. 2014. "'Every 'Never' I Ever Said Came True': Transitions from Opioid Pills to Heroin Injecting." *International Journal of Drug Policy* 25(2): 257–266.

Menjívar, Cecilia, and Néstor Rodriguez, eds. 2005. *When States Kill: Latin America, the U.S., and Technologies of Terror.* 1st ed. Austin: University of Texas Press.

Moreno, Kasia. 2014. The 67 people as wealthy as the World's Poorest 3.5 Billion. *Forbes,* March 25. http://www.forbes.com/sites/forbesinsights/2014/03/25/the-67-people-as-wealthy-as-the-worlds-poorest-3-5-billion/, accessed January 5, 2015.

O'Neill, Kevin. 2015. *Secure the Soul: Christian Piety and Gang Prevention in Guatemala.* Berkeley, CA: University of California Press.

Penglase, Benjamin. 2013. "Invading the Favela: Echoes of Police Practices among Brazil's Urban Poor." In *Policing and Contemporary Governance: The Anthropology of Police in Practice,* edited by William Campbell Garriott. New York: Palgrave Macmillan, 31–52.

Pine, Adrienne. 2008. *Working Hard, Drinking Hard: On Violence and Survival in Honduras.* Berkeley: University of California Press.

Quigley, John B. 1992. *The Ruses for War: American Interventionism since World War II.* Buffalo, NY: Prometheus Books.

Rodgers, Dennis. 2009. Slum Wars of the 21st Century: Gangs, Mano Dura and the New Urban Geography of Conflict in Central America. *Development and Change* 40(5): 949–976.

Rosenblum, Daniel, Fernando Montero Castrillo, Philippe Bourgois, et al. 2014. "Urban Segregation and the US Heroin Market: A Quantitative Model of Anthropological Hypotheses from an Inner-city Drug Market." *International Journal of Drug Policy.* DOI: http://dx.doi.org/10.1016/j.drugpo.2013.12.008.

Rosenblum, Daniel, George Jay Unick, and Daniel Ciccarone. 2014. "The Entry of Colombian-Sourced Heroin into the US Market: The Relationship between Competition, Price, and Purity." *International Journal of Drug Policy* 25(1): 88–95.

Scenario Team, Organization of American States. 2012. *Scenarios for the Drug Problem in the Americas, 2013-2025.* OEA/Ser.D/XXV.3. Washington DC: Organization of American States.

Scheper-Hughes, Nancy, and Philippe Bourgois. 2004. "Introduction: Making Sense of Violence." In *Violence in War and Peace: An Anthology,* edited by Nancy Scheper-Hughes and Philippe Bourgois. Oxford: Blackwell Publishing, 1–27.

Scott, Peter 1991. "Cocaine, the Contras, and the United-States—How the United-States Government Has Augmented Americas Drug Crisis." *Crime Law and Social Change* 16(1): 97–131.

Smilde, David. 2007. *Reason to Believe.* Berkeley: University of California Press.

Strathdee, Steffanie A., Remedios Lozada, Victoria D. Ojeda, et al. 2008. "Differential Effects of Migration and Deportation on HIV Infection among Male and Female Injection Drug Users in Tijuana, Mexico." *PLoS ONE* 3(7): e2690.

Tate, Winifred. 2013. "Congressional 'Drug Warriors' and U.S. Policy towards Colombia." *Critique of Anthropology* 33(2): 214–233.

Taussig, Michael. 2003. *Law in a Lawless Land: Diary of a "Limpieza" in Colombia.* New York: New Press.

Thomas, Deborah. 2011. *Exceptional Violence: Embodied Citizenship in Transnational Jamaica*. Durham, NC: Duke University Press.

Tucker, Katherine L., Josiemer Mattei, Sabrina E. Noel, et al. 2010. The Boston Puerto Rican Health Study, a Longitudinal Cohort Study on Health Disparities in Puerto Rican Adults: Challenges and Opportunities. *BMC Public Health* 10(1): 107.

United Nations. 2006. *Bulletin on Narcotics Illicit Drug Markets*. Vienna: United Nations.

United Nations Office on Drugs and Crime (UNODOC). 2013. *Global Study on Homicide 2013*. Retrieved at https://www.unodc.org/gsh/en/data.html. Accessed April 14, 2014.

US Department of State, Bureau for International Narcotics and Law Enforcement Affairs. 2014. *International Narcotics Control Strategy Report Volume II Money Laundering and Financial Crimes*. Washington DC: State Department Bureau Report.

Wacquant, Loïc. 2003. "Toward a Dictatorship Over the Poor?: Notes on the Penalization of Poverty in Brazil." *Punishment & Society* 5(2): 197–205.

Walter, Nick., Philippe Bourgois, and Margarita Loinaz. 2004. "Masculinity and Undocumented Labor Migration: Injured Latino Day Laborers in San Francisco." *Social Science & Medicine* 59(6): 1159–1168.

Zilberg, Elana. 2007. "Refugee Gang Youth: Zero Tolerance and the Security State in Contemporary U.S.-Salvadoran Relations." In *Youth, Globalization, and the Law*, edited by Sudhir Alladi Venkatesh and Ronald Kassimir. Stanford, CA: Stanford University Press, 61–89.

INDEX

interpersonal violence, definition, 193–194
  See also responses to interpersonal
    violence
interpersonal violence, Latin America
  protective factors, 8
  reasons for increases, 7–8
  risk factors, 8
interpersonal violence, US
  protective factors, 8
  reasons for increases, 7–8
  risk factors, 8
interrogation, example, 227–228
invalid *vs.* valid populations, 35
invisible barriers, 80, 86
I Swear I saw This, 266

Jader (case example), 22–26
jail. *See* incarceration
judicial system (US), racial and class bias, 7

kidnappable (*secuestrables*), 148–149
kidnappings, drug violence in Monterrey,
  144–145, 148–149
kinship's axiom of amity, 59
knives. *See* guns and knives

land invasions in the Catuche barrio, 168–170
La Salada (street fair), 192–193
Latin America
  drug trade
    domestic supply and demand, 314–315
    globalized narcotics industry, 309–310
    local addiction markets, 310–311
    neoliberalization of, 315–317
    punitive neoliberalism, 314–315
    theory of primitive accumulation, 306,
      316–317
    US war on drugs, 311–314
  homicide rates, 306
  interpersonal violence
    protective factors, 8
    reasons for increases, 7–8
    risk factors, 8
  non-linear politics of violence, 318
  police-criminal collusion, 7
  state violence, forms of, 7
  violence against women. *See* violence against
    women (Brazil & El Salvador).
  See also specific regions
legal cynicism, 198
Lencho (case example), 24–36
lethal stigmatization, 179

liberated zone (*zona liberada*), 204
life as an inmate, 80, 82–86
Ligas Camponeses, 270–271
Linda (case example), 222–237
little cartels (*cartelitos*), 32–34
livable lives, 268–270
livelihood strategies, destroyed by
  violence, 97–98
living
  with death below, 33
  onda (way of being), 26
  in the shadow of death, 25–26
  types of, 35
loquitas (sissies), 121
Los Angeles, CA. *See* Black and Brown
  tensions in Los Angeles
Luis Fanor Hernández (Managua) (case
  example), 22–34

machismo, 115
  See also masculinities
Malasuerte (case example), 83–84
male gang members, scripts of
  violence, 95–96
male identity formation. *See* masculinities,
  gangs of Medellin
male power as a cause of violence against
  women, 96
male promiscuity, 123–124
march against the death squads (*camanhada
  contra morte*), 289–292
marginal mass, 5
marijuana, in North Philadelphia, 48
Maritza (case example), 168–174
Marx, Karl, 66–69, 306, 316–317
masculine capital, accumulation of, 118–119
masculine habitus, 116, 118, 129
masculine shaming, 63–64
masculinities
  gangs of Medellin
    accumulation of masculine capital,
      118–119
    accustomization to violence, 117
    exclusion as emasculation, 115–118, 121
    guns and knives, roles of, 119
    image of success, 116
    interactions with girls and women, 114,
      122–123
    legitimate social mobility
      opportunities, 117–118
    loquitas (sissies), 121
    machismo, 115